SCOUNDRELS
AND
SHIRKERS

SCOUNDRELS AND SHIRKERS

Capitalism and Poverty in Britain

JIM SILVER

Fernwood Publishing
Halifax & Winnipeg

Copyright © 2023 Jim Silver

All rights reserved. No part of this book may be reproduced or transmitted in any form by any means without permission in writing from the publisher, except by a reviewer, who may quote brief passages in a review.

Copyediting: Jenn Harris
Text design: Brenda Conroy
Cover design: Housefires Design & Illustration
Printed and bound in the UK

Published by Fernwood Publishing
2970 Oxford Street, Halifax, Nova Scotia, B3L 2W4
and 748 Broadway Avenue, Winnipeg, Manitoba, R3G 0X3
www.fernwoodpublishing.ca

This book has been published with the help of a grant from the Canadian Federation for the Humanities and Social Sciences, through the Awards to Scholarly Publications Program, using funds provided by the Social Sciences and Humanities Research Council of Canada.

Fernwood Publishing Company Limited gratefully acknowledges the financial support of the Government of Canada through the Canada Book Fund and the Canada Council for the Arts. We acknowledge the Province of Manitoba for support through the Manitoba Publishers Marketing Assistance Program and the Book Publishing Tax Credit. We acknowledge the Nova Scotia Department of Communities, Culture and Heritage for support through the Publishers Assistance Fund. The Social Sciences and Humanities Research Council, through the Manitoba Research Alliance, provided support for the production of this book.

Library and Archives Canada Cataloguing in Publication

Title: Scoundrels and shirkers: capitalism and poverty in Britain / Jim Silver.
Names: Silver, Jim, 1946- author.
Description: Includes bibliographical references and index.
Identifiers: Canadiana (print) 20230000320 | Canadiana (ebook) 20230000355 | ISBN 9781773635996 (softcover) | ISBN 9781773636276 (EPUB) | ISBN 9781773636283 (PDF)
Subjects: LCSH: Poverty—Great Britain—History. | LCSH: Capitalism—Great Britain—History.
Classification: LCC HC260.P6 S55 2023 | DDC 305.5/690941—dc23

Contents

Acknowledgements x

1 Poverty in Britain: From Feudalism to Neoliberal Capitalism 1
   Main Themes 2
   The Razor's Edge 4
   "The Life of Savages" 5
   Perpetually Producing Poverty 8
   The Beliefs that We Hold 11
   Can It Be Otherwise? 13
   Situating Myself 15

2 Vagabonds and Beggars: Christianity and Enclosure
   and the Detritus of Crumbling Feudalism 17
   Medieval Christian Belief: Deserving and Undeserving, Charity
   and Punishment 18
   Masterless Men, Vagrants, Vagabonds and Paupers 22

3 Manage and Control: Two Centuries of the *Elizabethan Poor Law* ... 28
   A Rudimentary and Threadbare System of Poor Relief 29
   Evil, Destitute and Masterless Persons 31
   Precarious Labour, Precarious Lives: Making Shift
   and Other Means of Coping 33
   Idle, Ragged Children: Set Them to Work! 36
   Slavery: Producing Brutal Poverty, Massive Profits and Racism 38
   Punishment: The Workhouse as Incentive to Work 41
   The Growing Cost of Poor Relief and the Quest for Poor Law Reform 46
   "Within an Ace of a Revolution": Reforming the *Poor Law* 48

4 The Industrial Revolution: The New Poor Law and New
   and Horrific Forms of Poverty 51
   Factory Fodder for Industry 52
   The Poor called them Bastilles 54
   A Discipline So Severe and Repulsive as to Make Them a Terror to the Poor ... 57
   Cotton, Slavery and the Global Production of Poverty 59
   Were They Galley-Slaves Their Work Could Not Be More Oppressive 61
   The Factory Acts: The Beginnings of a Breach in Laissez-Faire 63
   A New Kind of Prison … a New Kind of Jailer 65

Pauperism was Always Near	68
The Dangerous Class, the Residuum	71
The Stench … Was Almost Sickening: Housing the Urban Poor	76
Exporting, Blaming and Counting the Poor	80
Warring Interpretations: What Causes This Poverty? What Should Be Done?	85
Still Making Shift	91

5 Great Unrest: Political Pressure and Social Reform, 1880–1914 ... 93
- Political Pressures 93
- New Ways of Thinking: Collectivism and the Positive State 96
- Only the Deserving Poor 98
- The Liberal Governments of 1906–1914 and the Social Services State 100
- Poverty Declines—Significantly 105

6 On the Dole: Mass Unemployment and Mass Poverty in the 1920s and 1930s 106
- To the Level of a Calamity: Unemployment, 1920–1921 107
- It Gets Worse: Mass Unemployment, Poverty, Privation and Destitution in the 1930s 110
- The Bitterly Hated Household Means Test 113
- Passivity and Resistance 114
- Women: Key Strategists in the Struggle against Destitution 119
- Sniggering Superiority; Vicious Hatred 120
- Vast Tracts of Slumdom: Housing in the 1930s 121
- Poverty Makes You Sick: Health in the 1930s 123
- Ideas that Led to the Welfare State 124

7 The End of Poverty? 1945 and All That 130
- The Most Advanced Welfare State in the World 130
- The Fight for the National Health Service 131
- Toward the Decommodification of Housing for Working-Class People 133
- The *National Insurance Act* and Its Limitations 134
- In the Face of Resistance: Full Employment and Related Gains 137
- Criticisms of the Labour Governments of 1945–1951 143

8 Mid-Century Retrenchment: The Welfare State Erodes, Poverty Re-emerges and Capitalism Goes into Crisis 147
- The Rise of Individualism and Consumerism 147
- Revisionism and the Abandonment of the Welfare State 150
- The Growth of Intellectual Opposition to the Welfare State 153
- Economic Decline 155
- The Rediscovery of Poverty 159
- A Drab Damp Flat on a Dump Estate 163
- Feckless Mothers and Feeble-Minded Children 171
- Racism: Legacy of an Imperial Past 173

9   Thatcherism: An Explosion of Poverty and Inequality 179
    An Intended and Inevitable Outcome: A Price Worth Paying 180
    Winning the Battle of Ideas 182
    No Economic Miracle: Restructuring and Deindustrialization..... 187
    Mass Unemployment: More of It and Longer than the 1930s........ 192
    Unforgiveable Treatment of the Poor 194
    But Poverty Had Not Disappeared 195
    Drab, Dreary, Depressing: Housing under Thatcher........................ 198
    Inequality 203
    Universality Erodes, Means-Testing Soars, Workfare and
    Private Delivery Emerge... 204
    The Importance of Redistribution 207

10 New Labour, New Revisionism: Thatcherism in Redux 210
    The New Party of Middle Britain 211
    New Welfare State: Make the Poor "Take Responsibility"............... 218
    Borrowing from America: Force Them to Work 221
    A Scar on Britain's Soul 227
    A Record beyond Abysmal: New Labour and Housing.................. 232
    Law, Order and Poverty Propaganda.. 235
    Low-Pay/No-Pay/No-Future 238
    A Savagely Unequal Society... 239
    Post–New Labour: It Just Keeps Getting Worse 242

11 Solving Perpetual Poverty: Can Capitalism Be Undone? 246
    Is Perpetual Poverty Inevitable?... 249
    Universal, Redistributive Strategies 251
    Two Roads.. 252

References 256

Index 283

*Dedicated to the memory of Loa Henry,
beloved wife and partner in all things, loving mother
and grandmother, long-time artistic director of the
community-based feminist theatre troupe Nellie McClung Theatre,
and long-time artistic director of the Winnipeg Labour Choir.*

Acknowledgements

I am happy to express my deep thanks to the many people I have worked with in Winnipeg's inner city over the years, whose dedication and skill is remarkable and from whom I have learned much about poverty.

For reading earlier versions of this manuscript and making very useful comments, I am particularly grateful to the late Leo Panitch. Leo not only offered useful suggestions but also was especially encouraging about publication. Henry Heller was similarly encouraging at an even earlier stage. Wayne Antony made this book possible and as always offered many detailed and positive suggestions, skilfully navigating the publication process. I am grateful to Wayne and the entire team at Fernwood—Bev Rach, Brenda Conroy for design and layout, Jessica Koricil for the cover design and Jenn Harris for copy editing.

I have worked for many years with the Canadian Centre for Policy Alternatives–Manitoba and the Manitoba Research Alliance and am happy to acknowledge the support and encouragement of the many wonderful people involved with those projects, especially CCPA–MB director Molly McCracken and MRA principal investigator Shauna MacKinnon.

I am pleased to acknowledge the Social Sciences and Humanities Research Council, through the Manitoba Research Alliance grant titled "Community-Driven Solutions to Poverty: Challenges and Opportunities," which provided generous financial support for this book and for much of my earlier work in Winnipeg's inner city.

Chapter 1

Poverty in Britain

From Feudalism to Neoliberal Capitalism

Capitalism is astonishingly productive. It produces commodities, which are sold to produce profits—massive profits—in the making of which a working class is produced and constantly reproduced and reshaped. The process of production is competitive and dynamic, so that change is constant. In this process, capitalism produces poverty. The perpetual production of ever-changing forms of poverty is an inevitable part of the creative destruction that characterizes capitalism. The remarkable growth over the centuries in the productivity of British capitalism has been accompanied at every stage by the production of poverty, and indeed, the production of poverty has been a *necessary* part of capitalism's growth.

In examining the constantly changing phenomenon of poverty in Britain, and particularly in England* since about the twelfth century, the necessary context is the dynamics of capitalism, from its origins in the long breakdown of and transition from feudalism, through the eras of mercantile capitalism and industrial capitalism, to the welfare state that began to be built by Labour governments in the immediate post–Second World War period. Poverty was significantly reduced by the Labour governments of 1945–1951—the result of what appears to have been the first real attempt in at least eight hundred years to significantly reduce the level of poverty. However, these gains were partial and proved to be temporary. By the mid-twentieth century, British capitalism had long been in decline relative to other capitalist powers, and the fledgling welfare state was not expanded and enriched as it ought to and could have been. For most of the second half of the twentieth century and into the twenty-first,

---

* This study does not systematically address the particular characteristics of poverty in Northern Ireland, Scotland and Wales. The primary focus, especially in the pre-Industrial Revolution years, is England.

the story is one of decline—of the British economy and the welfare state, with Britain going from social policy leader to social policy laggard—and the re-emergence of destructive and debilitating forms of poverty.

Poverty has taken many different forms over the centuries, always related closely to the dynamics of capitalism and the ever-changing structure of the working class. People are poor because of their relationship to the means of production—they have been pushed off the land, they do not have a job, or the job they have is poorly paid, part-time or irregular. This has been the case in Britain for centuries and continues to be the case today, although the particular form that poverty takes is constantly changing.

Why a book about poverty in Britain in particular? The answer has to do with the many ways that Britain has been first. Britain was the first industrial capitalist power, was the world's long-time leading imperialist power, and was first in developing the welfare state. The approach to poverty and the poor developed in Britain, especially under the *Elizabethan Poor Law* of 1601 and the *New Poor Law* of 1834—the centuries-long distinction between the deserving and undeserving poor, along with the stinginess and stigmatization of all forms of social assistance, for example—have come to characterize the approach to poverty and the poor adopted in the British settler colonies of Australia, the US and Canada. Margaret Thatcher's Conservative governments, acting in the interests of capitalism in Britain, were first in leading the dramatic shift to neoliberalism, the effects of which are still being felt, while Britain became the world's leading workfare state under Tony Blair's New Labour governments. Thus, an analysis of the production of poverty in Britain can yield insights into the relationship between capitalism and poverty more generally.

Main Themes

I draw a number of conclusions from this study. First, although the incidence and severity of poverty today are not as great as was the case in earlier centuries, the existence and many of the characteristics of poverty are strikingly constant over time. Poverty persists today as a major problem in Britain, as in most advanced capitalist societies. The production of poverty is, indeed, an intrinsic characteristic of capitalist production.

Second, although many among the poor have historically worked, and in fact for centuries a very high proportion of those who worked for wages were poor, nevertheless there has consistently been and continues to be a stratum of the poor—the poorest of the poor—who have not worked or have worked irregularly, for various reasons. They have been vilified and even hated as the "undeserving" poor, blamed for their poverty on the grounds that it is attributable to their moral failings and degenerate behaviour.

Third, there has never been in Britain, with the partial exception of the 1945–1951 Labour governments, a serious attempt to solve poverty—that is, to eliminate it or even dramatically reduce it. Rather, efforts have always been directed at managing and controlling the poor, to prevent them from starving or rebelling; punishing them for being poor; and pushing them by various forceful means into the lower reaches of the labour market, where they remain poor. In recent decades, so-called "anti-poverty" programs narrowly targeted at the poor have in some cases been successful in moving some people out of poverty, but these have had little if any impact on the existence and persistence of poverty.

Fourth, the ideas that have been prevalent at any given time—particularly ideas about poverty and its causes and appropriate responses—are an important part of any attempt to understand poverty. How poverty and its causes are understood contributes to shaping how people and governments respond to those who are poor. Those who are poor are seen by many, perhaps most, as scoundrels and shirkers and a wide range of other terms of vilification. This has been the case for centuries and is the case today.

A major question that arises from this study is whether it is at all possible for poverty to be solved within capitalism. The significant gains made by the 1945–1951 Labour governments were subsequently largely eroded, and poverty re-emerged and persists today. To solve the problem of the perpetual production of poverty would require a very large redistribution of resources from the top to the bottom of the income scale, continued over time, together with state-led efforts to create large numbers of good jobs. Those at the top would oppose such measures vehemently. Moreover, there is little public support for redistributive and state interventionist measures—a product at least in part of the ongoing fear and even hatred of those who are poor, along with the persistent belief that the poor are to blame for their poverty. Thus, it is a legitimate question to ask whether such redistribution and state intervention, aimed at eliminating poverty, is possible within capitalism.

The Razor's Edge

The characteristics of today's poverty are strikingly similar to those of previous centuries. For example, poverty has always been and continues to be about labour, about people's relationship to work: either their inability to find paid employment, the low wages and/or irregular hours of the work they are able to find, their structured subordination because of gender or "race," and/or the number of family members supported by a wage. Poverty in Britain, as in other advanced capitalist economies, has always been about low wages, precarious labour and the inability to find paid employment. As Blackwell and Seabrook (1985: 39) described it, "The single most unifying factor in working class culture has been poverty; the threat of poverty, the fear of poverty, the certainty of poverty." Precarious labour is not a new phenomenon. Work and life itself have always been, and continue to be, precarious—as Palmer (2014: 44) asserts, "work has never been anything but a precarious foundation of life lived on the razor's edge of dispossession."

It is not only that British workers have always lived on the razor's edge of dispossession; it is also that poverty is complex and multifaceted, and it often brutalizes those who are poor. Poverty is about much more than a shortage of income, although that is at its core. Complex poverty includes inadequate and often deplorable housing, inadequate diets, eroded health, dramatically reduced longevity, punishment, shame and humiliation, and hatred directed at those who are poor. This has been the case historically; it is the case today.

The poor have long been blamed for their poverty and have typically been despised and even feared. Punishment and incarceration, in a variety of institutions, have been and continue to be common responses to poverty, existing alongside various forms of charity for those deemed to be "deserving." Punishment and incarceration have been especially the case for those who are different, or who come from elsewhere, and those considered to be the "undeserving" poor. The distinction between the deserving and undeserving poor has been a constant in British history. So too have various charitable institutions aimed inevitably not at solving poverty, but at keeping the poor from starving and rebelling.

Those who are poor have long attempted to cope with their poverty-induced circumstances with various practices—most legal, some illegal, all poorly paid—by which they have scrambled to try to stay alive, historically called "making shift." As well, they have turned to the centuries-old practice of using various intoxicants to dull their pain and of turning to usurious moneylenders of various kinds to make it through the week. These types of responses have been more common than acts of rebellion.

However, various forms of resistance have been more prevalent than is often recognized. It was the many instances of rebellion by the poor that led to the *Elizabethan Poor Law* of 1601, and later to the *New Poor Law* of 1834. And it was pressure from below—from social democratic and socialist parties and trade unions—that led to the mild reforms enacted by the 1906–1914 Liberal governments and the major reforms of the 1945–1951 Labour governments. Human agency and pressure from below have always mattered in shaping the dynamic relationship between capitalism and poverty.

Precarious labour, low wages, poor housing, poor health, shame and humiliation, and blaming, punishing and offering handouts to the poor have a long history and persist to this day. Similarly, human agency and pressure from below have always been and will in future be crucial factors in shaping responses to poverty.

"The Life of Savages"

In producing poverty, capitalism has constantly generated a stratum of people who are not employed or only partially or irregularly employed. This is either because they are not needed by or do not fit in the production-for-profit process or because they choose not to be a part of that process. Or, in many cases, it is because they are by various means—for example, sexism and racism—actively excluded from full-time paid employment. This stratum is dynamic, constantly changing in numbers and composition. In the long period from the twelfth century leading up to the emergence of industrial capitalism in the mid-late eighteenth century, poverty was produced as people were pushed off the land as part of the demise of feudalism and the long transition to capitalism. The result was the creation of "masterless men" (Beier 1985)—people who were set free from the servitude required by, but also the obligations entered into by, feudal landlords. Masterless men—and women and children—tramped the country in search of livelihoods. They were identified as vagrants and vagabonds, rogues and scoundrels, paupers and other derogatory names. They were the "undeserving" poor, marginalized from the dominant society, blamed and even reviled for their poverty, and punished in various ways—an approach familiar to the late twentieth and early twenty-first centuries.

In the cities, this stratum was comprised of those outside of the paid labour force, or clinging to the edges of the labour market, who scrambled to make a living in whatever ways might be possible. These were, for example, the costermongers, chimney sweeps and organ grinders, the thieves and pickpockets and con artists, and those forced by poverty to sell sex for money. By the latter part of the nineteenth century, these were known as the "residuum" and were widely despised. Charles Booth, in some respects a relatively sympathetic observer, wrote in 1892 of category A, the "lowest class" in his categorization, that "their life is the life of savages.… They degrade whatever they touch, and as individuals are perhaps incapable of improvement" (Fried and Elman 1968: 11). Engels referred to "this scum of depraved elements" about which he said, "This rabble is absolutely venal" (quoted in White 1979: 2). Marx (1976: 797) referred to them as "the lowest sediment of the relative surplus population … the dead weight of the industrial reserve army." Later, in the twentieth and twenty-first centuries, this stratum of the poor would be identified by various other disparaging names—social problem group, scroungers and shirkers, problem families and—especially from the 1960s on, and strongly influenced by the American experience—the underclass and its later variants. Most recently such terms as shirkers, chav and venal scum have become common, and "poverty porn" has emerged as a means of further demeaning those who are seen to be poor because of their moral failings and degenerate behaviour (Jones 2012; Garthwaite 2016; Shildrick 2018).

Because capitalism and the capitalist labour process are dynamic, the numbers and social composition of those cast off or excluded and pushed into this surplus population have constantly changed in response. It is in this sense that they can be said to be created by capitalism. Capitalism produces this lowest stratum of the poor just as surely as it produces a working class. White (1979: 13–15), in describing Campbell Road, "a lumpen community in London," argued that this stratum of the poor "were defined, and often created, by capital. It was capital that labelled people as 'incapable' or 'inefficient'":

> Such words only have meaning where men and women are valued only for their labour-power. Where, as in some cases, that

labour-power is so worthless as to be unsaleable then its possessor is no longer even a commodity. He or she is rejected by capital and condemned to a life of dependency or pauperism, or to picking up a living by shifts and ruses of all sorts, living on their wits in the pores of society.

They are "useless to capital" (White 1979: 14). Capitalism aims only at profit making and thus employs only those people who can be profitably exploited. Those who do not, will not or cannot are surplus to the system. Today, in the third decade of the twenty-first century, the numbers of those who are "useless to capital" appear to be growing, necessitating a wide range of capitalist responses aimed at keeping those people from starving in the streets and from rebelling. In some cases, people choose "not to work in the jobs which society would have provided for them—back-breaking or mind-dulling work at the least 'skilled' and worst-rewarded end of the labour market" (Barrow 2020). They are forced to find other ways to make a living.

This lowest stratum, comprised of the poorest of the poor, also creates and re-creates itself, as its members struggle to find the ways to survive in their constrained and marginalized circumstances. Many have lived lives of quiet despair, struggling, often heroically, to do what could be done to keep their families afloat; some have resisted the plunge into abject poverty by means of criminal activity; others, in exasperation and often desperation, have resorted to drink or drugs. These behavioural responses to their circumstances have led to them being reviled and even hated and feared by the "respectable" working population, who too often have stigmatized and stereotyped the "undeserving" poor and blamed them for their poverty on the grounds of their personal failings. This demonization has then added to their exclusion and marginalization, deepening the sense of entrapment and despair, and even hopelessness, felt by at least some and likely many of its members.

This surplus population includes people who are damaged, physically or emotionally, by the system, as well as those who are needed only part of the time—seasonally, for example, or on the docks when a ship needs unloading or when there is a boom and not a bust. In addition, capitalism can and does act as a "filter." It rejects some people, on the grounds of "race" or gender, for example, even though they may be exploitable, or it may filter them into particular jobs for reasons that are cultural or ideological. For example, in the post-1945 era, West Indians and Asians in Britain were directed into menial and poorly paid jobs, in large part for reasons related to the legacy of colonialism and the racism it produced. When mass unemployment re-emerged in Britain in the 1980s, Black youth were both filtered out/rejected from wage-labour, and at the same time chose not to be exploited and humiliated in what many perceived as the never-ending, never-getting-ahead way that they saw as their future as wage-labourers. Some people have always chosen not to be exploited as wage-labourers and instead to live independently of the wage-labour system. All these various categories of people form the "undeserving" poor, the residuum, the scoundrels or shirkers or underclass or any of the various names that have long been applied to this stratum of the poorest of the poor.

Perpetually Producing Poverty

With the possible and partial exception of the 1945–1951 Labour governments, attempts have never been made to solve poverty. Rather, the centuries-long response to poverty by those with power and authority has been to manage and control, and all too often to punish, the poor—to allot to those who are poor just enough to prevent starvation and stave off rebellion. The result has been a terrible—almost certainly an incalculable—price paid by the vast numbers in poverty in terms of human suffering and early death. It would be a mistake to think that Britain is an exception to the violence and bloodshed that have characterized the path to industrialization taken by other countries. Capitalist industrialization in Britain was created by and relied upon a new and horrific form of poverty—that is to say, a brutal form of poverty was a *necessary* condition for its emergence and success. Those who were the poor paid a terrible price for any benefits that have emerged from this long process. As Marx (1976: 926) said, capitalism comes into the world "dripping from head to toe, from every pore, with blood and dirt." A dramatic and colourful statement, but the empirical evidence makes clear that it is scarcely an exaggeration.

Why are these central features of poverty so unchanged over the centuries, and why are efforts to eliminate poverty so rare as to be almost non-existent? The core of the explanation is that the logic of capitalism is such that it *produces* poverty. It does so because the surplus generated in the process of capitalist production is invested where it is thought it will make the greatest future profit. It is not invested in meeting peoples' needs if doing so is not expected to produce profits. It is not invested in a living wage, for example, because it is believed that doing so would reduce the total amount of profits to be earned or, as commonly expressed today, would damage the economy. Capitalists deliberately keep wages low and labour precarious in order to maximize profits, even though it is known that doing so will produce still more poverty. Adequate and affordable housing for the poor is not constructed, despite the great need, even though it is known that inadequate and unaffordable housing contributes to the production and reproduction of poverty. The result is the production not only of goods and services and of profits, but also of poverty. The entire point of the capitalist system is the maximization of profit, not the meeting of human needs and certainly not the elimination of poverty.

Solving poverty within capitalism may well be possible, but it would require very significant investment to meet the needs of, and to create meaningful opportunities for, those who are poor. If such investment were to be made—that is, if there were to be a redistribution of profits to meet the needs of and create opportunities, and especially employment opportunities, for those at the bottom of the income scale via a redistributive and interventionist state—the result would be a net reduction in the investment in otherwise profitable opportunities. Consequently, such investments are not made, unless they are demanded. Investments to reduce poverty—to improve the circumstances of those, both working and not working, who are poor—are only made when very significant collective pressure is put on states and governments to do so. Pressure from below, including especially that exerted by social democratic and socialist parties and trade unions, is essential in any strategy to significantly reduce poverty.

The gains made by the Labour governments of 1945–1951 in reducing poverty were the consequence of pressures from below that had been building from the 1880s, and especially during the Depression of the 1930s and the Second World War. Those gains have, especially since the 1980s, been largely reversed, with the result that poverty has re-emerged with a vengeance, taking forms and producing responses that have been, in virtually every important respect, constant over the centuries.

In recent decades, there have been periods when "anti-poverty" programs were put in place to address the needs of those in poverty.

However, these are narrowly targeted at a small group of those who are poor and have the effect of moving some out of poverty while leaving poverty in place. Anti-poverty programs cannot solve poverty, because they do not address the existing power relations that produce poverty.

It has to be acknowledged, however, that the process could have been worse. Today, tens and even hundreds of millions of people across the world are pushed off the land and forced into urban settings, as was the case in previous centuries in Britain. However, unlike the case of Britain, they do not find employment in, and are not exploited by, industrial capitalist enterprises. The process today is one of "urbanization without industrialization," creating a veritable "planet of slums" (Davis 2006).

But what is important about advanced capitalist societies such as Britain is that capitalism is sufficiently productive that, unlike any previous economic system, it produces enough surplus that poverty could be solved. We briefly saw a move in this direction—a significant but partial and incomplete move—in the immediate postwar years in Britain, and we can see a version of it in the Nordic countries. Capitalism inevitably produces poverty, but the incidence of poverty varies across capitalist nations. Poverty is lower where organized labour is stronger—that is, where rates of unionization are higher and where social democratic and socialist parties are stronger. This is exemplified by the historical experience in the Nordic countries, where rates of child poverty, for example, are far lower than in Britain. Conversely, where organized labour and social democratic and socialist parties are weaker, poverty and inequality are higher. We see this in the US, where social democratic and socialist organizations are especially weak, and rates of poverty are particularly high.

The argument being advanced in this study is not that only capitalism produces poverty; other ways of organizing economic activity also produce poverty. Rather, the argument is that capitalism necessarily produces poverty and that if poverty were to be eliminated within capitalism, it would require that large-scale collective demands be made to redistribute profits.

This in turn depends, in large part, upon the kinds of ideas that prevail at a given time, and the relative strengths of the social and political forces promoting contending ideas, for as Hobsbawm (quoted in Kaye 1984: 155) has written, "history is the struggle of men for ideas, as well as a reflection of their material circumstances."

The Beliefs that We Hold

Broad, cultural and political ideas about poverty matter in shaping responses to poverty. How we understand or explain poverty plays a significant role in determining how, or even if, we try to solve it. The belief that the poor are responsible for their poverty, because of their personal moral failings, for example, and the reliance upon punishment and charity as the dominant responses to poverty, have a long history and are still widely accepted. The Industrial Revolution was accompanied by the ideas associated with laissez-faire—that individuals should be left to their own devices, without support from the state. Thus, poverty was seen as an important stimulant to work and as "natural," and the poor were to blame for their own poverty; therefore, the society/the state need do nothing. These broadly held beliefs dominated the more than one hundred years from the last quarter of the eighteenth century to the latter decades of the nineteenth. They have re-emerged in force in the last decades of the twentieth and first decades of the twenty-first centuries.

However, starting in the latter part of the nineteenth century, the enormous human suffering caused by industrial capitalism and its laissez-faire accompanist led first some, then more and finally many to see the virtues of, and to fight for state intervention in pursuit of, a broader public interest. Such ideas may have had their origins in the early nineteenth century with the struggle for the Factory Acts and gained momentum in the late nineteenth century alongside the rise of an organized working class and socialist, social democratic and "new liberal" ideas and organizations. The powerful feared that such ideas might lead to socialism. They responded first with the limited but important liberal reforms of 1906–1914—partly the product of new ideas; mostly the result of fear of, and thus the need to placate, the forces that carried those ideas—and eventually with the social welfare regime of the Labour governments of 1945–1951.

Britain and the postwar Labour Party are important because they were forerunners in the creation of the welfare state. "For a few years after [the Second World War] this social democratic welfare state prevailed mainly in Britain. It was the most advanced welfare state in the world" (Sassoon 1997: 141). The National Health Service, for example, "was obviously one of the [Labour] government's outstanding triumphs, admired throughout the world, an immense landmark in the building of the welfare state" (Morgan 1984: 162). These postwar gains were by no means the automatic products of economic growth, as is sometimes argued; they were the products of determined struggle by unions and the working class in the face of severe financial restrictions and fierce opposition.

But even as the implementation of these social welfare, state interventionist ideas contributed dramatically to driving down the incidence of poverty, the seeds of neoliberal ideas were taking root again. They gradually emerged, embraced and pushed by British capitalists, at a time of economic crisis in the late 1970s, bringing with them a dramatic return of poverty.

The incidence and character of poverty is a product of broad economic forces, but such forces produce no automatic outcomes. There is no reason to believe, for example, that neoliberal ideas were a necessary or inevitable response to the crisis of capitalism in the last quarter of the twentieth century. Other responses were possible. Neoliberal ideas, and the social forces that promoted them, were victorious. Ideas matter, as Gramsci (1971) has argued, as do the social forces fighting to advance particular sets of ideas. Piketty (2020: 848) makes the same case, arguing, with respect to the causes of inequality, "everything depends on the mobilization strategies of the parties and the political-ideological balance of power." Ideas and broadly held beliefs are an important component of the pressure from below that can reduce poverty and inequality, as well as the pressure from above that can drive up its incidence. Dorling (2010: 308), in writing about a variety of injustices, including poverty and vast inequality, said, "it is beliefs, the beliefs which enough of us still hold, that today underlie most injustice in the world."

This is not to say that history is propelled by the struggle over ideas, but rather that conflicts over ideas reflect differing material interests. Ideas about poverty are an expression of the material interests of those who are benefiting from the system at a given time. What prevails in a given society at a given time is a "bundle of beliefs ... ideas beyond question, assumptions so deep that the very fact that they *are* assumptions is only rarely brought to light" (Hall, Massey and Rustin 2015: 14, emphasis in original). Central to that bundle of beliefs is the idea that the poor are to blame for their poverty.

An immediate and predictable objection is that the poverty in Britain today is not as severe nor as widespread as the poverty of the past. This is true. The incidence and severity of poverty today is less than it was in the past. This is because, since the 1880s, a part of the massive profits produced in Britain has been redistributed to those at or near the bottom of the income scale, particularly to the working class. This happened because of political pressure from below that insisted upon such a redistribution. However, the belief in the merits of redistribution has taken a battering over the past forty years. In all European social democratic parties, Britain's Labour Party included, "social redistribution, traditionally the first plank in social-democratic reformist action, is practically abandoned" (Moschonas 2002: 294; Piketty 2020: 40), leading to the dramatic resurgence of the complex poverty that scars Britain today.

Can It Be Otherwise?

It appears, at least at this historical stage in the third decade of the twenty-first century, that the conditions that made possible the relative and indeed significant improvements of the immediate post-1945 period may no longer pertain. Rates of economic growth have slowed, making redistribution potentially more difficult (Piketty 2017). Capitalism increasingly relies upon precarious labour, producing the low-pay/no-pay/no-future cycle that traps so many in poverty. And in the era of neoliberalism since the late 1970s, trade unions and social democratic parties have dramatically weakened and have abandoned most of their commitment to redistribution and equality, thus reducing the capacity to put collective pressure on dominant classes to share the wealth. The weakening of social democratic parties and their accommodation to global capitalism has happened all across Europe, but perhaps particularly in Britain and especially with Tony Blair's New Labour. As a result, the conditions that make possible significant reductions in the level and severity of poverty are now much diminished.

These conditions have been made the worse by the global pandemic of 2020, the long-term effects of which remain to be seen. The likelihood, therefore, although by no means the inevitability, is that capitalism as a system will continue to ignore the needs of the poor. Its benefactors argue that all efforts must be directed to restoring economic growth and that only with growth can the needs of the poor be met. Such claims are not to be believed. Unrestricted capitalism will continue to create still more poverty as a means of amassing profits. It will, as Seabrook (2013:

11) has argued, "guarantee the immortality of misery and hence, the necessity into the most distant of futures, for further economic expansion."

Therefore, contrary to what is undoubtedly the popular and dominant belief, history as it relates to poverty has not been a long, straight line of steady improvement. It is not the case that, although poverty was terrible in previous centuries and generations, it has improved gradually and steadily along with industrialization and the spread of the franchise and social welfare legislation. This is a constant right-wing refrain. Thatcher's Conservatives, for example, argued that by the time she took office, absolute poverty had been defeated. In 1980, the Conservative's secretary of state for social services said, "The harsh, grinding poverty that disfigured the 1920s and 1930s has gone" (quoted in Novak 1988: 18). To Thatcher, poverty meant not having enough for bare survival, and that level of destitution, she steadfastly maintained, no longer existed. Those claiming to be poor, it followed, were scoundrels and shirkers who had to be forced to work—for which she introduced various forms of workfare, a strategy extended and built upon by New Labour. Workfare is intended to force people into unattractive jobs, just as the *New Poor Law* of 1834 and the workhouse were intended to force people into the dark satanic mills of the Industrial Revolution.

The poverty of today in advanced capitalist nations such as Britain is a major problem—much greater than generally acknowledged. It is not as horrific as the worst of the Poor Law and Industrial Revolution experiences in previous centuries. Nevertheless, today housing conditions for many are appalling. Homelessness grows. Food banks are ubiquitous. Fuel poverty is widespread. The poor experience poorer health and significantly shorter lives than those who are not poor. Illegal drugs are rampant and destructive, as gin was in eighteenth-century Britain. Imprisonment of the poor is a staple of today's response to poverty, as it was under the Poor Laws. Charity takes the place of redistribution via the state. The poor are blamed, demeaned and shamed for their poverty. The results for many include despair and hopelessness, which add to their desperation. We have little to boast about, vis à vis past centuries, when it comes to the persistence of complex and debilitating forms of poverty and our collective treatment of the poor.

The current evidence suggests, unfortunately, that this is likely to continue to be the case (see, for example, Barrow 2020). As was the case in centuries past, we are likely to continue to respond with charity, punishment and efforts to force the poor into unattractive jobs that perpetuate their poverty, rather than taking the steps that are necessary—and are difficult—to eliminate the age-old scourge of poverty with all the human suffering that it produces.

Situating Myself

You may wonder why a non-historian (a social scientist, untrained in historiography) decided to write a history of poverty in Britain. The short answer is that this work has been curiosity-driven, and the curiosity has its origins in my years of close involvement in anti-poverty efforts.

For the past twenty-five years, I have worked in close association with community-based organizations on anti-poverty initiatives in the inner city of Winnipeg, Canada. Winnipeg's inner city is home to complex, often racialized and spatially concentrated, poverty. I have worked closely with and have come to know many outstanding individuals—people whose knowledge of complex poverty is deep and whose commitment to the poor is unwavering. Many of the community-based organizations that these individuals work with are highly skilled and genuinely creative in the work they do. They include women's resource centres, adult learning centres and training programs of various kinds, social housing organizations, neighbourhood renewal corporations, immigrant and refugee settlement houses, social enterprises and various community economic development initiatives, as well as a wide range of Indigenous organizations that work closely with families that are struggling in various ways. The ways in which these community-based organizations work would have to be a part of any successful effort to eradicate poverty.

I have had the good fortune of being a part of some successful projects. These include an intensive, seven-year community development effort in a deeply distressed public housing complex that has produced genuinely positive change (Silver et al. 2016; Mauro and Silver 2017), and the redevelopment of a crime-plagued hotel and adjoining city lots into a unique learning centre and student housing complex in one of Winnipeg's most troubled neighbourhoods (MacKinnon and Silver 2018). During this time, I have played an active role in the creation and operation of an independent, left-oriented public policy research institute—the Canadian Centre for Policy Alternatives–Manitoba. The CCPA–MB has been successful, through an arm's-length entity called the

Manitoba Research Alliance, in securing four large Social Science and Humanities Research Council (SSHRC) grants that have supported inner city and poverty-related research for almost two decades. This funding has contributed to the development of an intimate understanding of Winnipeg's grinding and debilitating poverty, along with the identification—working in close cooperation with community-based anti-poverty organizations—of a wide range of local solutions. I think that I have been deeply privileged to have had the opportunity to be so intimately involved in this work and to have learned as much about complex urban poverty as I think I have learned.

However, after twenty-five years of involvement and, indeed, immersion in this work, I have concluded that effective though it often is in responding to locally based problems, more is needed if poverty is to be solved. Community-based efforts alone are simply keeping the bottom from falling out completely. Many poor people have been moved out of poverty and into what for them have been better lives. But the poverty—a fiercely complex and debilitating form of poverty that is far more than simply a shortage of income—persists. These various "anti-poverty" initiatives do not solve or even significantly reduce the incidence of poverty. They are a necessary part of any meaningful solution to the problems of poverty, but they are not sufficient.

This has led me to wonder about the kinds of responses that have been taken to poverty in the past, and the different ways in which people have understood poverty in the past, in an attempt to determine how poverty might best be solved. Thus, this study.

Chapter 2

Vagabonds and Beggars

Christianity and Enclosure and the Detritus of Crumbling Feudalism

Throughout the Middle Ages, at least from the eleventh to the middle or end of the fifteenth centuries, feudalism prevailed in England. Some peasants gradually became able to purchase land and were successful landowners, or yeoman farmers (Brenner 1987b), able to invest in improved agricultural production and to hire wage labourers (Brenner 1987a). Many argue—and this has been the subject of intense debate (see, for example, Aston and Philpin 1987)—that these landowning peasants who came to employ wage labour and lease additional land were the embryo of the capitalist class and the basis of the emergence of agrarian capitalism. It was a centuries-long process (Hilton 1978; Dobb 1946; Brenner 1987a and 1987b; Byres 2006). Other peasants were less successful and were forced to work for wages, usually seasonally, with the poorer among them being "ruined by the effect of continuous demand for money rent, and by usury" (Hilton 1985: 271). Some borrowed when short of cash, but this often led to default on debts and the need to sell land to moneylenders or better-off peasants (Lis and Soly 1979: 6). Some would as a result become "masterless men" (Beier 1985)—those set adrift by changes in feudal practices—the vagrants, vagabonds and paupers who had access neither to land nor to wage labour and who tramped the countryside. By the end of the seventeenth century an estimated 40 percent of England's population had been forced off the land (Brenner 1987a: 52)—part of the long and complex process of enclosure that would continue into the nineteenth century. Widespread poverty, and harsh responses to poverty, were the result.

Medieval Christian Belief: Deserving and Undeserving, Charity and Punishment

The response to poverty in England and indeed much about life in historical and contemporary Britain has been shaped by the Poor Laws. The roots of the English Poor Laws can be found in early Christian thought. An entire body of ecclesiastical jurisprudence, dating from the twelfth century, was dedicated to thinking about how to deal with poverty and the needs of the poor. The reflections of Christian intellectuals on poverty were voluminous and sophisticated, and these laid the foundations of the *Elizabethan Poor Law* of 1601 and, indeed, for modern forms of poor relief. Early Christian thought was especially important in establishing the importance of charity as the dominant response to poverty and in raising the concern—central to all thinking about poverty over the centuries—about those who were perceived to be able-bodied and yet were not working. These were to become the "undeserving" poor.

Much of this Christian thought has its roots in the *Decretum*, written about 1140 by a monk named Gratian. At least a part of the *Decretum* assembles earlier Christian thought on how to respond to the needs of the poor. Medieval scholars then responded to and built upon this source. This body of thought is not merely an obscure historical artifact. On the contrary, "a large part of the law relating to poor relief is to be found in the *Decretum*" (Tierney 1959a: 8–9).

At one time it was believed by many Christians that to be poor was Christ-like. Morris (1953: 6–7) describes an early Christianity, around 200 AD, "whose ingrained habits of thought assumed that a Christian was a poor man, a rich Christian a contradiction in terms." It followed that poverty was not something to be prevented; rather, the poor were to be admired and supported, as was St. Francis of Assisi (Rubin 1987; Beier 1985). Those who were poor were to be responded to positively and generously, and generosity would be rewarded. In Matthew 19:21, Jesus said, "If you wish to be perfect, go and sell what you own and give the money to the poor, and you will have treasure in heaven."

Support for the poor was to take the form of charity: there was an obligation to give to the poor; giving to the poor—being charitable—was pleasing to God and would produce its own heavenly rewards. "Every deed of charity is counted towards the final reckoning and even a single act of charity could admit a man to heaven" (Rubin 1987: 86).

At the same time, however, early Christian thinkers argued that some who were poor were simply shirking work and/or leading "immoral" lives and so were not entitled to charity. Augustine recommended "denial of alms to those who could work or who led evil lives" (Rubin 1987: 70). In the Bible, 2 Thessalonians 3:10, Paul says: "We gave you a rule when we were with you; not to let anyone have food if he refused to do any work" (Quigley 1997: fn. 27).

This concern with those who can work but don't, and with those who are poor and are seen to live "immoral" lives, would grow over the centuries, becoming a defining feature of the English Poor Laws and of the response to mass unemployment in the 1920s and 1930s (Deacon 1978) and of the urban poverty of the post-1970s era. The concern with those who are able-bodied and not working, and whose perceived moral character and behaviour is deemed to be other than fully "respectable," continues to be central to social assistance policies to this day (see Katz 2013, for example). Complex rules and regulations are based on the perceived need to weed out those who are "welfare frauds," "scroungers" or "shirkers."

Medieval Christian thought struggled with the contradiction embodied in the obligation to give to the poor and the concern that to give indiscriminately, without due consideration of the characteristics of the beneficiary, was problematic. This led to the distinction in medieval Christian thought between the "deserving" and "undeserving" poor (Tierney 1959a: 56–61; 1959b; Rubin 1994). Some argued, "a man who was capable of working with his hands was not to be given anything but was to be corrected and told to go to work." Others added qualifiers such as "these things are true provided he can find someone to employ him" (Tierney 1959b: 367). By the beginning of the sixteenth century, when the elements that would become the *Elizabethan Poor Law* were being put in place, it was widely believed that the able-bodied poor who did not work were the undeserving poor (Slack 1988).

By the mid-sixteenth century, following the Tudor dissolution of English monasteries in 1536, attitudes to the poor had noticeably hardened. This is likely attributable to the fact that "pauperism began to increase seriously just after the traditional means for coping with it [i.e., the monasteries] had been destroyed" (Hill 1964: 262). There were references to the poor wandering "idly, lasciviously and dissolutely" about; to their "sundry and diverse diseases"; their being "contagious and infectious"; and their "heinous deeds, detestable sins, crime and offences." They were "lawless beasts," and "the very filth and vermin of the common wealth" (quoted in Slack 1988: 23, 25)—early examples of language that marginalizes and "Others" the poor, even dehumanizing them. From this time on, "most commentators agreed that some of the poor should be denied tribute, the benefits of beneficence, and a place in Christian society altogether" (Slack 1988: 22). Poverty had "ceased to be a holy state and [instead] become presumptive evidence of wickedness" (Hill 1952: 34).

Early Christian and medieval thinking about the poor, however much it struggled with when to be charitable and when not, was not at all concerned to find ways to "solve" poverty. Ending poverty was rarely, if ever, contemplated. "Medieval charitable relief was never intended to create a new social order, still less to eliminate poverty" (Rubin 1987: 292), and "one might almost say that throughout the early Middle Ages there was no public consciousness that poverty ought to be prevented" (Marshall 1969: 16). Rather, poverty was taken to be "natural," as were existing property relations and power structures. The widely held belief was that wealthy individuals were entitled to hold their property and their wealth, but the wealthy then had a duty to be charitable, especially with the poor and with that part of their wealth that was beyond their ordinary needs (Tierney 1959a: 24–35).

What followed was the belief that "the poor had a *right* to be supported from the superfluous wealth of the community" (Tierney1959a: 37–38, emphasis in original). That the English poor believed they had a right to at least a minimal level of subsistence was a dominant feature of the *Poor Law* of 1601 (E.P. Thompson 1971; Snell 1985). The trade-off for this right to a minimal subsistence was that the wealthy and powerful had a right to the maintenance of existing property and power relations; poverty was to be met merely with charity.

Charity has continued since medieval times to be a dominant response to poverty. "The impulse to remedy social ills through voluntary activity was perennial; watered usually by religious teachings, it sprouted anew in most generations" (Poynter 1969: 3). Charity was (and is) a part of an ideologically conservative approach to poverty. Classical conservatism believes in hierarchy, and knowing and accepting one's station in life, and it holds that those who are the "natural" rulers have obligations to those who are less fortunate (Oakeshott 1962). Throughout the centuries, the landed gentry in England were charitable to the poor (Dyer

2012; Jordan 1961), creating "almshouses"—residences for relief of the poor—and "hospitals" where the poor could be supported (Beier 1983: 3), along with establishing permanent endowments for the maintenance of the poor. Many small almshouses, funded by the charity of those with great or even modest wealth, were scattered throughout England (Jordan 1961).

However, these forms of charity were limited, and the corollary was always that the poor, on receipt of charity, should be grateful, meek and deferential—this too became part of the definition of "deserving poor" (Slack 1988: 20). The result was that far from "solving" poverty, only "extreme necessity among the poor parishioners is relieved" (Tierney 1959a: 78). Relief would always, throughout the period of the Poor Laws, be designed simply to keep the poor from perishing or rebelling. The same was the case with medieval monasteries, which appear to have provided—before their elimination in the Tudor era—for the most minimal and largely haphazard supports to the poor (Tierney 1959a).

Because charity was the means to bare survival only, and even that was delivered in the most haphazard fashion, the poor supported each other in times of need. Dyer (2012) describes the myriad ways by which English villagers in the decades prior to the 1601 *Poor Law* lent financial support to those among them who were poor. An example was the "help-ale or bid-ale: a communal drinking session to raise funds for an honest person fallen on hard times" (Bennett 1997: 23), an early version perhaps of the 1915 rent strikes in Glasgow (Thane 1982) or the 1920s Harlem rent parties (Lewis 1997). It has been argued that, "for many people in need, an ale probably provided much more immediate and substantial assistance than any charity offered by a monastery, almshouse or poor-law overseer" (Bennett 1997: 23). Whatever the limits of this form of self-help—including that it typically excluded vagrants and strangers—it is an important reminder that poor people were by no means simply passive recipients of relief. Indeed, they were often and in many ways anything but submissive—however necessary it might be on occasion to appear meek and deferential. Those with money and power were continually alert to the danger of rebellion by the poor. By the late sixteenth century, in the decades leading up the 1601 *Elizabethan Poor Law*, this was especially the case. A pamphlet of 1580 warned that the poor are "apt to assist rebellion," and it was further reported that not only did "the rich hate the poor," but also "the poor hate the rich" (Hill 1964: 275).

Masterless Men, Vagrants, Vagabonds and Paupers

After the twelfth century, forces were set in motion that would add to the numbers of the poor. The enclosure movement pushed people off the land, feudalism was in the early stages of its long decline and capitalist social relations gradually began to emerge. The sea change this centuries-long process would produce was severely aggravated by the Black Death of 1348–1349, estimated to have killed, at a minimum, 30 percent of the English population (Rubin 1987: 22; Fraser 1984: 31) and perhaps as much as 50 percent (Chambliss 1964: 69). The population of England and Wales in 1300 was about six million; that number was not reached again until the mid-1700s (Cantor 2001: 8). The result was major labour shortages, leading people to move about the country to secure the highest possible wages, in response to which an early *Statute of Labourers*—generally considered to be the first "full-fledged vagrancy statute"—was enacted in 1349 for the purpose of fixing wage levels at the level preceding the Black Death (Chambliss 1964: 68 and 70).

The gradual breakdown of feudalism and the "absolute impoverishment of the rural masses" (Lis and Soly 1979: 54) added to the numbers of beggars moving about the country. From the late thirteenth century the rural poor, no longer able to sustain themselves on the land, migrated in numbers to towns and cities in search of work (Rubin 1987). Kiernan (1953: 48) has called them "the detritus of a crumbling feudal society." By the sixteenth century, "vagabondage was on a new scale," their growing numbers "drawn largely from evicted peasants" (Hill 1952: 40). They caused fear. "The sixteenth century lives in terror of the tramp," wrote Tawney (1912: 270). Pinchbeck (1956: 275) described

> the bands of "sturdy beggars" who swarmed on the roads and terrorized both "towne and countrie".… There were families uprooted by agrarian change, industrial workers displaced by temporary fluctuations in industry and commerce, discharged soldiers, sailors and retainers, the old and impotent poor, the rogues and harlots, and the incorrigibly vagrant and idle, and accompanying many of these groups—the children.

Hill (1952: 34) wrote, "the fundamental causes of the increase of vagabondage in sixteenth century England are not in dispute. Some tenants were evicted, mainly by enclosure for sheep-farming. Others driven below the poverty line by loss of common lands." The long process of enclosure would last into the nineteenth century, unfolding in a complex and multifaceted fashion, forcing people off the land and, in a great many cases, onto the road in search of a means of survival (see, among many examples, Lazonik 1974; Slack 1974).

As ever more vagabonds and beggars were created as people were pushed off the land, ways of thinking about the poor shifted significantly. They were seen as outcasts and increasingly blamed for their circumstances, often in religious terms as sinners whose "only hope of salvation was to be set to work for wages" (Hill 1952: 44). In London, "beggars were demonized and equated with criminals and prostitutes." Golding and Middleton (1982: 9) refer to "god's poor and the devil's—the poor and the paupers"—the latter the object of fear and hostility for centuries.

The point was to push them, by whatever means, into the labour market. They were to be forced to work "under fear and terror of the whip and gallows" (Pinchbeck and Hewitt 1969: 94). Charlesworth (2010: 169) observes, "any reading of the statutes against begging reveals a continuous loathing and fear of beggars." As Tierney (1959a: 113) described it, "from mid-fourteenth century on, the problem of relieving poverty became inextricably intertwined with the problem of suppressing vagrancy." The preamble to a 1531 act of Parliament stated, "In all places throughout this realm, vagabonds and beggars have of long time increased, and daily do increase in great and excessive numbers, by the occasion of idleness, mother and root of all vices" (quoted in Quigley 1997: 12). Beier (1985: xxi) has argued that "the vagrancy laws were intended to deal with a new social problem, that is, a large landless element with no firm roots and no prospects. When uprooted, they became 'masterless men,' and dangers to the social order." Indeed, by the mid-sixteenth century "the vagrancy problem grew to alarming proportions; riots and unsettlement throughout the land created a state of panic which resulted in the *Act* of 1547, the most savage legislation of the century" (Pinchbeck 1956: 276–7; Charlesworth 2010: 169).

The long and complex process of enclosure by which people were forced off the land was resisted—constantly. Enclosure riots were more common than food riots from the mid-sixteenth to mid-seventeenth centuries. Hedges were often used to enclose land, and just as often these were torn down—levelled—in protest. "It became axiomatic that those who leveled hedges were bent also upon leveling social distinctions—

and it was from this time onwards that the term 'leveler' began to acquire the connotation of political radicalism" (Manning 1988: 30). The Midlands Revolt of 1607 was a "particularly significant" reaction against enclosures. Armed gentry killed some forty to fifty peasants and captured others, "some of whom were hung, drawn and quartered, and their remains displayed in local market towns" (Martin 1983: 167). Riots such as these were "an important mode of political expression for a population otherwise excluded from the political process" (Martin 1983: 177).

By the sixteenth century, the problem was no longer a shortage of labour, as in the years following the Black Death. "Rather it was the rising numbers of able-bodied poor that troubled officials" (Beier 1985: 9). Masterless men "existed in alarming numbers … and too often were unemployable rejects of a society in economic transformation" (Hill 1972: 32). Beier (1985: 3) equates these to "the unemployed of the Great Depression of the 1930s, or the jobless millions of today's inner cities." The responses by authorities—in the sixteenth century, the 1930s and today—were strikingly similar.

The vagabonds and beggars were frequently punished for their poverty. In the sixteenth century, a vagabond—someone who was able-bodied yet not working and therefore poor—could be "tied to the end of a cart naked, and beaten with whips … till his body be bloody by reason of such whipping," and a person's ears could be cut off (Quigley 1997: 12). In 1590, vagrants in Middlesex "were being whipped and branded … at the rate of one a day" (Hill 1964: 287). The idea was to force them into the labour market as wage labourers, "which many regarded as little better than slavery" (Hill 1972: 43). Although endorsed by law, such severe penalties were imposed in only a small percentage of cases (Slack 1988: 92), although in Salisbury alone ninety-six vagrants were whipped in 1598, and in Colchester in 1631, fifty-nine were whipped (Slack 1974: 369).

Naturally, children suffered from the poverty and punishment meted out to their parents. In the sixteenth century some relatively progressive measures were introduced for poor children—"children loomed large in the social legislation of the sixteenth century" (Pinchbeck 1956: 273)—but most of these initiatives were overturned quickly. The numbers of poor children streaming into cities overwhelmed the capacity of these limited attempts. Children whose parents were vagrants and idlers and petty criminals, of whom there were many, were at risk. For example, "children figured prominently among the inhabitants of the sixteenth century underground" (Pinchbeck 1957: 59). It was believed in the sixteenth century that such children "must be rescued from a life of idleness, and from growing up to swell the ranks of yet another generation of adult vagrants and criminals" (Pinchbeck 1956: 276).

One solution was to force poor children to work as apprentices. Legislation of 1536 enabled parish authorities to send all such children aged five to fourteen years to an apprenticeship. As Pinchbeck (1957: 61) argued, "While there was some justification for the removal of children from a vicious environment, and from parents leading a criminal way of life, the twentieth-century mind finds it both shocking and incomprehensible that family ties should have been so frequently broken by Tudor poor law legislation in the case of those whose only crime was poverty." For children aged twelve to sixteen years, it was worse—if they refused an apprenticeship they were to be whipped "with rods" (Pinchbeck 1956: 276).

As with children, so with adults. Those who were perceived to be the able-bodied poor were to be forced into the paid labour force. Indeed, poverty was inextricably intertwined with work and the need for wage labourers. "From feudalism through 500 years of regulation by the poor laws, work and poverty journeyed hand in hand" (Quigley 1997: 1). This comes out clearly in the *Ordinance of Labourers* of 1349. Its main purpose was to prevent labourers wandering away from their work to seek higher wages at a time when labour was in short supply due to the Black Death. To render this provision effective, "it forbade the giving of alms to able-bodied beggars under pain of imprisonment" (Tierney 1959a: 128–29) and ordered that towns build stocks "for the punishment of runaway labourers" (Charlesworth 2006: 8). All those who were able-bodied and under age sixty were required to work, and able-bodied persons without work were socially constructed as lazy and criminal (Rubin 1987). Failure to work, or quitting work, was subject to imprisonment. The entire purpose of the *Ordinance of Labourers* of 1349 was to secure a labour supply. All who might work

> were considered only a step away from being vagrants and beggars, thus they must be compelled to work, compelled to stay at work, compelled to accept lower wages, compelled to stay where they can be put to work, and imprisoned if they disobey.

Consequently, vagrants and beggars were compelled into joining the class of workers. (Quigley 1997: 12)

Laws in 1531, 1536, 1537 and again in 1563 and 1572 reinforced these provisions, while acknowledging that some might not be able to find work and establishing a public responsibility to provide employment in those cases. Failure to work was to be harshly punished.

A statute of 1547—"ferocious legislation" (Pinchbeck 1956: 278) withdrawn two years later—included particularly harsh measures. It provided that any runaway servant brought before a justice of the peace could be "marked with a hot iron on the breast with the mark of V," for vagrant, and could then be determined "to be slave to the same person that brought or presented him." If that same slave should run away again and be caught he shall be "marked on the forehead, or the ball of the cheek with an hot iron, with the sign of an S. and further shall be adjudged to be slave to his said master forever" (quoted in Erickson and Havron 1967: 125). The *Statute of Artificers* of 1563 "determined local wage rates, controlled employment conditions and restricted the mobility of labourers" (Golding and Middleton 1982: 10), and this statute "created the legal framework for English labour for over two centuries" (Woodward 1980: 42). The *Vagrancy and Poor Relief Act* of 1572 has been called the "most repressive vagrancy law of the Elizabethan period," involving whipping and burning of ears for a first offence and hanging for second offenders who ran away (Parker 2008: 45). The point was to force the poor, the paupers in particular, into the paid labour force.

As the sixteenth century moved to a close, the English governing elite was seized by the fear of rebellion and the perceived need to preserve public order—thus the harsh measures described above. Rebellions by the poor had rolled across Western Europe in the early sixteenth century. England was no exception. When the Duke of Norfolk asked to speak to the leader of a rebellious crowd he received an answer that reflects the angry mood of the times: "Since you ask who is our captain, forsooth his name is Poverty, for he and his cousin Necessity, have brought us to this doing" (Lis and Soly 1979: 85). Enclosure riots increased dramatically in the 1590s, as did outbursts of disorder and rioting in London (Manning 1988), and by the end of that decade "the problem of vagrancy threatened to overwhelm the courts" (Manning 1988: 166).

The result was to be the *Elizabethan Poor Law*. In explaining the introduction of that law in 1601, Solar (1995: 17) suggests, "the fear of social and political unrest played a major role." To deny relief was known to produce "riots." For elites, "relief protected them from a host of disorders that might otherwise have threatened their social supremacy" (Beier 1983: 36). For its recipients, relief would come to be seen in future centuries as an English right, part of the "moral economy" of the poor (E.P. Thompson 1971; Snell 1985).

Chapter 3

Manage and Control

Two Centuries of the *Elizabethan Poor Law*

The series of statutes put in place from 1349 to 1601 constituted an attempt to find a solution to the large numbers who were destitute and able-bodied but not working. In many cases they moved about the country as vagrants, scoundrels and beggars, often engaging in various forms of civil unrest. The *Poor Law* of 1601 and later the *New Poor Law* of 1834 were all about pushing such people into the paid labour force, forcing them to work. As Marx (1976: 899) described it:

> Thus were the agricultural folk first forcibly expropriated from the soil, driven from their homes, turned into vagabonds, and then whipped, branded and tortured by grotesquely terroristic laws into accepting the discipline necessary for the system of wage labour.

Feudalism was in the last stages of giving way to capitalism, England was embarking upon colonial adventures, and the coming century was to be one of particularly dramatic changes. The result of such changes—and the poverty they created, and the risks to established order that poverty posed—was the *Elizabethan Poor Law* of 1601. The *Poor Law* was an essential part of the transition from feudalism to capitalism.

The entire transition process can be seen as the making of a working class. This process occurred physically via the enclosure movement, which cut people off from their traditional means of livelihood, thus making them available for and in need of wage labour. It was also a behavioural process, via the *Poor Law*, intended to afford people only enough to keep them from starving or rebelling, thus making wage labour more attractive by comparison.

A Rudimentary and Threadbare System of Poor Relief

The *Poor Law* established the legal right to relief for the deserving poor, those who were destitute and unable to work—the aged, the sick, those with disabilities, for example. It excluded from the legal right to relief those deemed able to work—the undeserving poor—and authorized parish officials to set them to work or to impose punishments of various kinds (Hill 1986). The *Poor Law* of 1601 also represented a transition from the ancient English tradition of voluntary charity, into a national—albeit parish-based and thus highly differentiated—system "that placed a legal obligation on each parish to supplement the incomes of those whose idleness was involuntary" (Hindle 2004a: 227). The *Poor Law* was in effect a rudimentary, and particularly threadbare, social assistance system. The idea that any form of relief that was offered should be directed at the "deserving" poor and consist of a bare minimum would persist for four centuries and beyond.

From its declaration in 1601 to its replacement in 1834, responsibility for the administration of the *Poor Law* was carried out at the parish level. The relief provided was financed by taxes levied on income earned by those who owned property. England became the only country in Europe with a system of poor relief paid out of local taxes, or rates. Some have argued that by comparison with other European countries, English poor relief was "relatively generous and certain in its benefits" (Solar 1995: 2), although others have demonstrated there was "great variation at the individual parish level" (Williams 2016: 951–53). It was in effect a national system, but its administration—who was entitled to benefits and how much they were entitled to, for example—differed widely from parish to parish.

There were some fifteen thousand parishes in England. Most were very small: in twelve thousand of the fifteen thousand parishes there were fewer than eight hundred inhabitants (Solar 1995: 12). Each parish had its own traditions and practices regarding the administration of relief. Each had an overseer of the poor. Overseers were residents of the parish appointed and supervised by local magistrates and/or the parish vestry. Magistrates typically settled disputes related to the denial of relief.

The advantage of the parish-based delivery of relief, its advocates argued, was that those who were its administrators—overseers, magistrates, the parish vestry—were likely to know the personal circumstances of applicants, because applicants for relief were their neighbours. The administration of relief was not a distant and impersonal bureaucratic system. Persons seeking relief had first to approach the overseer to ask for assistance. They then had to demonstrate that they were destitute and had a "settlement" in that particular parish. As Lees (1998: 11) has described it, in each parish "rich and poor faced one another to contest the distribution of local resources and to reallocate them according to some locally recognized standard of need."

The personalized character of this system of relief required that applicants behave in a meek and deferential manner. "Deference was the lubricant that greased the machinery of [relief]" (Hindle 2004a: 447). Often, however, this involved a "micro politics" of complex negotiations and strategies by which the poor sought ways to express their agency in pursuit of relief—they were not simply the passive recipients of aid (Hindle 2004a: 362).

Not surprisingly, each parish sought to hold down costs, and thus rates or taxes, by excluding applicants deemed able to work or insufficiently deferential. There was a strong unwillingness to pay taxes to provide benefits for the poor.

A crucial part of the relief system, and a product of its parish-based character, was the need to determine which parish was responsible for providing relief to any given individual. Starting with the 1662 *Act of Settlement,* after the *Poor Law* was already in place, there emerged what would become a bewildering web of laws intended to determine in which parish any individual had "settlement"—that is, which was their "home" parish and thus the only parish in which they were legally entitled to relief. Settlement in a given parish could be established by birth, but also by being hired there for a year, serving an apprenticeship, holding a local office, owning or renting land or paying taxes. Women acquired their husband's right to settlement and legitimate children acquired their parents' right (Lees 1998: 28), although in a minority of cases children and unmarried mothers were removed to different parishes, thus separating mother from child (Levene 2010). All those unable to prove settlement in a particular parish were denied relief and were subject to being removed, often forcibly, to that parish in which they did have a settlement and therefore a legal entitlement to relief. The exception was those parishes experiencing labour shortages (Solar 1995) or those cases in which the poor could negotiate non-removal. The purpose of the laws of settlement and associated practices was to hold down the rates by removing those among the poor who came from outside a given parish. Thus, built into the system was the ancient fear of the vagrant or the vagabond, of the outsider or the "Other."

Evil, Destitute and Masterless Persons

Many of the poor, both prior to and after the *Poor Law* of 1601, were "vagrants"—able-bodied people, mostly but not only men, on the road looking for work and begging or stealing when work was not to be found. Begun in earlier centuries, this phenomenon worsened in the later centuries. "Petty theft in particular was the activity of a stranger to a village or parish, stealing clothes drying in gardens and almost anything that could be reached through open windows" (Slack 1988: 101). This problem was seen to be serious enough that a 1597 vagrancy statute authorized whipping and the removal to their parish of birth of all "rogues, vagabonds, and sturdy beggars over the age of seven, found 'begging, vagrant, wandering or misordering themselves'" (Slack 1975: ix). People left their villages to find work—Beier (1983: 8, 11) estimated that as much as 15 percent of the population per year left their villages in search of work in the 1520s, and by the 1600s that proportion was one third per decade.

In every city the poor were concentrated in neighbourhoods characterized by poor housing and poor health (Slack 1988). "From the 1580s in London and elsewhere, the suburbs were on the point of being overwhelmed with the hordes of displaced indigents." Conscripts for military service overseas were mostly "rogues, vagabonds and other evil, dissolute and masterless persons" (quoted in Hill 1986: 253). In London a criminal underworld developed, with "organized prostitution and large scale receiving of stolen goods" and "schools for pickpockets." Public drunkenness was a problem. Alehouses were seen as "centres of disorder, where stolen goods could be disposed of, whores picked up, money wasted and youth corrupted" (Slack 1988: 102–3). Thus was created "a massive poverty problem which posed a real threat to public order," including "popular rebellions in which the poor participated, and in which egalitarian ideas surfaced" (Beier 1983: 13).

The 1640s saw "a vigorous policy of colonial expansion starting with Cromwell's annexation of Jamaica in 1655" (Hill 1985: 320) and the intensification of the slave trade as vast profits poured into England. The English Revolution laid the basis for the further development of capitalism. The aristocracy was not eliminated, but it was weakened; a capitalist class had not yet emerged, but it was in the making; and the constraints on the further development of capitalism had been considerably weakened (Heller 2011). As Hill (1955: 6) described it: "The English revolution of 1640–1660 was a great social movement like the French Revolution of 1789. The state power protecting an old order that was essentially feudal was violently overthrown, power passed into the hands of a new class, and so the free development of capitalism was made possible." To a considerable extent this was still agrarian capitalism, involving the concentration of larger amounts of land into fewer hands and leading to still more people becoming landless.

It was during this time of "unique intellectual ferment" (Wood 2012: 224) that the True Levellers or Diggers advanced radically egalitarian ideas about the promotion of political democracy and the redistribution of land from rich to poor. As Gerrard Winstanley (quoted in Hill 1955: 52) wrote, "The poorest man hath as true a title and just right to the land as the richest man." In response to such rebellious ideas, attitudes toward the poor hardened. It was argued in the seventeenth century that the poor were wicked, and like the biblical Cain, were cast out of godly society, becoming "a cursed generation" (Hill 1964: 283–85).

Throughout the seventeenth and eighteenth centuries, market relations more rapidly replaced the land-based feudal system. The centuries-long process of enclosures had intensified by the mid-eighteenth century (Plumb 1981)—between 1750 and 1850 more than 4,000 enclosure acts were passed in Parliament (Lazonick 1974: 26). The numbers of those who were poor grew steadily, because so many had lost access to the land. Enclosure, a key element in creating capitalism, produced poverty. As Beier (1983: 4–5) described it, "there were multitudes who had little to fall back on.… Reliable taxation records suggest that a third to a half lived in or near poverty in the 1520s and again in the 1670s." In the second half of the 1700s it is estimated that over 10 percent of England's population was in receipt of relief, and that "up to 60 percent … experienced significant poverty at some point during their lives" (Hitchcock and Shoemaker 2015: 5). Using more colourful language, Porter (1991: 13) says, "The Grim Reaper harvested the poor. Pauper children died like flies during the 1720s and 1730s."

Precarious Labour, Precarious Lives: Making Shift and Other Means of Coping

Prominent among the poor were workers who either were paid too little to support themselves and their families or were temporarily out of work. Labour was then, as it is now, precarious. Life was precarious, lived on the razor's edge. Most labourers were "only a farthing away from destitution's door: the slightest accident, illness or trade downswing would instantly turn a sturdy family into beggars" (Porter 1991: 130). Parish surveys done at the end of the sixteenth century include lists of "labouring persons not able to live off their labour" (Slack 1988: 28) and throughout the seventeenth century, growing numbers of the poor were those who found work but whose wages were so low or whose employment so precarious that they still lived in poverty (Slack 1990).

The Irish, who came to England to escape even greater poverty at home, were seen by the English as a threat to their already threadbare wages and as a potential draw on parish funds. "British rate-payers resented the heavy burden of Irish paupers on their poor-rates, and further feared them as disease-carriers" (O'Tuathaigh 1985: 21). In London, "the Irish poor were often forced to become among the most desperate and marginal of Londoners in some of the capital's most filthy and decrepit districts" (White 2013: 161). In 1815 it was reported that in London's East End, seven hundred Irish were found living in twenty-four small houses (George 1965: 116)—almost thirty per house.

The parish relief system was there as a legal entitlement for those designated to be the deserving poor, but it was residual, inconsistent and, at best, offered just barely enough to stay alive. This was especially the case in the north and west of England, where parish relief has been described as "ramshackle and parsimonious" (King 2000: 262).

Workers therefore relied upon an "economy of makeshifts"—income generated from a wide range of other sources, including cottage gardens and livestock, the mutual support of kin and neighbours, taking in lodgers, begging and engaging in "crimes of necessity." Hindle (2004a: 93) argues, "The resonance of the phrase 'to make shift' lies in its very vagueness: contriving to get by somehow—anyhow—without actually specifying the expedients involved." Children, too, contributed to "making shift." Hindle (2004a: 224) refers to the "extraordinarily ambiguous role of children in the makeshift economies of the poor. Children's hands might equally be busied spinning in the family home or outstretched in a gesture of importunity at the kitchen door of their neighbours." In some cases children would be farmed out to relatives or friends, sent out to work for wages or even sent temporarily into a workhouse. In London, children were on the streets begging, selling whatever they could get their hands on and engaging in petty crime as part of a family's survival strategy (Levene 2012, 2010). In some cases, they were hired out to beggars who used the children as begging aids and "presumably made a profit from their bargain" (White 2013: 203). Parish relief was generally a last resort (Hindle 2004a). King (2000: 135), drawing upon the evidence of letters written by (or for) paupers, finds that a dominant theme is "the extraordinary lengths that people claim to have gone to in order to keep away from dependence on the communal welfare system." On the other hand, Harley (2015) provides evidence that in some cases the poor would use the workhouse as part of a survival strategy—part of making shift—particularly when hit with sickness or unemployment. Unmarried mothers, for example, were known in some cases to place their children in a workhouse in order to find work, and then take the children back when circumstances allowed (Levene 2008; Harley 2015).

Gin was another response to poverty. In the first half of the eighteenth century, "gin became the quickest way to oblivion for the poor…. It offered speedy if temporary relief from the anxieties of poverty, hunger, homelessness and abuse" (White 2013: 239). George (1965: 27–28) describes this as "the orgy of spirit-drinking which was at its worst between 1720 and 1751 … whose effects were seen in the streets of London, in the workhouses, in the growing misery of the poor, in an increase of crimes of violence." Hitchcock and Shoemaker (2015: 170) argue that "women were prominent participants in the gin trade." They quote a 1736 justices' report:

> With Regard to the Female sex we find the Contagion has spread even among them, And that to a Degree hardly possible to be Conceived. Unhappy Mothers habituate themselves to these distill'd Liquors, whose Children are born weakly and Sickly and often look Shriveld and old, as tho they had Numbered many Years; Others again daily give it to their Children whilst young and learn them even before they can go to taste and approve of this Certain great Destroyer.

In St. Giles in the East End of London in 1750, it was claimed that "every fourth house at least was a gin-shop. Its eighty-two 'two-penny houses' were also brothels of the lowest class and places for receiving stolen goods" (George 1965: 42). Prostitution was common. In the streets of eighteenth-century London "it seemed that prostitutes were everywhere" (White 2013: 346), recruited largely from the vast numbers of "deserted boys and girls" of London (George 1965: 7) and appropriately seen as a part of making shift.

Women especially were poor—their disproportion among the ranks of the poor throughout the seventeenth and eighteenth centuries has been described as "striking and significant" (Oxley 1974: 59). The nature of the work available to women was the main cause of their poverty. A poignant example is washerwomen in eighteenth century London:

> Perhaps there is not a class of people who work harder than those washer-women who go out to assist servants in what is called a heavy wash; they may be seen in the winter-time, shivering at the doors at three or four in the morning, and are seldom dismissed before ten at night. (Quoted in George 1965: 208)

Women were paid less than men, and employment was often seasonal:

> Even if women enjoyed regular wages, they were often not sufficient to guarantee survival. Many women were forced to use an "economy of makeshifts." They worked in a variety of jobs, they sold their clothes, asked family, friends and neighbours for help when they needed it. They applied to charities and to the parish for relief. Others were forced to turn to crime to survive by stealing or prostitution. (Evans 2005: 30)

These conditions were worsened when, because of the early death of a husband or abandonment by a lover, women were left to raise young children on their own. Levene (2012: 40) describes "the extreme fragility of families which did not consist of two parents, or when one parent was sick or otherwise incapacitated." The laws relating to settlement were especially damaging to women. In many cases overseers would drive a pregnant single mother out of a parish in order to prevent the child from becoming a "burden" on the parish rates. As a result,

> the roads were thick with wandering women in a pregnant condition. No other word than brutal can describe the treatment which these women received from the parishes through which

they strayed…. The parish officers did everything they could to check the growth of bastardy, a thing which they abhorred, not on moral grounds, but because it was likely to cost the parish money, and so raise the rates. (Marshall 1969: 210, 221)

An example is the case of a pregnant woman abandoned by her lover and pushed out of a parish "by constables fearful of the cost of maintaining her bastard." She gave birth "in a little straw under a tree in the common highway in a cold night … after a cruel and savage manner." In Oxford, justices "made vagrants distribute their children in the parishes where they happened to have been born and had a settlement, while the parents were ordered elsewhere. They quite deliberately broke up families" (Slack 1988: 99). In some cases unwanted children were deserted by parents and "found dead on the roads from exposure and starvation" (Pinchbeck and Hewitt 1969: 22). In other cases, unmarried mothers in London would be left no choice but to turn their children over to the London Foundling Hospital, which opened in 1741. From that date until the end of the century, 18,539 infants were left there and "two thirds perished in infancy or early childhood" (Berry 2019: 58).

Idle, Ragged Children: Set Them to Work!

Concerns about poor children during the era of the *Old Poor Law* and again in the nineteenth century under the *New Poor Law* had to do, almost exclusively, with their relationship to the labour market. The most common complaint made about poor children was that they were not working; thus, the most common response was to set them to work. In the eighteenth century much concern was expressed about the "idleness" of children, which was a "great scourge" (Cunningham 1990: 131). In Manchester in the eighteenth century, the streets were full of "idle, ragged children, who are not only losing their time, but learning habits of gaming." In 1770 it was recommended "that poor children be sent at the age of four to workhouses…. There is considerable use in their being, somehow or other, constantly employed at least 12 hours a day" so that they might be "habituated to constant employment" (quoted in E.P. Thompson 1974: 59). London in the eighteenth century "teemed with abandoned children. Over a thousand a year were being left on the rubbish heaps, in the streets, alleys and other public thoroughfares of the city" (Evans 2005: 129). "Each year nameless children died wretchedly on the streets of London" (White 2013: 113–15).

Those who survived were often on the streets, where they were seen as a threat. For example, in Exeter in the sixteenth century there were "troupes of children, boyes and older persons, [who] lye loitering and floistering in every corner of the citie." In eighteenth-century London, idleness was seen as "the Parent of most Disorders in Society, as Housebreaking, robbing on the High-way, thieving of all kinds, Beggary, Lying, Sedition, and even a total Depravity of Manners" (quoted in Cunningham 1992: 21). The vast numbers of children who "infested" the streets of London were described by a magistrate in the mid-eighteenth century as "Shoplifters, Pilferers and Pickpockets," adding that "these deserted boys were Thieves from Necessity, their Sisters are Whores from the same cause" (Pinchbeck and Hewitt 1969: 110, 117). So dangerous were these children seen to be that "by 1740, for stealing a handkerchief worth one shilling, so long as it was removed privily from the person [i.e., pickpocketed], children could be hanged by the neck until dead" (Plumb 1981: 17).

Overseers wanted such children gone from their parish, "and there was consequently enormous pressure to apprentice a child in a neighbouring or more distant parish in order to avoid any long-term costs" (Cunningham 1990: 132). In some cases, "it was a norm to bind out [place into apprenticeship] nearly all the children of the poor at the age of eight, nine or ten" (Cunningham 1992: 30). In many cases, a fee was paid to a master in another parish to encourage him to take on as apprentices those young children who were on relief:

> This was usually about 5 pounds; to a poor man, who was usually a journeyman weaver, this was a fortune, and children could be useful in weaving at a very early age. The parish regarded the money as well spent—they were rid of supporting a potential pauper. But the results for the child were too often disastrous. (George 1953: 125)

In each parish, a balance had to be found: enough had to be paid in relief to keep people from starving or rebelling; yet relief payments had to be held down to control taxes.

From the early seventeenth century, some vagrant children and youth were transported to the Caribbean and the American colonies where the demand for labour was insatiable. Exporting poor children began in 1617 "in the immediate context of relieving pressure in the poorest parts of London swarming with homeless waifs, orphans, foundlings, runaway apprentices and unemployed servants" (Coldrey 1999: 35). In 1648, Liverpool City Council responded to growing numbers of paupers and street children by passing an order delegating a group to "go through and about the town and take their names and examine them and cause such as are fit and able to work in the Plantations to be shipt for Barbadoes" (quoted in Law 1981: 1). In parishes across Britain, overseers were known to purchase clothing for poor children in order that they could be exported to America. In other cases, children were kidnapped and sent for service in America (Coldrey 1999). In 1793, it was reported that "three army regiments of 1000 each were formed of pauper boys. This was to meet recruitment targets, and also to take children off the hands of the parish" (Levene 2012: 187). All these attempts to remove poor children from the responsibility of a particular parish have been described by Pinchbeck and Hewitt (1969: 109) as "attempts to shovel out some of the human debris of the streets and alleyways into merchant ships and distant colonies," albeit without solving the problem they purported to address.

Slavery: Producing Brutal Poverty, Massive Profits and Racism

Particularly in the seventeenth century, Britain's focus shifted to the insatiable appetite for labour in the Caribbean colonies—primarily African slave labour, but also the British poor and working class, many of whom became Caribbean plantation overseers. The seventeenth century sugar trade relied upon the massive transport of African slaves to the Caribbean. As the number of slaves grew—to extract huge sugar-based profits in Barbados and Jamaica in particular—and their rebelliousness in response to their brutal treatment also grew, slaveowners came increasingly to rely upon indentured servants and others exported from Britain as overseers. They were offered material rewards to set themselves against the slaves and in support of the slaveowners. Thus was created a cross-class alliance of all those of European descent, created for the purpose of controlling Black slave labour and leading to the belief in "whiteness." To better exercise their control of Black slaves, those from Britain, no matter their social class or religion, came to imagine themselves as "white." Prior to this, there would have been no reason for indentured servants, for example, to imagine themselves as "white." They would be likely to identify along class or religious lines—as Catholics or Church of England—or along national lines—as English or Irish, for example. Those not "white," those who were Black, were the "Other," the dangerous classes, those who were inferior to "whites"—and to justify their oppression, they were denigrated.

Liverpool slave merchants, who controlled as much as 85 percent of the British slave trade (Beckert 2015: 213), as well as slave merchants in Bristol and London, mounted vigorous defenses of their inhumane business. They justified it on various grounds, including its important contribution to the economy and to job creation, but most importantly on the false grounds that Africans were inferior to "whites"—lascivious, promiscuous, more like animals than humans. "Slavery's defenders portrayed the Negro as stupid, indolent and promiscuous" (Myers 1996: 42) or "libidinous and shameless as monkeys or baboons" (Lorimer 1978: 24). Such ideas were advanced to justify the slave trade—African slaves were commodities to be bought and sold, and they were brutally treated. Indeed, the profits flowing from slavery fuelled Britain's Industrial Revolution (Fryer 1984), as first argued by Eric Williams (1944). In the US, the profits from slave-produced cotton fuelled that country's industrialization. Slaves as financial assets were so significant that "the capital stored in slaves exceeded the combined value of all the nation's railroads and factories" (Beckert and Rockman 2016: 1). Thus, the denigration and dehumanization of Africans had its origins in the massive profits that derived from the slave trade. "To justify this trade, and the use of slaves to make sugar, the myths were woven into a more or less coherent racist ideology" (Fryer 1984: 7–8).

Liverpool's economy was built upon the slave trade and slave-produced cotton—for example, in 1799, it comprised 50 percent, and by the late 1830s almost 90 percent of all British cotton imports entered the country through Liverpool (Beckert 2015: 212). It is estimated that 4,051 slaving voyages left Liverpool in the eighteenth century (Longmore 2007: 231). The city's entire power structure was populated by those directly involved in and benefiting from the slave trade. In 1787, thirty-seven of the city's forty-one councillors "were slave-ship owners or major investors in or suppliers to the trade. All of the twenty mayors between 1787 and 1807 financed or owned slave-ships." Tens of thousands of working-class jobs depended upon the trade in slaves. Most in Liverpool "vehemently defended the slave trade" (Myers 1984: viii). "The slave trade was 'the pride of Liverpool,' for it flooded the town with wealth," and it was this wealth that was invested to create Liverpool's major banks (Fryer 1984: 33, 42–3). These banks, in turn, made vast profits by advancing the credit needed to build the cotton plantations in the American Deep South, without which the plantations would have crumbled (Beckert 2015). Collateral for that credit was typically the slaves themselves (Baptist 2016). The same was the case in London, where those who traded in slaves disproportionately held major political offices, including mayor, and developed and invested in innovative credit systems to facilitate the trade in slaves (Fryer 1984). In fact, those supporting what Taylor (2020: 311) has called the "West Indian Interest" in slavery included "hundreds of MPs, peers, civil servants, businessmen, financiers, landowners, clergymen, intellectuals, journalists, publishers, soldiers, sailors, and judges, and all of them went to extreme lengths to preserve and protect colonial slavery" (see also Sanghera 2021).

The case of Bristol is similar, except that Bristol was built on the trade in slaves and slave-produced sugar: "every brick in the city had been cemented with a slave's blood" (Fryer 1984: 33). Some 40 percent of the city's income at the time derived from the slave trade (Longmore 2007: 243). In the nine years after 1698, "Bristol alone shipped 160,950 Black slaves to the sugar plantations" (Shyllon 1977: 8), and between 1630 and 1807 British slave merchants bought and sold an estimated 2,500,000 Africans (Fryer 1984: 33).

Capitalism generated, at the same time and as part of the same process, both massive profits and horrific poverty and grief. The production of poverty was a bloody and a global business. The belief in the inferiority of those of African descent was, of necessity, built into the very structure of the slave-trading economy and society (Law 1981).

Anti-slavery forces, which grew in the late seventeenth and early eighteenth centuries, typically made the case that Africans were indeed human but child-like, "noble savages" who needed the benefits of Christian training to make them "civilized," as were, so the argument went, the British (Myers 1996: 47). The abolitionists' attitude was a "condescending paternalism which claimed to care for the black man's welfare, but assumed he would remain a ward of his guardians" (Lorimer 1978: 122). This abolitionist depiction of Africans was similar to the way charitable societies treated the English poor, especially the "respectable" or "deserving" poor. Thus, in the eyes of both the defenders and opponents of slavery, Africans in England, as in the colonies, were considered inferior. The abolitionists, Wilberforce in particular, were deeply conservative, and adopted a similar attitude toward British workers—they were inferior to those of a higher class and should accept their position.

In the seventeenth and eighteenth centuries Blacks in England—those of African and Asian descent—were relatively few. Myers (1996: 27) estimates their numbers in London at 5,000, perhaps somewhat more, and it is generally believed that in Britain the number was about 15,000, although it is almost impossible to be precise. Many came as slaves brought by planters returning from the colonies; others had been seamen or Loyalists who left America after the War of Independence (Braidwood 1994: 22; Fryer 1984: 191). Most lived in the major slaving ports, Liverpool, Bristol and London. They were subjected, in a great many cases, to discrimination and racism (Shyllon 1977), although Chater (2009: 166, 171) argues that those of African descent were no more discriminated against than were the poor—class and religion, more than "race," were the more typical sources of discrimination. Most people of African descent were poor, largely because they were unable to find employment, and many were beggars. Disproportionately they lived among the English poor—many, for example, lived in London's East End (Myers 1996: 21)—and appear to have been accepted (Lorimer 1978: 27).

In the post–Second World War era, Caribbeans, Africans and Asians from the colonies moved from the periphery to the heart of the once-sprawling British empire. Here they continued to be confronted with racism and came to include disproportionate numbers of the poor, increasingly creating the late twentieth and early twenty-first century notion of "racialized poverty."

Punishment: The Workhouse as Incentive to Work

Another response to the ever-growing numbers of the poor and the constantly rising costs of relief throughout the seventeenth and eighteenth centuries was to require those on relief to wear a badge indicating they were entitled to relief in a given parish. There is evidence that as far back as 1370—not long after the *Statute of Labourers*—some parishes required that paupers wear badges (Hindle 2004b: 11). More than three hundred years later, an act of 1697 required that "all poor persons receiving parish relief must wear a badge in red or blue cloth on the shoulder of the right sleeve in an open and visible manner" (Hindle 2004b: 10). Wearing a badge was intended to provide evidence that a beggar was both from the parish and was "deserving." Those without badges, therefore, were able to work but would not, or they were insufficiently meek and deferential and thus lacking in moral character, enabling almsgivers to know who should receive charity and who should not.

The badge was also intended to be a symbol of shame, and the inculcation of shame was aimed at holding down relief costs, becoming but one of an endless series of measures aimed at doing so. Hindle (2004b: 19) argues, "badging the poor was a modification of the sixteenth-century practice of branding or whipping the idle, a way of inscribing an external physical sign on the clothes, rather than on the body."

Paupers, however, were not just passive recipients of the badging process. Badges became "objects of counterfeit and fraud," used by paupers to "pretend" to be deserving recipients of alms in a particular parish (Hitchcock and Shoemaker 2015: 50). Paupers exercised their agency in a multiplicity of ways, doing what they deemed necessary to survive.

A more long-lasting response to the rising costs of relief was the workhouse. In the late seventeenth and early eighteenth centuries especially, many writers—perhaps most significantly Jeremy Bentham (Stokes 2001)—promoted plans for workhouses (Orsi 2017). Bentham drew up detailed plans for workhouses all over the country, "each containing up to 2000 paupers, arranged in such a way that their every action would be visible to those governing the establishment" (Seabrook 2013: 82). The original "Bridewell" was created in London in 1555, intended for "sturdy beggars" (Golding and Middleton 1982: 12). Various forms of workhouses existed in the seventeenth century, but *Knatchbull's Act* of 1723 facilitated and encouraged their further creation. As a result, "between 1723 and 1750 approximately 600 new workhouses were established in England and Wales" (Orsi 2017: 456). In London alone, there were some eighty workhouses in 1776, able to accommodate sixteen thousand people (Levene 2012: 108). By 1782, as the Industrial Revolution was fully taking off, one third of parishes either had a workhouse or had access to one (Slack 1990: 32–35), and by 1802–1803, there were 3,765:

> The Webbs believed that this figure had risen to 4000 institutions by 1815, with a resident population of 100,000. By 1831, there were almost 4800 institutions, and while that number fell under the new poor law, workhouses became progressively larger and more grandly constructed. (King 2000: 3)

Most workhouse inmates were women. At the London workhouse for which the best records exist, there were just over ten thousand admissions in the period 1738–1748, of which 51 percent were adult women and 26 percent were children under fifteen years (Hitchcock and Shoemaker 2015: 139)—that is, just over three in four inmates were either women or children.

> The inmates lists show young, deserted, unmarried and widowed mothers as the largest able-bodied group in most workhouses…. In the workhouse a few could look after the children while the remainder were set on useful tasks. In any case, nobody had any qualms about forcing unmarried mothers, whose plight aroused hostility rather than sympathy, into the workhouse. (Oxley 1974: 90)

Workhouses were often places of misery. This appears to have been especially the case when management of a workhouse was contracted out (Marshall 1969). In some cases workhouses were "hired out to any manufacturer who, in return for keeping the inmates alive, obtained cheap labour" (Plumb 1981: 20), a practice similar to that used profitably in the post-Reconstruction era in the American South (Blackmon 2009). Nevertheless, eighteenth-century workhouses "proved hopelessly unprofitable" (Pinchbeck and Hewitt 1973: 496). George Rude (1971: 139) describes workhouses in London as "dumps and dosshouses for the destitute and unemployable." Overseers were often arbitrary in their use of punishments. Harley (2015: 88) describes the case of a workhouse where inmates not complying with rules lost their next meal, "and if they told lies they had to stand on a chair in the dining room with a Paper fixed on his or her Breast, whereupon shall be written, *Infamous Liar*" (emphasis in original). Marshall (1969: 55) described inmates punished with "three whippings, with a week's interval between each." On the other hand, there is evidence that "material life in the workhouse was adequate and that inmates were well fed," and in some cases they "could expect to receive better provisions than they could when living independently outside the workhouse" (Harley 2015: 85, 95). Conditions undoubtedly varied from workhouse to workhouse (Pinchbeck and Hewitt 1969: 170–1), and in all cases, conditions outside the workhouse were especially harsh for the poor.

Overcrowding was often a major problem. "Shoreditch parish complained that their workhouse was so crowded that 39 children had to sleep in three beds" (George 1953: 70). Even the better workhouses "slept the elderly two to a bed and children three to a bed" (Harley 2015: 86). In the case of London's St. Marylebone workhouse, between 1769 and 1781, approximately one in every six children was apprenticed out. Doing so relieved the parish of the responsibility to pay for the children. "This, and not a desire to provide a training for the young, was the real motive that made the overseers zealous to place out their poor children" (Marshall 1969: 188). As for the masters to whom the children were apprenticed, they were typically paid by the parish to take on the children, and so "cared little what happened" to them (Marshall 1969: 193).

Those many children who remained in workhouses suffered grievously. For instance, "of more than 2300 children taken into London workhouses between 1750 and 1755, only seven percent survived until the end of that period" (Lees 1998: 54; Porter 1991: 132). A 1767 Committee of the House of Commons reported that from 1741 to 1748, of the 1,419 children who either were born in a London workhouse or had come to a workhouse at less than one year of age, only nineteen survived (Marshall 1969: 145)—a survival rate of slightly better than one percent. Hitchcock and Shoemaker (2015: 252–53) conclude, based on 1746–1750 data from a London workhouse, that "St. Margaret's workhouse was quite simply a place of death." They add that for the first half of the 1750s, London's Foundling Hospital experienced a mortality rate of 72 percent. Reformer Jonas Hanway visited every workhouse in London between 1757 and 1763 and found horrendous death rates for children under age five: at St. Luke's workhouse, all fifty-three children (100 percent) perished; St. Giles workhouse, it was 169 of 415 children (41 percent); St. Martin in the Fields workhouse, 158 of 312 children (51 percent); and St. George's workhouse, 137 of 288 children (48 percent) (Pinchbeck and Hewitt 1969: 181).

Workhouses were, of course, an essential component of the emergent industrial form of capitalism. Vast numbers of people continued to be severed from their means of livelihood as the result of enclosure, and they had to be forced into the new Industrial Revolution factories. Profits depended upon forcing people into the paid labour force; workhouses were one of many means of doing so. As Marx described it, "a matter of a million paupers in the British workhouses is as inseparable from British prosperity as the existence of eighteen to twenty millions in gold in the Bank of England" (quoted in Palmer 2019: 54).

The costs, in terms of human well-being, were immense.

The high death rates led to some children in workhouses being farmed out to nurses in the countryside. Here, too, death rates were shockingly high, so much so that "those nurses who could keep their charges alive for at least 12 months received a premium of 10 shillings" (Green 2010: 138).

The purpose of the workhouses was to deter those able to work from seeking relief. This was achieved in either of two ways: make the workhouses so unattractive that those able to work would do so rather than enter a workhouse; or use the workhouse as a venue in which to impose a regime of "moral reform." This was consistent with the long-standing belief that poverty was attributable to the moral failings of the poor.

Not surprisingly, as Marshall (1969: 151) observes, "as a rule, the workhouse was detested by the poor."

Prisons were worse, though. And in eighteenth-century London, they were everywhere. "Of all the miserable places to live and die in eighteenth-century London none was more terrible than the prison, [which] touched the lives of a large minority of Londoners and hung like a pall over the lives of many more." Many inmates were debtors, and the debtors' prisons were "the apex of terror facing all borrowers who could not pay their debts" (White 2013: 446–47). In the 1750s, authorities in London acted aggressively against the city's poor.

> Women and men deemed disorderly, whose begging was too aggressive, who worked as prostitutes or who were deemed unwilling to work for a living, were arrested and prosecuted for vagrancy, including all the ill-defined "crimes" of "wandering and begging" and of being "loose, idle and disorderly." (Hitchcock and Shoemaker 2015: 305)

Conditions in the prisons were terrible. "Overcrowding, filth and the ubiquitous louse produced endemic sickness among the prisoners"

(White 2013: 452). Prison reformer John Howard claimed that prisons were so filthy and "the air was so corrupted that he could not travel by stage coach after visiting a prison because of the stench on his clothes" (Henriques 1979: 158). In 1776, prisoners were incarcerated in the hulks of ships on the Thames River. "Conditions on the hulks were intentionally poor.… In the first twenty months over a quarter of the prisoners died (176 of 632); and 138 more perished in the following year" (Hitchcock and Shoemaker 2015: 335).

Public whippings and hangings were common, especially in the first half of the eighteenth century, intended as a public warning and deterrent (White 2013: 456–57), although such events were typically treated as a spectacle by the public. Later in the eighteenth century, especially following the week-long Gordon Riots of June 1780, public whippings and hangings grew in number—"all told, 500 people were hanged in London in the seven years following 1780, almost a third of all those hanged in the century" (Hitchcock and Shoemaker 2015: 363). All of this was in addition to the large numbers transported to Australia for their crimes—164,000 from 1787 to 1868, while "just under two-thirds of all Old Bailey punishments between 1718 and 1776" were sentences of transportation (Hitchcock and Shoemaker 2015: 374).

At the same time, the poor and those enmeshed in the prison system resisted authorities in a wide variety of ways. The "imaginative engagement of the pauper and the criminal" were a "force for change," although Hitchcock and Shoemaker (2015: 21) argue that they acted "independently of any systematic politics," as a type of "class struggle without class."

The Growing Cost of Poor Relief and the Quest for Poor Law Reform

Throughout the seventeenth and eighteenth centuries, and particularly toward the end of the eighteenth, both the numbers of the poor and the costs of poor relief grew steadily (Slack 1990), producing growing levels of concern from ratepayers about the need for Poor Law "reform." Lees (1998: 84) reports that "yearly expenditures on poor relief, as reported to Parliament, were more than five times as great in 1803 as they had been in 1750." By the early nineteenth century, "beggars were to be found everywhere," and many of the poor "lived lives of squalid misery" (Innes 1999: 252). King (2000: 254) describes a spiraling eighteenth and nineteenth century poverty problem which could leave well over two-thirds of people in many communities by the late 1820s "in poverty".... In particular, we can see an underclass of poor people emerging from the mid-eighteenth century onwards who would spend much of their lifetimes in poverty and who were likely to pass on that poverty to their own children and to share their poverty with brothers, sisters and friends.

Farm labourers were particularly hard hit. By the middle of the eighteenth century the still unfolding enclosure movement was hitting rural workers especially hard (Plumb 1981), and conditions worsened in the late eighteenth and early nineteenth centuries as industrial capitalism emerged (Polanyi 1944). E.P. Thompson (1963: 217) wrote, "In agriculture the years between 1760 and 1820 are the years of wholesale enclosure, in which, in village after village, common rights are lost," leaving the landless and "pauperized labourers." Hobsbawm and Rude (1969: 15) describe "the English farm-labourers' long and doomed struggle against poverty and degradation," adding, "their history between the industrial revolution and the middle of the 19th century is a tragic one." Because of the emergence of capitalism, the world they knew was transformed, and the farm labourer "became not merely a full proletarian, but an underemployed, pauperized one" (Hobsbawm and Rude 1969: 15).

New charitable bodies emerged in response. "Ten were launched in London from 1771 to 1780, eighteen from 1781 to 1790, and thirty from 1791 to 1800" (Porter 1991: 297). They sought to reform the morals of the poor—on the long-held grounds that poverty was the fault of the poor, attributable to their many moral and other failings. As White (2013: 480) notes, "There continued to be an aggressive Christian proselytizing about [charity] that required subjection, obedience and gratitude from all who received its bounty." These efforts, however, were typically met with scorn and derision—"sermonizers and snoopers met catcalls, hecklers and stones" (Porter 1991: 298). The poor resisted not only their impoverishment, but also the charitable efforts aimed at encouraging them to bear their pain more respectably.

For agricultural labourers, who suffered from seasonal unemployment and rising food costs, the Speenhamland system provided what were, in effect, unemployment benefits (Boyer 1990). The Speenhamland

Scheme of 1795, adopted especially throughout southern England, was in effect a strategy to subsidize the wages of those who were the working poor, the subsidy amount based on family size and the price of bread. Not surprisingly, employers then deliberately held down wages, knowing that subsidies were available to close the gap between what workers were paid and what they needed to stay alive. Farmers in the south of England favoured Speenhamland subsidies because they prevented rural labourers from seeking work elsewhere while seasonally unemployed, thus retaining an agricultural labour supply (Polanyi 1944). Hobsbawm (1968: 105) saw Speenhamland as "a last, inefficient, ill-considered and unsuccessful attempt … to maintain a traditional rural order in the face of the market economy" (see also Macnicol 1980).

The inevitable effect was to add further to the costs of relief. Poor Law reformers were especially critical. For them, the "generosity" of the *Poor Law* was blamed for its rising costs, although Blaug (1974: 143) argued that "hardly any of the dire effects ascribed to the *Old Poor Law* stand up in the light of available empirical evidence." Nevertheless, calls for Poor Law reform became a major part of the public discourse in the late eighteenth and early nineteenth centuries. By the latter part of the eighteenth century, there was a "general hardening of attitudes to the poor and especially the able-bodied … which occurred as the costs of relief rose" (Levene 2012: 9).

Overall, the parish-based relief system of the 1601 *Poor Law* was not generous. Relief was intended not to "solve" poverty, "which was seen as a normal, God-ordained and desirable part of the social order" (Lees 1998: 14), but to keep the poor from either perishing or rebelling. The risk of rebellion was always a concern. As King (2000: 21) argues, "the threat of public disorder loomed large in the elite psyche," which "meant that the old poor law was always geared to confronting pauperism rather than treating and preventing poverty and destitution."

"Within an Ace of a Revolution": Reforming the *Poor Law*

Nevertheless, the *Poor Law* of 1601 established the legal right to relief if destitute, and the *Settlement Act* of 1662, while often harsh in its consequences, confirmed that "every person born in England and Wales possessed a settlement somewhere, and in that place a settled person was legally entitled to relief if destitute" (Charlesworth 2010: 4). The *Old Poor Law* was thus becoming a constraint on the emergent industrial capitalism. The vast numbers of poor in England were a potential labour force; the problem—and this had long been the problem—was the need to reform the *Poor Law* to more effectively *force* the poor into the paid labour force.

Poverty and the *Poor Law* occasioned much debate in the late eighteenth and early nineteenth centuries, as industrial capitalism was taking off. "No less than 44 parliamentary enquiries took place on the poor and the poor law between 1750 and 1834 and enough books and pamphlets were published to fill a small library" (Green 2010: 5). New ideas about the *Poor Law* were struggling to be formulated in the face of the expanding labour needs of industrial capitalism.

What emerged reinforced the long-held belief that the poor had to be made desperate in order to force them into the emerging industrial mills and factories. An eighteenth-century writer asserted, "everyone but an idiot knows that the poor must be kept poor, or they would not work" (quoted in Poynter 1969: xvi). A prominent writer of the day, Joseph Townsend, wrote, "it is only hunger which can spur and goad [the poor] on to labour" (quoted in Boyer 1990: 52). Cunningham (1990: 127) describes "the doctrine of the utility of poverty," which "taught that there must always be a large mass of people driven to work by want."

The *Elizabethan Poor Law* of 1601 was seen to be too soft on the able-bodied poor. The Poor Law Commission established in 1832 identified the able-bodied poor, the paupers, as the "master evil" of the relief system (Great Britain 1834: 114). Nassau Senior, later to be one of the New Poor Law Commissioners, wrote in 1831, "the relief of the able-bodied is itself the grand abuse of the English Poor Laws—the source from which all other abuses have flowed" (quoted in Dunkley 1982: 9). The *Old Poor Law*, it was increasingly argued, had to be "reformed," so that more of the poor could be forced to work for wages.

On the other hand, complete abolition of the *Poor Law*—called for by many intellectuals of the time, including perhaps most notably Thomas Malthus (Innes 1999: 253–54)—was not an option because "the ruling classes were always aware of the usefulness of the *Poor Law* as an insurance against rebellion" (Poynter 1969: xxiv). By the late eighteenth and early nineteenth centuries, rebellion was widespread and seen by the establishment as a genuine threat. As food costs rose, poor people frequently resorted to food "riots." Called such at the time, "riots" suggests a greater mindlessness than was typically the case —they were more organized than that. The collective determination was made by the poor that prices of bread had risen so high that they eroded the standard of living to which they believed they had a "moral" right. Between 1792 and 1815, for example, "155 military barracks were built in industrial areas" (Beckert 2015: 196), while those with means responded with more charity. "A disposition to riot was certainly effective as a signal to the rich to put the machinery of parish relief and of charity—subsidized bread and corn for the poor—in good repair" (E.P. Thompson 1971: 79). This drove up the costs of poor relief and thus local rates that supported relief, further increasing the demands for reform of the *Poor Law*.

In parts of southern England, there were "almost continuous individual acts of violence in the form of incendiarism, cattle-maiming, fence-breaking and so on. These sporadic and localized protests were punctuated by upheavals of greater intensity and scope in 1800–01, 1816, 1830–31 and 1835–36" (Dunkley 1982: 40). In the Midlands and north, there were Luddite riots in 1811 and 1812 (Plumb 1981). Particularly significant were the Swing Riots in southern England in 1830–1831 (Hobsbawm and Rude 1969), government fears about which "are woven through its [the *Poor Law Commission Report* of 1834] pages as one of its most disconcerting themes" (Dunkley 1982: 97). Sidney and Beatrice Webb (1927: 45) argue that the Swing Riots "put the fear of revolution into the hearts of the English governing class." E.P. Thompson (1963: 898) wrote that "England was within an ace of a revolution which once commenced, might well have prefigured, in its radicalization, the revolutions of 1848 and the Paris Commune." To the fear that this dissent would lead to higher wages and relief costs was added the fear of broader insurrection. As Brundage (2002: 25) put it: "to the issue of growing poor rates and a supposed decline of the work ethic among the poor was added a fear of their revolutionary potential."

There were many other expressions of discontent in the early nineteenth century—"Luddite and Radical, trade unionist and utopian-socialist, Democratic and Chartist" (Hobsbawm 1968: 55). In addition, there was the emergence early in the nineteenth century of a working class increasingly conscious of itself as a class and of its differences with those who ruled (E.P. Thompson 1963). Arising out of all this turmoil, and the fear it inspired in the governing elite and the need to find a way to force more of the poor into the burgeoning factories of industrial capitalism, was the *New Poor Law* of 1834.

Chapter 4

The Industrial Revolution

The *New Poor Law* and New
and Horrific Forms of Poverty

The *New Poor Law* of 1834 represented a massive shift away from the "moral economy" in which the poor had a legal right and a community obligation to at least minimal relief to "the new political economy of the free market" (E.P. Thompson 1971: 136), a system much more punitive. The *New Poor Law* was a centralized and bureaucratic system controlled from London and administered by three Poor Law commissioners. It sought to overcome the fragmentation of the parish-based system of relief by requiring that parishes join in Poor Law unions, managed by elected boards of guardians. The guardians in turn hired salaried officials, replacing the voluntary officials of the *Old Poor Law*. The fifteen thousand parishes in England were amalgamated into approximately six hundred Poor Law unions. Outdoor relief was to be abolished, each union was to have a workhouse and each workhouse would impose upon the able-bodied poor the harsh regime of "less eligibility." Less eligibility meant that those in a workhouse would be less eligible for benefits of any kind—that is, they would in every way be worse off—than the poorest-paid worker outside the workhouse.

Novak (1988: 46–47) argues that this principle of less eligibility "has ever since been at the heart of the system of social security," embodied in the late twentieth and early twenty-first centuries in the "modern-day social security office, with its wire meshes and glass screens, its chairs bolted to the floor, its interminable queues and waiting and its persistent treatment of claimants as second class citizens," an image indelibly conveyed in the film *I, Daniel Blake* (Loach 2016).

The intent of less eligibility was to remove the historic right to relief except for those prepared to enter the workhouse. This was the "workhouse test"—conditions in the workhouse were to be so bad that those who entered would have passed the test, their entry being proof positive that they were unable to work and were therefore eligible for relief. As Polanyi (1944: 101–2) described it: "It was now left to the applicant to decide whether he was so utterly destitute of all means that he would voluntarily repair to a shelter which was deliberately made into a place of horror." The alternative to that horror, and this was the *Poor Law*'s purpose, was wage-labour in the "dark satanic mills" of industrial capitalism (Blake 1810).

Factory Fodder for Industry

The 1834 *Poor Law* "was specifically designed to provide factory fodder for industry" because, as William Cobbett described it, workhouses were to be so oppressive that "labour would be prepared to work for any wages they could get" (Knott 1986: 252). George Nicholls, who was to become an important member of the Poor Law Commission, was clear: "I wish to see the Poor House looked to with dread by our labouring class … for without this, where is the needful stimulus to industry?" (quoted in Fraser 1984: 41). Hobsbawm (1968: 69) concluded, "There have been few more inhuman statutes than the *Poor Law Act* of 1834."

The *Poor Law* was made necessary by the needs of industrial capitalism. It made an important—indeed, essential—contribution to the economic success of the Industrial Revolution, by forcing able-bodied people into the labour market. The price was the devastation it imposed on wage labourers and the poor. As Toynbee describes it, "side by side with a great increase in wealth was seen an enormous increase in pauperism" (quoted in Cannadine 1984: 136). The two were part of the same contradictory process: the growth in one was made possible by the growth of the other. De Tocqueville, referring to Manchester in 1835, wrote at the time:

> From this foul drain the greatest stream of human industry flows out to fertilize the whole world. From this filthy sewer pure gold flows. Here humanity attains its most complete development and its most brutish, here civilization works its miracles and civilized man is turned almost into a savage. (Quoted in Hobsbawm 1962: 44)

Prime Minister Benjamin Disraeli said the same: "while immense fortunes were accumulating, while wealth was increasing to a super abundance ... the working classes, the creators of wealth, were steeped in the most abject poverty and gradually sinking into the deepest degradation" (quoted in Dorey 2011: 52).

There has been a long debate—the "standard of living" debate—about the impact of the Industrial Revolution on the well-being of British workers. The "optimists" take the view that real earnings grew from the 1780s to 1850 (for example, Lindert and Williamson 1983), while those labelled "pessimists" argued that any gains that might have been made in a narrowly constructed real wages index were offset by the damage caused by poor housing, working and environmental conditions, including their adverse impacts on health and longevity (for example, Hobsbawm 1964; Feinstein 1998). Complex and often narrowly constructed quantitative evidence might show some gains, but the more broadly defined quality of life of working people during the late eighteenth and the nineteenth centuries certainly doesn't. Even so optimistic an analyst as Hayak (1954) allows that, as what follows will show, "there is every evidence that great misery existed."

In the 1840s, seventy thousand tons of human feces per year were thrown onto the streets of Manchester—those same streets on which, said de Tocqueville, "pure gold flows." The city's assistant Poor Law commissioner wrote that streets were "so covered with refuse and excrementitious matter as to be almost impassable from depth of mud, and intolerable from stench." Together with the industrial poisoning from the factories, this produced "a small, sickly, pallid, thin ... degenerate race—human beings stunted, enfeebled, and depraved," wrote a surgeon at the time (Hunt 2005: 35, 26). Engels (1987: 89) said it was impossible "to convey a true impression of the filth, ruin, and uninhabitableness, the defiance of all consideration of cleanliness, ventilation and health" in Manchester's New Town slum, the result of which was "a physically degenerate race, robbed of all humanity, degraded, reduced morally and physically to bestiality." Throughout England and Wales, poor sanitation "cost the lives of 137 persons per day; annual deaths from typhus fever amounted to 16,000 along with another 150,000 to 200,000 affected by this wholly preventable disease" (Hunt 2005: 33–34). The Industrial Revolution, with the help of the *New Poor Law*, not only created a working class; it also created a new and brutal form of poverty.

The *New Poor Law* was never instituted in its pure form. For a variety of practical reasons—not least the constant growth in the numbers of the poor and unemployed beyond the capacity of workhouses to accommodate them all (Green 1995: 214)—the use of outdoor relief continued throughout the nineteenth century, especially but not only for the "deserving poor," namely widows and those who were old or sick. "The number of people receiving relief in money or goods outside the workhouse was never less than twice the number of inmates" (Crowther 1981: 6). Kidd (1999: 34) adds that of the one million on relief in 1849, 88 percent were not in the workhouse, and by 1869 that figure was still at 84 percent.

At least some of those in receipt of outdoor relief were part of the reserve army of labour, enabling flexibility to be built into the labour process. Nevertheless, the *New Poor Law* principle of "less eligibility" resulted in a cruel regime imposed on inmates.

The Poor Called Them Bastilles

There are different opinions among historians and others about the level of cruelty in the workhouses of the *New Poor Law* (Roberts 1963: 101). Crowther (1981: 3) observes that workhouses served as hospitals, schools and homes for the aged as well as fulfilling their *New Poor Law* functions; thus, they ought to be seen as "the first national experiment in institutional care." Even before the *New Poor Law*, "along with the sick, the ill and the injured, pregnant women and new mothers helped transform the workhouses of London into de facto hospitals for the poor" (Hitchcock and Shoemaker 2015: 146). Crowther argues that despite mistakes and cruelties, "the state was led into creating the specialized institutions which eventually replaced the workhouse," adding that "physical cruelty was neither the intention nor the usual practice of the system. Where cruelty did occur, it resulted from problems which were common to all residential institutions" (Crowther 1981: 270). Fraser (1984: 54) similarly argues,

> destitute indoor paupers were undoubtedly better housed, better fed and better cared for than those "merely poor" outside the workhouse, and Poor Law officials were trying to raise standards rather than depress them. Where scandals occurred they were often the result of unsupervised local abuse, rather than of central policy direction.

Nevertheless, the evidence of cruelty in workhouses is strong. The poor did not call them "bastilles" without reason. The Webbs (1929: 138) describe them as "shocking to every principle of reason and every feeling of humanity." Polanyi (1944: 101) calls them "places of horror" and G.D.H. Cole (1941: 16) says they were "odious and cruel" (quoted in Roberts 1963: 100). Dickens's *Oliver Twist,* published three years after the *New Poor Law* in 1837, was a passionate critique of workhouses. Marx (1976: 808) referred to "the growing horror in which the workers hold the slavery of the workhouse."

Some contemporary stories of workhouse cruelty were indeed exaggerated, and the New Poor Law commissioners worked to prevent the most deplorable conditions (Roberts 1963: 102). But families were separated while incarcerated—not only husbands and wives but also, in some cases, mothers from children. Workhouse staff were disproportionately recruited from the military and "on the whole demonstrated little sympathy for the inmates, even for the children, aged, and infirm who were supposed to be treated kindly" (Brundage 2002: 78).

The *Poor Law Report of 1834* set out the means of transformation applied to those entering the workhouses:

> First came disinfection and a bath. After paupers gave up their clothes for fumigation, they were washed by an attendant and inspected by a doctor. An ill-fitting, ugly uniform and a standard haircut began the process of homogenization that continued until they left the house.... Bells announced the hours for sleep, work, meals, and religious services ... paupers were to rise at 7:00 a.m. in winter, and 5:00 a.m. in summer, put in a nine-or ten-hour workday, and go to bed at eight in the evening. They ate together silently, worked and slept together, rigidly separated by sex and age. The ideal workhouse regulated every minute of the paupers' day, trying to teach discipline through regimentation. (Lees 1998: 147)

It could on occasion be worse. In 1845 in the Andover workhouse, paupers ate hogwash and chicken feed, and gristle and marrow from bones. A Select Committee of the House of Commons set up to investigate "found a long list of cruelties and mismanagement in the workhouse" (Henriques 1979: 55). Roberts (1963: 104), even while arguing that the horrors of the workhouses were often exaggerated, acknowledged that terrible conditions prevailed in many workhouses, citing, among others, examples such as a "nursery of filth, vice and fanaticism" and "a large number of unfortunate human beings afflicted with loathsome diseases in a ward too small." King (2000: 68) acknowledges that "most of the major scandals were fakes," but adds that "the discovery of paupers in Bolton workhouse so infested with lice that their skin was hanging off provides ample testimony of just how dreadful these conditions could be."

Not surprisingly, the *New Poor Law* was "viewed with hatred and horror by most of the labouring population of Britain" (Knott 1986: 7; Lees 1998: 114). Its introduction was greeted by "a storm of popular protest…. Mass meetings were organized and protest marches held." There were attempts to burn down workhouses, and "the epidemic of workhouse fires and the obvious hatred that people had for the new workhouses kept Boards of Guardians on edge." Guardians were directly attacked: "in one case an "entire board of guardians [was] pursued and showered with stones and other missiles"; in another, "a large crowd of women booed and hurled stones at officials transferring paupers from small parish workhouses to larger ones," while "a separate crowd rescued paupers being conveyed in a cart" (Hitchcock, King and Sharpe 1997: 13; Brundage 2002: 74).

The fierce opposition to the New Poor Law workhouses was put down, in many cases, by force.

> The authorities responded with brutal repression. Special constables were sworn in, the military placed on alert and detachments of Metropolitan Police quickly moved into troubled areas. Throughout south-east England all organized protests against the 1834 Poor Law were ruthlessly crushed. (Knott 1986: 269)

In the north of England, opposition was even stronger than in the south, because temporary unemployment was virtually inevitable for mill workers, "and the prospect of virtual imprisonment in a workhouse terrified men whose trades were liable to sudden fluctuations" (Fraser 1984: 50). Riots in several northern towns in 1837 and 1838 were put down by troops. Opposition to the *New Poor Law* subsided in part because the protests "gave impetus to the embryonic Chartist movement in northern England" (Rose 1972: 10; Fraser 1984: 50–51).

Resistance and insubordination by the poor continued inside the workhouse. "Riots in casual wards and workhouse yards were not uncommon, [so that] far from being a total institution that fostered docile bodies, the workhouse, especially in the early stages of the new poor law, needs to be understood as a deeply contested site of resistance" (Green 2006: 156). Paupers' resistance to the workhouse regime can be seen in the context of the centuries-long beliefs held by the English poor regarding "customary rights and expectations in relation to poor relief" (Green 2010: 187).

A Discipline So Severe and Repulsive as to Make Them a Terror to the Poor

An assistant Poor Law commissioner told factory reformer Richard Oastler, "the object in building these union [work] houses was to establish therein a discipline so severe and repulsive as to make them a terror to the poor and prevent them from entering" (quoted in Ward 1962: 173). An examination of the nineteenth-century labour market—the types of jobs on offer—makes clear why those behind the *New Poor Law* believed it necessary to force able-bodied people into the labour market.

Consider the case of children as workers. Child labour was a crucially important—indeed, it can safely be argued, a necessary—component of the Industrial Revolution, especially in its early years. Cruickshank (quoted in King 1998: 142) writes of "employers scouring the countryside to recruit children" for the mills. The Hammonds, social historians who were husband and wife, write, "During the first phase of the Industrial Revolution the employment of children on a vast scale became the most important social feature of English life" (quoted in Cunningham 1992: 16). In 1833, just over one third of workers in Lancashire cotton mills were less than sixteen years of age (Beckert 2015: 189). Children could be paid much less than men, and even less than women; moreover, they were "more tractable and less militantly organized ... than men" (Porter 1991: 325), and with their smaller and more flexible bodies they could do jobs in the cramped confines of mills and mines that adults could not do.

Cotton manufacturers contracted with parish authorities to take pauper children as apprentices. As described by a contemporary,

> It is a very common practice with the great, populous parishes in London to bind children in large numbers to the proprietors of cotton-mills in Lancashire and Yorkshire, at a distance of 200 miles. The children, who are sent off by wagon loads at a time,

are as much lost forever to their parents as if they were shipped off to the West Indies. (Quoted in Porter 1991: 325)

This process began in the 1780s, as the Industrial Revolution was taking root. In the case of one London parish, "after several months' negotiations, the parish agreed to supply a steady stream of parish apprentices, as young as eight, to the new mills of Lancashire and Yorkshire. In the next five years, twenty-two girls and sixty-one boys were apprenticed by the parish." Most London parishes soon followed. "Between 1784 and 1814, some 4,414 of the country's most vulnerable children were apprenticed to the new industrial mills of the north, the vast majority from the capital" (Hitchcock and Shoemaker 2015: 383–84, 396).

Poor Law overseers had an incentive to meet the demand for child labour, because by sending pauper children off to work in another parish, they could reduce their parish's relief costs and thus drive down poor rates:

> Parish authorities gladly relieved the Poor rates by virtually selling batches of children to northern manufacturers; a Parliamentary Committee was told, in 1815, that the London parishes claimed "the exclusive right of disposing, at their pleasure, of all the children of the person receiving relief." (Ward 1962: 15)

In the mills, child labourers were subjected to horrific conditions.

> Exhausted children were beaten to work, and sickness, mutilation by machinery and even deaths from malnutrition and long confinement were regular occurrences…. Children started work at 5, 6, 7 or 8 and toiled for 14 or 15 hours in high temperatures, without proper meal breaks. (Ward 1962: 16, 26)

An examination of the skeletons of children who worked in the mills produced "evidence of children's stunted growth, bone deterioration, rickets, and traces of inherited degenerative diseases that came with hard labour, inadequate diet, poor medical care, and other problems associated with intergenerational poverty" (Berry 2019: 187). As technology improved, the price of such "progress" was that accidents became "increasingly ferocious, as ever larger and swifter revolving belts and shafts caught tired or careless millworkers by sleeves or aprons or hair, and tore off limbs or scalps" (Henriques 1979: 108). In some mills there were schools, yet twelve- to eighteen-hour workdays remained the norm and the "schools" often offered conditions little better than the mills (Cruickshank 1978). In Dundee, children worked fifteen-hour days, and as a contemporary wrote, "the lash of the slave driver was never more unsparingly used in Carolina on the unfortunate slaves than the canes and 'whangs' of mill foremen were then used on factory boys" (quoted in Ward 1962: 17).

A parliamentary committee of 1833 heard from former child mill workers, including Joseph Habergram, then disabled from work in the mills. Habergram told the committee, "I had 14 1/2 hours actual labour, when 7 years of age … strapping was the means by which children were kept at work." Ellen Hooten, aged seven years, said her overseer beat her twice a week, so that "her head was sore with his hands" (quoted in Beckert 2015: 177). The son of factory owner and reformer, David Owen, wrote, "In some large factories, from one-fourth to one-fifth of the children were either cripples or otherwise deformed, or permanently injured by excessive toil, sometimes by brutal abuse" (quoted in Ward 1962: 22).

Such are the origins of industrial capitalism in Britain. To return to Marx's (1976: 926) phrasing, it came into the world "dripping from head to toe, from every pore, with blood and dirt." As Beckert (2015: 441) describes it: "Slavery, colonialism, and forced labour, among other forms of violence, were not aberrations in the history of capitalism, but were at its very core."

Cotton, Slavery and the Global Production of Poverty

The capitalism that created the Industrial Revolution was global, as was the exploitation of the labour that drove it. Children were driven in cartloads to be forced to work in the Lancashire cotton mills; Africans had been captured and transported as slaves across the "middle passage" to the Americas—eight million of them in the three centuries after 1500 (Beckert 2015: 36). In the American Deep South, African-American slaves were brutally exploited, forced to plant and pick the raw cotton that was grown on land forcibly expropriated from Indigenous inhabitants. Baptist (2016, 2014) argues that "torture" was the primary management technique used to drive up slave output: "The whip made cotton"

(Baptist 2016: 52). The slave system of the American Deep South, precisely because of its appalling cruelty, was enormously productive and profitable; its profits fuelled the Industrial Revolution in the US (Baptist 2014). "Slavery and land expropriation on a continental scale created the expansive, and elastic, global cotton supply network necessary for the industrial revolution" (Beckert 2015: 92). The cotton produced by African-American slaves was then processed by wage slaves—often children—in the Lancashire mills, fuelling the Industrial Revolution in England. The social and economic gains eventually made possible by the Industrial Revolution were paid for by the deliberate destruction of untold numbers of lives.

Particularly in the latter eighteenth and early nineteenth centuries to the 1840s, the Industrial Revolution in England was driven by cotton. "Whoever says Industrial Revolution says cotton," observes Hobsbawm (1968: 40; see also Landes 1969: 82). "No other industry could compare in importance with cotton in this first phase of British industrialization." About 50 percent of British exports and 20 percent of imports were raw cotton and cotton products. By 1830, "one in six workers in Britain laboured in cottons," and 70 percent of them worked in Lancashire (Beckert 2015: 73). The factories made "massive use of cheap (women's and juvenile's) labour" (Hobsbawm 1968: 51). And cotton was intimately and necessarily linked to slavery:

> Slavery and cotton marched together.... After the 1790s the slave plantations of the southern United States were extended and maintained by the insatiable and rocketing demands of the Lancashire mills, to which they supplied the bulk of their raw cotton. (Hobsbawm 1962: 52)

The finished product—cotton clothing—was exported, primarily to British colonies such as India, undermining the production of clothing there. For centuries, India had been the world's leading producer of cotton, the best of which was of "legendary" quality, of "almost incredible perfection" (Beckert 2015: 7–8). However, what Beckert (2015: xv) describes as "war capitalism"—the use of force and violence to open markets and secure labour and resources—virtually destroyed the Indian cotton industry. "India was systematically deindustrialized and became in turn a market for Lancashire cottons: in 1820 the subcontinent took only 11 million yards; but by 1840 it already took 145 million yards"

(Hobsbawm 1962: 53). Slaves picked cotton under brutal conditions in the American South; women and children processed it in Lancashire mills under brutal conditions; and the sale of the resulting products caused "virtual destruction" of a thriving clothing industry in India (Hobsbawm 1962: 198). Poverty—brutally inhumane poverty—was produced at every point in what was a global capitalist process.

Were They Galley-Slaves Their Work Could Not Be More Oppressive

This was the case in the British coal mines as well, where children were similarly exploited. The 1842 *Report on the Condition and Treatment of the Children Employed in the Mines and Collieries of the United Kingdom* describes "the sufferings and degradation, physical and moral, of large numbers of young children" (United Kingdom [UK] 1842: 6). Typically, children started work in the mines at age eight or nine, taken down into the pits by their fathers, because of "the inadequacy of their own earnings to support their families" (UK 1842: 36, 41). Women took their daughters into the pits, in some cases to assist mothers "whose health had been ruined by too early a return to work after childbirth." In such cases, as the 1842 report indicated, "Women soon get so weak that they are forced to take the little ones down to relieve them; and even children of six years of age do much to relieve the burden.... Many declared that they could not exist without the wages of their children" (Pinchbeck and Hewitt 1973: 401–2).

Women forced to take their very young daughters into the pits sometimes used drugs—often dangerous drugs like opium—to keep the little ones quiet.

> The result of this terrible practice is that a great number of infants perish from an overdose, or, as more commonly happens, slowly, painfully and insidiously. Those who escape with life become pale and sickly children, often half idiotic, and always with a ruined constitution. (Quoted in Pinchbeck and Hewitt 1973: 406)

Boys, girls and women hauled cartloads of coal from the mine face to the pithead, typically with belts around their waists and chains that passed between their legs attached to the cart, and often on all fours when the seam was low. In some cases, seams could be "no more than eighteen inches, or perhaps twenty inches. The boys crawl on their hands and knees" pulling the cartloads (UK 1842: 76). So did girls, who in some instances worked naked from the waist down. The length of the workday was typically between eleven and thirteen hours. Women and children were known to be beaten if they did not work fast enough. Betty Harris, aged thirty-seven, told the commission that she worked in the pit at Bolton:

> It is very hard work for a woman…. I am very tired when I get home at night; I fall asleep sometimes before I get washed…. I have drawn [cartloads of coal] till I have had the skin off me; the belt and chain is worse when we are in the family way. My husband has beaten me many a time for not being ready. I were not used to it at first, and he had little patience, I have known many a man beat his drawer. (UK 1842: 51)

Margaret Harper, aged thirteen, described the work that she and other girls did:

> We hurry the carts on the railroads by pushing behind; I frequently draw with ropes and chains as the horses do; it is dirty, slavish work, and the water quite covers our ankles. I knock my head against the roofs, as they are not so high as I am, and they cause me to stoop, which makes my back ache. (UK 1842: 128)

The report describes these employment conditions as "oppressively hard work performed by young females," adding, "were they galley-slaves their work could not be more oppressive" (UK 1842: 79–80).

Pauper children sent by parish overseers to the mines as apprentices were especially badly treated. The 1842 report says, "these lads are made to go where other men will not let their children go. If they will not do it, they are taken to the magistrates who commit them to prison" (quoted in Pinchbeck and Hewitt 1973: 354). A surgeon found on the body of a boy apprenticed to a collier by a Poor Law overseer "from twenty-four to twenty-six wounds. His posteriors and loins were beaten to a jelly; his head, which was almost cleared of hair on the scalp, had the marks of old wounds upon it which had healed up" (UK 1842: 106–7). While this case was an exception in the degree of its brutality, cruel treatment of young children and women was common; the work itself was abominable.

The Factory Acts: The Beginnings of a Breach in Laissez-Faire

So horrific were these conditions that they produced an effective movement of opposition. Reformers appalled by the treatment of child labour fought for legislation that would place limits on the age at which children could be employed and the number of hours per day that they could work (Driver 1946; Ward 1962). They promoted the Factory Acts on the grounds that this "particular form of child labour was so inhumane that it was incumbent upon them to campaign for its abolition" (Cunningham 1992: 59).

The campaign was also in pursuit of a shorter workday for all. "Short-time committees" were formed, starting in 1831 and led by textile workers and reform-minded members of the gentry like Richard Oastler and Michael Sadler. The short-time committees "were the storm troops of the factory campaign and were composed mostly of operatives themselves, together with sympathetic tradesmen" (Fraser 1984: 16). The success of this movement in winning the 1847 *Factories Act*, the *Ten Hour Act*, was at least in part a result of the belief that the damage done to children was so great that Britain's future—the successful reproduction of society—was being placed at risk. The concern of many adult workers was that the competition created by child labour was driving down their wages and creating unemployment (Cunningham 1992: 65, 165).

Much of the Factory Act legislation applied to the textile industry, especially the cotton mills. The *Cotton Mills and Factories Act* of 1819 prohibited children under nine years from working in the cotton mills and limited the length of the workday to twelve hours for children aged nine to sixteen years. The *Factory Act* of 1833 further limited the workday to eight hours a day for children ages nine to thirteen, and even then only if they attended two hours of school per day, although this provision in particular was little enforced. The 1833 *Act* also limited the length of the working day to twelve hours for those aged fourteen to eighteen years, prohibited night work for anyone younger than eighteen years and extended those regulations to all the textile mills except silk mills. The *Factory Act* of 1833 also introduced a four-person inspectorate to enforce the legislation, making at least a small measure of enforcement possible for the first time, although Henriques (1979) describes the many limitations of this enforcement and the endless ways that mill owners were able to subvert inspection efforts because there were too few inspectors.

Nevertheless, Henriques (1979: 95) argues that, however reluctantly, "The state control of private industry began seriously in 1833." Begrudging though it was, "the 1833 *Factory Act* clearly marks a great turning point in the history of social policy" (Fraser 1984: 22). It established the principle, contrary to the dominant laissez-faire ideology, that the state had a right to intervene in economic matters in pursuit of broader public interests. This principle would gain traction half a century later in the 1880s and would eventually find expression in the 1906–1914 Liberal government reforms, and more fully in the welfare state reforms of the 1945–1951 Labour governments.

The biggest immediate gain was the 1847 *Factories Act*, called the *Ten Hour Act*, which limited the length of the workday for all mill workers to ten hours. In some respects, it was the culmination of the efforts of the short-time committees, but the struggle to improve working conditions continued. "In 1867 factory legislation was for the first time seriously extended beyond the textile industries, and even began to abandon the fiction that its only purpose was to protect children—adults being theoretically capable of protecting themselves" (Hobsbawm 1968: 101). The 1878 *Factory Act* prohibited the employment anywhere of children less than ten years of age, limited those ten to fourteen years to half days of work, and limited women to fifty-six hours of work per week. However gradual and hard-fought, these were significant gains that "marked a definite breach with laissez-faire" (Briggs 1961: 236).

Factory owners reacted strongly against the restrictions imposed upon child labour by the Factory Acts, instituting, for example, relay systems—calling children in to work on a flexible, as-needed basis. And "on their surprise visits" early factory inspectors "discovered children hidden away, secreted under baskets or behind trap doors" (Cruickshank 1978: 112). Inspecting and policing was difficult, however, because the number of factories and workshops vastly exceeded the number of factory inspectors.

The long struggle to prevent child labour and its particularly exploitative character and damaging consequences has typically been described as a success story, "a romance in which both children and nation entered into hell, and were rescued to lead a new and better life" (Cunningham 1992: 17). Another way of seeing this struggle, however, is to conclude that industrial capitalism needed this level of brutal exploitation, including the abuse of children, to "succeed."

A New Kind of Prison ... a New Kind of Jailer

Factories and mines brought enormous change to English workers, not just child labourers. As Landes (1969: 43) observes, "the factory was a new kind of prison; the clock a new kind of jailer." For the English labouring poor, their "traditional world and way of life" was destroyed by the Industrial Revolution (Hobsbawm 1968: 66). As Beatrice Webb (quoted in Cannadine 1984: 135) put it:

> To the working class of Great Britain in the latter half of the eighteenth and first half of the nineteenth century—that is fourfifths of the entire population—the "Industrial Revolution" ... must have appeared ... as a gigantic and cruel experiment which, insofar as it was affecting their homes, their health, their subsistence and their pleasure, was proving a calamitous failure.

Most did not want to enter the factory. Those who did went despite "an aversion to supervision and discipline, and resentment of the unremitting demands of the machine" (Landes 1969: 114). The *New Poor Law* was needed to force people into these dangerous mills in the face of their perfectly reasonable reluctance to enter.

Massive numbers of Irish farm labourers were pushed into Lancashire mills by the even more difficult economic conditions in Ireland—they were "pauperized beyond belief," especially after the 1846–1847 famine in which almost one million Irish starved to death (Hobsbawm 1968: 73). Irish workers did much of the most arduous, dangerous, seasonal and poorly paid work, and they faced relentless discrimination (Hickman 1998: 142–44), partly because Irish workers were seen as competitors who drove down wages. Wages paid to male workers—Irish and English alike—were so low that children and women were also pushed into the factories, their even more meagre wages serving to assist in keeping their families economically afloat.

Much work continued to be done in small workshops and at home, often including all members of a family, as the putting-out system existed alongside the emergent factory system, paying similarly meagre wages. As Samuel (1977: 15) argues, "modern (factory) industry is exaggerated, while its artisan components are ignored, and comparatively little notice is taken of production in the workshop and at home." The clothing trades, for example, "which increased by leaps and bounds in the 1840s and 1850s, depended on the poor needlewoman's fingers" (Samuel 1977: 17).

Poverty was widespread—most English workers were poor—and it was a direct product of the characteristics of the wage labour available to those who had no other options. The "less eligibility" principle of the *New Poor Law* forced them into poverty-producing work. The Industrial Revolution generated commodities, profits, a working class that gradually became aware of itself as a class—and poverty. Poverty was an essential part of the "success" of the process.

Although child labour was heavily relied upon in the mills early in the nineteenth century, by 1833 children represented only about 5 percent of the total labour force, replaced in large part by women. By the late 1830s, "females constituted over 64 percent of all employees in cotton aged between sixteen and twenty-one," and by the 1840s women of all ages constituted over one third of the total labour force in the cotton mills (Morgan 1992: 30). For most women, factory work was part of a family wage strategy. "Factory work was generally episodic and largely confined to the years prior to marriage and child-bearing. In later years of the life cycle, women moved in and out of the workforce according to family need" (Morgan 1992: 39).

Women were thus available to be "drawn in as cheap labour that could be discarded as the market contracted or shifted" (Boyd and McWilliam 2007: 31). They were crucial parts of the reserve army of labour.

In the 1820s and 1830s, women were paid half of what male factory operatives were paid (Morgan 1992: 25), and they faced discriminatory practices not only from cotton mill owners, but also from male factory workers and especially the "elite" male mule spinners. The mule spinners managed to carve out a relatively privileged place in the cotton mills, in part by working to exclude women, arguing that women were "a threat to male unionized jobs" and should work "only under 'exceptional' circumstances or when the male unions allowed it" (Valverde 1988: 629).

All workers—men and women—feared the consequences of pauperism, because they feared the workhouse.

> Misery or pauperism, perceived not only as economic deprivation but as human degradation, was the spectre that haunted the working class in its formative years; the fact that pauperism often meant going into the workhouse and having one's family

split up only helped to reinforce the ideological link between the desire to avoid pauperism and shame and the pursuit of the male-breadwinner family model. (Valverde 1988: 620)

Valverde (1988: 632) describes this reality as "the important role of the fear of pauperism in the self-construction of the 'respectable' working class."

The *New Poor Law* contributed to creating the "respectable" working class in various ways, including its inhumane treatment of unmarried mothers. "The bastardy clauses of the New Poor Law were the harshest of the new code" (Williams 2016: 946) and "unmarried mothers took centre stage with the able-bodied poor in the reform of the Poor Laws in 1834" (Evans 2005: 209). The *New Poor Law* "characterized single mothers as 'pests of society' [a term used in the 1834 report of the Royal Commission on the Poor Law], burdens, villains, strumpets, and cunning manipulators of men and charities" (Cody 2000: 132). The argument made was that under the more lenient provisions of the *Old Poor Law*, women were seducing men in order to produce children and earn higher relief payments—an early version of what US president Ronald Reagan called "welfare queens" (Nadasan 2007). Illegitimacy rates had been rising since at least the 1770s, as had population and relief costs (Cody 2000. 133–35), and this, the argument went, was because the *Old Poor Law* was too lax, thus promoting sexual promiscuity. Women, it followed, were to blame, and thus under the *New Poor Law* no relief whatever was to be made available to unmarried mothers and their children unless they entered the workhouse.

As had been the case under the *Elizabethan Poor Law*, most adult paupers after 1834 were women. "A depressingly long list of familiar problems—widowhood, longevity, desertion by husbands, child-rearing responsibilities, poor diets, low wages—led them into welfare offices" (Lees 1998: 196). Policy makers assumed the traditional two-parent family; women were treated not as independent individuals, but as dependents of a man. Women who were deserted or widowed or never married were ignored, or worse. For example, a widow or abandoned wife seeking relief could be removed to the parish where her husband had settlement, even though she might know nobody there and thus be severed from any local supports she might have had (Levine-Clark 2000). Worse, she could lose her children. For some single mothers, children were to be taken into the workhouse school, "in preference to giving outdoor relief, on the grounds that the children would be better cared for in the institutions" (Thane 1978a: 39). Even when single mothers kept their children, "almost nowhere was the amount of relief sufficient for barest subsistence; mothers had always to find means of supplementing it," and often this meant sending children out to work at the earliest possible age (Thane 1978a: 41).

As the nineteenth century progressed, it increasingly became the case that applications for relief by unmarried mothers "would be accompanied by close investigation into their ways of life" (Thane 1978a: 38). For example, in the 1870s "cross-visitors" were hired to make "detailed checks on the circumstances of paupers and relief applicants—in effect, they snooped on paupers … to ensure that deserted wives and widowed or unmarried mothers were not secretly co-habiting with men who could be held responsible for their support" and to exclude those of "immoral habits." Snooping came to include judging the "morality" of the relatives with whom a relief applicant was living and the cleanliness of their accommodations (Thane 1978a: 40–42). Intrusive and unwanted inspections of the homes and families of the poor would become a common thread in the response to poverty, used, for example, by the dominant charitable organizations from the late eighteenth century and as a central part of the hated means test of the 1920s and 1930s.

Pauperism was Always Near

The *New Poor Law* forced all able-bodied adults into the labour force, where the precarity of labour defined their lives.

> If any single factor dominated the lives of nineteenth century workers it was insecurity. They did not know at the beginning of the week how much they would bring home at the end. They did not know how long their present work would last or, if they lost it, when they would get another job or under what conditions. (Hobsbawm 1977: 258)

This was the case in the cotton mills: "stability of employment was the last thing to expect from a cotton manufacturer. The industry was prone to intense cyclical fluctuations, with mill closures or short-time working an almost universal feature of depressions" (Dutton and King 1982: 62).

As a result, "pauperism was always near" (Hobsbawm 1977: 269). Small-scale operations existed side by side with the new factories, "putting out and subcontracting were widespread," and "the worst conditions, long hours, irregular payment of wages, truck, gross exploitation of female and child labour were to be found in small-scale and domestic industry" (Plumb 1981: 88; Henriques 1979: 2).

The case of mid-nineteenth-century London has been particularly well described, especially by Henry Mayhew—"altogether it [Mayhew's body of work] is the most impressive survey of labour and of poverty at the midcentury which exists" (Thompson and Yeo 1984: 24). Thompson and Yeo (1984: 94) argue that Mayhew identified the problem of "casual labour" in London, and in so doing he came to see the cause of the city's widespread poverty in "irregular work and fluctuating wages" rather than the moral habits of the poor. "Mayhew was concerned to document what Charles Booth and Seebohm Rowntree rediscovered fifty years later—that the overwhelming problem of London poverty was not one that could be dismissed by moralizing or by appeals to exertion and self-help, but was one of absolute insufficiency of wages" (E.P. Thompson 1967: 59).

The docks were "London's largest single enterprise," and their reliance on casual labour epitomized the "high incidence of cyclical unemployment" (Briggs 1963: 339). Kidd (1999: 47) describes London at the time as "a pool of unskilled casual labour, living precariously on the margins of the labour market." On the docks, casual labourers were hired by the day or half-day, and the men lined up in search of work exceeded the jobs available—"the pool of labour available was about 30 percent above the average demand," although the available work fluctuated wildly (P. Thompson 1967: 49)—creating intense competition among workers. "Casual dockers were thus forced, day by day, to queue up at the "cage" in the hope of securing a work ticket from the ganger" (P. Thompson 1967: 49).

> The social consequences of this hiring policy were deplorable. Many of those weakened or made chronically infirm by such a life simply gave up: at the very bottom of this human pile were the "loafers," men who had become so demoralized as to be unemployable. Safety was a farce. Ben Tillett recalled that 'every dock was a shambles,' with bodies flattened out to unrecognizable human wreckage. (Tully 2014: 28)

Charles Booth, writing about the 1890s, found that while some 22,000 men sought work on the London docks, only 14,000–15,000 jobs were available at any given time (Gazeley and Thane 1998: 185). In examining the case of London dockworkers, Mayhew reports that "I was unprepared for the amount of suffering that I have lately witnessed. I could not believe that there were human beings toiling so long and gaining so little, and starving so silently and heroically" (quoted in P. Thompson 1967: 46).

Conditions at home were no better. As described by a local priest at the time of the 1911 London dockers' strike: "Home conditions are terrible. I often have to visit dying people in a room where a family of seven or eight lives. I have seen many instances approaching starvation" (quoted in Roberts 1971: 73). Weavers in London's Spitalfields experienced similar despair, as described by a medical doctor of the time:

> It is not in the power of language to describe their long and continued miseries, miseries not brought on by idleness, intemperance or a dissolute course of life, but human wretchedness, absolutely produced by want of employment … whole families without fire, without raiment, without food. (George 1965: 186)

The wives of dockworkers suffered from the irregularity of wages. Eleanor Rathbone writes that dockworkers' wives in Liverpool were forced "to plan out the expenditures of a weekly income that zig-zags in this bewildering way. It is by the wives and children that the hardship of irregular earnings are felt most keenly" (quoted in Pederson 2004: 103). Casual labour—workers who waited on the docks in hopes of being hired by the day or half-day—caused many problems, but

> worst of all was its effect on family life. The hard-drinking, freewheeling culture of the port victimized wives and children in particular, for dockers tended to give only the smallest weekly sums to their wives for household expenses, 'all above this sum being spent by the husband on his pleasures'. (Pederson 2004: 104)

Chief among those pleasures was drink: "drunkenness was by far the commonest cause of dispute and misery in working class homes" (Roberts 1971: 96).

Further, wives were often widowed with young children. The 1842 *Report on the Sanitary Condition of the Labouring Population of Great Britain* found the average age of death of tradesmen in Manchester to be twenty years and of labourers to be seventeen years (Briggs 1963: 98). This is a significant part of the reason that women and children comprised the majority in the workhouses. Lone mothers living in poverty has a long history.

The Dangerous Class, the Residuum

By the last decades of the nineteenth century, skilled workers were making gains in wage levels and standards of living. But most workers—casual workers in particular—were not. They came to be known as part of the "dangerous class, the casual poor or most characteristically, 'the residuum'" (Jones 1971: 11):

> Numerous popular and official studies from the 1880s onwards commented on and explored the emerging syndrome of urban degeneration, drink, early marriage, feckless procreation, hereditary disease and chronic social dependency, which characterized the "residuum" and its various synonyms: the "hopeless classes," "the unfit," "the abyss," the "quagmire," the "pauper Frankenstein" and the "submerged tenth" (Harris 1995: 68)

Barrow (2020: 69) describes this "dangerous class" as the lumpenproletariat—identified as such by its detachment from the labour market and its disreputable lifestyle. This class became separated from the bulk of the working class, particularly as industry employed ever more skilled workers whose wages and conditions gradually improved toward the end of the nineteenth century (Hobsbawm 1968). "A fissure therefore ran through what was increasingly becoming 'the working class.' It separated 'the workers' from 'the poor,' or alternatively 'the respectable' from 'the unrespectable'" (Hobsbawm 1977: 263). The residuum were thus left out, left behind, and could more easily be blamed for their condition. Their problem, it was generally held by contemporaries, "was not structural but moral" (Jones 1971: 11). They were the "undeserving" poor, identified not only by their precarious or non-existent attachment to the labour market, but also and especially by their purported "moral degeneracy," as evidenced by behaviour deemed other than respectable. The undeserving residuum, *The Times* reported in 1886 (quoted in Golding and Middleton 1982: 25), were "recruited from the incapable or immoral," and for them "the old remedy would have been a sound whipping at the cart-tails," a strategy *The Times* recommended.

The residuum, members of the dangerous class, were left to their own devices to find ways to survive. In London there were endless opportunities to scrape together some kind of living via casual employment and/or a wide variety of activities, at least some of which were outside the law. This was the "making shift" of earlier centuries, by which poor families did what they had to do to stay alive. There was in London "a glut of unskilled labour" and widespread unemployment—the predominance of seasonal unemployment "can scarcely be overstated." Casual, or what we now call "precarious," employment was the norm. The result was an unpredictable volatility, without coherent political direction. "At a political level, the most striking characteristic of the casual poor was neither their adherence to the left, nor yet their adherence to the right, but rather their rootless volatility" (Jones 1971: 343). As in the nineteenth-century mills and mines, child labour was a factor. The casual labour market was reproduced by the large demand for what came to be known as "boy labour," and typically these child labourers would be turned adrift by employers upon reaching adulthood, adding to the ranks of unemployed casual labour (Jones 1971: 42).

Women in the late nineteenth century worked at low-paid, irregular and often subcontracted jobs, typically in crowded and often insanitary workshops or in their own equally crowded homes. They worked long hours making clothing, shoes or matchboxes and other forms of "sweated labour"—in some cases supplementing the irregular wages of their husbands, in other cases struggling as single working mothers to keep their children fed and clothed. A contemporary account describes an East End London woman making trousers in her home, working seventeen hours a day to scrape out a bare living (Mearns in Keating 1976: 100). Children, too, did this work, typically of necessity, those employed in matchbox making being described by a contemporary as "the child-slavery of the East End" (Pinchbeck and Hewitt 1973: 562).

The care of children, usually the responsibility of women, was a significant burden. Titmuss (1958: 90) argues that by late in the nineteenth century, "about half of working class wives over the age of forty had borne between seven and fifteen children." He adds, "The typical working class mother of the 1890s, married in her teens or early twenties and experiencing ten pregnancies, spent about fifteen years in a state of pregnancy and in nursing a child for the first year of its life" (Titmuss 1958: 91). Nor did men contribute. "Men in the lower working class ... displayed virility by never performing any task in or about the home, which was considered by tradition to be women's work" (Roberts 1971: 36).

Women's wages were typically so low that other means of earning an income had to be pursued. E.P. Thompson (1967: 47) describes Mayhew's finding that "thousands of the girls in the outwork dressmaking and clothing trades earned piece-rates so low that, as a matter of course, they supplemented these by occasional prostitution." In the last decades of the nineteenth century, large numbers of women in London—Booth estimated between sixty thousand and eighty thousand—were pushed by such circumstances into full-time prostitution (Tully 2014: 82). Wives of casual workers pawned items to manage precarious household finances, took on boarders and washing in their neighbourhoods, and supported—and were supported by—neighbouring women to manage precarious finances (Ross 1993). Shopkeepers in poor neighbourhoods "sold goods 'on tick' or ran a 'slate' for reliable customers," enabling poor families to survive by making shift (Kidd 1999: 148).

Pawning and other forms of local credit were in fact essential means of survival, and the women negotiated these often intricate and typically furtive strategies. Trips to the pawnbroker were, for many, a weekly occurrence. Clothing was pawned, to be used as security for a small loan to make it through the week. Families' Sunday-best clothing was pawned on Monday—why leave good clothes hanging in the house when they could be used as security for a loan to buy food for the week, or to repay other outstanding debts? Wedding rings were saved for particularly serious financial crises, and some pawnshops had rows of wedding rings in their windows. In some cases, women who could not leave the house, perhaps because they were new moms or were aged, would rely upon what in the Midlands was called a "popper" and elsewhere a "bundle woman" or "runner." This was a woman who would pick up clothing door to door, negotiate with the pawnbroker for the best price and earn a small commission for services rendered (Tebbutt 1983: 44). "There was a woman in nearly every street of the East End of London who got a living taking neighbours' things to the pawn shop" (Samuel 1981: 90).

In many low-income working-class communities, virtually every family had clothing at the pawnbroker's (Tebbutt 1983: 13–14). In most low-income communities, in addition to the pawnbroker, there was a woman whose family was a bit better off and who made small loans. "Small-scale borrowing frequently took place at this time of the week when funds had been exhausted, the man's wages had not yet arrived and there was nothing to take to the pawnbroker" (Tebbutt 1983: 51). In all cases, effective interest rates were high—in some cases shockingly high—and the smaller the loan, the higher the rate, so that the poorest paid most (Tebbutt 1983). After 1872, on a loan of less than two pounds, the legislated maximum rate was 25 percent, but if, as was often the case, "an item was continually re-pledged throughout the year, the real rate of interest could range from …100 to 1000 percent" (Vincent 1991: 12). Yet women borrowed, no matter the interest rate, because wages were not high enough or work steady enough to cover the costs of food, rent and other necessities. In almost all cases, these complex and stressful financial gymnastics were carried out without the knowledge of the man in the house, in many cases for fear of a beating (Tebbutt 1983).

Large numbers of children were on the streets in London and other major British cities, especially in the second half of the nineteenth century. The Webbs (quoted in George 1965: 58) describe "the dense swarms of pallid, undersized and wretchedly clad wage-earners, who constituted all but a tiny minority of the population" in early nineteenth-century London. Variously referred to as "savages," "waifs" and "strays" or "street Arabs" (Samuel 1981: 68), they were viewed either with alarm and fear or, particularly toward the end of the century, with pity and concern. "Such children, it was thought, would acquire a propensity to crime. This, of course, was a longstanding fear" (Cunningham 1992: 103). For example, in Manchester in 1840, each year about 3,650 children were lost "and found straying in the streets by the police." A contemporary reported that there were many "shoeless, half-naked, uncombed, and dirty little urchins, who, from two to six years old and upwards, swarm in the streets," seen by many as "savages" (quoted in Cunningham 1992: 103–4).

In testimony before the Select Committee on Criminal and Destitute Juveniles in 1852, it was said about the large numbers of children on the streets, "they have in truth all the vices and some of the virtues of savages." These "City Arabs," as they were called, were described as "indolent, averse from any settled or steady employment, averse from restraint of any kind" and unwilling to "be at school or at work, under the restraints which belong to a civilized society" (quoted in Cunningham 1992: 112–13). In short, and as always, the explanation for these children's poverty was their moral degeneracy—their "indolence"—seemingly developed from a particularly early age.

Much of the worst of the poverty experienced by casual labour, the residuum and street children was concentrated in London's East End, described by Engels as "that immense haunt of misery" (quoted in Palmer 2014: 54). As Jones (1971: 100) observes, "from the end of the 1860s to the First World War, the East End was a byword for chronic and hopeless poverty, and endemic economic malaise" as people scrambled for what jobs there were in "industries characterized by low wage rates, irregular employment, and the subdivision of skilled processes into unskilled ones." This created a "casual labour market of unprecedented dimensions."

Racism was a factor in this poverty, directed as always at the Irish but also, by the end of the nineteenth century, at Jews who had fled the pogroms of the 1880s and 1890s in Eastern Europe. From the early 1880s until 1914, some 250,000 Jews arrived in England, many settling in London's East End, eking out a living in the casual labour market (Thane 2018: 11). They had fled pogroms only to arrive in a country "which was itself profoundly anti-Semitic" and which had a long history of extreme discrimination against Jews (Cohen 1985: 74). Indeed, Jews had been expelled from England in 1290 until the seventeenth century (Kimber 2010: 31). Opposition to Jewish immigration was intense and included opposition from organized labour, British workers and leading members of the progressive trade union movement. Jewish workers, however, were militant and won some trade union support following a series of "major Jewish strikes," especially between 1890 and 1903 (Cohen 1985: 78). Nevertheless, anti-Semitism was the driver behind the 1905 *Aliens Act*, which restricted further Jewish entry to the country and made most Jews ineligible for the welfare benefits—especially unemployment and health insurance—introduced by the Liberal governments of 1906–1914 (Cohen 1985: 81–82). The long history of blaming and attacking the "Other" was far from over.

The Stench … Was Almost Sickening: Housing the Urban Poor

Housing conditions in nineteenth century England were appalling, consistent with the precarious character of the labour market and resulting low incomes.

> Descriptions of working class housing in the early part of Victoria's reign are uniform in their portrayal of filth, stench and inadequate water and sanitary facilities. The first reaction of many sanitary officials on entering the dwellings of the poor was to force, or even break open the windows to try to relieve their heaving stomachs with the comparatively fresh air outside. (Wohl 1971: 21)

John Hollingshead, author of *Ragged London* in 1861—called "one of the most accurate and compelling descriptions of working class London"—describes entering a London house. "The stench throughout the house, although the front and back doors were open, was almost sickening; and when a room-door was opened this stench came out in gusts" (Wohl 1971: 22).

Overcrowding worsened these conditions. A majority of London's workers lived in overcrowded housing, with most families occupying a single room (Wohl 1977). In Church Lane, "in the notorious St. Giles district of London," 655 people lived in twenty-seven houses that averaged five rooms per house in 1841, and six years later, in 1847, 1,095 people lived in those twenty-seven houses (Flinn 1965: 5)—about forty people per house and eight people per room. By the end of the nineteenth century, little had changed. In London's Notting Dale neighbourhood in 1896, many houses had twenty or more people "often sharing a single toilet. Here, 43 children out of every 100 would die before reaching their first birthday" (White 2016). The same was the case in other English cities. When Robert Blatchford was asked in 1889 "Where are the slums of Manchester?," he answered, "They are everywhere. Manchester is a city of slums" (quoted in Burnett 1986: 175).

Disease was rampant. "The history of British towns in the first half of the nineteenth century is, to a considerable extent, the history of typhus and consumption." From the 1780s, every medical writer knew this was "the direct product of overcrowded slums and insanitary squalor" (Flinn 1965: 10). John Haygarth, pioneer of epidemiological studies, wrote as early as the late eighteenth century that disease "is the offspring of filth, nastiness and confined air, in rooms crowded with many inhabitants" (quoted in Flinn 1965: 25). Typhus, associated with overcrowded, insanitary housing, was known as a "poor man's disease." Little was done to control it or tuberculosis, the latter of which accounted for one third of all deaths in the first half of the nineteenth century. These epidemics were so common "as to be deemed a natural hazard of life about which nothing could be done," particularly since they were diseases of the poor (Fraser 1984: 60).

The work of Edwin Chadwick, particularly his report on public health and its huge costs, led to the *Sanitation Act* of 1866. This "marked a significant turning point in the history of public health" (Fraser 1984: 74) and represented another case—along with the Factory Acts—in which, contrary to the tenets of laissez-faire, the state intervened in the economy to promote the broader public interest. Yet appalling housing conditions and the diseases they caused persisted throughout the nineteenth and into the twentieth centuries.

A major cause of these housing problems, particularly but not only in London, was "relentless demographic pressure" (Chapman 1971: 11; Briggs 1963: 81). As people and especially the impoverished poured into London, its population grew from just under two million in 1841 to just under five million in 1881 (Hobsbawm 1968: 132), reaching seven million in 1911 (P. Thompson 1967: 5). In the 1840s, 500,000 Irish migrants inundated Lancashire cities, "spurred by famine and lack of poor relief in Ireland" (Boyer 1990: 247). "Irish immigration was a trickle in the 1790s, a stream in the 1820s, a river in the 1840s, and a flood from the late 1840s" (Swift and Gilley 1985: 1). One quarter of Liverpool's population was Irish-born by 1861 (O'Tuathaigh 1985: 13). By 1913 the population of Ireland had been reduced by half relative to its pre-famine total, "a depopulation without equal in Western Europe since the Black Death" of 1348–1349 (Searle 2004: 8). Many had emigrated to English cities.

Even as this population growth was taking place, more residences were being bulldozed than built, because of street improvements, railway expansion and the massive building and extending of dockyards, warehouses and other commercial enterprises that were the product of dynamic capitalist growth (Wohl 1977: 3). Between 1850 and 1900, an estimated 100,000 people were, as a result, pushed out of their London homes (Haggard 2001: 153). Those most affected "were casual and poorly paid workers. Factory, railway and dockyard extensions were almost exclusively achieved at the expense of the poorest neighbourhoods" (Jones 1971: 170; see also Wohl 1977: Ch. 2). In Birmingham, downtown "improvements" in the 1870s "displaced far more than they re-housed," with the result that "slum dwellers ... were packed more and more closely together in the already crowded courts and alley-ways out of the public gaze" (Wohl 1968: 199). The impact upon the poor was so dramatic "that contemporaries likened the coming of the railways to the invasion of the Huns" (Wohl 1971: 18). Constantly forced to move, the displaced poor were "an almost nomadic tribe, changing homes at very frequent intervals, with their goods pushed on hand-barrows" (Gauldie 1974: 90).

In his influential pamphlet, *The Bitter Cry of Outcast London*, published in 1883 along with a rapidly growing volume of tracts about England's poverty and poor housing, Reverend Andrew Mearns decried the "pestilential human rookeries ... where tens of thousands are crowded together amidst horrors which call to mind what we have heard of the middle passage of the slave-ship" (Keating 1976: 94). The impact of Mearns's pamphlet was so dramatic that it "awoke deep feelings of indignation, pain and sympathy in every direction" (Wohl 1968: 190). The outcry led to the 1885 Royal Commission on the Housing of the Working Classes.

Typically, the poor had been blamed for these housing conditions. It was "assumed that where slums existed they were the haunts of the morally depraved only and the inevitable consequence of grave personal failings" (Wohl 1977: 8; see also Poovey 2007). In his 1832 study of Manchester cotton workers, Dr. James Phillips Kay (quoted in Burnett 1986: 55) described their appalling housing conditions and blamed the inhabitants for being "spendthrifts and destitute—denying themselves the comforts of life in order that they may wallow in the unrestrained license of animal appetite."

First among those to be blamed were the even "less civilized" Irish. As O'Tuathaigh (1985: 16) observes, "their living conditions were generally the very worst which the Victorian industrial slum could offer." A contemporary commentator writes:

> The poverty, the quarreling, the drunken disturbances, the dirt, and the excessive crowding together of the Irish, wherever they form a London colony, cause that they lower the character of every neighbourhood in which they settle, and landlords are of-

ten glad at length to refuse them as tenants, and to sweep them away. (Quoted in Wohl 1977: 9–10)

The echoes of such claims would be heard in the second half of the twentieth century, referring to those arriving in British cities from other, more distant colonies.

Many Irish had no choice but to live in cellars. Engels (1844: 26) describes a case in Manchester where "the water constantly wells up through a hole stopped with clay, the cellar lying below the river level, so that the occupant, a handloom weaver, had to bale out the water from his dwelling every morning, and pour it into the street." In Liverpool in the 1840s, between 25,000 and 38,000 people, most of them Irish, lived in cellars (Burnett 1986: 61).

The Irish were caricatured in cartoons in *Punch* magazine as "the ape-faced, small-headed Irishman … [with] the unmistakable width of mouth, immense expanse of chin, and 'forehead villainous low,' so characteristic of the lowest Irish" (quoted in O'Tuathaigh 1985: 22). A Birmingham surgeon told the 1836 Commission to Inquire into the State of the Irish Poor that "the Irish in Birmingham are the very pests of society. They generate contagion" (quoted in Hickman 1998: 151).

The housing problem was, however, a poverty problem, not a moral problem. Because people were so poor, they could not afford adequate housing; because there were no profits to be made in building adequate and affordable housing for the poor, it didn't get built. More profitable commercial enterprises were built instead (Jones 1971).

> For building entrepreneurs and property developers the poor were an unprofitable market, compared to the rich pickings from the new specialized business and shopping districts and the solid houses and apartments for the middle class, or the developing suburbs. (Hobsbawm 1977: 249)

Capitalism produces what will earn a profit; decent housing affordable by the poor was not then, and is not now, profitable. Therefore, it did not get built. With no new supply being built, and so much existing supply bulldozed, the housing that remained was partitioned into ever-smaller units and the poor squeezed into ever more marginal and overcrowded spaces.

As housing conditions continued to deteriorate and rents continued to rise faster than wages in the 1880s, poverty came grudgingly to be seen as "the root of the housing crisis" (Wohl 1971: 37–38). The 1885 Royal Commission on Housing of the Working Classes reported that the primary cause of poor housing was poverty, since the problem was "the relationship borne by the wages they receive to the rents they have to pay" (Gauldie 1974: 289), or as Wohl (1977: 243) describes it, "wages were low and rents were high."

Dyos (1967: 27) advanced a deeper explanation, saying the "slums were necessary … [and] helped to underpin Victorian prosperity." He argued that, had capital been invested in building better housing and paying higher wages for the poor—for workers—it would not have been available for the economic expansion that characterized the Industrial Revolution of the nineteenth century. Therefore, "one of the real costs of industrial expansion was the making of slums, then and since." It can be fairly said that capitalism produces slums.

The ubiquitous slums became a problem for the governing classes in the last decades of the nineteenth century. The simultaneous growth in the 1880s of trade unions and industrial militancy, and socialist and social democratic organizations, together with massive demonstrations in London in 1886 and 1887, created fear of an uprising, "the fear that the overcrowded rooms of the poor were breeding grounds for malcontents and revolutionaries" (Wohl 1968: 224). "London was haunted by the spectre of Parisian barricades. The housing problem comprised a direct threat to social stability. A solution had to be found" (Jones 1971: 178; Wohl 1977: 212–13).

The Royal Commission did, in fact, lead to a series of housing acts—"remarkably radical acts"—that enabled municipal governments to construct housing for the working class (Wohl 1968: 233–4). There was, by this time, a growing but reluctant acceptance of the fact that private enterprise could not meet the housing needs of low-income workers, let alone the residuum (Burnett 1986: 220). The result was another step along the long path away from laissez-faire.

Exporting, Blaming and Counting the Poor

In lieu of attempts to find solutions, an important response to England's poverty was to export the poor, as in previous centuries. This not only got rid of some of those who were poor, but also helped to meet the labour needs of the colonies and build colonial markets for English manufactures. Parr (1980: 27, 33) argues that emigration of the poor increased in times of economic distress, and in the case of poor children, exporting them to the colonies was "a safety-valve for internal disorder," a means to "tide over the troubles at home." By the last third of the nineteenth century, Poor Law authorities were given permission to spend money raised on the rates "for the purpose of emigrating children" who were poor, and thousands of poor children were removed by way of emigration from the English relief rolls, many going to Canada (Snow 1931: 259). Parr (1980: 11) estimated that from 1868 to 1925, "eighty thousand British boys and girls were sent to Canada to work under indentures as agricultural labourers and domestic servants."

While many thrived, some were badly treated (Parr 1980). "The high hopes invested in the various schemes were regularly punctuated by news of some scandalous treatment of a child on the Canadian frontier" (Cunningham 1992: 148). An inspector sent to Canada in 1874 believed that many were being exploited because of their precarious position and "were in a plight more serious than they would have been in England" (quoted in Pinchbeck and Hewitt 1973: 567–68).

Charities such as the Charity Organization Society and the Salvation Army developed programs in support of emigration, "particularly among the poorest classes." The charitable Dr. Barnardo's Homes "was especially prominent in the transfer of destitute children from Great Britain to the Dominions," sending 22,000 children to Canada alone between 1867 and 1910 (Snow 1931: 259). In at least some cases, Barnardo exported poor children without parental consent "in order to save them" (quoted in Parr 1980: 67) from the moral degeneracy that was seen to be the cause of their poverty.

The moral failings of the poor were depicted in a narrative that included such terms as "disease" and "savagery" and "moral deficiency," which were threatening the health of society and making the poor, including children, dangerous. "Savage, uncontrolled children ... were seen as only one of many infections that threatened the social body" (Lees 1998: 126–27). It was feared that there might be emerging from amongst the poor "a truly degraded race of sub-human beings, a kind to be recoiled from, a kind whose reactions might be animal, revengeful, unpredictable" (Gauldie 1974: Introduction). The Irish were especially targeted. "Dislike of the Irish, especially destitute ones, ran rampant in

England" (Lees 1998: 217). They were "shiftless, dirty, primitive, drunken, wild and generally to be deprecated" (Gauldie 1974: 63). A physician in Liverpool wrote in 1845, "The Irish seem to be contented amidst the dirt and filth … they merely seem to care for that which will support animal existence" (quoted in Law 1981: 22).

That poverty continued to be a major problem late in the nineteenth century was made clear by the detailed surveys conducted in London by Charles Booth. "Before the Booth survey there were no scientifically reliable estimates of the actual extent of poverty" (Jones 1971: 10). Booth's work changed that. The Social Democratic Federation (SDF) had completed a survey showing that one in four residents in London lived in abject poverty. Booth did not believe it and was determined to do his own survey. Starting in the East End of London and then extending throughout the city, Booth systematically collected the observations of school board visitors and other local investigators along with using of his own field workers, one of whom was Beatrice Potter, later to be Beatrice Webb. He ultimately produced a seventeen-volume study—*Life and Labour of the People in London*. The first four volumes focused on poverty, finding that instead of the 25 percent estimated by the SDF, a full 30 percent of those living in London were "in poverty or want." Booth defined poverty as "having no surplus" or having nothing left after paying for bare necessities, and thus nothing left to be able to respond to the emergencies that were part of precarious lives. Poverty was, he found, especially high among those over sixty-five years of age, a large proportion of whom ended up in a workhouse. Booth went on to become a major advocate of England's first pension plan, introduced in 1908.

But perhaps Booth's most significant findings were that the level of poverty was high—just over 30 percent—and that poverty was attributable less to personal failings than to low pay and irregular work (Thane 1982: 4–8). The main problem was not yet unemployment. As Gazeley (2003: 41) argues, in comparison with what was to follow in the early 1920s and especially the 1930s, "it is striking that unemployment is usually fairly low down the list of 'causes of poverty' provided by investigators at this time." The problem was low pay, in jobs that we might today describe as precarious, low-pay/no-pay jobs.

Booth identified eight categories, labelled alphabetically. Category A was "the lowest class, which consists of some occasional labourers, street sellers, loafers, criminals, and semi-criminals"; B was the "very poor," living on "casual earnings"; and C was unskilled labourers with small and intermittent earnings who, together with D, earned regular but low incomes, as the "poor" (Booth 1889: 33–61). Booth argued that the "poor," those in classes C and D, "could make ends meet if they lived frugal and rigorously self-disciplined lives, if their wants were simple and their 'vices' few—and if their luck held out" (Fried and Elman 1968: xix). It is important to note, especially considering debates in the 1960s and 1970s following the "rediscovery of poverty," that Booth's interpretation of what it meant to be poor was at least in part consistent with the later use of the concept of "relative poverty." The poor, Booth writes, "are those whose means may be sufficient, but are barely sufficient, for decent independent life; the 'very poor' those whose means are insufficient for this *according to the usual standards of this country*" (Booth 1889: 33, my emphasis).

Significantly, Booth recommended that all those in category B—casual labourers working irregular, part-time hours and representing some 100,000 people in London, whom Booth described as "industrially valueless and socially pernicious" (quoted in Haggard 2001: 49)—should be sent outside the city to labour colonies. This, he argued, would improve the economic prospects of those workers just above them, in C. "The entire removal of this very poor class [B] out of the daily struggle for existence, I believe to be the only solution to the problem" (quoted in Brown 1968: 351). This recommendation was not implemented. However, it was consistent with a long tradition of "solving" poverty by exporting the poor—to another parish to avoid paying relief, to mines and mills as child labour to meet the needs of the emergent Industrial Revolution and avoid paying relief, and to Barbados, Jamaica and North America to meet the demand for labour there—and to avoid paying relief in Britain.

Seebohm Rowntree completed a similar study in York in 1899, with findings that were "remarkably similar" to those of Booth in London (Thane 1982: 6). Ten percent of those living in York had earnings below "the minimum necessary for the maintenance of merely physical efficiency" and lived in "obvious want and squalor"; these he identified as the "primary poor" (Rowntree 1901: 8). An additional 18 percent of York residents had income "sufficient for the maintenance of merely physical efficiency were it not that some portion of it is absorbed by other expenditures, either useful or wasteful." This Rowntree (1901: 8) called "secondary poverty." He concluded, "we are faced with the startling probability that from 25 percent to 30 percent of the town population of the United Kingdom are living in poverty" (Rowntree 1901: 17). He also found, consistent again with Booth's findings, that more than half of the poor held regular jobs—low wages were the problem, particularly in the case of families with large numbers of children. Rowntree's studies also identified the life cycle character of poverty—that individuals and families were more likely to be poor at particular times in their lives. These times included when they had young children or when women were widowed, otherwise abandoned or elderly.

There were other studies of the incidence of poverty in the pre–First World War era. A 1912 study conducted by the Liberal Christian League found that in Norwich, "children were often living on a diet consisting solely of white bread, jam and tea … [and were] chronically hungry, stunted and undernourished, ill-clad and ill-shod, and notably below the physical average of other children" (quoted in Gazeley 2003: 13). Bowley and Burnett-Hurst (1913: 46–47), in their study of four towns, found "permanent, as distinct from occasional, poverty exists in certain places on a scale which is appalling," and 27 percent of children "are living in families which fail to reach the low standard taken as necessary for healthy existence." Low pay and large family size were the primary causes. A previous study by Florence Bell in 1907, undertaken in a northern industrial town, found that approximately 14 percent were "absolutely poor," by which she meant, "they never have enough to spend on food to keep themselves sufficiently nourished" (quoted in Gazeley 2003: 38). In each of the pre-war social surveys, "it is the fragility of the position of households with a regularly employed breadwinner and how easily their circumstances could be transformed, that is apparent" (Gazeley 2003: 40). Maude Pember Reeves, in a London study published in 1914, concludes, "to the insufficiency of a low wage is added the horror that it is never secure" (quoted in Gazeley 2003: 42). Precarious employment and precarious lives were the norm.

Women suffered particularly. Pregnancies were especially difficult: miscarriages ended 15 percent and still-births another 6 percent of pregnancies. Women who survived were back with never-ending household tasks "after no more than a fortnight's rest, and often less, faced with all her old tasks, in addition to the loss of sleep and energy which feeding and caring for a new-born baby entailed." A working-class mother of the times described the reality of women who were poor:

The toil, the grind, the struggle, the poverty of it all, and of the even more barren lives of those about her; of how in time it stifled human qualities—kindness, sensitivity, intelligence, and left no way out—the "too much sacrifice" that "turns the heart to stone." (Quoted in Vincent 1991: 21)

Constant poverty can produce a sense of hopelessness and resignation to the reality that life is not going to improve. This internalization of the effects of poverty can in turn lead to behavioural consequences that reinforce the all-too-common "blame the poor" trope.

Warring Interpretations: What Causes This Poverty? What Should Be Done?

Nevertheless, the empirical sociological work done by Booth, Rowntree and others contributed to the late nineteenth-century change in thinking about the causes of poverty—perhaps poverty was not, in fact, simply a matter of personal failings. This belief would grow slowly in the late nineteenth and early twentieth centuries and would exist alongside the persistence of the centuries-old belief that poverty was caused by the depravity and immorality of the poor themselves. Booth himself embodied these warring interpretations. He was a major figure in promoting the old age pension introduced by the Liberal government in 1908, as were Sidney and Beatrice Webb (see Cooper 2017: Chapter 4). However, Booth also advocated labour colonies, believing that members of the residuum were unsalvageable and undeserving. For the poorest of the poor, such interpretations remained dominant.

The term "feeble-minded," for example, began to be used to describe the residuum, and by early in the twentieth century, the eugenics movement was gaining strength (Searle 2004). This was in part a response to the 1899–1902 Boer War, when it was found that large numbers of would-be recruits—perhaps as many as 40 percent—were not physically fit to fight (Harris 2004: 156). This was undoubtedly a consequence of the severe poverty, poor diets and disabling working and housing conditions of the nineteenth century. Nevertheless, some in Britain saw the cause in "hereditary weakness" among those for whom "there was not much hope" (Harris 1972: 46–47). Feeble-mindedness as the explanation for such poverty was even adopted by some progressive thinkers, as eugenics "enjoyed a minor vogue." For example, eugenic ideas "affected the Webbs who advocated the segregation of the 'feeble-minded'" (Thane 1982: 59). A 1905 Fabian pamphlet said, "the weak-minded and incompetent must be dealt with in farm colonies … the deliberately idle must be set to hard labour, and their social vice, if it may be, sweated out of them" (quoted in Jones 1971: 334). William Beveridge—who, more than thirty years later, would write the document that became the cornerstone of the postwar welfare state (Beveridge 1942)—wrote in his 1906 publication, *The Problem of the Unemployed*, that those who are unemployable should be "removed from free industry and maintained adequately in public institutions, but with a complete and permanent loss of all citizen rights including not only the franchise, but civil freedom and fatherhood" (quoted in Jones 1971: 335). On another occasion, however, Beveridge acknowledged, "only an insignificant proportion of the unemployed are unemployable" (quoted in Macnicol 1989: 150).

Despite the changes in thinking about the poor that were beginning to emerge in the minds of at least some thinkers late in the nineteenth century—that the cause of poverty had more to do with the way the capitalist economy worked than with the moral and behavioural failings of the poor—there was still the belief, even in progressive quarters, that at least some of the poor, because of their own moral or even genetic failings, were beyond redemption and had best be removed from society.

The Webbs later recognized that the problem of the casual poor, the residuum, was "a social and not a biological creation. Their lifestyle had not been the result of some hereditary 'taint' but the simple consequence of the offer of poor housing, inadequate wages, and irregular work" (Jones 1971: 336). This was more typical of the shift in thinking that led to the 1906 Liberal government initiatives by which the state would begin, very gradually and outside the terms of the Poor Law, to assume some responsibility for the fate of at least some segments of Britain's still very large population of poor people.

Yet charity continued to be the primary response to poverty, as it had been for centuries. Not only was it a long British tradition, but also and especially importantly, it required no change to existing structures of power and privilege. Those with wealth considered charity a small enough price to pay to keep the system intact. Much charity was driven by "a genuine and persistent fear of social revolution" (Fraser 1984: 126), so that for the Victorians it became "an accepted tenet that the burden of the poor was one which would always have to be borne by the superior classes" (Gauldie 1974: 214). Many among the "superior classes" were in fact charitable, as had been the case throughout the centuries of the *Old Poor Law*.

By the mid-nineteenth century, "the scale of private charity expanded remarkably ... and offered considerable protection to the poor against the rigours of the Poor Law. A very large sum indeed was thus redistributed from rich to poor annually." One estimate is that there were 640 charities in London in 1861 with a collective annual income of 2.5 million pounds; the amount of this private charity exceeded the amount spent on relief under the provisions of the *New Poor Law* (Thane 1982: 19–21). This was a part of the price paid to stave off the structural changes that the poor might otherwise have demanded.

An important example of private charity was the Charity Organization Society (COS), created in 1869. The COS—whose full title was the Society for Organizing Charitable Relief and Repressing Mendacity—drew considerable support from the governing classes, including Queen Victoria herself as patron, the Archbishop of Canterbury as honorary president, and a host of dukes, earls, bishops, parliamentarians and other dignitaries (Haggard 2001). The COS practised what the organization called "scientific charity." Their mostly female and middle-class staff made home visits to interview and classify relief applicants, in the belief that its "scientific" casework could best distinguish between the deserving and the undeserving poor. Once the deserving poor were identified—via the "intense moralizing" to which they were subjected by COS visitors (Brundage 2002: 118)—work would begin to assimilate them into middle class values and standards of behaviour. Given the strong evangelical thrust of the work of the COS, this meant attempting to Christianize the poor, "to extirpate vice and to encourage the growth of virtue" (Kidd 1999: 72). Those who, by contrast, were identified "scientifically" as "undeserving" would remain under the control of the *New Poor Law*, whose "less eligibility" principle was intended to force them into the paid labour force, or failing that, the workhouse.

The COS opposed state involvement (Woodroofe 1962: 34–35), including state pensions and free school meals for poor children, asserting that when parents were negligent it was always best "to allow in such cases the sins of the parents to be visited on their children." To do otherwise would erode the sanctity of the family (Mooney 1998).

To the COS, personal failings caused poverty. Mooney (1998: 64) quotes a COS publication of 1881: "there can be no doubt that the poverty of the working classes of England is due ... to their improvident habits and thriftlessness. If they are to be more prosperous it must be through self-denial and forethought." The COS rejected most applicants because they were undeserving (Kidd 1999). Their use of casework was "professionally pioneering but ideologically reactionary" (Fraser 1984: 131). As Paul Thompson (1967: 22) put it: "It is easy to understand why no Victorian institution was more disliked by the working classes than the Charity Organization Society." In the East End of London, for example, the COS was "deeply resented," particularly the "patronizing attitude accorded to them by the 'old women and earnest young men' of the COS" (Brodie 2004: 79–80).

Most of the charitable work done by the COS and the many other charitable organizations of the time was done by middle- and upper-class women, "for whom unpaid charitable work was one of the very few socially acceptable occupations." Such women "supplied a willing and almost endless supply of volunteers for such activity" (Thane 1982: 27; Kidd 1999: 69–70).

An example was Octavia Hill. She was highly successful at securing charitable donations, which she used to acquire housing in the poorest areas of London. At the height of her influence, some three thousand to four thousand people lived in her various East End London properties (Wohl 1977: 180). She had the housing renovated and then carefully selected the families to be housed there, seeking to identify the deserving poor. The "undeserving" poor were excluded. Poor but "deserving" families were visited "by volunteer rent-collectors whose task was to advise tenants on the management of the household or other aspects of their lives—how to sweep the floors, wash their children and clothing and to conduct themselves with propriety" (Thane 1982: 26; see also Jones 1971: 193–95). Hill believed that her housing efforts should include "improvements in the 'character' of the poor," making her "just one of many middle class women who invaded the homes of the poor to preach bourgeois respectability" (Wohl 1977: 180, 184). Like the COS, Hill remained steadfastly opposed to government intervention, in favour of a "stern insistence on self-reliant individualism" (Rose 1972: 26). Wohl (1977: 199) summarized Hill's efforts: "Her activities, so sound, altruistic and godly, tended to push into the background the real crises which had to be met, caused by widespread poverty and the inconsistency of wages and rent."

Another important and only slightly different example of this charity-based approach was the settlement house movement, founded in the 1880s by Samuel and Henrietta Barnett. They opened Toynbee Hall in London's East End in 1884, and other settlement houses followed in London and elsewhere, so that by the end of the century there were some thirty settlement houses in poor urban areas (Fraser 1984: 135). The idea was that bright young Oxford graduates would live at Toynbee Hall to develop personal relationships with the poor residents of the East End. This was because "estrangement between classes would be brought to an end only when the educated and well-to-do went among the poor" (Woodroofe 1962: 65). They did in the East End what could be called "community work," as opposed to the casework of the COS. This included, for example, adult education classes, clubs for children and musical and other cultural evenings. Cooper (2017: 16) describes "a never-ending stream of the brightest graduates from Balliol in particular and from Oxford generally [who] were directed to take up residence in the settlement," and he adds that many of these young people "later had a huge impact" as civil servants or elected officials. Some were socialists—Clement Attlee and R.H. Tawney, for example (Cooper 2017: 22). About Attlee, later to be prime minister during the 1945–1951 Labour governments, it has been said that "his eyes were opened when he commenced social work with the poor in the East End of London in 1905" (Boyd and McWilliam 2007: 13), where he lived for fourteen years. Others involved with this movement became civil servants active with the 1906–1914 Liberal government and its program of modestly progressive and conceptually important social service changes (Hay 1975). In the case of Attlee, who gave away significant amounts of his own money to those in need, "the people of the East End were the touchstone of his political life" (Addison 1975: 272).

Jones (1971) offers an interpretation of this kind of settlement work—which involved middle-class people living side by side with the poor—that is based on the observation that the spatial distance between rich and poor had widened dramatically in London in the latter decades of the nineteenth century. The poor—dockworkers, for example—were increasingly segregated from the more well-to-do. The latter moved to the suburbs; the poor could not. This geographic segregation existed in all major British cities. Hobsbawm (1968: 68) quotes a Manchester clergyman who wrote, "there is not a town in the world where the distance between the rich and the poor is so great or the barrier between them so difficult to be crossed." Another contemporary wrote, "owing to the vastness of London ... the rich know nothing of the poor; the mass of misery that festers beneath the affluence of London ... is not known to [its] wealthy occupants" (quoted in Woodall 2005: 44). The poor were spatially segregated, as well as socially and economically segregated. Skilled workers were increasingly separated in all these ways from unskilled workers and especially from the residuum. By the late nineteenth century, better-paid workers "could take advantage of cheap workmen's trains and the expanding network of trams, which offered an escape from the overcrowding, squalor and expense of inner-city life. Unskilled workers, trapped in casual employment, could seldom take this option," because as in the case of dockworkers, for example, they had to be close to their place of employment to be able to know when work was available (Searle 2004: 94).

The result of such changes was that there was no longer any direct, social connection between rich and poor. This was in contrast to conditions that prevailed under the *Old Poor Law*, when the landed gentry and the poor lived in the same parish and relief was administered by overseers who personally knew those seeking relief. The late nineteenth-century solution, as seen by those involved with the settlement movement, was to close the spatial gap that had emerged between urban rich and poor by having some of the well-to-do take up residence in low-income areas such as the East End of London, thus re-creating the supposedly more intimate connections between rich and poor that had prevailed under the *Old Poor Law*. As Jones (1971: 261) describes it, the underlying premise was that when those of means returned to live in the low-income neighbourhoods, London "would be turned into a gigantic village, and its poor would be led back to manliness and independence under the firm but benevolent aegis of a new urban squirearchy." This is another version of a response to poverty that requires no change in the structure of power and privilege in English society. It is an early version of the late twentieth and early twenty-first century mixed-income approach to housing, which has been rooted in the mistaken and simplistic belief that the mere presence of middle-class people living alongside the poor would in itself improve the circumstances of the poor (August 2008).

Still Making Shift

By the late nineteenth century, even though Poor Law expenditures continued to rise (Thane 1982), only a small proportion of those who were poor were getting Poor Law relief. While work done by both Booth and Rowntree suggested that approximately 30 percent of the English population was poor in the 1890s, "there were no more than 2.7 percent in receipt of poor relief in any one year" (Kidd 1999: 12; Searle 2004: 188). Those getting Poor Law relief were primarily women and children, the aged and sick. The able-bodied poor had been effectively denied relief and thus were forced into the paid labour force, as was the intent of the 1834 Poor Law. "The Poor Law had been most effective in forcing all those who could to be self-helping. It had not succeeded in eliminating poverty" (Thane 1982: 32). Eliminating poverty was, of course, not its purpose.

However, even those relatively few who were the recipients of relief provided by the *Poor Law*, or of benefits provided by the many existing forms of charity and community work, remained poor. "Almost nowhere was the amount of relief sufficient for barest subsistence" (Thane 1978a: 41), and "the most miserable poverty was concentrated among older women" (Thane 2000: 83). The poor still had to rely upon "making shift." Some took on various casual jobs "such as cleaning, running errands and child-minding" (Thane 1982: 18).

Others used various illegal means:

> Gangs of burglars, garroters, and pickpockets operated almost without check in many parts of the Metropolis [London], [while] poverty and a lack of decent employment opportunities in the slums induced a large number of young women to sell their sexual favours in the music halls, public houses, or streets of the Metropolis, if only for a couple of years in their late teens and early twenties. (Haggard 2001: 39–40)

As in previous centuries, poor people also turned to friends and neighbours, as well as family, in time of need. "Time after time [they] came to the rescue, helping with food and shelter, clothing, attendance as the case may require ... it is only in the most serious pressure that help is asked either of the clergyman ... or to one of the numerous charitable societies that distribute relief in food and clothing" (Rathbone 1913, quoted in Thane 1982: 19).

In many cases, this mutual aid was formalized in burial clubs and the "friendly society" movement, which emerged in the seventeenth century and became especially strong as the working class began to become conscious of itself as a class early in the nineteenth century (Kidd 1999: 111–12). By 1803, an estimated 8 percent of the population of England and Wales were members (Mann 1992: 68), and by 1900 friendly societies, with about 5.6 million members in Great Britain, were the largest working-class organizations of the time (Thane 1984: 21), pooling individual workers' resources to provide sickness and burial benefits to their members. By 1911, close to one half of male labourers were members of friendly societies (Searle 2004: 187). These and other forms of self-help and making shift would persist well into the twentieth century, existing side by side with the state-provided social service and later social welfare systems. Poverty persisted and was reflected, for example, in the much poorer health of lower-income workers and their families. A 1910 study that found that the average weight of thirteen- to fourteen-year-old children whose parents earned over twenty-five shillings per week was one hundred pounds, while children of parents earning only twelve to fourteen shillings per week weighed an average of seventy-one pounds (Searle 2004: 405).

In the last two decades of the nineteenth century and up to the beginning of the First World War, significant changes occurred in Britain. The dominance of laissez-faire was gradually eroded, although by no means replaced, while state delivery of social services slowly emerged. This was the product of practical responses to real problems enacted by governments concerned both with responding to the human carnage created by unregulated, laissez-faire capitalism and with staving off the possibility of more dramatic, socialist-oriented changes. The source of the threat to the existing order was the growth in the numbers and demands of the trade union movement and socialist and social democratic political formations. To fend off these threats, British governments made concessions in the form of increased state-delivered social services.

Chapter 5

Great Unrest

Political Pressure and Social Reform, 1880–1914

Throughout the nineteenth century, the poor—much of Britain's population—fought against their poverty and against those they deemed responsible for their poverty. Sometimes they did this openly— Jacobin movements, Luddite demonstrations, the Peterloo Massacre, the Captain Swing revolt, the campaign for parliamentary reform, opposition to the *New Poor Law*, the rise of Chartism and more. Always, they did this in more hidden and individualistic ways—making shift, negotiating with overseers, resisting workhouse rules. The governing classes responded with both repression and accommodation. The *New Poor Law* of 1834 was perhaps the chief instrument of repression. However, there was accommodation, too—for example, in the long, gradual working-class gains embodied in the Factory Acts, and the even slower gains represented by public health and housing legislation (Harris 2004: 130–31; Henriques 1979). It might be argued, therefore, that the first steps away from laissez-faire and toward state intervention had their origins early in the nineteenth century.

However, it was in the last two decades of that century, with the growth in trade union membership and militancy and small but vocal socialist organizations, that the speed of this transition accelerated. The view emerged that the state would have to respond in the same way that Chancellor Otto von Bismarck was responding to similar but even stronger demands in Germany— "in an explicitly conservative manner," aimed at dampening militancy by offering to working class people social services such as pensions and unemployment insurance (Hay 1975: 30).

Political Pressures

With continued industrial growth, the numbers of trade union members grew rapidly, from 750,000 in 1888 to two million in 1900 and four million in 1913 (Searle 2004: 93). The "new unionism" of the late 1880s "was built on the foundations laid by a series of remarkable industrial struggles over 1888–89. Most notable were the Dock Strike, the gasworkers' strike, and the matchgirls' strike" (Tully 2014: 19). Engels considered 1888–1889 and the dockworkers' strike to be "the real beginning of a movement" (quoted in Tully 2014: 38). There were riots of the unemployed in London's Trafalgar Square in 1886 and 1887, their anger directed at "the propertied and privileged people in London" (Briggs 1963: 340). In Germany, whose rapidly growing economy threatened British economic dominance, the German Social Democratic Party had won 500,000 votes and thirteen seats in the Reichstag as early as 1877 (Pelling 1965: 13). This led to Bismarck's reforms—"three groundbreaking compulsory social insurance schemes between 1883 and 1889 which covered workers against industrial accidents, illness, invalidity and old age" (Perry and Reiss 2011: 20). Their purpose was to prevent socialism.

In Britain, there were similar pressures:

> Both the Labour Party and the Trades Union Congress had extensive social reform programs by the early 1900s, including free education for all, assisted by scholarships; old age pensions; the abolition of the Poor Law; and measures to deal with unemployment. (Hay 1975: 27)

In 1900, the Labour Representation Committee (LRC) was formed by the rapidly growing union movement. The Fabian Society was formed in 1884 and the Independent Labour Party (ILP) in 1893. By 1905, the LRC included 158 trade unions, seventy-three trades councils plus the Fabian Society and the ILP, making the LRC the "largest and strongest political organization in Britain" (Russell 1973: 45). Growing levels of unemployment led in 1908 to riots, strikes and hunger marches (Novak 1988: 129). The strike wave from 1910 to 1914 was labelled the "Great Unrest" (Hannah 2018: 10).

In addition, workers were steadily gaining the vote. While the 1832 *Reform Act* had excluded almost all of the working class, the 1867 *Reform Act* extended voting rights to "a large number of working class householders in urban areas" (Harris 2004: 153). It added one million people to the voting rolls, which doubled the number of eligible voters in England and Wales "and propelled the British electoral system into the age of mass politics" (Saunders 2007: 571–72). Nevertheless, the enfranchisement process was relatively slow. Less than 30 percent of the adult population was on the electoral register following the *Reform Act* of 1884–1885. By 1911, sixty percent of the adult male population was entitled to vote, but large numbers of others—most notably women, but also anyone receiving Poor Law relief—still could not vote (Blewett 1965: 27). In addition, the system of registration was "so replete with technicalities, and anomalies, that every obstacle is put in the way of getting on, and every facility exists for getting struck off, the register" (quoted in Blewett 1965: 28). For example, twelve months' residency was required before being placed on the electoral rolls, thus disadvantaging large numbers of workers who moved in search of jobs. Blewett (1965: 36–37, 43) estimated "at least half" of those nominally entitled to vote "were eliminated by the working of the registration system."

Nevertheless, "the 1884 extensions of the electorate meant the end of the already moribund principle of government non-intervention in the economic sphere" (Pelling 1965: 39). By 1906, workers comprised 75 to 80 percent of the electorate—"a majority in one half to two-thirds of all seats" (Russell 1973: 21). By 1918, "the English adult male enfranchisement level was 94.9 percent, and only 39 out of 509 constituencies in England and Wales had levels of less than 85 percent for males over 21" (Matthew, McKibbin and Kay 1976: 731).

Simultaneously, women—textile workers, shopkeepers and other working-class women, as well as middle-class women—had been organizing since at least the 1860s for voting rights. Women secured the right to vote in school board and Poor Law boards of guardians elections in the last decades of the nineteenth century, and in municipal council elections in 1907. The struggle to vote at the national level accelerated in the last decades of the nineteenth and first decades of the twentieth century. In 1897, women formed the National Union of Women's Suffrage Societies (NUWSS), followed in 1903 by the more militant Women's Social and Political Union. The latter adopted increasingly militant tactics, including interrupting ministers' speeches with shouts of "Votes for Women" and demonstrations that often led to arrests and to the media disparagingly referring to them as "suffragettes" (Thane 2018: 22–24). Their efforts, derailed by the First World War, resulted in the partial victory embodied in the 1918 *Representation of the People Act,* by which women over the age of thirty and who paid taxes secured the right to vote. The last barriers to women's right to vote were removed in 1928.

This long struggle for the right to vote mattered. "The more the poor acquired votes in the wake of suffrage reform, the more bread and butter issues dominated the political arena" (Fraser 1984: xxix). By 1897 a *Workmen's Compensation Act* had been passed, "partly the result of trade union pressure" (Thane 1982: 44). "Public health, housing, education and working conditions all became issues of political importance following the widening of the franchise" (Fraser 1984: 139). Sidney Webb had warned the 1905 Royal Commission on the Aged Poor that when working people had the vote, they would use it to change "the conditions under which they live and work" (quoted in Gilbert 1970: 305). He was right.

It was to such pressures that the Liberal government of 1906–1914 responded. They could make the reforms being demanded or face the likelihood of even greater change being imposed. As Hay (1975: 62) argued, "the desire to retain as much as possible of the existing capitalist economic system, at a time when it was under increasing pressure from within and without, seems to have been the most important motive in the origins of the Liberal reforms." Fraser (1984: xxx) concurs: "Concessions to working-class welfare were rarely made through altruism; more often than not it was for fear of something worse." Social reforms were the means to dampen class conflict. They were the price that had to be paid for political peace and the maintenance of the system.

New Ways of Thinking: Collectivism and the Positive State

At the same time, new ways of thinking emerged—a shift was in process, away from the strict individualism of classical liberalism to a more collective approach that began to look to state intervention as a response to problems created by nineteenth-century industrial capitalism. The origins of this changed thinking about the role of the state can be seen earlier in the nineteenth century in the Factory Acts, and later the *Sanitation Act* of 1866 and related initiatives, and it accelerated in the 1880s as the labour movement gained strength. In 1883 *The Economist* wrote, "it required very little observation of current politics to see that the principle of laissez-faire is no longer in the ascendant" (quoted in Haggard 2001: 117). A "new liberalism" emerged in the late nineteenth century, embodied in the work of T.H. Green, J.A. Hobson, L.T. Hobhouse and others. It called for a more positive, but far from socialist, role by the state (Rose

1972: 31), and these "new liberal" views were buttressed by the more socialist views of the Fabian Society and Independent Labour Party.

What Cooper (2017) described as a "counter-elite" emerged, promoting the ideas of "new liberalism." These middle-class reformers—the small membership of the somewhat socialist Fabian Society, for example, was dominated "by the emerging middle class professional groups of late Victorian England" (Hay 1975: 37)—would benefit enormously from the creation of state-run programs, because they would be employed by the state to administer them. The modest pension, health and unemployment insurance programs introduced by the 1906–1914 Liberal governments would benefit those among the working class who were the respectable and deserving poor.

As important as these working class and socialist pressures were, the Liberal reforms of 1906–1914 should not be thought of as pure products of working-class demands or socialist ways of thinking. After all, as Haggard (2001: 115) observes, "socialism remained the province of an isolated, marginalized and tiny minority of social reformers." Hobsbawm (1974: xxii) says of the state of late-nineteenth century British socialism, "with the exception of a few of the Social-Democrats of the Left, and a very few Fabians on the Right, no Socialists had a clear idea of what they were after, and most confined their theory to moral fervour and a few statistics." Most trade union leaders were Liberal Party supporters. Engels, writing in 1881, describes the English working class as the "tail of the great Liberal Party" (quoted in Pelling 1965: 3), and socialist organizations at the time were "pitiably weak" (Pelling 1968: 4). Tully (2014: 135) observes that "Popular music hall songs scoffed at the puny efforts of the socialists, whom they lumped in with Christian evangelists and other 'do-gooders.'" So, while the rise of trade union militancy and the beginnings of socialist ideas and organizations and the resultant creation of the Labour Party were important, it was also the case that to a considerable extent the Liberal reforms were practical responses to real problems created by industrial, laissez-faire capitalism:

> any explanation [of the emergence of these reforms] which does not emphasize the practical, pragmatic, unplanned, *ad hoc* response of the state is in a major respect deficient. It cannot be overemphasized that social policies and their administration were geared to meet real and pressing problems.... It was the

pressure of facts, and unpalatable ones at that, which produced … administrative growth. (Fraser 1984: 117; see also Briggs 1961: 253)

Among those facts was the new empirical evidence about the incidence, depth and persistence of poverty, which became more widely known because of the work of Charles Booth, Seebohm Rowntree and others. "The findings of Booth had shown that the major problems of chronic poverty were beyond the scope of charity and would have to become the responsibility of the state" (Jones 1971: 328). Booth's findings, soon supported by those of Rowntree and a host of other detailed studies—many conducted by women between 1909 and 1913 (Thane 1984: 55)—contributed to producing "a guilt-ridden, fearful recognition that poverty and squalor were not the product of individual shortcomings, but were endemic in a system that created so much want in the midst of so much plenty" (Cannadine 1984: 133).

Only the Deserving Poor

Yet this "fearful recognition" applied only to the deserving poor; it did not extend to the "undeserving" poor—those long described as vagrants and vagabonds, scoundrels and shirkers, paupers and, more recently, the residuum. As Himmelfarb (1991: 12) writes, it "was the poor, rather than the very poor, who were the beneficiaries of most of the reforms."

Indeed, these reforms accentuated the marginalization and stigmatization of the "undeserving poor." Reforms for the deserving poor

> would allow a much harder line to be taken with members of the residuum, who were regarded as beyond hope…. late Victorian and Edwardian social legislation is thoroughly permeated by the desire to provide decent treatment and social incentives to the respectable, and to separate them from the residuum. (Hay 1975: 34)

Many working-class families were moving out of poverty, because average real wages had grown by about 60 percent between 1860 and 1900 (Hopkins 1991: 5). Those left behind and still mired in poverty—casual and other precarious workers, those outside waged labour entirely—were further marginalized. Increasingly, the mainstream working class blamed them for their poverty, as had been done for centuries by more establishment elements.

As outlined in previous chapters, the seeds of this interpretation were centuries old, initially in the early Christian concerns about the able-bodied poor and in subsequent centuries in the fear of vagrants and vagabonds, scoundrels and masterless men. However, for centuries, a very large proportion of British people and families had been poor, and there existed a collective sense of empathy for those in need, as expressed in the idea of a "moral economy"—the widespread belief that English people were owed at least a bare minimum under the *Elizabethan Poor Law*. Nevertheless, as more workers made economic gains in the late nineteenth century, they came to separate themselves from the residuum:

> The dangerous classes were perceived as a "residuum," left behind by the mid-Victorian march of moral and material progress. The values and behaviour attributed to them—violence and licentiousness, thriftlessness and dependence, criminality and political volatility—were those which many believed had now been spurned by the respectable majority of the English nation. (Davis 1989: 11)

The behaviour of the residuum reinforced these perceptions of their moral failings, and the media of the day fed those perceptions, attaching to the undeserving poor such derogatory labels as the unemployable, the social problem group, the problem family, the underclass and, often in a more vitriolic fashion, scroungers, shirkers, social scum, dregs, diseased, degenerate, parasites and the feeble-minded.

The state-delivered social service gains of 1906–1914—what Titmuss (1958: 18) would later call, with some exaggeration, "the great collectivist advances at the beginning of the century"—benefited the deserving poor. Their gains were limited but significant. However, the residuum, the undeserving poor, gained little, perhaps nothing. What is more, the lowest-income labourers—casual and other precarious workers—did not experience the more general wage growth of the 1880–1914 era (Gazeley 2003: 16). The Liberal legislation of 1906–1914, important as it was as an expression of new thinking about the role of the state and the circumstances of the working poor, was a relatively modest way station on a longer journey.

The Liberal Governments of 1906–1914 and the Social Services State

In 1906, a majority Liberal government was elected with 401 seats. The Conservatives won 157 and the Labour Representation Committee, which, after Parliament had met, "decided to adopt the title of Labour Party" (Russell 1973: 209), won 29. The strong LRC/Labour representation added to the pressure for state-delivered social services.

A series of important but limited measures followed. The details are perhaps less important than the fact that the social services introduced in the early twentieth century represented a significant conceptual break with the past, because they were delivered by the state and outside the purview of the *Poor Law*. Briggs (1961: 228) calls the results of the Liberal initiatives a "social service state" but not yet a "welfare state." A social service state is one "in which communal resources are employed to abate poverty and to assist those in distress," while a welfare state "is concerned not merely with the abatement of class differences or the needs of scheduled groups [specifically identified categories of people] but with equality of treatment and the aspirations of citizens as voters with equal shares of electoral power." Solving poverty was not the purpose of the Liberal reforms of 1906–1914, although poverty was in fact abated as a result, in part, of these new state-delivered services.

In their first year, 1906, the Liberal government passed the *Education Act*, which authorized free school meals and medical inspections of children. These measures were "products of the climate of opinion created by the Boer War," which had "highlighted the poor health of army recruits" (Hay 1975: 43). The inspector-general of recruiting "reported that up to 40 percent of those who were willing to join the army were unfit to serve" (Harris 2004: 156), and a 1904 report by the Interdepartmental Committee on Physical Deterioration concluded that "a low standard of health prevails among the working classes" (Hay 1975: 54). Adding to these concerns were fears of growing international industrial competition, especially from Germany and the US (Haggard 2001: 13), leading to demands from all sides to lay the basis for a healthier and thus more productive working class. The Labour Party, whose backbenchers had previously introduced bills along these lines (Thane 2000), together with progressive medical doctors, "took the lead in demanding that local authorities be compelled to feed needy children" (Hay 1975: 43). The Liberals' efforts in this regard "were designed to convince working-class voters that a Liberal government could work to their advantage" (Thane 2000: 84). The Conservative Party also supported subsidized meals for children of the poor because they were concerned that "economic and military superiority was incompatible with a feeble, malnourished and impoverished workforce" (Gazeley 2003: 23). These reforms were aimed at working-class children and not the children of the residuum, who were considered "almost beyond hope" (Hay 1975: 44). This was a holdover from earlier in the nineteenth century when charitable organizations provided school meals to "necessitous children," while making sure not to cater to children of "undeserving and worthless parents" (quoted in Briggs 1961: 225). In fact, the 1904 Interdepartmental Committee on Physical Deterioration recommended that what they called the "waste elements" be transported to labour colonies (Gazeley 2003: 24). The assumption, as had long been and would continue to be the case, was that their poverty was caused by their moral failings and degenerate behaviour.

In 1908, the Liberal government introduced old age pensions. This idea had been publicly debated since at least the 1890s and was the subject of select committees of the House of Commons and the 1895 Royal Commission on the Aged Poor (Haggard 2001: 166–71). The pension plan decided upon was limited to those who were seventy years and over, it was means-tested and nobody on poor relief—no pauper—was entitled to receive the weekly pension. Again, those deemed to be the undeserving poor, the residuum, those guilty of "habitual failure to work," those who were known to be "shirkers and shams," were omitted (Golding and Middleton 1982: 36; Deacon and Bradshaw 1983: 7). More than that, the weekly pension of five shillings amounted to only about one quarter of a labourer's wage (Clarke 2004: 56) and was one shilling less than what Rowntree had deemed to be the lowest amount that could support an individual for a week (Thane 1984).

Limited though it was, this reform was nevertheless especially important because it was "the first anti-poverty measure to be financed out of central taxation," and one analyst of poverty policy has argued that "[it] marked the beginning of the trail to the modern welfare state" (Glennerster 2004: 69). Booth and the Webbs were especially important in making the case for non-contributory old age pensions (see Cooper 2017: Chapter 4), but "the driving force in the movement for old age pensions were the trade unions through the National Committee of Organized Labour on Old Age Pensions set up in 1899" (Cooper 2017:

61–62). Women also played a key role: "the impact of the women's organizations on the legislative record of the Liberal governments was much more dramatic than has so far been admitted" (Cooper 2017: 32).

The first pensions were paid out January 1, 1909. Approximately 490,000 people qualified, "a striking testimony to the extent of severe poverty in old age untouched by the Poor Law. A majority of them were women" (Thane 1982: 84). Because of the payment of pensions, the number of people over seventy years of age who needed outdoor relief declined dramatically from 312,235 in 1910 to 8,240 in 1911 (Vincent 1991: 40), further evidence of a great and unmet need.

In 1905, just prior to the Liberal election, the Royal Commission on the Poor Laws and the Relief of Distress had been struck. It reported in 1909, producing both majority and minority reports. The *Majority Report* was written by Helen Bosanquat, long a central figure in the Charity Organization Society and whose ideas were tinged with that experience (Cooper 2017). The Webbs, leaders of the Fabian Society, wrote the *Minority Report*, about which Fraser (1984: 161) writes, "the whole *Minority Report* outlook anticipated much of the modern Welfare State, and though in the short term its influence on policy (though not on ideas) was negligible, in the longer term much of the Webb's vision has materialized."

This progressive vision notwithstanding, the Webbs continued to believe there was a lowest stratum of the poor who were beyond hope and for whom coercion of some form was the only solution. Both reports of the Royal Commission on the Poor Laws "assumed the existence of a ne'er do well class at the base of society, for whom punitive labour colonies or similar institutions would be required" (Thane 1984: 90). These are the kinds of persistent views that, even with the first and partial steps toward the welfare state, excluded the lowest stratum of the poor.

In 1909, with the *Labour Exchange Act*, the Liberal government created a national network of labour exchanges or what today might be called job centres (Harris 2004: 160). Their purpose was to support the unemployed. The initiative was driven by William Beveridge, who in turn had been influenced by, and recommended for a civil service position by, the Webbs (Hay 1975). As Fraser (1984: 171) describes it, "the introduction of state-run, nationally financed labour exchanges (whose use was to be voluntary) was a notable innovation in a free market economy." Other pro-labour initiatives included the *Trades Disputes Act*, "restoring the legal immunity of trade unions, and the *Workmen's Compensation Act of 1906*" (Hay 1975: 52), which was the expanded version of the original 1897 *Workmen's Compensation Act*.

While the intention to bring together jobs and job seekers to reduce unemployment was a good one, there were other, more sinister motives. The labour exchanges were also intended to identify and weed out those of the "undeserving poor," who, it was thought, were not really looking for work and had to be excluded from benefits. Churchill made this clear when, in 1909, he emphasized the punitive role of the labour exchanges by saying: "there is no reason at all why people should wander about in a loafing and idle manner; if they are not earning their living they ought to be put under some control" (quoted in King 1995: 38). The labour exchanges and their successors would exert this control throughout the twentieth century and particularly during the 1930s and after 1979. Their purpose was at least as much to deny benefits to those they deemed to be "undeserving" as it was to find jobs for the unemployed (King 1995: 80).

In addition, the *Trade Boards Act* of 1909, which was pushed especially by the Fabian Women's Group and the Women's Trade Union League, introduced a minimum wage in several poorly paid, female-dominated trades (Thane 2000: 85). By this time, at least some working-class women were becoming directly engaged in politics at the local level. In most cases these were married women from politically active families in London districts that were Labour strongholds (Stenberg 1998).

These and later initiatives were made possible by the modernization of the tax system, producing significantly more government revenue. The Liberal government's "Great Budget" (Cooper 2017: 6) or "People's Budget" (Fraser 1984: 156) of 1909 introduced a graduated income tax and a supertax on incomes over 3,000 pounds [more than 120,000 British pounds today] (Searle 2004: 367). The budget was "overtly redistributing wealth through taxation. It was seeking to raise revenue by taxing the wealthy few for the benefit of the penurious many" (Fraser 1984: 156–57). These tax measures, not surprisingly, generated significant opposition (Searle 2004: 395).

In 1911, the Liberal government introduced what was perhaps the centrepiece of its program, the *National Insurance Act,* which covered both medical care and unemployment. This was a social insurance plan: those who were employed paid contributions, along with their employers; the unemployment component of the plan applied, at first, only to manual workers in selected trades, although its coverage was steadily extended until most were covered by the late 1930s (George 1968).

Unemployment insurance was a response to working-class pressure, which included the great strike wave of 1910–12. In 1909, 3.5 million days were lost due to strikes and lockouts; by 1912 the number had increased tenfold to 38 million days (Roberts 1971: 68). Unemployment insurance has been described as "probably the boldest experiment in social legislation of the entire period of the New Liberalism." Nevertheless, it was limited. It covered only about one quarter of the male working class—those in engineering, shipbuilding and construction. It deliberately excluded women "unless the woman was in full-time insurable employment," which was the case for only 10 percent of women (Lewis 1992: 163). The maximum duration of benefits was fifteen weeks per year, and no benefit was payable unless applicants had contributed for twenty-six weeks before a claim (Garside 1990: 33). "In every way the programme was tentative, narrow and carefully guarded" (Gilbert 1970: 52–53). It was aimed at the "respectable" working class; it excluded the "undeserving" poor.

The medical coverage, as was the case with school meals and inspections, "derived much more directly from the concern for national efficiency at the turn of the twentieth century" (Hay 1975: 54). It was intended to improve the health and productivity of the English working class when England was losing economic ground to international competitors, especially Germany and the US.

Both the health and the unemployment components of the legislation required that workers, as well as employers and the state, pay a flat weekly amount—it was contributory insurance. This generated opposition from some workers because it amounted to a regressive tax. Workers earning eighteen shillings per week were required to pay over 10 percent of their income in indirect taxes and contributions, while better-paid artisans on thirty-five shillings per week paid only 3.65 percent (Searle 2004: 405). Again, the wide-ranging Liberal initiatives, important though they were in moving beyond the *Poor Law* to state-delivered social services, were limited. Women, for example, were entitled to health benefits at only three quarters the level for men (Williams 1993: 84), while the "undeserving" poor were again completely excluded. "National insurance was clearly for the deserving, and the fact that entitlement to benefits rested upon the prior payment of contributions was believed to remove the need for explicit tests of moral character" (Deacon 1976: 11).

Limitations notwithstanding, all of this was historic. For the first time the state was providing publicly funded benefits:

> the introduction of free school meals, the establishment of old age pensions and the creation of the unemployment and health insurance schemes marked the beginning of a new approach to the development of welfare policy which offered a genuine alternative to the deterrent and stigmatizing policies of the Poor Law. (Harris 2004: 165)

As Vincent (1991: 41) describes it: "In the penny economy in which the poor lived, 5s. for a pension, 7s. for unemployment and 10s. for health insurance, unencumbered by pauperization, were solid sums of money which placed real meals on actual tables."

Poverty Declines—Significantly

The First World War put people to work and drove up wages into the 1920s—in 1920, real wages were 11 percent higher than they had been in 1914; by 1929 they were 18 percent above the 1914 level (Clarke 2004: 133). This affected poverty levels: "By the early 1920s the quantity of severe poverty had diminished" (Thane 1982: 169). For example, a study conducted in 1924 by Bowley and Burnett-Hurst (1925) repeated a five-town study they had done in 1913, finding the incidence of poverty at about one third its pre-war level, while child poverty had dropped from one in five to one in sixteen (Gazeley 2003: 65, 77, 79). These gains were partly attributable to wage increases during the war, and this mattered because, as argued above, "pre-war surveys had consistently shown low pay to be a more serious cause of poverty than unemployment" (Thane 1984: 148).

But the gains in combatting poverty were also a consequence of Liberal social legislative measures, "which together lifted a sizeable proportion of the population out of poverty and laid the foundations of the Welfare State. There was a marked transfer of income to the poorest members of the community" (Cooper 2017: 292). What worked in reducing poverty in the 1920s—and this has continued to be the case—was the combination of economic growth and a government prepared to redistribute some of the proceeds of that growth to those at the lower end of the income scale.

Chapter 6

On the Dole

Mass Unemployment and Mass Poverty in the 1920s and 1930s

In the pre–First World War era, it was low and irregular wages and large families that were the primary cause of poverty. While these continued to be important causes of poverty, in the postwar era the primary cause became unemployment, specifically *mass* unemployment.

The term "unemployment"—referring to those who had in earlier times most typically been called able-bodied paupers, vagrants, vagabonds or masterless men—appears to have come into common use in the 1880s, although it had been used in English trade union and radical literature in the 1820s and 1830s (E.P. Thompson 1963: 853–54). Large-scale demonstrations against unemployment occurred in the mid-1880s, leading to the Select Committees on Distress from Want of Employment (Harris 1972: 90). Unemployment statistics began to be kept by the British government in 1886 (Gazeley and Thane 1998: 186). The term first became part of the economic lexicon when used by English economist Alfred Marshall in 1888. As early as the 1890s, Independent Labour Party MP Keir Hardie raised the issue so often that he was referred to as the "Minister of the Unemployed" (Pelling 1965: 155). By 1914, unemployment had become "a central problem of public administration," in large part because of "massive demonstrations of the unemployed" (Harris 1972: 4–5, 152), similar to those that occurred in the 1880s. Unemployment was a major issue for the 1905–1909 Royal Commission on the Poor Laws.

A wide variety of solutions were debated and tried over these years—labour colonies; emigration; public works; labour exchanges—and a vigorous public debate took place. But in the period leading up to and immediately following the First World War, no adequate solutions were found. Indeed, "the history of the unemployment policies introduced before

1914 was a history of almost unmitigated failure" (Harris 1972: 367). This was the public policy experience leading into the unemployment crisis of 1920–1921, which "inaugurated mass unemployment" (Garside 1990: 8).

To the Level of a Calamity: Unemployment, 1920–1921

By the end of 1920, two years after the end of the Great War, two million people were unemployed in Britain, approximately 18 percent of the labour force (Gilbert 1970: 46). The years 1921 and 1922 were called "the worst in the records of unemployment in this country" (Astor et al. 1922: 3), and some scholars have said that the unemployment problems of the early 1920s "were at least as serious as those of the 1930s" (Butchart 1997: 5). Britain was to experience two decades of mass unemployment.

The 1911 unemployment insurance legislation was extended with the *Unemployment Insurance Act* of 1920, and "between 1920 and 1931, over twenty different unemployment acts were introduced," each aimed at reducing public expenditures without promoting political backlash (Ward 2013: 34). Each was limited, "the product of a series of expedients, of political concessions made necessary by previous concessions" (Gilbert 1970: 56). Like the *Poor Law*, they were intended simply to prevent starvation and rebellion. They were the result of political pressure from and fear of the working class, "the fear of popular violence if something were not done to provide economic security for the British working man" (Gilbert 1970: 66).

British workers were more threatening because of the dramatic increase—a tripling—of trade union membership, from 16 percent of the labour force in 1910 to 48 percent in 1920 (Thane 2018: 71). Strike activity jumped from just over 450 strikes in 1905 to almost 1,500 in 1913 (Matthews 2018: 7) and increased again from 1919 to 1922 in the wake of the 1917 Bolshevik Revolution (Clarke 2004: 107). In 1919 alone, 2.8 million workers were on strike (Perry 2000: 38). Of particular concern were the large numbers of unemployed ex-servicemen:

> Wandering the streets at a time of great social tension were hundreds of thousands of men with experience of warfare, 'four million trained and successful killers' as Churchill described them, many still with their weapons that they had kept in the confusion of rapid demobilization, but without work. (Flanagan 1991: 91)

By May 1919, 408,000 ex-servicemen were without work (Flanagan 1991: 93) and "a political explosion seemed inevitable" (Saville 1957: 12). The home secretary warned in December 1920, referring specifically to the large numbers of unemployed ex-servicemen, "the temper of the men is becoming increasingly bitter.... There is much muttering about the ostentation and luxury of the 'idle rich' and agitators have seized upon the real discontent to carry on a ceaseless propaganda of class war" (quoted in Garside 1990: 37). Whether or not the early 1920s threat of revolution was genuine "must remain a matter of interpretation, but there is no doubt as to the sense of fear and even panic which pervades the Cabinet and departmental papers" (Deacon 1976: 15).

Despite these fears, and the constant adjustments made to unemployment benefits, no solutions were found. The Unemployment Insurance Acts of the 1920s and other measures—short-time work, changes to the age at which workers entered and left the labour market, juvenile unemployment centres (Garside 1990)—were ineffective in addressing mass unemployment.

The mass unemployment of 1920–1921 through to 1940 was concentrated in specific industries and geographic areas, a defining feature of unemployment in the interwar period. While the overall national rate was 10 percent, in shipbuilding it was over 28 percent in 1923–1924 and in cotton textiles, which still employed some 800,000 people, it was typically 16 percent (Gilbert 1970: 87). It was this structural unemployment in old and increasingly uncompetitive industries to which the Unemployment Insurance Acts of the 1920s could not adequately respond. Instead, governments tightened the criteria for receiving unemployment benefits to restrict eligibility and hold down costs.

Two measures were applied to those who had exhausted their right to insurance benefits and who were seeking "extended" or "transitional" benefits. The first was a "genuinely seeking work" test, introduced in 1921. The second was a means test, introduced in 1922, subjecting those seeking extended benefits to intrusive investigations of family incomes. As a result of these two policies, three million claimants were rejected between March 1921 and March 1930 (Deacon 1976: 9).

The 1921 *Unemployment Insurance Act* required all claimants who were seeking extended benefits to prove they had been "genuinely seeking work" (Garside 1990: 47–48)—claimants were otherwise assumed to be malingerers or shirkers and thus not entitled to extended insurance benefits. This was the legacy of centuries of blaming and denigrating the poor for their poverty. The Ministry of Labour "left its officers in no doubt as to what was expected of them. Their task was to detect and penalize malingering, and the accomplishment of this purpose was to override all other considerations" (Deacon 1976: 88). Claimants appeared before a Local Employment Committee, which in many cases made a determination about eligibility within two or three minutes. If claimants were inarticulate or nervous, as many were, or insufficiently meek or deferential—the long-standing de facto test under the *Poor Law*—they were deemed not to be genuine in their efforts to find work and were denied benefits. This occurred even though the report of the Unemployment Insurance Committee of 1925 could find little evidence of malingering (Deacon 1976), nor could a similar 1922 study (Astor et al. 1922: 11). Yet this was, in effect, the sole "solution" to the poverty created by the mass unemployment of the 1920s. It was, of course, no solution at all. "The seeking work test was a futile and sometimes brutal ritual. No one pretended that the work which claimants were supposed to be seeking actually existed, least of all the Minister involved." The result was "hundreds of thousands of unemployed men and women being arbitrarily deprived of benefits which they desperately needed" and many more forced "to make repeated journeys in search of jobs that they knew did not exist" (Deacon 1976: 61, 89).

The means test was first introduced in 1922, one year after the genuinely seeking work test, and its administration involved investigating officers who, typically without notice, entered the homes of claimants and questioned neighbours about claimants' "character." This emphasis upon "character"—upon demeanour and behaviour and thus whether a claimant was deserving or undeserving—brought the "taint of pauperism" to insurance benefits (Deacon 1976: 33). A divisional controller in southeast England is quoted as having written that, although grocers and insurance agents were often questioned,

> in actual practice it has proved more fruitful to call, ostensibly in error, at a neighbour's house instead of at the correct address and to allow the line of enquiry to develop in accordance with the reception given by the neighbour. Although neighbours are often vindictive, generally it can be stated that very little information is obtained regarding the decent type of claimant,

whereas the life history of the ne'er do well is readily volunteered. (Quoted in Deacon 1976: 60)

This was nothing less than the historical disdain for able-bodied individuals who were out of work. The means tests "restored the full glory of the ethics and psychology of 1834 to the administration of relief," the purpose being to discourage "the pauper habit of mind, and pauper way of life" (Golding and Middleton 1982: 43). The organized labour movement, which for the most part represented the "respectable" working class, was similarly "no more concerned with the welfare of the undeserving than was the opposition" (Deacon 1976: 38). In the 1920s it was as it had always been—those who were able-bodied and not working, and who were not meek and deferential or were behaving in ways not seen to be "respectable," were the cause of their own problems. The seeking work test and the means test would find them out.

The treatment of the very poor is exemplified by the account of Jessie Stephen, a female Labour Party member elected to the Bermondsey Board of Guardians in 1921. Ms. Stephen was appalled by "the rituals of deference which obliged old people to stand up when a [Poor Law] guardian entered the room," and she could not "stomach this kow-towing to elected representatives" (quoted in Jones 2019: 102).

It Gets Worse: Mass Unemployment, Poverty, Privation and Destitution in the 1930s

Unemployment would worsen dramatically at the end of the 1920s and throughout the 1930s—even while average real wages rose with declines in prices and in average family size (Harris 1988). Many who were able to hold onto full-time employment during the 1930s did relatively well. But most of the millions who were unemployed were plunged into genuine poverty.

There are those who argue that the crisis of the 1930s has been exaggerated, especially by writers on the political left. These leftist writers, some conservative historians argue, have sought to use the 1930s as a means of discrediting capitalism and demonstrating the need for the postwar welfare state. In doing so, they have ignored the gains made by working people in the 1930s in real income, health and leisure opportunities such as cinema and radio (Stevenson and Cook 1994; Pugh 2008. For a critique, see Howkins and Saville 1979; Perry 2000). It is true that for many British workers who held permanent, full-time jobs, real wages and living standards rose throughout the 1930s. Nevertheless, the 1930s were a time of mass unemployment—albeit differing by region—and genuine poverty.

Throughout the 1930s, the unemployed constituted never less than one million and rose as high as three million in 1932. The unemployment rate in the UK jumped from just over 3 percent in 1920 to 17 percent in 1921. It stayed at or above 10 percent throughout the 1920s, peaked at just over 22 percent in 1932, remaining higher than 20 percent from January 1931 to May 1933, and declined slowly in the later 1930s while constantly staying well above 10 percent (Eichengreen and Hatton 1988: 6–8). Unemployment was especially concentrated, as in the 1920s, in northern industrial areas and among older men—those over forty years of age—and especially older, "unskilled" manual workers. In 1932 the unemployment rates in cotton textiles, coal mining, pig iron making and shipbuilding—industries that had driven the Industrial Revolution and were disproportionately located in the north—were 28.5, 33.9, 43.5 and 62.2 percent, respectively (Hopkins 1991: 29). Although unemployment rates for women were generally lower than for men, this was not the case for women in the Lancashire cotton mills. In the cotton mill towns of Blackburn, Darwen and Great Harwood, unemployment rates for female cotton workers in 1931 were 56.3, 59.5 and 61.1 percent, respectively (Pope 2000: 746). In Jarrow, a northern shipbuilding centre from which the famous Jarrow Crusade was staged in 1936, 75 percent of men were jobless, and as Wilkinson (1939: 8) said at the time, "one thing is common through the whole story of Jarrow … and that is the poverty of the working people of Jarrow."

Unemployment in the 1930s was both massive in terms of numbers and, on average, longer in duration than ever before. In September 1929, just fewer than 5 percent of applicants for unemployment benefits had been without work for over a year; by 1931 the proportion had grown fivefold to 25 percent (Butchart 1997: 4). The average duration of unemployment doubled from twenty-two weeks in September 1929 to forty-three weeks in December 1935, then dropped slowly to thirty-eight weeks in June 1938. The average duration was even longer in the north and among older workers (Gazeley 2003: 103–8). In 1938, for example, the average uninterrupted spells of unemployment for workers sixty years and older was just over one year; 12 percent had been unemployed for more than five years (Thomas 1988: 120).

In many parts of Britain, poverty became the norm. Historians G.D.H. and Margaret Cole (quoted in Ward 2013: 51), describe this by saying that "destitution has stalked out from its lurking places in the slums and spread its contagion over the homes of respectable people—even over whole towns and once flourishing villages in the depressed areas." Hobsbawm (1995: 92) writes: "There had been nothing like this economic catastrophe in the lives of working people for as long as anyone could remember."

As unemployment became so much the norm, ways of thinking about it, and about poverty, began to change. Many came to believe that mass unemployment and the poverty it produced had less to do with individual's moral failings than with the character of the economic system. This was hard to miss when so many who had recently been working were now out of work. A 1928 Ministry of Labour report was emphatic in saying, "the body of unemployed is not a standing army of vagrants and loafers, but a number of genuine industrial workers whose composition is constantly changing" (quoted in Garside 1990: 25).

A decade later, in 1938, the Unemployment Assistance Board found that only "a very small percentage" of the long-term unemployed could be characterized as "workshy" (Thomas 1988: 129). Bakke (1933: 143, 128), in his study of the unemployed in the London borough of Greenwich in 1931, concluded, "The behaviour of the unemployed in searching for new employment gives no evidence that the possibility of drawing Unemployment Insurance benefit has retarded the efforts of the unemployed to get back to work." He estimated that, on average, they spent twenty-three hours per week looking for work. The problems were less moral and behavioural than structural, as had always been the case.

In northern industrial communities where unemployment was staggeringly high, working-class families that had experienced some limited improvement in their standard of living since the end of the First World War were plunged into poverty. Brockway (1932: 12) describes the case of two Lancashire towns: "In Blackburn there are 60 mills closed down, and most of the mills which are open—about the same number—are only working intermittently. In Great Harwood only eight of the twenty-five mills have worked during the last two years." The move from being employed in the mill, to relying on unemployment benefits, cut many family incomes by half or more and children were "growing up undernourished" (Brockway 1932: 17, 20, 222). Registrar-General figures reveal that in 1932, two unemployed men were committing suicide every day (Perry 2000: 68).

The Bitterly Hated Household Means Test

In the early 1930s, unemployment benefits were administered by locally based public assistance committees (PACs). A woman in a northern industrial community who served on a PAC, making decisions about who was to receive relief payments and who not, admitted,

> The Means Test is so cruel that I don't want to have anything to do with it, yet I know I've been able to get a few extra shillings for this family, and I feel for their sakes I ought to go on…. We are being asked to administer an Act which no one with human feelings can administer with a clear conscience. (Brockway 1932: 26, 28)

As of 1935, unemployed workers who qualified for twenty-six weeks of unemployment insurance benefits but were still without work at the end of that period came under the scrutiny of the newly created Unemployment Assistance Board (UAB). The UAB was created to overcome what was considered to be the generosity of some locally controlled PACs and to institute a tougher and more standardized and centralized extended benefits payment regime (Ward 2013, 2011).

The UAB administered the household means test, introduced in 1931. As Ward (2011: 246) explains, this was "the first time that all the long-term unemployed were required to undergo a public assistance-style household means test," which was, "in effect, a Poor Law evaluation of their circumstances" (Whiteside 1987: 19). If any member of a household found paid employment, even an unrelated lodger, their earnings could be deducted from the UAB benefit (Deacon and Bradshaw 1983). Savings had to be exhausted and furniture sold to qualify for benefits. If an unemployed man, out of desperation, took a job at a lower wage than his original job, that lower wage became the new standard, and the UAB benefit was deducted accordingly (Wilkinson 1939).

Labour MP Ellen Wilkinson (quoted in Ward 2013: 202) writes that the means test was "so bitterly resented, that in an area like Jarrow a local speaker has only to hiss out the words to rouse any working-class audience to the same fury which they would have shown at the mention of the Poor Law in pre-war days."

Even those who, after investigation, were deemed deserving were awarded benefits that typically were minimal, being given "just enough to exist themselves and keep their families alive, not even in good health, but just alive" (Wilkinson 1939: 225). Keeling (1961: 43), who worked in Liverpool's poorest areas during the 1930s, adds, "The Liverpool PAC scale was meagre—it did little more than prevent starvation—and the standard of life was miserably low." Between 25 and 50 percent of children "must have been deprived of the basic diet to sustain normal life and development" (Webster 1983: 79). This was the long-standing, minimalist approach of the *Poor Law*—just enough to keep the poor from starving or rebelling.

There was no real strategy for solving unemployment throughout the 1920s and 1930s. Rather, as Gazeley and Thane (1998: 198) argue, the "strategy" was to wait for an economic revival while in the meantime "balancing the pressure to minimize the cost of unemployment benefit whilst keeping it at a sufficient level to prevent social unrest and political outbursts."

Calls for public works expenditures to put the unemployed back to work went largely unheeded; the few such programs, such as the *Special Areas Act* of 1934, were far too limited to have a significant effect (Perry 2000).

Passivity and Resistance

To what extent did mass unemployment and the hated means test generate political opposition? There is a range of views on this.

The prevailing argument is that unemployment produced passivity: "Poverty and privation leading to fatalism, hopelessness and social divisiveness are prominent parts of the story" (Eichengreen and Hatton 1988: 42). Studies in the 1930s found that the unemployed were disinterested in politics, considering political involvement to be futile (Perry and Reiss 2011). In their study of the Austrian village of Marienthal in 1930, Jahoda and her colleagues (1971: 2–3, 54) found that unemployment produced "a steady decline into apathy," resulting in "despair, depression, hopelessness, and a feeling of the futility of all efforts, and therefore no further attempts to find work or to ameliorate the situation." The psychological damage was enormous. The UAB referred in 1939 to "applicants who would probably accept work if it were offered to them but have fallen into such a condition of body and mind that they make no personal effort to attain it." They had become "victims of their own prolonged unemployment, which has produced a state of indifference and lassitude that tends to become progressively worse" (quoted in Thomas 1988: 132–33).

Nevertheless, there was organized protest. Perry and Reiss (2011: 6) argue that for the unemployed, "despair and starvation did not preclude some of them from making themselves heard or following those who offered to lead them in clearly defined campaigns."

In the 1920s, a number of organizations of the unemployed engaged in protests. In September 1920, one of them produced a draft "unemployment bill" that has been described as a "radical working-class manifesto," calling for a minimum wage, equal pay for women and men and other left-wing measures. In October 1920, they carried a placard in a peaceful London demonstration that read: "Oh that bread should be so dear, and flesh and blood so cheap" (Flanagan 1991: 110–11). On the other hand, some unemployed ex-servicemen became involved in racist and misogynistic confrontations. Some joined Oswald Mosley's British Union of Fascists, which Mosley created in 1932 after leaving the Labour Party in frustration with their responses to mass unemployment (Perry 2000). It was often the case that unemployed ex-servicemen were "profoundly reactionary" (Flanagan 1991: 114). Flanagan describes a delegation of five thousand ex-servicemen that met with the deputy lord mayor of Liverpool in 1919 to "complain that women and 'coloured men' were occupying jobs that were rightly the ex-servicemen's." The political activities of unemployed ex-servicemen were complex and contradictory, but nevertheless, not all the unemployed were passive and politically inactive.

Throughout the 1930s, British governments struggled with the ballooning costs of unemployment insurance. By May of 1931, 400,000 of the two million unemployed were receiving extended benefits, costing the government thirty million pounds (Ward 2013: 85). Cuts to benefits produced public protest: "The early 1930s were the bloodiest era of the politics of the unemployed in Britain, with pitched street battles between police and unemployed throughout the major industrial centres of

Britain." "At one stage in 1932 it was estimated that over 400 unemployed were serving sentences in prisons for offences related to their political work with the unemployed" (Flanagan 1991: 185, 187). Proposed cuts to relief in 1935 were met with another "wave of public protest and indignation" and produced "widespread and spontaneous demonstrations" (Garside 1990: 77) "on a scale never witnessed before" (Ward 2013: 161):

> The events in January and February [1935] were remarkable, and throughout Britain, hundreds of thousands of the unemployed took to the streets, often in displays of united community action. At times, even a Popular Front appeared to be in evidence as divergent political parties, trade unions, movements of the unemployed, religious bodies and other community organizations stood united in the streets against a common threat. (Ward 2013: 188)

The largely Communist-led National Unemployed Workers' Movement (NUWM) formed in 1921 (it was called the National Unemployed Workers' Committee Movement until 1929) and became "by far the most substantial movement of the dispossessed this [20th] century has produced" (Vincent 1991: 56). Six national hunger marches were organized by the NUWM between 1922 and 1936 (Kingsford 1982: 73). The 1932 march was called the "National Hunger March against the Means Test." Contingents from various parts of Britain were met in London by 30,000 supporters in Hyde Park (Deacon and Bradshaw 1983: 20). The first five hunger marches were met with police repression and in some cases became violent, which was relentlessly condemned in the mainstream media (Perry 2000). The sixth hunger march, in 1936, generated a positive public response, including overt support from the Labour Party and organized labour, perhaps evidence of the shift in public attitudes that would lead to the gains made by the 1945–1951 Labour governments.

While most attention has been focused on the hunger marches and the NUWM, many other forms of protest—perhaps less openly militant—were widespread (Ward 2011). Local marches against the means test "were held on a weekly, if not daily, basis" in the early to mid-1930s (Ward 2011: 246). There were demonstrations numbering thirty thousand on the Tyneside, and forty thousand in Sheffield, and according to the *Manchester Guardian,* 150,000 in south Wales (Perry 2000: 111). In addition, "opposition to the Means Test led to an outpouring of literature in the press, letters, social surveys, pamphlets, histories and working class novels" (Ward 2011: 247). Resolutions against the means test were passed by union locals, churches, seniors' clubs and women's councils, resulting in "an almost constant barrage of criticism against the government" (Ward 2011: 261).

The Labour Party gained control of many local councils throughout the 1930s, with rapidly growing numbers of women elected to local office, and as Thane (2000: 93) argues,

> Labour's welfare activities at local level, building new housing and clearing old "slums," subsidizing rents, improving working class education, increasing expenditure on health care and improving local transport, helped to build hopes of what it might achieve nationally.

Whatever the level of protests, and however much Labour and growing numbers of women succeeded at the local level, relatively little was gained at the national level—at least immediately. The struggles of the unemployed via the NUWM were plagued by the passive opposition of organized labour and the Labour Party (Vincent 1991). The Labour Party was largely ineffectual in responding to unemployment throughout the 1930s, sticking closely to conventional economic policies. "There was little to distinguish Labour from the economic thought of mainstream parties and economists of the time" (Perry 2000: 83). The labour movement was cautious and conservative and largely opposed to direct action. Unions were, in fact, "primarily concerned with their working members rather than with the unemployed" (Perry 2000: 99). Many individual trade unionists, Labour Party members and some MPs were active in supporting those taking action (Ward 2013), as were "a majority of local trades council members in Britain who valued the mobilizing efforts of these marches on local workers" (Perry and Reiss 2011: 28). But the official stance of the Labour Party and organized labour was different. There were still over two million unemployed in 1934, "yet the Labour Party and the TUC viewed all rank and file action with acute suspicion" (Pimlott 1971: 33). The Labour Party's focus was on "electoral advance rather than the momentum of the attack on poverty" (Vincent 1991: 65), and the party was determined to keep its distance from the Communist Party of Great Britain, with which the NUWM was closely associated.

In any event, even at its peak, only about one in eighty of those who were unemployed was involved with the NUWM (Kingsford 1982: 235). Perry (2000: 113) argues that in the early 1930s, when three million were unemployed, the NUWM had only forty thousand members. In his study of the unemployed in Greenwich in 1931, Bakke (1933: 60 and 62) found that "talk of revolution is conspicuous by its absence," and when the call went out from the NUWM to join what became the largest demonstration of the year, only ten of Greenwich's unemployed responded, and "ten men are not conspicuous among the more than 3000 unemployed in Greenwich."

The bulk of the unemployed were struggling simply to feed and house themselves and their families. Aneurin Bevan presented a petition in the House of Commons on behalf of the hunger marchers at the last hunger march in 1936, referring to

> the grievous hardship which is being endured by great numbers of unemployed men and women by reason of their loss of physical well-being, the breaking up of many of their homes, the wretched condition of the villages and towns, and the harsh incidence of the family means test. (Quoted in Kingsford 1982: 216)

While the NUWM can be seen as largely unsuccessful—Stevenson and Cook (1994: 216) claim they "achieved very little and faded into obscurity"—British governments were nevertheless constantly alert to the potential danger to political and social stability posed by the unemployed (Perry and Reiss 2011). Further, it is likely that the NUWM-led hunger marches contributed to the growing understanding that the system just wasn't working. Kingsford (1982: 237) argues that the NUWM had an impact on people's consciousness of unemployment, perhaps especially on the consciousness of those in the south of England where unemployment was much less severe:

> There was nothing like a repeated invasion by large bodies of hungry men to spread awareness of them from the distressed to the prosperous areas. In hundreds of towns people saw for the first time the victims of unemployment.... The marches may be seen, in A.J.P. Taylor's words, as "a propaganda stroke of great effect. The hunger marchers displayed the failure of capitalism in a way that mere figures or literary description could not."

Further, the "failure of capitalism" can lead and has led to fascism. Because at least some ex-servicemen were attracted to the British Union of Fascists, it is significant that Wal Hannington, leader of the NUWM, wrote in a 1959 letter, "I have always considered that one of the most important political achievements of the NUWM was our defeat of Mosley's efforts ... to get control of the unemployed" (quoted in Flanagan 1991: 199).

It would take the war effort to truly reduce unemployment. Addison (1975: 116) observes that "during Dunkirk there were still 645,000 men and women registered as unemployed; by the time of the Normandy landings in June 1944 the figure was down to 54,000." Prior to the war in 1938, approximately 400,000 were in the armed forces; by 1940 that number had grown to two million; by 1942 it was four million; and by war's end in 1945 approximately five million were in the armed forces (Clarke 2004: 200).

Women: Key Strategists in the Struggle against Destitution

As had been the case in the nineteenth century, it was women who struggled in the 1930s to feed and clothe the families of unemployed workers, often on half or less of what until recently had been the family's normal income. The woman in a working-class family was "the key strategist in the struggle against destitution" (Vincent 1991: 94). The constant tightening of entitlement to unemployment benefits hit women especially hard. The 1931 *Anomalies Act* made married women who left the labour force for any reason ineligible for benefits. Seasonal and part-time workers were also disqualified. "By March 1932, more than 82 percent of married women claimants had been disqualified" (Perry 2000: 94).

To feed and clothe their families during the 1930s, working-class women, as they had done in the nineteenth century, often relied upon pawnbrokers and local grocers and moneylenders for credit. Their financial juggling was typically kept secret from the husband, for fear of disapproval or, in some cases, domestic abuse if a husband thought shame was being brought on a family (Ayers and Lambertz 1986). In Liverpool in the 1930s, women were described as "living in a state of daily terror, both of the lender and their husbands" and it was said that "violence lay just beneath the surface in many marriages" (Ayers and Lambertz 1986: 204, 208). Keeling (1961: 111) describes cases in Liverpool of women being charged rates of interest by local moneylenders and pawnbrokers in excess of 400 percent per annum, and in one case of 1500 percent per annum, adding,

> many of these loans were taken out by wives without their husbands' knowledge, and the women lived in daily fear of being found out. Indeed two mothers known to us committed suicide, leaving families of young children.

Women's health suffered: "years of feeding herself last and least weakened her ability to cope with bearing children; in the 1930s it was estimated that one pregnant woman in ten was disabled by the experience of childbirth." Even in 1939, one third of British families continued to subsist on what were identified as "inadequate" diets (Vincent 1991: 94, 83). A 1939 survey found that 45 percent of working-class women suffered from anemia, and fewer than one in three described herself as consistently in good health (Perry 2000: 67). Those women who could find paid work outside the home carried an immense load. A working-class woman in Lancashire described the life of such women:

> The weaver's wife works harder than any woman on earth. She starts at the mill at seven and works until quarter past eight. She has three-quarters of an hour to get breakfast and get the children off to school—she's had to bath them the night before. Then back to the mill at nine until half past twelve. An hour's break for dinner for her husband, herself and the children; the mill again until 5:30. Then tea and the housework and the cooking and baking and the washing up and the mending and the clothes-making, and bathing the children and putting them to bed. I don't know how she does it. (Quoted in Brockway 1932: 40)

Sniggering Superiority; Vicious Hatred

The class system remained firmly in place throughout the 1930s. "Common" people were treated by the upper class with "an attitude of sniggering superiority punctuated by bursts of vicious hatred," and "the average middle class person is brought up to believe that the working classes are ignorant, lazy, drunken, boorish, and dishonest" (Orwell 1962: 109, 112). These were the attitudes that drove the intrusive means test and its assumptions about malingerers and shirkers.

The overwhelming evidence was quite the contrary: extremely hard work went into keeping working class families alive. For example, "Baby care among the poor included relentless physical labour: heating water for bathing and laundry, carrying heavy buckets, emptying coppers; all at a time when breast-feeding seriously undermined a woman's stamina" (Ross 1986: 79). And yet middle-class observers blamed poor mothers for high rates of infant mortality. Their distorted, class-biased view was "that the poor valued infant life cheaply, and accusations of neglect, ignorance, and even deliberate infanticide run as a *leitmotiv* through official discussions of working class infant health" (Ross 1986: 82). Women were similarly blamed by middle-class agencies "for not being thrifty or not budgeting properly" despite the enormous financial challenges they faced (Ayers and Lambertz 1986: 207). The poor were yet again stereotyped, stigmatized and blamed for their poverty.

The same attitude characterized the typical British person's view of those in the then sprawling British colonies. Those not "white" were seen as inferiors, just as the upper class saw the British working class as inferior. Much of the language and imagery used to describe British workers and especially the poor had its origins in colonialism and imperialism. The working-class poor were described as "savages" or "primitive tribes" or "races" different from the British, and "explorers … went 'slumming' 'down among the poor' who lived in the parishes 'as dark as Africa'; in 'darkest' Liverpool or London, or in *Darkest England*," as General Booth of the Salvation Army titled his 1890 book (Mooney 1998: 63).

The racism that was an intrinsic part of British colonialism divided the working class and the poor from Black and Asian workers in the colonies and would create the same division when those colonial workers came to Britain in their numbers after the Second World War to fill poorly paid, menial jobs. Racism directed against Blacks and Asians has remained largely unchanged across the decades of the second half of the twentieth and early decades of the twenty-first centuries.

Vast Tracts of Slumdom: Housing in the 1930s

Also unchanged throughout the 1930s were housing conditions. Housing continued to be appalling, compounding the pain and distress of those who were poor. Gains made in the early 1920s had been the product of working-class pressures during and immediately after the First World War. The 1917 Commission of Inquiry into Industrial Unrest identified housing as a leading cause of working-class discontent "and called for the mass provision of cheap housing as a necessary remedy." The Liberal government of Lloyd George responded by introducing "almost unlimited subsidies for the construction of municipal homes" (Matthews 2017: 47), setting a goal of 300,000 houses, seen as "the largest single contribution to the unemployment problem" (Johnson 1968: 65, 113). However, the money to provide these housing subsidies had to be borrowed (Gilbert 1970), and the subsidies were terminated when the London financial industry "was disturbed by the dislocation of the capital market and the pressure on interest rates brought about by large-scale local authority borrowing for housebuilding" (Thane 1984: 146). In 1920–1921,

> the British government was forced to choose between the claims of the City of London as the central financial market of the world and the claims of domestic reconstruction. In this struggle, the City prevailed and one of the important casualties was housing. (Gilbert 1970: 144)

Addison (1922) calls it, as his book was titled, *The Betrayal of the Slums*. In a capitalist housing market investment would not, without a fight, be directed away from profit-making to housing needs. Quite a bit of government-subsidized housing was built—"about 273,000 houses under various acts"—but the government "demolished at the same time 242,000, mostly in slum clearance" (Gilbert 1970: 201). This dynamic happened often: in the 1870s and 1880s, in the 1960s and 1970s and in the first decades of this century.

In the industrial north, where mass unemployment hit hardest, "great numbers" of the working class and especially the poor continued to live in housing "not fit for human habitation," located in "filthy slums round belching foundries and stinking canals and slag-heaps that deluge them with sulphurous smoke." There was not enough decent quality, affordable housing to meet the needs of working families, let alone the poor, which meant

> people will put up with anything—any hole and corner slum, any misery of bugs and rotting floors and cracking walls, any extortion of skinflint landlords and blackmailing agents—sim-

> ply to get a roof over their heads. [In the] fearful northern slums [there was massive overcrowding]—so there are eight or ten people sleeping in two small rooms, probably in at most four beds. (Orwell 1962: 45–46)

In Manchester, a 1933 study of housing in a working-class area of the city found

> there are many houses that can only be described as slums, which are old, damp, ill-ventilated and verminous. This part of the ward is squalid and grimy; many of the streets are little better than alleys, sun and air are kept out by the proximity of mills and warehouses, and the inhabitants are poverty-stricken. (Inman 1934: 4)

Vast slums existed in all major British cities. In 1935 it was said, "No other civilized country has such vast tracts of slumdom.... For size and density, foul air and wretchedness, the slums of Britain are in a class apart" (quoted in Burnett 1986: 243). In 1928 there were one million houses unfit for human habitation and another two million overcrowded. By 1939 it was estimated that about one third of British housing was substandard, "much of it slum or rapidly becoming so" (Burnett 1986: 249).

These were the conditions that had been so familiar in the nineteenth century. Even by 1945 housing remained, for the British working class, "the most pressing issue" (Gilbert 1970: 201).

Poverty Makes You Sick: Health in the 1930s

The poor were sicklier throughout the 1930s than those not poor, as had long been the case. As Thane (1984: 56) points out: "Poor children who survived infancy were predictably shorter and thinner than others and the differential widened as they grew older." Women suffered particularly poor health, "often the result of repeated pregnancies, miscarriage, sometimes illegal abortions without qualified medical care, all worsened by poverty and bad housing" (Thane 2018: 134). In the industrial north, few people over thirty years of age had any teeth, and "the death rate and infant mortality of the poorest quarters are always about double those of the well-to-do residential quarters—a good deal more than double in some cases." Little had changed by 1935, when roughly the same proportion of volunteers for the armed services were rejected as had been the case during the Boer War at the turn of the century. "The central cause of ill-health was, as Rowntree pointed out, poverty, which caused poor diet and living conditions" (Thane 1984: 190). Rowntree's 1936 study of York found that 31 percent of the working class population was poor, and "rickets, the most direct manifestation of early malnutrition was still found in as many as two out of three working class children" (Vincent 1991: 72, 74).

Ideas that Led to the Welfare State

Public support for the "welfare state" implemented by the 1945–1951 Labour governments was laid partly in the latter years of the Great Depression. As Briggs (1961: 229) argues, "it is unemployment more than any other social contingency which has determined the shape and timing of modern 'welfare' legislation." The devastating effects of the Depression made it clear to many, and not just the working class, that the old ways were failing, and something new was needed:

> Britain's political leaders finally agreed, almost unconsciously, that society in some way or another would have to find a means to support all its citizens at a decent level of civilized life—in effect the national minimum. This understanding, whether or not publicly accepted, was a private political consensus by the end of the 1930s. (Gilbert 1970: vii)

Hobsbawm (1995: 102) concurred: "The great slump confirmed intellectuals, activists and ordinary citizens in the belief that something was fundamentally wrong with the world they lived in."

Nevertheless, in the 1930s, ideas regarding a state-driven movement toward a more collective and egalitarian society were being advanced. This was at least in part the result of the fear of political upheaval and, in particular, of socialism. "Socialism … did not become in fact the only issue in British parliamentary affairs in the 1920s and 1930s, but the fear of it was the catalyst of social politics" (Gilbert 1970: 305). There was protest—not only the hunger marches, but also in many other ways. There was seething resentment of the means test. Left ideas were spreading. The Left Book Club launched in the mid-1930s and had 45,000 members by 1937. Sir Stafford Cripps, later a key cabinet minister in the postwar Labour governments, was the major funder and a leader of the Socialist League, a left-wing grouping within—and, in 1937, expelled from—the Labour Party. The Socialist League called for "a sharp and decisive transformation to socialism" (Addison 1975: 48; for a critical evaluation of the Socialist League, see Pimlott 1971). It included some prominent British intellectuals, many of whom had been with the ILP and remained in the Labour Party (Desai 1994a). The young economists in the New Fabian Research Bureau created by G.D.H. Cole in 1931 were working on progressive economic ideas (Pelling 1984)—"putting forward the case for a gradualist parliamentary, Keynesian socialism" (Desai 1994a: 60)—although most of them, including especially future Labour Party leader Hugh Gaitskell, would later become intellectual leaders of the post-1951 "revisionist" movement. For example, Evan Durbin's *The Politics of Democratic Socialism* has been described by Panitch (1986: 68) as a forerunner to Crosland's *The Future of Socialism,* the central text of the revisionist movement.

Nevertheless, their intellectual efforts were prodigious. "Throughout the 1930s [Evan] Durbin and Gaitskell were the philosophical and social organizers of an extraordinary level of unofficial intellectual activity on behalf of the Labour Party, for which there is no parallel before or since" (Durbin 1985: 108). Reconstruction committees were debating the postwar world, including a Keynes-Beveridge group, "which met together in Bloomsbury in the winter of 1939–40 and drafted the proposals for family allowances, food subsidies, compulsory savings and postwar credits embodied in Keynes's influential little book on *How to Pay for the War*" (Harris 1986: 237). The Labour Party itself had long since adopted a policy statement, *Labour and the New Social Order,* which laid the ideas basis for a new approach. It included:

> a "National Minimum," an idea first advanced by the Webbs in 1897 (Harris 1986: 250): "a minimum wage and a minimum standard of working conditions, together with a maximum working week of 48 hours"
>
> the "Revolution in National Finance," which meant in practice the subsidization of social services by heavy taxation of large incomes;
>
> the "Surplus for the Common Good," which proclaimed that

the balance of the nation's wealth should so far as possible be devoted to expanding opportunities in education and in culture for the people as a whole. (Pelling 1968: 44–45)

This was, in broad terms, the outline for an aggressive social democratic approach to governance. It was the product of many years, even decades, of high-level intellectual engagement with alternative policy ideas. "Reconstruction plans usually attributed to the master designs of Beveridge and Keynes in fact owed much to the intellectual sedimentary deposits of academics, journalists and editors and bodies like the Oxford Institute of Statistics and the National Institute of Social and Economic Research" (Middlemas 1979: 272).

The 1942 Beveridge Report, *Social Insurance and Allied Services,* updated these ideas, and was sufficiently important that it has been called the "Beveridge Revolution" (Briggs 1961: 231). It did not produce a revolution, but it did provide a "comprehensive blueprint for post-war welfare policy" (Clarke 2004: 213). It was also "an unprecedented bestseller" (Campbell 1987: 126), with 635,000 copies sold and 86 percent of respondents to a survey at the time saying the report should be implemented (Addison 1975: 217). Beveridge (1942: 9) called for "a scheme of social insurance against interruption and destruction of earning power and for special expenditures arising at birth, marriage or death." Every working-age citizen would make a compulsory weekly, flat-rate contribution to a single social insurance fund, added to by contributions from employers and the state. From it, payments would be made "for unemployment, disability and retirement," all without a means test (Beveridge 1942: 16). Beveridge was strongly opposed to means testing (Harris 1977). Benefits were to be fixed at subsistence level, except for pensions, which were to build up to subsistence level over twenty years, and "subsistence" was to take into account "changing perceptions of a decent standard of life" (Harris 1977: 418, 394). Benefits were to last as long as needed, although in practice that did not happen—ultimately requiring the dramatic growth of means-tested supplementary benefits, which, as Donnison (1982: 12) later argued, "divide society, creating second class citizens who get second class treatment." The real limitation of the Beveridge Report was that it attempted to base a universal program of benefits "on a very restricted source of income (flat-rate contributions tied to what the poorest could afford)" (Lowe 2005: 145).

Nevertheless, "the principles of universalism, collectivism and subsistence rates were central" (MacGregor 1981: 11). The intent was "to win freedom from want by maintaining incomes" (Beveridge 1942: 153) and, by making those services equally available to all, to create a sense of social solidarity. This social insurance plan required for its success that there also be children's allowances paid to those responsible for the care of children, comprehensive health services and a strategy to maintain full employment and prevent mass unemployment. The latter was essential because the social security plan "is impracticable if it has to be applied to men by the million or hundred thousand" (Beveridge 1942: 163).

The entire Beveridge strategy implied a collective and universal response to poverty, a dramatic turnaround from the individualistic approach of laissez-faire that had so dominated the nineteenth century. It implied a new "theory of poverty"—a move away from the long-held view that poverty was the result of moral, behavioural or other personal failings and that government intervention would erode people's independence. The new theory assumed that a positive role could be played by the state to achieve a collective overcoming of want. So too did the ideas of John Maynard Keynes, who advocated the management of demand in pursuit of the goal of full employment (Pelling 1984) and who closely advised Beveridge. Keynes's ideas—as expressed in 1936 in his *General Theory of Employment, Interest, and Money*—were embodied in the 1944 White Paper on Employment Policy in which the wartime Coalition government committed "to maintain full employment after the war by Keynesian techniques of demand management" (Campbell 1987: 130). It was Beveridge's view that all of this was affordable, to be achieved by a redistribution of income, primarily to occur not by redistributing income and wealth from the rich by means of taxation, but rather by redistribution *within* the working class. He said,

> abolition of want by redistribution of income is within our means.... Better distribution of purchasing power is required among wage earners themselves, as between times of earning and not earning, and between times of heavy family responsibilities and of light or no family responsibilities. (Beveridge 1942: 167)

This would later become a problem because many low-income people came to resent the fact that their hard-earned but modest incomes were being taxed to support the poor, whose numbers grew dramatically starting in the mid- to late 1970s, leading to a resurgence of the traditional blame-the-victim interpretation of poverty. For example, a working-class couple worried in the mid-1950s about their long-term financial stability said: "We have worked hard and saved all our lives.... Can't the government, who do everything for the lazy and extravagant, do something for the thrifty and careful?" (Kynaston 2013: 13).

However, it was the experience of war, and not just the damage created by the mass unemployment of the 1930s, that made these new, collective ideas palatable to the beleaguered British population. The evacuation of Dunkirk, the Battle of Britain, the shared, cross-class experience of wartime rationing and queuing for food—"queues were a great leveler" (Clarke 2004: 207)—the widespread belief in the idea of "fair shares" and the powerful rhetoric of Churchill all combined to create a sense that "we are all in this together." A sense of common citizenship and equality took hold in the minds of many. People began to see themselves and their relations with others in a more collective way. They also saw the state less as the oppressive force of the Poor Laws and the means test and instead more as a potentially positive force for change (Titmuss 1950). In 1943–1944 there emerged "an elite consensus" about the failures of the 1930s and the need for a new set of policies (Lowe 1990: 158).

Even the establishment newspaper, *The Times*, writing in 1940 following the Dunkirk evacuation, called for the creation of "a sense of common values," saying, "the new order cannot be based on the preservation of privilege, whether the privilege be that of a country, a class or of an individual" (quoted in Vincent 1991: 112). Titmuss (quoted in Gazeley 2003: 158) argues that by the end of the Second World War, "it was increasingly regarded as a proper function or even obligation of government to ward off distress and strain among not only the poor but almost all classes of society." Indeed, the number of poor children being fed by government, 130,000 in 1940, had grown more than tenfold during the war to 1,650,000 in 1945 (Vincent 1991: 115).

The war effort was a massive undertaking that had to be managed and planned. The fact that Labour Party representatives played a lead role—at least six leading Labour Party members were key figures in Churchill's wartime government, including Attlee, who would later be prime minister (Pelling 1984: 11)—was an important factor in proving their worth and that of their more collective and egalitarian social welfare ideas. The war effort also made clear that sufficient money could be made available to mount a peacetime war against poverty and unemployment. Government expenditures grew sixfold, from a billion pounds in 1939 to six billion pounds in 1945 (Clarke 2004: 210). "The knowledge that large sums of money, raised through taxation at a level without precedent, were being used to wage war led without difficulty to the conclusion that smaller sums of money could produce a 'welfare state' in times of peace" (Briggs 1961: 227).

The emergence of the welfare state can best be seen as the product of a process that goes back at least to the 1880s and in some respects perhaps earlier. This process combined political struggle by trade unionists and socialist and other left organizations of various kinds; concessions made by various governments in the face of those demands in order to stave off even greater gains by those calling for change; and the long, gradual growth of ideas opposed to laissez-faire and in favour of more collective, state-interventionist strategies.

The Labour governments' immediate postwar achievements would occur despite exceptionally difficult economic circumstances. Five million British armed forces members were decommissioned, producing fears of the mass unemployment that followed the First World War. Britain was desperately short of money and was forced to turn to the US for loans that came with tough conditions. Housing, which for most working people had been a crisis for centuries, was worsened by wartime bombing. Nevertheless, very substantial social democratic gains would be made, in the face of almost overwhelming challenges.

Chapter 7

The End of Poverty?

1945 and All That

The Labour governments of 1945–1951 had a dramatic impact on poverty. Morgan (1984: 2–5) calls their policies a "seismic transformation" and "a sustained shift to the left, unique in our history," referring to "that heroic period, however unfulfilled or shackled by financial constraints." Thane (2000: 98, 102), although critical of the limits and the enduring impact of Labour's anti-poverty initiatives, argues that given the challenges they faced, "the outcome was a remarkable transformation" and "in the circumstances, it was magnificent."

The Most Advanced Welfare State in the World

Other social democratic governments were elected in Europe immediately after the war, but the British Labour Party, led by Prime Minister Clement Attlee, was the first with an absolute parliamentary majority (Sassoon 1997). To a considerable extent, what Labour achieved was a product of the postwar boom and the pent-up public demand for change following the long years of the Depression and the Second World War. After all, even the Conservatives had made commitments about full employment and reforms to health care. However, the British public believed that Labour was the party most likely to implement the changes needed, and they did. "For a few years after the war this social democratic welfare state prevailed mainly in Britain. It was the most advanced welfare state in the world" (Sassoon 1997: 141). As the leaders in this process, the postwar Labour governments faced enormous challenges, which they met with courage and determination. The gains they made did not come automatically, with the rising tide of postwar economic growth. They were not voluntarily agreed to as a means of stabilizing and reproducing capitalism. These were gains that had to be fought for.

The ideas driving the welfare state and its response to poverty were expressed in the 1945 Labour Party manifesto, *Let Us Face the Future* (Blair 1995) which described a move away from a targeted, residual and charity-based approach to an egalitarian, inclusive and universal approach. All citizens were to have equal access to services of a roughly equal standard, and by this means a floor was to be established for all. This shift in the approach to poverty was dramatic, proving to be effective, and it is an essential aspect of any strategy to eliminate poverty.

All of this was driven by the crucial principle of universality—"the provision of free medical treatment, family allowances, pensions and insurance benefits to rich and poor alike." This insistence upon universality can legitimately be seen as an attack on class privilege (MacGregor 1981: 18).

So too can changes to taxation. The Labour government placed a surtax on incomes over 10,000 pounds and death duties of 75 percent on estates worth more than 21,500 pounds. By 1951 the marginal tax rate on high incomes was over 90 percent, while the basic rate for lower earners was reduced (Thane 2018: 191–92; Daunton 2002).

The *Poor Law* was finally gone, abolished by the 1948 *National Assistance Act*. Section 1 of that Act says: "The existing poor law shall cease to have effect." This was, at the level of ideas, an entirely new way of thinking about and responding to poverty.

The Fight for the National Health Service

Perhaps the major success of the 1945–1951 Labour governments was the creation of the National Health Service (NHS), under the leadership of the minister of health, Aneurin Bevan. A universal, single-payer, publicly funded health care system was an especially significant anti-poverty measure, given the extent to which a lack of access to adequate health care had been such a crucial contributing factor to poverty in the previous two centuries of the Industrial Revolution and prior. During that industrialization, the English population experienced precariously poor health for reasons related both to the social determinants of health— poverty, poor housing, long hours of work in dangerous conditions, for example—and to the cost and thus inaccessibility of medical care. The road to the NHS, which came into effect July 5, 1948, goes back at least half a century to the Liberal *National Insurance Act* of 1911 and to the health insurance plans run by unions in Welsh mining towns in the late nineteenth century (Rozworski 2018: 10).

In giving birth to the NHS, Bevan faced powerful opposition (Jones 2019). Kynaston (2008: 297) describes Bevan as being "engaged for two years in a fierce war with the British Medical Association" (see also Pelling 1984; for a different interpretation of the role of the BMA, see Eckstein 1960). Bevan also faced opposition from the Conservative press and at least some of the British establishment—Churchill, for example, expressed his opposition by labelling Bevan the "minister of disease" (Addison 1975: 273). The challenges were immense in other ways as well. Many of the 2,700 hospitals then in existence were "obsolete," and those that had been Poor Law hospitals were described as "dark, old, devoid of modern sanitary conveniences, death traps in the case of fire; and in short unfit for the Nursing of Chronic Sick or any other form of Sick Person" (quoted in Addison 2010: 38). Bevan's solution was to nationalize the hospitals.

Bevan benefited from almost forty years of progressive work on health care, from the Webbs' 1909 *Minority Report of the Poor Law Commissioners* to the work in the 1930s of the Socialist Medical Association (SMA). As Morgan (1984: 152) describes it, "The SMA had succeeded in forcing the idea of a non-contributory, comprehensive state medical service on the Labour Party programme in 1934." Radical physicians who were Labour Party members and working-class women who were local party council members contributed throughout the 1920s and 1930s to the development of progressive health care policy (Jones 2019). Bevan's work was also bolstered by the fact that by 1939, there was a "clear commitment of the labour movement to major reform of the health service" (Webster 1990: 148).

While the historical origins of the NHS are complex and interpretations differ, what is clear is that Bevan committed immense energy and skill over the three years following the Labour Party election in 1945 to creating the National Health Service and insisting upon the highest standards. The result was that the NHS "was obviously one of the government's outstanding triumphs, admired throughout the world, an immense landmark in the building of the welfare state" (Morgan 1984: 162). However, Bevan had been forced, in the face of intense opposition, to make several important concessions, most notably abandoning both salaried physician payment and the promise of community health centres—which had been promoted especially by the SMA—and these would have future consequences. As Webster (1990: 150) argues, "The

NHS fell short of the revolution wanted by its more idealistic architects." Nevertheless, Bevan had secured the essential socialist principle that health care should be available based on need, not ability to pay. As Rozworski (2018: 10) describes it, the NHS "quickly became a beacon of what a decommodified public service could be: open to all, free at the point of service and paid out of taxes." Given the extent to which poor health and poverty had been intimately and causally connected over the centuries, the NHS was an immense anti-poverty measure.

Toward the Decommodification of Housing for Working-Class People

Also of crucial importance were the steps taken to build affordable, decent housing for low-income people, an effort also led by Bevan. Appalling housing conditions were for centuries a defining feature of poverty in England, including but not limited to what Morgan (1984: 164) describes as "the appalling heritage of slum property in inner-city areas." These conditions were worsened when as many as half a million houses were destroyed during the war, a third of all houses needed serious repair (Pearce 1994: 51), about seven million homes lacked hot water and six million did not have an indoor toilet. At the same time, there had been two million marriages during the war, and the birth rate was rising rapidly (Burnett 1986: 285). Not surprisingly, opinion polls in 1945 identified housing as voters' number one concern (Francis 1997).

Labour responded with a conceptually simple but expensive policy initiative—they built more low-income rental or "council" housing. And they did so based on Bevan's "most cherished socialist assumptions, notably the motifs of provision on the basis of 'need' and the right of all to receive high quality social services irrespective of purchasing power" (Francis 1997: 9). Subsidies were channelled through local authorities, and Bevan required that building private homes be limited to one for every four council houses built, "in order to direct limited resources to those most in need." He also ensured that new council houses "were of a good standard and size" (Pearce 1994: 51). In fact, Bevan's council houses were of unprecedented size and quality (Campbell 1987): the average floor area of a three-bedroom council house was 25 percent greater than the pre-war average (Donnison and Ungerson 1982: 143). His commitment was to "the overwhelming direction of resources into public house-building, with stringent limits on private building" (Campbell 1987: 138). Almost 1.2 million houses were built between 1945 and 1951 and Bevan insisted that "the main emphasis should be on council houses built by the local authority with a high element of Treasury subsidy, that is, on houses for rent, rather than houses for private sale" (Morgan 1984: 164). The result was that the focus of the Labour governments' housing strategy "was placed squarely on those least fortunate, on working-class people without adequate housing and caught in huge waiting-lists, seeking housing at low rents" (Morgan 1984: 170).

Because housing is foundational in pulling families out of poverty, this, like the NHS, was an enormously important anti-poverty measure. And it was achieved despite immense difficulties, including shortages of supplies, labour and foreign exchange. Building costs in 1945 were almost double what they had been in 1939 (Great Britain 1965: 12). That these formidable obstacles were overcome was attributable in large part to Bevan's fierce commitment to egalitarian socialist principles (Campbell 1987). As described by one analyst writing in 1948, Labour built houses "for those who needed them most," as opposed to the 1930s, when "people got houses not because they needed them, but because they could pay for them" (quoted in Francis 1997: 122). This approach was an important step in the direction of the decommodification of housing.

The *National Insurance Act* and Its Limitations

The *National Insurance Act* of 1946 was another crucial plank in Labour's foundation for the welfare state and for driving down the incidence of poverty. The *Act* introduced a universal, compulsory, contributory plan that paid unemployment and sickness benefits plus maternity, death and pension benefits (Pearce 1994). The pre-existing system had been "characterized by complexity and incoherence," with public and private components, "both contributory and non-contributory, means-tested and non-means-tested, and drawing on both insurance and Poor Law principles" (Colwill 1994: 54). The *National Insurance Act* outlined a single, coherent plan, intended to produce "the security from the cradle to the grave which was the essence of the Beveridge Report" (Hopkins 1991: 95). Benefits were payable as a matter of right, earned via contributions, and thus were not to be thought of as "handouts." Two years later, the *National Assistance Act* of 1948 "confirmed the new concept of social citizenship first outlined in aspects of Lloyd George's bill of 1911." It provided supplementary benefits for those not covered by the national insurance plan. Morgan (1984: 173) argues that it "dealt the final blow to the old poor law of nineteenth-century notoriety."

Morgan's interpretation is, however, too generous. Thane (2000) offers a less enthusiastic interpretation of the 1948 *Act*, arguing that it maintained some elements of the Poor Law tradition, including means testing of the poorest when seeking supplemental pensions and other benefits. As time progressed, more and more benefits for the poor would be means tested—thus eating away at the crucial principle of universality. Among the many problems of means testing, including attached stigma and the eroding of social solidarity, is the fact that so many of those eligible for benefits do not apply (Thane 2010), a problem that would grow dramatically in subsequent decades. For example, in the 1960s and 1970s, fewer than 50 percent of those entitled were applying for means-tested supplementary benefits (Lowe 2005: 159). Further, the benefits flowing from the *National Insurance Act* and the *National Assistance Act* were, consistent with the principles set out in the Beveridge Report, insurance-based rather than tax-based—that is, they were based on individual contributions rather than from general taxation—and were set at a bare subsistence level. In his 1942 report, Beveridge had argued that benefits should guarantee "the minimum level needed for subsistence." However, rates were set very low from the beginning, consistent with the well-worn *Poor Law* principle of "less eligibility." As Berthoud and colleagues (1981: 138, 144) argue: "The most serious weakness of the 1945–1948 legislation was the inadequacy of the benefit rates," in part because "the yield of flat-rate contributions would always be limited by what the lowest-paid worker could afford to pay." Almost immediately, one million pensioners applied to the new National Assistance Board (formed in 1948) for a means-tested supplement because the pension was too low (Thane 2010: 11). Many more who needed the supplement did not apply. The fact that Labour persisted in Beveridge's contributory rather than tax-based approach, that contributions were on a flat-rate basis and thus "highly regressive" (Townsend 1972: 7) and that benefits were too low from the beginning would become even more of a problem over time. Even by the early 1960s, the real value of benefits had dropped to the extent that they made possible "what can only be described by twentieth century standards as a pitiably meagre living" (Wootton 1963: 192). In 1993, for example, pensions were worth about 15 percent of average males' gross earnings (Pierson 1996: 144), and by 2008 pension benefits had declined further to their lowest level since 1945 as a percentage of average earnings (Thane 2010: 16). The declining real value of *National Assistance Act* benefits "limited the redistributive potential of the emerging welfare state" (Francis 1995: 227–28).

Moreover, because of its contributory rather than tax-based focus, the Beveridge Report had largely excluded women. It was assumed that women would return to the household after the war, seen as wives and mothers in two-parent households whose access to benefits would be primarily through husbands as breadwinners (Thane 1982). A "dual insurance/assistance model" was created, "with first class (insurance) benefits going mainly to men and second class (welfare/assistance) benefits to women" (Lewis 1992: 161). Wilson (1977: 148) describes the Beveridge Report, with some exaggeration, as "one of the most crudely ideological documents of its kind ever written." She makes this claim on the grounds that its underlying assumptions "were not those of socialism, but the principle of insurance; the principle of subsistence income; and the principle of the sanctity of the family." Harris (1996) offers an important partial corrective, suggesting that Beveridge's rationale for the insurance principle was, in fact, sensitive to the needs of women, at least as perceived at the time. For example, when Beveridge wrote in 1942, most women were not working due to the "marriage bar" by which employers expected women to give up work upon marriage. Further, as Thane (2018: 175) argues, Beveridge took the view, realistic at the time, that many women would remain at home "given the difficulties of combining work inside and outside the home and the inadequacy of affordable childcare"; furthermore, at home they would be doing work that was "vital though unpaid, without which their husbands could not do their paid work and without which the nation could not continue" (Beveridge 1942: 49). Nevertheless, it is certainly the case that the use of a contributory scheme, restricted to those who were employed, had the effect of discriminating against women—and against all of those outside of the paid labour force. The structure of the plan was regressive. Beveridge himself wrote in the report that in a contributory scheme, "the poorer man (sic) and the richer man are treated alike," whereas in a taxation scheme, "the richer man, because of his capacity to pay, pays more for the general purposes of the community" (quoted in Colwill 1994: 57). This was a major design flaw, a non-socialist aspect of the plan that differentiated social insurance from, for example, the taxation-funded National Health Service. The contributory character of the plan would cause increasing problems as poverty worsened from the mid- to late 1970s.

Any redistribution of income that did occur was within the working class, rather than from the rich to the poor and near-poor. As Morgan (1984: 185) describes it: "Many of the new social reforms were financed by transfer of income within lower-income groups themselves, rather than by transfers from the rich to the poor." This would later be at least a part of the cause of an emergent resentment of the welfare state by stable working-class and middle-class families when the British economy faltered in the late 1960s and 1970s. The construction of the Beveridge Report and the *National Assistance Act* were such that it was low-income working-class people—rather than those with higher incomes—who were being asked to pay for welfare benefits.

Nevertheless, the *Poor Law* was gone, albeit with lingering elements of that centuries-old approach, and a national minimum had been put in place. A foundation had been laid; much building remained to be done.

In the Face of Resistance: Full Employment and Related Gains

Finally, and of particular importance in fighting the centuries-old poverty that had plagued the British, was full employment. Unemployment had devastated vast stretches of 1920s and 1930s Britain, and during the Second World War "widespread apprehension" was reported about what might happen at war's end. "People dread and expect mass unemployment.... Most people remembered the aftermath of World War I and expected the same heavy unemployment to recur" (Addison 1975: 248). Further, Beveridge's report was predicated upon the essential, underlying principle that a welfare state was not possible when very large numbers were unemployed.

The Labour governments of 1945–1951 overcame the 1930s' curse of unemployment, along with the widespread fear that the mass unemployment that followed hard on the heels of the First World War would re-emerge at the end of the Second World War. It did not—even though some four million men and women in the armed services were demobilized in the eighteen months between June 1945 and January 1947 (Kynaston 2008: 97). The postwar boom, fuelled in part by the Marshall Plan, deserved much of the credit (Tomlinson 2000). Industrial production in Britain grew by one third between 1946 and 1951; exports increased 77 percent while imports grew 15 percent during the same period; trade was in balance by 1948 (Pearce 1994: 43). The shift could also be chalked up to the diversion of scarce resources to industrial production for export, even at the expense of rationing and austerity. In addition, Labour nationalized basic industries and took the Bank of England into public ownership, set up planning committees and controlled capital exports. The result was a dramatic change from 1945, realizing Labour's commitment to full employment as initially set out in Keynes' 1944 White Paper. Wootton (1963: 181) writes, "this, more than anything else, is the dramatic social revolution of our time."

> From the start of 1948 onwards, the rate of unemployment fell consistently, to well under 2 percent of the insured labour force. The north-east of England, which had known unemployment of 38 percent in 1932, in 1949 showed a total of only 3 percent; in industrial Scotland, the rate was 4 ½ percent where it had once been 35 percent; South Wales had an unemployment rate of 5 ½ percent in 1948–9 when it had been crucified by a rate of 41 percent in 1932, at the height of the depression. (Morgan 1984: 183)

At least a part of this decrease was attributable to the substantial growth in the number of people, women especially, who were employed by the state to deliver social services, a number estimated at more than 1.3 million by 1951; in this way, "the new welfare state created a new labour supply" (Tomlinson 1995: 207). The nationalization of the coal, electricity, gas, railway, iron and steel industries also contributed to full employment. By 1949, the average manual worker was earning almost 2.5 times in real terms what had been the case in 1937 (Addison 2010: 61).

These gains—the National Health Service, the building of more than one million good quality housing units for low-income people, the *National Insurance Act* and *National Assistance Act*, full employment—represented in their totality a massive anti-poverty effort. Thane (2000: 102) argues that the "welfare state" put in place by the 1945–1951 Labour governments "provided as never before a secure basis for the lives of the mass of people who could not provide for all their own needs—at last a 'national minimum'—whilst carrying out a massive task of economic reconstruction." Although barely redistributive, Labour initiatives "provided a real safety net which prevented the poorest falling too far behind the rising standards of the remainder, at least until the 1980s."

There was a price to be paid for these gains. An important part of that price was the severe austerity of the period: individual consumption was limited via rationing in order to invest to meet the collective needs of creating the NHS, constructing social housing and reinvigorating industrial production. Investing in industry was prioritized over individual consumption, in the belief that doing so would maximize human welfare. The result was what Morgan (1984: 297) describes as "a puritan regime of Cromwellian austerity," which included rationing of food, petrol and other commodities, as well as queueing for whatever commodities were available. A London schoolteacher wrote in 1948, "dreariness is everywhere. Streets are deserted, lighting is dim, people's clothes are shabby and their tables bare" (quoted in Kynaston 2008: 298). At the end of 1947 it was estimated that the average British woman spent an hour per day in a queue (Pearce 1994: 38). Churchill called it "Queuetopia" (Addison 2010: 20) while staunch Labour Party supporters appealed to the wartime slogan of "fair shares" (Pelling 1984: 267). But it was in large part against these personal privations that voters, especially "middle class" voters, reacted in 1951, the Conservatives campaigning with the phrase "setting the people free" (Morgan 1984: 317; Pelling 1984: 268), which would echo across the decades to Margaret Thatcher in 1979 and beyond.

The Labour governments of 1945–1951 adopted a clearly ideological approach—invest in collective measures that would benefit all, including and especially those at the bottom of the income scale. This approach stood in stark contrast to the traditional laissez-faire approach, which gave free rein to the pursuit of individual gains while producing widening disparities between rich and poor and worsened conditions for those at the bottom. The poor benefited enormously from the radical reformism—limited and flawed though it was—of the immediate postwar Labour governments. Investment in the collective measures made possible by this approach produced exceptionally positive gains in human well-being:

> All the indices—for instance, the statistics of medical officers of health, or of school medical or dental officers—suggest that the standard of health and of robust physique steadily improved during the entire 1945–51 period, from infants, whose survival rates continued to improve, to old people, whose expectation of a long and happy retirement steadily lengthened. (Morgan 1984: 370)

Rowntree and Laver's final study of poverty in York, published in 1951, showed a dramatic decrease—"perhaps in exaggerated fashion," as Morgan (1984: 371) notes—in the incidence of poverty because of Labour policies and investments. It was not eliminated, as Abel-Smith and Townsend (1965) would later reveal, but it was significantly reduced—even as measured by a revised analysis of the 1951 study (Hatton and Bailey 2000).

All of this was achieved despite Labour governments facing severe financial crises, especially in 1945 and 1947. Keynes called the 1945 financial crisis, following the termination in August of Lend-Lease—by which, in 1940, the US had agreed to lend military supplies to Britain with payment deferred—"a financial Dunkirk" (Pelling 1984: 54). The chancellor of the exchequer called it "total economic ruin" (Pearce 1994: 33). This was followed by "the grave financial crisis over the convertibility of sterling in August 1947, the worst Britain had experienced since August 1931. With Britain facing bankruptcy, the Cabinet was brought to its knees" (Morgan 1984: 334). The 1947 financial crisis led to conflict over whether to "consolidate," as argued especially by Herbert Morrison, or to continue to push ahead with reforms, as advocated particularly by Aneurin Bevan (Schneer 1988: 94). For the most part, consolidation won the day, even though the Marshall Plan of 1948 significantly improved Britain's finances—to the point that "the Board of Trade established in 1948 that but for Marshall Aid," rations of a wide range of daily necessities would have been cut even further (Coates 1975: 68).

Nevertheless, the reformist zeal of the Labour governments was tamed in large part by the 1947 financial crisis. Their approach to economic management shifted away from physical controls toward the adoption of Keynesianism (Addison 1975). "After 1947, physical planning and the ideology of socialist planning, as it had developed between 1931 and 1945, was on the wane while the Keynesian star rose" (Brooke 1991:

700). Nationalization came almost to a halt, with some 80 percent of industry still in private hands (Hopkins 1991: 91). Pressure was placed on the Labour cabinet to curb welfare expenditures on the grounds that they were a burden on the economy. Only Bevan argued that such expenditures could offer economic benefit. The result was the tendency to hold down welfare expenditures (Tomlinson 1995). And Keynesianism implied working within the system, rather than pushing its limits, since "this approach to planning is quite compatible with private ownership, competition and profit-making" (quoted in Brooke 1991: 701). By 1949, the government had "lost both momentum and direction" (Francis 1997: 34). Cabinet members were exhausted; many were experiencing poor health; some had died; and "after six exhausting years in power," they were "running out of energy and out of ideas" (Morgan 1984: 460).

Over that period, 1945-1951, the forces of political opposition had been intense. Kynaston (2008: 172) describes the hatred directed at the Labour government by the British establishment and by British capitalists. He quotes a junior Labour minister, John Freeman, who described the mood in the House of Commons:

> The tension of rising to answer questions or conduct a debate under the cold, implacable eyes of that row of well-tailored tycoons, who hated the Labour government with a passion and fear which made them dedicated men in their determination to get it out of office and to limit the damage it could do to the world which they saw as theirs by right.

Kynaston (2008: 172) adds, "though we cannot recover those lost conversations in saloon bars or at 19th holes or local Rotaries, it is pretty clear that a strong, almost tribal middle class backlash was well underway within a year of Labour taking power." Rose (1960: 90) describes "an outburst of middle class resentments" to what was seen as the "hardly interrupted drudgery" of 1945-1951. Townsend (1973: 7) writes of the response later in the 1950s as a "middle-class counter-revolution." The rest of the century would see what has been described as the "withering of the Welfare State" and a steady retreat from the principles of collectivism and universality (MacGregor 1981: 24). This would subsequently be dramatically accelerated, especially in the years following the 1979 election of Margaret Thatcher and her return to policies more consistent with the laissez-faire approach of the nineteenth century and the 1930s.

Today, what has been described as the "brief life of social democracy" (quoted in Kefford 2018: 230) seems, in many important respects, long in the distant past.

But when examined from the point of view of poverty, the achievements of the Labour governments of 1945–1951 were historic. Never had poverty been reduced so dramatically—indeed, never before, with the possible, partial exception of the 1906–1914 Liberal governments, had an attempt even been made. Further, it was done despite enormous financial challenges. Churchill had made it clear in 1945 that given Britain's fragile financial condition, the measures advocated by the Beveridge Report were not affordable (Pelling 1984). The Labour government pushed ahead anyway, despite the financial constrictions and despite vigorous opposition from business and a quickly reinvigorated Conservative Party (Francis 1997). An important conclusion to be drawn is that the best—maybe the only—anti-poverty strategy is a broadly based, genuinely social democratic strategy that includes such collective measures as universal, single-payer health care, the building of subsidized, low-income housing, universally available social assistance and the promotion of full employment. Such collective measures will, with certainty, be opposed by those with power, and thus their implementation requires government leaders with vision, courage and a commitment to the dramatic reduction of poverty.

In 1951, much still remained to be done. Social assistance benefits were too low, still coloured by the principle of "less eligibility" to which Beveridge had clung. Women's entitlements were still largely dependent upon wage-earning husbands. The hated means test was still in place, and although it affected relatively few by 1951, the numbers who would receive means-tested benefits would grow significantly in coming decades. Poor quality housing was still a major problem and wait lists for council housing were long—over 65,000 in Birmingham alone in 1951, for example (Chinn 1991: v). Health centres where various practitioners could work together and where preventative medicine could be practised—long a socialist goal—had been abandoned, and no new hospitals were built. Although grammar schools had been made free of charge in 1944 and the school-leaving age was raised to fifteen years in 1947, no new schools were built and deep inequalities continued to be reproduced by a class-based educational system about which Labour had done little (Kynaston 2008).

Perhaps more importantly, especially if one sees the 1945–1951 achievements as a foundation that would have to be built upon if poverty were to be fully and permanently overcome, there were some major problems. The social welfare gains made by Labour had been, for the most part, financed by a redistribution of income not from rich to poor and near-poor, but from within the working class—what Panitch (1976: 124) derisively calls "socialism in one class." When economic conditions deteriorated in the 1970s, the result was not only middle-class but also working-class resentment of the cost to them of the welfare state, in the face of which Labour governments largely abandoned redistribution to those at the lower end of the income scale. Further, the Labour Party became disconnected from many of those who were poor and who ought to have been their constituency. This was the case with Black youth, for example, as will be shown. It was also the case even with council housing tenants. In Manchester, for instance, the local Labour Party lost touch with council housing tenants and with "non-political community groups" of various kinds that emerged at that time (Shapely et al. 2004: 430–31).

Criticisms of the Labour Governments of 1945–1951

Many have criticized the Labour governments of 1945–1951. Those on the right have argued that the welfare state produced a culture of dependency that eroded the animal instincts of a dynamic capitalism, leading in Britain, as expressed perhaps most colourfully by Barnett (1986: 304), to the "dank reality of a segregated, sub-literate, unskilled, unhealthy and institutionalized proletariat hanging on the nipple of state maternalism." More significantly, perhaps, the right, and others not on the right, have correctly argued that the Labour governments—and British capitalists—failed to modernize an aging industrial base that was increasingly uncompetitive globally, and the price for this began to be paid in the 1960s and 1970s. The left (see Miliband 1972 and Coates 1975, for example) has argued that socialism was not achieved—this was true—and that to varying extents what Labour did in laying the foundations of the welfare state was but "a modest program" (Saville 1957: 17), largely indistinguishable from what was implemented in most advanced capitalist societies to varying extents. In this same vein, some Marxist scholars (O'Connor 1973; Glyn 1979, for example) have argued that the postwar welfare gains served to stabilize capitalism, reproduce the labour force and tame the working class. Thus, Saville (2003: 78) argues that the achievements of the Attlee governments "are a necessary and essential part of the structure of advanced industrial societies" because they remove "the harshness and insecurity which is a built-in characteristic of industrial life." What is very clear, from a left perspective and with the enormous benefit of hindsight, is that more should and could have been done.

These criticisms, however, underestimate the achievements of 1945–1951 and the fierce struggle to attain them, and they turn out to have been far too complacent about capitalism's, and the broad public's, acceptance of the welfare state.

A more fundamental critique is the argument that social democracy of the type practised by the 1945–1951 Labour governments is incapable of achieving socialism (Coates 1975) and therefore incapable of delivering the redistributive policies that are needed to defeat poverty. There is a rich debate (Coates 2003; Panitch and Leys 1997, for example) about the limits of social democracy, especially of the Labour Party's approach to social democracy. Important as it is, this is not the place to enter that debate. What is important, from the point of view of poverty, is that if poverty is to be dramatically reduced, then any government in power must deliberately divert very substantial fiscal resources to meeting the collective needs of those at the bottom of the income scale. To a considerable extent, the Labour governments of 1945–1951 did that. In subsequent years and decades, however, the demands of immediate consumption and the growing weakness of the British economy, especially in manufacturing, pushed out that diversion of resources, as individualism increasingly replaced collectivism and as the Labour Party revised its ideological approach.

Criticisms of the Labour governments of 1945–1951 ignore or make too little of the enormous achievements of these governments, and the massive financial, political and logistical challenges that had to be overcome in order to do so; they also ignore the enormous efforts of workers and their organizations over many decades to achieve these gains. While there is undoubtedly intellectual merit in evaluating these Labour governments relative to some theoretical depiction of a socialist society, it is more important to acknowledge that the Labour governments went an enormous distance in a remarkably short time in significantly reducing poverty. They diverted fiscal resources from individual consumption to the creation of collective services that pulled millions out of poverty, and as Dorothy Thompson (quoted in Palmer 2002: 202) describes it, these collective services provided benefits "purely on the basis of need and not of cash payment.... This conception is a profoundly anti-capitalist one. It had to be fought for at every stage"; therefore, "these are, objectively, victories for working class values within capitalist society." Matthews (2018: 41) makes the same case, arguing, for example, that the NHS "arose after decades of class struggle over access to medical care" and "embodied principles of universalism and collectivism." Hall (1988: 226) writes, with respect to the NHS, "We—rightly—want to see more of this, not less: more aspects of life organized on a similar principle." These are anti-poverty principles.

Attlee and his governments were not revolutionaries. "All these men were by temperament social reformers rather than leaders of the class struggle ... they were driven far more by the desire to achieve things than by the desire, common enough in politics, simply to be at the top of the greasy pole" (Addison 1975: 15–16). Attlee's wife Violet is reported to have said, "Clem was never really a socialist, were you dear? Well, not a rabid one" (Brown 2001).

But this underestimates Attlee's radical impulses, at least as regards poverty. Although raised in a well-off Conservative family, he spent fourteen years in London's East End working with impoverished youth. He wrote, "I found abundant instances of kindness and much quiet heroism in these mean streets. These people were not poor through their lack of fine qualities. The slums were not filled with the dregs of society." This practical experience shaped his politics. "From this it was only a step to examining the whole basis of our social and economic system." He became a socialist, joined the Independent Labour Party and for years worked as an active Party member in London's East End, where he lived, often speaking multiple times per week on street corners and at factory gates (Attlee 1954). This political background was no doubt instrumental in his strong support of Bevan and of Labour's creation of the welfare state and his commitment to the redistributive measures that would improve the lives of the poor. As Tony Benn argued (quoted in Hobsbawm 1981: 80), "these things didn't happen inexorably, they happened because a form of socialist, democratic and activist leadership was given at a critical moment." As Pimlott (1995: 237) has describes the struggle for these gains:

> It is easy to take for granted hard-won reforms, and to forget how bitterly they were contested at the time. When one policy triumphs over another, it is tempting to regard the change as inevitable.... Yet the reality of radical reform is that it has seldom come without a fight.

It makes good sense to conclude that although the Attlee governments were not revolutionaries, "revolutionary changes" did occur in the lives of many of the poor, "as shown by oral history studies of the impact of the NHS. We do well to respect such testimony" (Pearce 1994: 76). Benn argued (see Hobsbawm 1981: 79) that given the circumstances of the time, the 1945 Labour government achieved a "social revolution." These changes laid the foundation for what could have been a lasting end to poverty, had their initial steps been built upon and had their vision and political courage been carried on by their successors. But that did not happen. As Miliband (1972: 307, emphasis in original) expresses it, the activist in the Labour Party "saw the welfare state and the nationalization measures of 1945–1948 as the beginning of the social revolution to which he believed the Labour Party was dedicated; while his leaders took these achievements to *be* the social revolution." It is Attlee's Labour Party successors who must bear the responsibility for the failure to build upon the foundation laid by the 1945–1951 Labour governments.

At the same time, opposition to the welfare state was building right from the Labour victory in 1945. The observation of Ken Livingstone, former mayor of London, is germane here: "In politics nothing is ever wholly a defeat or a victory. Even when you think you are coasting home to a great victory, things are probably happening as a by-product of your success which are laying the seeds for future problems and which might mushroom into future defeats" (quoted in Seyd 1987: 142). This accurately describes the work of the British political right that was underway in 1945 and which led ultimately to the 1979 victory of Margaret Thatcher.

Chapter 8

Mid-Century Retrenchment

The Welfare State Erodes, Poverty Re-Emerges and Capitalism Goes into Crisis

The foundation built by the 1945–1951 Labour governments remained largely in place for at least a decade and perhaps longer following their 1951 defeat. While it was not further built upon, as was needed and possible, there was, at least initially, a broad consensus about the virtues of the fledgling welfare state. This was evidenced by the Conservative Party's "One Nation" group, formed in 1950, which wrote, "the social services for the most part are here to stay ... our contemporaries and descendants will take them ... for granted" (quoted in Jones and Lowe 2002: 23).

The Rise of Individualism and Consumerism

But individualism, especially as expressed in the mass consumption that started what for Britain was a brief postwar boom, increasingly took ever-deeper hold. Not only did this produce "the joyous ringing of capital's cash-tills" (quoted in Panitch and Leys 2020: 10), but also, as Hobsbawm (1981: 176) observed, "the values of consumer-society individualism and the search for private and personal satisfactions above all else, have been daily taken into every living room for a generation by the media." Indeed, as Seabrook (1985: 8) argued, "the dismantling of the identity of the old working class, and its replacement with a new, more individualistic, more consumer-driven identity in which the personal acquisition of commodities came increasingly to be the means by which human needs are met" was occurring. An example is home ownership, which was "being powerfully promoted by cultural and political elites," the implied and intended corollary being that "universal, socialized forms of provision could never be a desirable alternative to the private sector" (Kefford 2018: 257).

These would in time become virtually a revolution in values, relative to those of the 1945–1951 Labour governments. It was a revolution "according to Marks not Marx" (quoted in Tiratsoo 1991: 47), a reference to British retailer Marks and Spencer. In 1959, compared to the year previous, sales of refrigerators, washing machines, vacuum cleaners and cars had grown by 89, 37, 36 and 13 percent, respectively (Kynaston 2013: 337). The proportion of people with a television set rose from 42 percent in 1950 to 82 percent in 1960; unemployment rarely rose above 3 percent in the 1950s and 1960s; average real incomes doubled between 1950 and 1973 (Addison 2010: 56, 168). Capitalism "had been transformed from satanic mill to shopping mall" (Blackwell and Seabrook 1985: 150). Under the new prosperity, Prime Minister Harold Macmillan famously asserted in July 1957, "most of our people have never had it so good" (Kynaston 2013: 56)—and it had an understandable impact on people's consciousness. So too did the fact that pension benefits were rising—by 1964, their real value was 50 percent greater than in 1951—and the number of medical doctors and nurses rose at a rate faster than population growth (Pinto-Duschinsky 1970: 56). Full employment and the welfare state gradually came to be taken for granted, especially by the young (Rose 1960). Collectivism increasingly gave way to individualism. The welfare state gradually atrophied, beginning what would be a decades-long process that continues today.

Rather than fighting to build the rest of the welfare state and extend collective benefits, British people became "much more interested in the new culture of affluence, with its expanding opportunities for leisure, labour saving and mass consumption" (Harris 2000: 32). This may have been especially the case for women, "notably middle-class women, who particularly disliked the daily queueing and skimping that widespread rationing produced" (Tomlinson 2000: 58) and who protested via middle-class organizations such as the Housewives' League. McKibbin (2010: 165) describes this as "a revolt of women against the 'collectivist, productionist agenda' of the Labour Party in favour of the Conservative Party's consumptionism."

But it is also undoubtedly the case that for women especially, given the gendered division of household labour, the ready availability of washing machines and vacuum cleaners was the kind of tangible benefit that had genuine meaning. How could such gains be seen as anything other than the just rewards for the hard, depression-era, wartime and postwar struggles?

> A washing machine, especially for a woman who saw her mother used up with work at the dolly tub and labouring over the wooden handle that turned the heavy mangle as she struggled to force her husband's reluctant overalls through the tight grey rollers to press out the water, is an unqualified and incalculable good; a blessing, even. (Blackwell and Seabrook 1985: 106–7)

The Conservative opposition had used these sentiments to build a successful election campaign in 1951 by promoting "disaffection with austerity, rationing and controls" (Zweiniger-Bargielowska 1994: 176). As a result, from 1951, unlike in 1945, "there was a strong female presence in the Conservative Party" (Zweiniger-Bargielowska 2000: 252).

Yet, despite the prosperity brought by the brief postwar boom, basic problems were far from solved. For example, poverty was soon to be "rediscovered":

> by the end of the [1950s] decade … it was clear that a new housing crisis was looming…. Behind the "affluent society" still lay much private squalor in the housing conditions of lower-paid workers, immigrant groups, old people and others who had not been in a position to push their claims on national prosperity. (Burnett 1986: 286–7)

In his last major speech in the House of Commons in 1959, Aneurin Bevan made this case:

> In the years immediately after the war we made very great efforts to build up fixed capital equipment and sacrificed our Parliamentary majority. Our name became identified with greyness and dullness, frugalities, shortages … holding back present consumption, holding back immediate satisfaction, holding down the standard of living, to canalize and divert resources into building up the economy…. It was absolutely necessary that personal consumption at that time should hold back so that we could build up the resources of the nation. So the problem for us today … is to try to reconcile popular representative government with setting aside sufficient of the national income in or-

der to expand productive resources. (Quoted in Campbell 1987: 365)

Another way of saying this is that the Labour governments of 1945–1951 promoted the collective good, the "common wealth," as opposed to the pursuit of individual gains (Jackson 2018: 293), making life better for the working class than it had been in the 1930s. "For them the comparative poverty of the interwar years was a type of rationing more stringent than anything experienced in the late 1940s." But Bevan presciently expressed the concern that "popular representative government," especially in an era of growing individualism and consumerism, would reject the diversion of resources to broader public purposes—including, and as would become increasingly clear, especially—to meet the needs of the poor.

Revisionism and the Abandonment of the Welfare State

During Labour's 1964–1970 and 1974–1979 terms, the effective anti-poverty initiatives that were part of the welfare state put in place by the Attlee governments were not built upon, even though "the post-1945 'welfare state' was not in itself a final destination" (Briggs 1961: 222). Beveridge himself had seen the Beveridge Report as "merely the first installment of a much more far-reaching program of radical reform" (Harris 1977: 450). Yet "instead of realizing that their work was only beginning, the Labour Party leaders thought it was at an end" (Townsend 1973: 4). The 1945–1951 initiatives should have served as the foundation upon which more was built. They did not.

Instead, the post-1951 Labour Party moderated its policies, abandoning the genuinely social democratic drive of 1945–1951 that had diverted scarce resources to rebuild the economy and meet the needs of those at the bottom of the income scale. Post-1951, the revisionists adopted policies aimed at securing middle-class votes, policies described by Miliband (1960: 7) as "a programme of tinkering empiricism within the framework of capitalist society." Hugh Gaitskell became the party's leader in 1955. He was surrounded by Labour Party intellectuals who sought to revise the social democratic impetus of 1945–1951 in favour of a more "modern" party that would work within the system, would rely more upon public relations experts to shape party policy and would see its central purpose as winning elections (Haseler 1969: 144).

"Butskellism"—derived from the names of Conservative MP Rab Butler and Gaitskell—was the term used to describe the consensus arising from the apparent melding of Labour's ideology with that of the Conservative Party. Crossman (1952: 2) argued that in the wake of their 1951 defeat, "the Labour Party was unsure where it was going" and had "lost its way."

The "revisionists"—those who wanted to moderate the more socialist aspects of Labour's policies—quickly filled that gap. They took the view, expressed most importantly by Anthony Crosland (1956), that capitalism had changed significantly; that class conflict was outdated. This was the era of the "embourgeoisement thesis," the argument that an increasingly affluent working class was abandoning their values and adopting those of the middle class (Zweig 1961). This was an exaggerated view. Nevertheless, Goldthorpe et al. (1967) found that while workers generally retained their class consciousness, they were doing so in an increasingly instrumental fashion—less and less did they perceive themselves as part of a movement. The collectivism that is an inherent part of a working-class movement was giving way to individualism.

The revisionists argued that capitalism was now held fully in check by unions and other social forces, that the mass unemployment of the 1930s would never return and, therefore, that Labour's long-time commitment to socialism—or at least to a robust welfare state—had to be revised and moderated.

Crosland's *The Future of Socialism* was an especially important part of this revisionist "counter-revolution." Some of his claims about the extent to which capitalism had changed are, especially with the benefit of hindsight, wildly mistaken. His central argument was that capitalism had been so tamed that the redistributive measures of 1945–1951 were no longer necessary, and poverty would no longer be a problem (Crosland 1956: 517). Lipsey (1981: 37), a strong Crosland supporter, agreed with Crosland that poverty would end "almost as a natural process." However inaccurate this laissez-faire, "trickle-down" approach proved to be, the policies of the Labour "revisionists" reflected this interpretation (Coates 1975), and Crosland's "*The Future of Socialism* signaled a sea-change in the undercurrent of Labour's social and political philosophy" (Harris 2000: 36). This would echo some forty years later: as Coates (2003: 6) suggested, Gaitskell's leadership saw the first period of revision, and "Tony Blair's rise to power began the Party's second period of revision." Blair agreed, describing Crosland's *The Future of Socialism* as "a magnificent essay in bringing Labour to the reality of life in the 1950s, but we only really imbibed it and digested it by the late 1980s" (Blair 2010: 214).*

Also undergoing a sea change was the country's class structure. Capitalism is dynamic, including its class structure—constantly structured and restructured to meet the needs of capital. The "traditional" British working class—the manual worker in mine, mill and factory— was being eroded by deindustrialization, replaced by white-collar workers in the service sector and financial and related industries, particularly in the south and southeast of England. Manual workers, 75 percent of Britain's population in 1911, were by 1976 barely over half the population (Hobsbawm 1981: 3). The traditional working class had been largely white and male; increasingly workers were non-white and female. Hall (1988: 5) described this as a "profound reshaping of the classes of contemporary British society." Miles and Savage (1994; see also Savage et al. 2013) describe further the fragmentation of the "traditional" working class and the abandonment by some on the left of the very idea of the working class. This, together with the growth of individualism and consumerism and the sense that the welfare state had been won for good, is what found expression in Crosland's work and what led the Labour Party to its growing stagnation.

Nor was there an attractive alternative—one rooted in the benefits of collectivism, solidarity and egalitarianism—available for those who were enamoured of the individualistic attractions of consumerism. "Socialism has no privileged pathway to the heart of the working class; on the contrary, it has to fight every inch of the way" (Blackwell and Seabrook 1985: 48). That fight was in many important respects abandoned by the post-1951 Labour Party. Meanwhile, in the mid- to late 1960s and 1970s, the forces of a revitalized and much more aggressive political right were mobilizing, especially at the level of ideas.

---

* It is important to note, however, that Crosland remained committed to the pursuit of equality and the relief of poverty, advocating taxes on the wealthy in pursuit of these socialist goals. This was to be quite unlike the later revisionist efforts of Tony Blair, who was "decidedly post-Crosland.... Blair stands far closer to Margaret Thatcher than he does to Tony Crosland" (Heffernan 2000: 130–1), as described herein in Chapter 10.

The Growth of Intellectual Opposition to the Welfare State

The 1950s and 1960s saw anti-welfare forces gaining strength, with a wide range of publications and effective appeals to the broader public (Titmuss 1958). The seeds of these ideas, which would ultimately undermine so much of what had been achieved, were already being planted prior to 1945 in the work of Friedrich von Hayek, embodied in a variety of publications (Harris 1986), most famously *The Road to Serfdom*, published in 1944. As early as 1942, a secret Conservative Party committee had rejected as too expensive the Beveridge Report's commitment to benefits at a subsistence level, a position supported by 90 percent of Conservative Party MPs (Deacon and Bradshaw 1983: 43). From that time through the 1950s and 1960s, and in contrast to the consensus of Butskellism and the moderation of the Macmillan and One Nation factions of the Party, "there is evidence of deep-seated Conservative hostility, especially in the middle and lower ranks of the party, to the development and impact of state intervention in the economic and social spheres" (Green 1999: 22).

In 1950 and again in 1952, a Conservative Party group that included Enoch Powell—who wrote, "Often, when I am kneeling down in church, I think to myself how much we should thank God, the Holy Ghost, for capitalism" (quoted in Nairn 1977: 280–81)—called for the replacement of universality with means testing (Deacon and Bradshaw 1983). As Powell and Iain Macleod wrote in 1952, "the question that poses itself is not 'should a means test be applied to a social service?' but 'why should any social service be provided without a test of need'" (quoted in Green 1999: 25). The establishment in 1957 of the Institute of Economic Affairs added weight to the opposition against the principle of universality, in favour of the private, for-profit provision of services. By the late 1960s, "the welfare state was being attacked as an expensive and wasteful anachronism which should be replaced as far as possible by private markets in education, housing, life assurance and medical care" (Deacon and Bradshaw 1983: 51). The Edward Heath Conservative government of 1970–1974 attempted to introduce a range of aggressive neoliberal initiatives, and although they backed off—"it was too soon for the neoliberal counter-revolution" (Golding and Middleton 1982: 223)—nevertheless, "universal measures were reduced and withdrawn ... and in their place means-tested measures were introduced." This was accompanied by the resurgence of "pathological perceptions of the problem of poverty as being due to the inadequacy and incompetence of the poor themselves rather than the limitations and failures of policies for state support" (Alcock 1987: 63).

Even trade unions, seemingly unconcerned about the poor, expressed opposition to the "generosity" of the welfare state. Crossman wrote that after a meeting in his Coventry constituency, "the trade unionists want to see us spending less on social services so there'll be more for wage packets" (quoted in Deacon and Bradshaw 1983: 67). This was, at least in part, because redistribution to fund the welfare state came more from the working class—many of whom themselves struggled to pay their bills—than from those with higher incomes. The collective consciousness of the industrial working class was being replaced by an individualism and more narrowly economistic unionism that focused on wage increases rather than the broader, collective concerns of the labour movement (Martin 2009).

Ironically, this retreat from the radical reformism of the Attlee governments was happening just as the student and anti-Vietnam War and women's movements, as well as young workers' wildcat strikes, were happening around the Western world, including Britain. The Labour Party was largely disconnected from these movements, as it was from Black youth and, increasingly, even from council housing tenants. Samuel (1960: 13) argues that even by the late 1950s, the Labour Party "scarcely touch[ed] the lives of many working class people." It had become "a party of modest social reform in a capitalist system within whose confines it is ever more firmly and now irrevocably rooted" (Miliband 1972: 376).

Labour Party membership declined sharply during this period: from just over one million members in 1952—membership had "increased fivefold between 1942 and 1952"—to just under 700,000 in 1970 (Kynaston 2013: 277). These numbers are contested, and there exist several estimates, but in each case the sharp downward trend in Party membership is clear (Seyd 1987). Such data are evidence of the Labour Party's decline and of the fact that it was no longer the driving force for change for working people and the poor that it had been from 1945–1951.

Townsend (1966: 31) argues that the reforms of the 1964–1970 Harold Wilson Labour governments were no more "than hot compresses on an ailing body politic." Poverty had grown during this time, "and the best that Government spokesmen could do to counter the argument was that it had, at most, been marginally alleviated," even while "massive deprivation remained a permanent feature of life in Britain" (Miliband 1972: 368).

Wilson made reforms: pensions were substantially increased, but nevertheless remained too small to live on without a supplement. Access to social services for people with disabilities was improved. Gains were made in housing: significant numbers of council homes were built, subsidies were increased, rent controls were reintroduced and the *Prevention from Eviction Act* was introduced in 1965. Each of these was important, but in their totality they did relatively little to improve upon the "massive deprivation" in Britain.

Crosland and the revisionists mistakenly assumed that the postwar boom would be permanent. It was not. It ended in the late 1960s to early 1970s. Yet the Labour Party revised its policies as if capitalism had become permanently more benign. The naiveté of that belief would be made fully clear, less than a quarter century after Crosland's "revisionist bible," by Margaret Thatcher, who would oversee a massive resurgence in the incidence of poverty.

Economic Decline

Economic growth in Britain in the 1950s and early 1960s was satisfactory, albeit relatively slow compared to other European countries (Skidelsky 1988: 3) or, as described elsewhere (Berthoud et al. 1981: 3), "modest in comparison with some other countries," but for Britain, "exceptional by historical standards."

But the increasingly obvious reality was a British economy struggling from the mid-1960s and especially the early 1970s, adding to the growing backlash against the welfare state. The problems had been there throughout the twentieth century—in 1901, for example, *The Times* ran a series titled "The Crisis in British Industry" (Middlemas 1979: 53). Britain's economic weaknesses related primarily to loss of empire and a failure by British capitalists to make the investment and strategic managerial decisions needed to be competitive with other economies.

Growth in manufacturing was especially weak, and it would worsen following the 1973 world recession, driving up levels of unemployment (Coates 1983: 33–35). Unemployment had averaged just under 2 percent for the twenty years ending in 1966, then accelerated sharply after 1973.

One million manufacturing jobs disappeared—relocated to low-wage countries and displaced by automation—in the 1970s (Sinfield and Showler 1981: 3). Old British industries, most in the north, were especially hard hit: from 1957 to 1974/75, employment in coal plummeted from 704,000 to 246,000 workers; from 1958 to 1963, employment in British shipbuilding dropped from 215,000 to 160,000 (Addison 2010: 169). In the early 1950s, Britain contributed 38 percent of the world's share of shipbuilding; by the early 1960s, its share was 16 percent (Kynaston 2014: 136). Nor was it just the north: Greater London lost almost a quarter of a million jobs in the 1960s, and manufacturing jobs there declined by 25 percent (Shankland et al. 1977: 1). In 1950, the UK share of the global export of manufactured goods was 25.5 percent; by 1975 it was 9.3 percent. Britain's share of total world trade was cut in half, from 19.3 percent in 1953 to 10.5 percent in 1970, while the volume of imported manufactured goods almost quadrupled, creating balance of payments problems (Coates 1975: 112). Looked at in longer perspective, the UK's share of world trade dropped from 40 percent in 1880 to 8 percent a century later in 1980 (Jackson 1992: 23).

A massive wave of industrial militancy in the late 1960s and early 1970s—characterized by the frequency of unauthorized wildcat strikes and related in part to the political and cultural upheaval symbolized by May 1968—added to economic concerns. Days lost due to strikes went from 2.8 million in 1967 to eleven million in 1970 (Panitch 1976: 214).

Stagflation—rising levels of both inflation and unemployment—became an issue. "In 1974 retail prices rose by 19 percent, wage rates by 29 percent, and industrial production fell by 3 percent (all postwar records); by August 1975 the price rise over the previous eleven months was a new record—26.9 percent" (Kavanagh 1990: 129). Labour governments tried incomes policies, especially from 1964—including the contentious *In Place of Strife* document of 1969—in repeated attempts to control wage gains, but these had little success (Addison 2010). Evidence from Britain and elsewhere was "that incomes policy makes little difference to the rate of inflation" (Oppenheimer 1970: 141).

Expenditures on welfare services rose rapidly, from just over 16 percent of GDP in 1955 to 28 percent by 1975 (Clarke and Langan 1993: 33). As a result, Britain faced intense pressures from global financial institutions—particularly the International Monetary Fund, as part of its 1976 rescue package—to cut social expenditures (Coates 1975).

The result was "something of an intellectual revolution in economic policy" (Kavanagh 1990: 129)—a revolution that started three years prior to Thatcher's 1979 election victory. Prime Minister James Callaghan's Labour government abandoned its commitment to full employment—a commitment that went back to 1944—choosing to cut public spending rather than increase the deficit. In 1976, Callaghan famously told Party members,

> We used to think that you could spend your way out of a recession, and increase employment by cutting taxes and boosting Government spending. I tell you in all candour that that option no longer exists, and that insofar as it ever did exist, it only worked on each occasion since the war by injecting a higher dose of inflation into the economy, followed by a higher level of unemployment as the next step. Higher inflation followed by higher unemployment. (Labour Party Annual Conference Report 1976: 188)

The Callaghan government then agreed to conditions for a loan from the IMF—namely large cuts in government spending, of a billion pounds in 1977–1978 and a billion and a half pounds in 1978–1979. In a letter to the IMF on December 15, 1976, the Labour government agreed to "a continuing and substantial reduction over the next few years in the share of resources required for the public sector" (quoted in Seyd 1987: 200).

Total welfare expenditures in real terms fell in 1977 and 1978—the only time in postwar Britain (Jones and Lowe 2002: 12). In one of its relatively few "radical" reforms, the 1974–1976 Labour government cut the child tax allowance, which advantaged men, and in its place increased "the family allowance, paid in cash, usually to women, by an equivalent amount" (Jones and Lowe 2002: 69). Barbara Castle, the minister responsible, described in her diaries a Treasury official's fierce opposition to this universal benefit. "He waxed eloquent about the wickedness of universal benefits—the need for greater selectivity" (quoted in Jones and Lowe 2002: 70). Donnison (1982: 209), based on his experience in trying to reform the supplementary benefits system, referred to "the wolves in the Treasury, always ranging abroad in hopes of bringing down a social benefit." Bosanquet and Townsend (1980: Preface) describe the results of the 1974–1979 Labour governments, especially regarding poverty and inequality, as being "intensely disappointing."

In 1978, Callaghan called for a maximum 5 percent increase in pay levels but was "overwhelmed by a flood of far higher pay claims in what became the 1978–79 Winter of Discontent" (Hopkins 1991: 201). Labour's incomes policy was shredded. Once the terms of the IMF loan—the first made to a major industrial nation—had been agreed, the Labour government was no longer able to deliver its part of the social contract—especially increased public expenditure. About a capitalism clearly in crisis, Middlemas (1979: 459) writes: "Like an overloaded electrical circuit, the system began to blow more fuses than electricians could cope with in that dismal decade." In the face of these problems, the Party leadership "inspires no sacrifice, blazes no trails, bodes no fundamental changes, and meets no spiritual needs" (Coates, quoted in Panitch 2003: 167).

The economic crisis demanded a new approach; Margaret Thatcher would soon deliver it. As Stuart Holland (quoted in Panitch 2003: 168) puts it, "Certainly, the edge of Mrs. Thatcher's axe was first ground and then fell under successive Healey [Callaghan's chancellor of the exchequer] budgets." The Labour Party was bereft of ideas. Their electoral support collapsed "from 47 percent in 1966 to 37 percent in 1979" (Kavanagh 1990: 169), resulting in Thatcher's 1979 election.

Hay (2010: 447) argues that "the Winter of Discontent was in many aspects a manufactured crisis" that was "politically orchestrated." The four major union disputes of that winter created the impression of a country at the mercy of a union movement that had grown far too powerful. The media promoted this idea. However, far from being too powerful, Hay argues that in fact the events of that winter were evidence of union weakness—union leadership could not control their membership. Hay (2010: 461–62; see also Thane 2018) argues further that during this period inflation was being brought down and most economic indicators were "moving in the right direction." Yet the situation was constructed as a crisis, primarily because of "the existence of an alternative paradigm—in the form of Thatcherism—capable of providing such a construction" (Hay 2010: 465). This was possible in the absence of any coherent left alternative. The right seized the initiative—Hay (2007: 184) refers to "the importance of the Thatcherite narration of the crisis of the 1970s"—in the face of an economy that was struggling.

Capitalism was in crisis. Britain had become the "sick man of Europe" (Martin 2009: 50). In this context, the "re-emergence" of poverty was virtually inevitable.

The Rediscovery of Poverty

Soon after the end of the Second World War, it came to be widely believed that the problem of poverty had been solved. Rowntree and Lavers (1951: 32, 40, 45) had done a third survey of poverty in York in 1950. They found a "remarkable decrease in poverty between 1936 and 1950," from just over 31 percent in 1936 to just under 3 percent in 1950, arguing this was largely attributable to Labour's welfare legislation and to "the disappearance of unemployment as a cause of poverty." The *Manchester Guardian* proclaimed the "ending of poverty" (Gazeley 2003: 159) and the 1950 Labour Party manifesto declared that "today destitution has been banished" (quoted in Vincent 1991: 133). Crosland wrote in 1956 that "nine-tenths of the poverty which existed in 1936 had disappeared" (Crosland 1956: 43). Townsend (1979: 160–61) later identified several weaknesses in the 1951 Rowntree and Lavers study, but concluded that even correcting for these, there was nevertheless "a diminution of poverty" to "between 6 and 10 percent" (for a similar conclusion, see Hatton and Bailey 2000). He attributed these gains to the decline in unemployment, plus various government initiatives regarding family allowances, social insurance, pensions and food subsidies.

Between 1945 and 1960, unemployment remained below 2 percent. Between 1956 and 1968, "average money wages more than doubled and average money earnings nearly tripled." Most of the welfare state remained in place. Nutrition improved, and infant mortality declined (Gazeley 2003: 160–64). The real incomes of the poor increased by some 60 to 70 percent between 1953 and 1973, by which time poverty reached its lowest level in statistical terms since the Attlee years; the numbers in *absolute* poverty decreased substantially (Fiegehen et al. 1977: 27–31).

Then in 1965, Brian Abel-Smith and Peter Townsend published *The Poor and the Poorest*, and poverty was "rediscovered." They found that poverty, when measured in relative terms—taking account of the generally accepted standards of the time—was still widespread. One in every seven households in 1960—approximately 7.5 million, of whom about 2.5 million were children—was in or on the margins of poverty (Abel-Smith and Townsend 1965: 65–66).

Further, inequality was re-emerging (Townsend 1970: 116). The share of personal earnings going to the lowest paid declined between 1949–1950 and 1959–1960 (Gazeley 2003: 161). Post-1951 tax adjustments benefited upper-income individuals and families, so that "ancient inequalities have assumed new and more subtle forms" (Titmuss 1962: 187). As Lowe (1999: 4) writes, "the secret history of the British post-war welfare state is the decreasing progressiveness of the tax system."

The rediscovery of poverty was a function, at least in part, of its redefinition as relative. Townsend (1975: 268) developed "a distinct conceptual approach based on relative deprivation," arguing that "any rational definition of poverty must be relative." People are in poverty, Townsend (1975: 270) writes, "when they lack or fall seriously short of the resources required to share in the customs and style of life approved and commonly available in society."

This was important, Townsend (1975: 269) argues, because when the minimum needs, or subsistence approach, is used to define poverty, the result is the claim that only a small minority of the population is poor, which in turn leads to "selective, ameliorative and isolated rather than universal and reconstructional policies to relieve poverty." Further, because poverty was widely thought to have been eradicated post-1951, it was therefore no longer seen as a class issue, as it was in the 1930s and 1940s. Rather, poverty was increasingly seen as a residual issue, affecting only isolated "pockets" of people—the elderly, the sick and large families, for example. What necessarily followed from such an interpretation was isolated, narrowly targeted and ameliorative policies that are simply not capable of responding adequately to poverty.

Further, social assistance rates—consistent with the long-held principle of "less eligibility"—were so low that they kept people in poverty. Means-tested supplementary benefits, originally intended as "a last resort, a safety net to catch the few not covered by national insurance," had instead become "the mainstay of the social security system" (MacGregor 1981: 30). As Abel-Smith (quoted in Jones and Lowe 2002: 66) observed in 1968, "Poor families are already caged in a veritable labyrinth of means tests." The means test process had become so complicated that "approximately 10,000 pages of new or amended rules were added in 1975 alone. The only way in which staff could reduce their work-load to manageable proportions (as suggested in Section 3.1.3) was actively to discourage people from making claims" (Lowe 2005: 160; see also Donnison 1982).

By the late 1970s, three million people were receiving and five million were reliant upon means-tested supplementary benefits, and there were some fifteen thousand "unique local authority means tests" (Field 1982: 99). "Wherever you looked, there were no common principles or practices to protect poor people who were the bewildered victims" of this system that had taken on a form and character never intended by its founders (Donnison 1982: 42). The supplementary benefits system, originally intended to respond to the needs of those few not qualifying for national insurance benefits, produced "poor take-up of benefits, enormous variations in practice from place to place, and a growing sense of injustice and hostility afflicting claimants, staff and the public at large" (Donnison 1982: 43). This represented a dramatic turning away from the collectivist and universalist approach of the Attlee governments and a return to the hated means tests and Poor Law indignities of the 1930s. Along with the erosion of the British economy, this undermined support for the welfare state.

In the late 1950s and early 1960s, an internal government review of the adequacy of social assistance benefit levels was conducted. The review was at least in part the result of work being done by those—Richard Titmuss in particular—who had identified and were critical of the re-emergence of poverty. There was a wide-ranging and sophisticated discussion within government at the time regarding the adequacy of existing social assistance benefit levels. There appears to have been an acceptance within the civil service that social assistance levels were set at a level too low to meet the needs of the poor.

However, rather than raise benefit levels, Harold Wilson's Labour government acted timidly. For example, the response to the family poverty campaign waged in large part by the Child Poverty Action Group starting in 1965 "was clearly a disappointment to everyone ... over half the children involved were still below the Supplementary Benefits level the day after the increases came into effect" (Banting 1979: 106). This was borne out by a 1976 Labour government memo explaining that "families with children were now getting substantially less support than the Tories provided in 1970, 1971 and 1972, and less than the Labour Government provided in the late 1960s" (Field 1982: 154–55).

Similarly, major concerns about poor housing and especially about predatory landlords led to the 1965 *Rent Act*. But Banting (1979: 65) described the *Rent Act* as "simply a holding operation in a decaying sector of the housing market. It strengthened the legal protections available to poor tenants, but it did not improve the housing in which they lived. It built no new houses; it redistributed no houses."

Rather than build upon the gains of the 1945–1951 Labour governments, the Labour governments of the 1960s and 1970s allowed the welfare state to atrophy. Relatively minor reforms were introduced by the 1964–1970 Labour governments. These were added to by the 1974–1979 Labour governments, which introduced the 1975 *Sex Discrimination Act* while making domestic violence a legal offence for the first time and launching the State Earnings-Related Pension Scheme in 1978, a genuinely progressive measure. The circumstances of lone parents, mostly mothers, and their children were improved with a universal, non-contributory child benefit and with the 1977 *Housing (Homeless Persons) Act*, which gave them access to council housing from which they had previously been largely excluded. But these reforms were, in their totality, relatively minor. As a result, conditions for the poor were bleak: "Poor housing, rent arrears, fuel shortages, second hand clothing, a limited diet and constant financial anxiety—this was the real meaning of the Welfare State for these families" (Banting 1979: 67).

Worse, the recipients of welfare benefits were blamed and attacked. An example is the July 1968 introduction of the "four-week rule," intended to make it harder for those who were unemployed to qualify for supplementary benefits—they were withdrawn from those not finding work within four weeks. The reason was the widely held view that young people were abusing the system. Repeated studies had shown low levels of abuse—far lower than abuse of the tax system by higher-income individuals (Meacher 1974). Nevertheless, with unemployment rising especially since 1966, the media publicized isolated cases of abuse, and the centuries-old hatred of the unemployed re-emerged.

In the late 1960s, they were labelled "scroungers" (Meacher 1974: 40). The media condemned "Britain's army of dole queue swindlers…. A plague was diagnosed, the symptom was the scrounger, the cause was the state's slush fund and the victim was the people" (Campbell 1984: 20–21). All of this is a product of the centuries-old and "deep-seated hostility toward the unemployed," which had led Beveridge to describe unemployment as "the misery that generates hate" (quoted in Deacon 1981: 84).

There emerged in 1976–1977 a "scroungerphobia" (Deacon 1978), promoted by a hostile media. Countless newspaper stories and vicious headlines—"Get the Scroungers!" was the *Daily Express* headline on July 15, 1976 (McArthur and Reeves 2019: 1007)—fuelled the belief that the central poverty problem of the late 1970s was abuse by "scroungers" who were able to work but chose to abuse the system. Golding and Middleton (1982: 178) found that the media response to growing levels of poverty was "hostility to welfare claimants." Based on an empirical analysis of five British newspapers between 1896 and 2000, McArthur and Reeves (2019: 1022) identify a pattern: "as unemployment increases so does newspaper stigmatization of the poor."

That poverty had re-emerged in the post-1950 period was clear. Abel-Smith and Townsend (1965: 57) analyzed two sets of data, from 1953–1954 and 1960, to identify changes in the numbers of those at or near the national assistance rates for each year—rates that were sufficiently low that they did not make possible a satisfactory standard of living. The proportion almost doubled, from 7.8 percent of persons in the UK—about four million people—in 1953–1954 to 14.2 percent—almost 7.5 million people—in 1960. Then in the late 1960s, Townsend (1979: 895) found that somewhere between 6 and 9 percent were in poverty, and 22 to 28 percent were "on the margins of poverty." He observes, "these are strikingly, depressingly, similar proportions to those found by Booth, Rowntree and Bowley in the generation before 1914" (Thane 1982: 288). A later study (Layard et al. 1978: 13) found that in 1975, 26 percent of the population was in, or on the margins of, poverty.

These numbers were the subject of considerable debate, which turned in large part on how poverty was defined. However, what was irrefutable was that a considerable minority of the British population remained poor. The elderly were especially likely to face poverty, but women and large families, as had been the case for centuries, were also disproportionately among the poor. Women continued to be discriminated against in the labour market. Toynbee (2003: 231) describes the written agreement between auto manufacturer Vauxhall and the unions representing workers there, which included that "women will not be engaged if suitable men are available" and "women will only be employed on jobs broadly specified and agreed," which meant that women were blocked from the highly paid jobs and confined to those at the lowest pay levels.

A Drab Damp Flat on a Dump Estate

When Labour regained office in 1964, some three million families were still living in "slums" or near slums in "grossly overcrowded conditions" (Crouch and Wolf 1972: 27). Some 2.5 million households in the 1960s still had no running water and three million—just less than one in four households—had no indoor plumbing (Townsend 1973: 19). The Milner-Holland Report (Great Britain 1965: 21) found that in London alone in 1960, just under one-half of all rental units had been built prior to 1918. "Large numbers of people" in London were "living in conditions which are more akin to those prevailing in the middle of the nineteenth century." By 1964, 1,500 families—about 7,000 people—were homeless in London, and 180,000 were on council wait lists. The rate at which those lists were being cleared was such that it would have taken sixteen years for all to be housed (Great Britain 1965: 57, 101, 129). All of this is depicted in Ken Loach's powerful and emotional film *Cathy Come Home*, a 1966 BBC-TV production that features a working-class family struggling to find housing, coping with overcrowded and decrepit housing, and eventually falling into homelessness and losing their children as a consequence.

In the private rental market, predatory landlords were buying large numbers of older, undervalued rental properties, and in the wake of the 1957 *Rent Act*, which lifted rent controls on all properties when tenants left, were pushing out sitting tenants in order to be legally entitled to raise the rent and drive up profits. Banting (1979: 18) found that when the 1957 *Rent Act* phased out rent controls, "high rents, homelessness, eviction and exploitation were the consequences." The Milner-Holland Report (Great Britain 1965: 229) examined "the extent of abuses by landlords," concluding that while "they affect only a small proportion of tenants," they were "too numerous to be dismissed as isolated instances" and "constitute a serious evil which should be stamped out." The "intense housing shortage" led to the doubling of rents in unfurnished accommodation between 1957 and 1963 and trebling of rents in cases where occupancy had changed—forcibly or otherwise (Davis 2001: 71).

Townsend's (1973) descriptions of low-income neighbourhoods in the 1960s make clear the continued existence of much depressing, complex poverty. Similar conditions were identified by Coates and Silburn (1970: 73) in their detailed examination of an inner-city neighbourhood, St. Ann's, in Nottingham, where 91 percent of households did not have an indoor lavatory and 85 percent had no bathroom. They compared their findings to those of Abel-Smith and Townsend (1965). "Where [Abel-Smith and Townsend] found 17.9 percent of households at or near the poverty line, we found over 37 percent; where they found 14.2 percent of the population to be poor, we found nearly 40 percent" (Coates and Silburn 1970: 55).

The Child Poverty Action Group campaigned against the 1964–1970 Labour government with the slogan "the poor got poorer under Labour" (Field 1982: 4). Despite Prime Minister Wilson's claim that he and the Party had a "burning desire" to abolish poverty, and despite the relatively minor reforms discussed above, Field (1982: 24) argued that "right to the end of the Government's life, the Wilson Administrations would fail even to develop an effective strategy against poverty, let alone begin to implement one."

Many urban centres were devastated. In certain parts of Liverpool, for example, "it is an understatement to speak of massive unemployment: unemployment has become as normal as work" (Seabrook 1981: 19). So had deplorable housing:

> Housing standards are bad and accommodation is overcrowded; there are few amenities; the environment is inhospitable; 15 percent of the land is actually vacant or derelict; apartment blocks ... have been vandalized beyond repair, boarded up or torn down—all adding up to the atmosphere of decay. Other indicators of malaise are just as bad: poor health, low educational achievement, low incomes, high crime rates, many problem families and, of course, massive unemployment. (Ridley 1981: 21–22)

This was a product, in large part, of the geographic relocation of the cotton textile industry, which along with the slave trade had been the basis of Liverpool's economy. By the late 1960s, Britain accounted for only 2.8 percent of the world's cotton exports, where once it had been the world's leading exporter. While 600,000 British workers had once worked in British cotton mills, now there were only thirty thousand (Beckert 2015: 428). Yet right-wing newspaper *The Spectator* claimed, "Unemployment in Liverpool, like famine in Africa, is almost entirely caused by human folly and wickedness" (quoted in Dorey 2011: 141).

From 1955 to 1975, massive "slum" clearance programs were undertaken: "no other country anywhere has demolished and rebuilt so much slum housing" (Donnison and Ungerson 1982: 63). But while slums kept on being cleared in the 1960s, "waiting lists are not cleared ... and the slum clearance goes on forever" (Samuel et al. 1962: 65). The result was that "year by year we are pulling down the older parts of our cities with a savage and undiscriminating abandon which will not earn the gratitude of posterity" (Briggs 1990: 18).

Slum clearance was largely a top-down exercise, with virtually no input from those being re-housed. Canon Norman Power wrote in 1965, referring to "slum" clearance in Birmingham—"site of arguably the most rapid and fundamental change anywhere in urban Britain" (Kynaston 2014: 76):

> In all this redevelopment, during which I saw a living community torn to pieces by the bulldozers and scattered to the four corners of the city, there was no consultation with the people most affected and concerned. Neither was any opinion sought from local teachers, social workers, organization-leaders or clergy. (Quoted in Kynaston 2013: 84)

Most of the displaced poor were moved into high-rise public housing complexes—which came to be seen by many as "slums in the sky" (Addison 2010: 166). This process was driven in large part by architects inspired, as was the case in the US, by Le Corbusier and by developers who made vast fortunes. This kind of building had boomed from 1955 to the1970s—"by the end of the 1970s, 4500 tower blocks had been built in Britain" (Hanley 2007: 114)—but the quality of construction suffered from the "drastic reductions in the space standards and amenity of public housing" put in place by Conservative governments (Dunleavy 1981: 35). Contrary to the principles and practice of Aneurin Bevan, the 300,000-plus new homes per year built by the Macmillan governments in the mid-1950s were constructed cheaply and with reduced quality standards and size (Donnison and Ungerson 1982: 148). What characterized the Conservatives' housing strategy was

> its small size and quality-skimping construction—internal walls made of plasterboard rather than brick, smaller and fewer windows, yards rather than gardens—[which] showed that Macmillan's policy was dangerously preoccupied with short-term results at the expense of the long term health of both the housing stock and, ultimately, society as a whole. (Hanley 2007: 90)

Rather than see council housing as serving a cross-section of society, including the families of skilled workers, the Conservatives saw it, and legislated that it be, "housing for the poor," or "housing of last resort—a safety net for the poorest or most vulnerable" (Boughton 2018: 107; 143–44). Labour introduced legislation in 1977 confirming that councils were to give priority to the most vulnerable. However well intentioned, it was this "residualization," as much as the reduced construction standards, that led to the denigration and stigmatization of council housing.

In their 1953 White Paper, *Housing: The Next Step*, the Conservative government committed to allowing the housing market to run with minimal intervention from the state and to promoting the private market. The result was that "in many ways the housing sector had turned back to the model of the 1930s" (Jones 1991: 41). The houses built "were cheap, and nasty, and we now have a housing crisis which will endure beyond this century. Already the mass housing programs of the fifties and sixties are the new slums having to be rebuilt or torn down" (Campbell 1984: 33).

Many were torn down, "with the demolition of tower blocks in London and Merseyside appearing as slow-motion spectaculars on television, hundreds of homes up for less than a lifetime now squandered" (Campbell 1984: 41). By the end of the 1970s, some high-rise complexes had become unlettable and were demolished a mere twenty years after construction. In Manchester, massive "slum" clearance policies had created such a demand for new housing that the local council was pressured to build high-rise towers, which quickly deteriorated. "Tenants who moved into the new developments soon began to realize that their new modern homes were fraught with social and structural problems" (Shapely et al. 2004: 427). In 1968, a twenty-two-storey block called Ronan Point, located in London, partially collapsed. Its building had been plagued with problems, from lack of skilled workers to shoddy materials (Hanley 2007: 107–11). An explosion caused by a gas leak in the kitchen of one of the flats "blew out the external walls of the living room and bedroom, and this structural failure developed progressively so that the whole of the south-east corner of the building collapsed from the top down to the level of the podium." Four residents were killed and seventeen injured (Cooney 1974: 169). The Hulme development in Manchester was touted as the modernist centerpiece of this brave new world of council housing. However, "Hulme became a national symbol of the horror of 1960s housing developments. Only four years after its completion, residents were demanding to be rehoused" (Shapely et al. 2004: 427). In Sheffield it was reported, shortly after the construction of a massive, high-rise housing project, that "Life in Sheffield's new multistorey Park Hill flats is becoming a nightmare for many tenants" (quoted in Kynaston 2014: 30). The nightmare worsened with the June 2017 Grenfell Tower fire that killed at least seventy-one tenants in London. The fire was attributed to poor-quality cladding; a higher quality fire-resistant cladding had been ruled out because of cost (Shilliam 2018: 165–72). Poor construction and maintenance, together with the fact that such developments have become the "housing of last resort" (Boughton 2018: 6) for the poorest of the poor, created conditions comparable to the massive housing problems especially in the US but also, to a somewhat lesser extent, in Canada (Venkatesh 2000; Silver 2011).

All of this, not surprisingly, eroded support for such projects. Dunleavy (1981: 354) argues that the problems with high-rise housing contributed to the "de-legitimization of public housing."

Yet council housing is not necessarily poor housing. On the contrary, council housing has been a crucial part of the century-long push in Britain in the direction of egalitarianism. In the 1930s, Labour governments in London built what an American critic described as "the finest low-cost housing in the world" (Hatherley 2020: 91). Despite all the problems with housing estates, especially since 1979, "it is undoubtedly the case that estates are overwhelmingly now decent places to live" (Boughton 2018: 4). Romyn (2016) shows that at the vast Heygate complex in South London, tenants had a high level of satisfaction, in stark contrast "to the reductive, all-encompassing idea that social housing estates are simply 'problem places,' home to 'problem people'" (Romyn 2016: 199). When the Heygate was demolished to make way for an urban regeneration scheme, residents "were treated as an afterthought. The 1998 poll where 80 percent of the tenants wanted to remain on the estate, and a subsequent 1999 MORI survey in which 29 percent of residents were dissatisfied with the Heygate, were ignored" (Romyn 2016: 215; Boughton 2018).

All of this, Romyn (2016: 221) argues, was part of the deliberately negative portrayal of social housing—its reduction to "negative stereotypes and caricatures"—that served to delegitimize the public provision of essential goods.

By 1976, there were approximately "2.6 million houses—15.6 percent of the total in England—which needed rehabilitation," and 3.6 percent of the total housing stock was "unfit for human habitation" (Donnison and Ungerson 1982: 187–88). Importantly, however, these "are not principally housing problems at all. Bad housing conditions are a product of poverty" (Donnison and Ungerson 1982: 235). Poverty and poor housing had been causally connected for centuries.

Coates and Silburn (1970: 50) emphasized the "complex" character of this inner-city poverty and the way it becomes internalized by those who are poor. "In nearly every interview we undertook, we detected a basic sense of hopelessness, or powerlessness." Writing about Glasgow, McGarvey (2018: 61–62) observes that when you grow up in such communities, "the biggest impact is on your emotional life, specifically emotional stress, which plays a significant role in shaping how people think, feel and behave … stress is all-consuming; it's the soup everyone is swimming in all the time. Stress is the lens through which all life is viewed." In this kind of environment, "the anger and frustration tend to turn inwards. People turn on each other, or even on themselves. Violence, family breakdown, mental illness are part of the price people pay" (Seabrook 1981: 13). As Friend and Metcalf (1981: 122) describe it: "The cyclone of social change that has enveloped the old working class areas has ripped its way through the old family structures and flung out atomized individuals." Many, especially lone mothers, have recourse to "a drab damp flat on a dump estate, the remorseless struggle to survive on social security, the enforced isolation when there's no one to babysit, the weight of sole responsibility for the kids, the doctor's tranquillizers."

This deterioration had taken place in the context of the long process of deindustrialization, "as Britain sinks into the low-wage, de-industrialized pit of Europe" (Campbell 1984: 169). In the older industrial regions, "massive redundancies in factory after factory became an almost monthly event" (Friend and Metcalf 1981: 68) as capitalists relocated factories to low-wage jurisdictions and replaced labour with technology to maximize profits. A return to the mass unemployment of the 1930s was the result, producing idleness, "depression, self-hatred and pessimism" (Campbell 1984: 209).

By the late 1970s, the point had been reached that "mild redistributive social policies have become less effective and are thoroughly inadequate" (MacGregor 1981: 79). Coates and Silburn (1970: 217) state what should have been obvious: "Clearly what is needed is a systematic, simultaneous and integrated assault upon all these areas of deprivation."

This did not happen. The economy was in freefall. Labour struggled to cope with what was in fact a crisis of capitalism. Poverty was not a priority—for the Labour Party, for unions or for the electorate. A Conservative MP "claimed that ordinary people were sick and tired of seeing their taxes squandered on people who would not know what a day's work looked like if it stared them in the face" (quoted in MacGregor 1981: 157). Prime Minister James Callaghan agreed:

> He sensed the current of public opinion turning against social spending and in favour of tax cuts, and he argued that middle-income groups, including skilled manual workers, were unwilling to sacrifice their standard of living so that social security could be improved. (Banting 1979: 97)

The poor had been abandoned.

At the same time, the beleaguered welfare state faced massive opposition. This assault was led "by insurance companies, banks, investment and hire purchase firms, the *British Medical Journal,* the Institute of Chartered Accountants, the British Employers' Federation, the Association of British Chambers of Commerce, the Institute of Directors, actuaries, judges and other professional men" (Titmuss 1960: 17).

Labour's response was tepid. "The story of post-war welfare administration is one of repeated retreat from the aims of the Beveridge Report." The elimination of poverty was not at all a priority. "A careful reading of [Labour] Party conference reports reveals only rare discussions of poverty" (Golding and Middleton 1982: 206, 216). Regarding poverty and social justice more broadly, they were out of ideas. More toxic and harshly punitive ideas would soon fill that gap.

The postwar boom—brief though it had been in Britain—was well and truly over, in Britain perhaps even more than other capitalist states. The capitalist economy was in crisis; the commitment to full employment had been abandoned; stagflation was a new and unprecedented reality; public expenditure cuts were the response. Labour governments had become the vessels through which conventional, IMF-inspired programs were delivered, but these produced no solutions. Many blamed the welfare state and especially the poor, who were its intended beneficiaries. The anger long directed at the "non-respectable" poor—the vagrants and vagabonds, the scoundrels and shirkers, the rogues and sturdy beggars, the residuum and now the scroungers—had once again pushed through to the surface. The poor were to blame.

Feckless Mothers and Feeble-Minded Children

Researchers such as Titmuss, Townsend, and Coates and Silburn had offered structural explanations—economic decline, mass unemployment, slum clearance and inadequate housing, the erosion of universalism and the return of narrow, targeted, means-tested benefits, for example—for the dramatic re-emergence of poverty in the 1960s and 1970s. Such analyses stood in stark contrast to the enduring and centuries-long focus on poverty as caused by the moral failings and "degenerate" behaviour of those who are poor. As Mann (1994: 86) observed, "In Britain each generation seems to 'discover,' like some lost tribe, the hopeless and the dangerous class."

For example, from its formation in 1907 and reinforced by the arguments advanced by the 1929 Wood Report on mental deficiency, the Eugenics Society had promoted a pathological interpretation of poverty, rooted in the idea of "feeble-mindedness" and "mental defectives" as the cause of poverty (Macnicol 1987: 300). Similar eugenics-based arguments would re-emerge in the 1930s in the face of mass unemployment. At least some eugenicists argued then that "parents on public assistance should be compulsorily sterilized" (quoted in Macnicol 1980: 82). Other eugenicists argued that "a large proportion of the slum populations were 'morons,'" the unemployed "consist very largely of hereditary defective individuals" (quoted in Searle 1979: 161–62), and that "society was becoming increasingly burdened with an ever-expanding 'social problem group' of unemployables, lunatics, criminals caused by the growth of 'bad stock'" (Macnicol 1980: 79). As Macnicol (1989: 149) argues, "the explicit policy outcomes of eugenics were few," and so the importance of the movement should not be exaggerated. Nevertheless, the eugenics movement's interpretation of the causes of poverty found expression in the 1930s in the widely held idea of the "social problem group" (Welshman 1996: 449), an ill-defined concept promoted by eugenicists (Macnicol 1987). This concept would re-emerge in the 1940s and 1950s as the "problem family," still heavily influenced by eugenics thinking and social pathology (Starkey 1998: 423), rooted in the centuries-old belief that the moral and behavioural failings of the poor were the cause of their poverty. These concepts and this way of thinking would ultimately meld with the notion of the "underclass" and other related "blame-the-victim" understandings of poverty.

Starkey argues that the blame was focused especially on mothers in so-called problem families. They were "feckless mothers," whose homes were chaotic and whose children were "always ragged and dirty" (Starkey 2000: 542–44). In such homes children were "dull and feeble-minded … [and] clothing is dirty and torn," while the home was characterized by lack of cleanliness and "nauseating odours" (quoted in Starkey 1998: 430–31). Yet, as Macnicol (1999: 81, 90, emphasis in original) argued, "most of the definitions of 'problem families' were essentially *descriptions* of household squalor, piled high one on top of the other." Such interpretations of poverty never mentioned the lack of running water and indoor plumbing that was still such a common feature of postwar British housing.

This interpretation bears a striking similarity to that of Daniel Moynihan (1965), who argued that in the US, Black mothers' lack of parenting skills resulted in "the deterioration of the Negro family," as evidenced by its matriarchal structure. The resultant "tangle of pathology" in female-led African-American families was a root cause of poverty. There soon followed the culture of poverty and underclass debates largely rooted in a blame-the-victim mode of explanation (O'Connor 2001; Katz 2013). Interpretations such as these made their way to Britain as "ideas drifting casually across the Atlantic, soggy on arrival, and of dubious utility" (quoted in Welshman 2013: 2). Indeed, Robert Walker (1999: 680) describes this as the "Americanization of British welfare," and Kiernan and her colleagues (1998: 15), writing about the 1980s, say that "the transfer of policy ideas from the USA to Britain about all aspects of social provision became striking."

The end of poverty that had been celebrated in the early 1950s, just like Crosland's (1956) taming of capitalism, proved premature. Poverty persisted, and it was the fault of the poor themselves—an interpretation now reinforced by its popularity in America.

Racism: Legacy of an Imperial Past

Racism complicated the resurgence of poverty. The problem was not new. During the Second World War, the relatively limited number of Black servicemen had often been badly treated. In the immediate postwar period, when there were only some twenty thousand to thirty thousand non-whites in Britain, there was racism, including at the workplace (Kynaston 2008: 271, 518). And the British colonial project included, as a defining characteristic, the racist treatment of Africans and Asians.

In the late 1940s and 1950s, Black and Asian workers were recruited from the colonies—"those vast and cheap resources of labour" (Sivanandan 1982: 102)—to solve Britain's postwar labour shortage. Unemployment was exceptionally low and some industries were experiencing severe labour shortages. In the NHS, for example, "the manpower shortage was catastrophic." A factory manager said in 1954 that "any worker could leave the works and get a job literally within three or four minutes simply by going to the factory next door." This manager did not want to hire Black workers, "but eventually we succumbed ... there was no-one else" (Wills 2017: 89, 196).

Black and Asian workers disproportionately occupied "positions of structured subordination" (Hall et al. 1978: 346). In the workplace, "there was a hierarchy of labour, and it was coloured" (Wills 2017: 196). This was readily apparent in the case of Black women employed by the NHS, where "patients saw it as fitting that we should be doing Britain's dirty work and often treated us with contempt" (Bryan et al. 1985: 43).

Many West Indian parents complained that their children were disproportionately relegated to "ESN" (educationally subnormal) schools and classrooms (Sivanandan 1982: 110; Carby 1982). White landlords and homeowners were generally reluctant to rent or sell to West Indians. A controlled test "in which the [real estate] agents were approached with identical requests by a West Indian, a Hungarian, and an Englishman" confirmed this (Peach 1965: 87). The 1965 Milner-Holland Report on housing in London found "a marked degree of reluctance among private landlords to let to coloured tenants and, where these lettings occur, the rents are in general higher" (Great Britain 1965: 189). Glass (quoted in Davis 2001: 78) labelled this the "foreigners' levy." Building societies created "blue zones" to exclude immigrants from access to mortgages (Jacobs 1985: 14).

As a result, Black and Asian families were pushed into inner city slums, in a process similar to that in US cities (Hirsch 1983). Overcrowding—that long-familiar characteristic of poor peoples' housing—was endemic. "In one Paddington ward, 497 households were crammed into 26 dwellings." Wait lists for council housing were decades long. Those Black applicants finally able to secure council housing were typically "confined to the worst, inner city 'problem' estates" (Jacobs 1985: 15). Typically, "systematic racial differences exist in the allocation of council housing: Black people usually have to wait longer for council housing and when rehoused tend to be given lower quality accommodation" (CRE 1984: 9).

In London and the Midlands especially, immigrants lived in overcrowded inner-city areas from which many white working-class families had fled, creating a spatially concentrated and racialized layer of the poor whose living conditions reinforced racist views (Hansen 2000: 81). The weakening of the British economy in the 1960s and 1970s, and the resulting competition for jobs, then fuelled that racism.

Black and Asian workers resisted their "structured subordination" by engaging in industrial militancy in the face of racist treatment at the workplace. Often, they were "either unsupported or opposed by the trade union to which they belonged" (Sivanandan 1982: 22). A particularly egregious example was the 1974 Imperial Typewriter strike in Leicester. More than two-thirds of the 1,500 workers were Asian, many of them women. The strike was caused by "the usual practices of racial discrimination and exploitation … the white workers, management and unions worked hand in glove and were backed up by the violent presence of the National Front at the factory gates" (Sivanandan 1982: 37). A manager at a non-union factory said, "whenever I have to put off staff I sack the coloured ones first. There would be a riot if I did anything else" (Wills 2017: 196–97).

Part of the challenge, Novak (1988: 147) argued, was that "social democracy was very much the politics of a white male working class." For the traditional white working class there was loss—not only of jobs, but the sense that a way of life was being lost (Blackwell and Seabrook 1985: 43).

In London's East End, for example, members of the white working class saw their neighbourhoods and "their" welfare state undergoing dramatic change—in favour of newcomers. For example, council housing had traditionally been allocated based on people's connections in tightly knit communities, so that over time and with good behaviour one could expect to earn better housing. Then the rules changed, so that the allocation of housing was based on need, and newcomers were seen by the state to have the greatest need. Many interpreted this as being unfair. Newcomers, whom they saw as having contributed nothing to the building of the welfare state, were now at the head of the queue to derive its benefits (Dench et al. 2008). To many in such white working-class communities, the welfare state had become "a complex, centralized and bureaucratic system run by middle class do-gooders who gave generously to those who put nothing into the pot while making ordinary working people who did contribute feel like recipients of charity when drawing their entitlements" (Dench et al. 2006: 208).

All of this was taking place in the context of the erosion of their livelihoods.

> After 1970, the secure post-war world of the white East End working class suddenly began to crumble around them, as they saw their docking, factory and warehouse jobs disappear in the great de-industrialization of the 1970s and 1980s, only to be replaced with a new economy for which they were not prepared. (Dench et al. 2006: 121)

These interconnected changes resulted in white youth clashing with Black and Asian youth. The first major confrontation was at Notting Hill and in other parts of London in August and September 1958, when "white youth went on self-described 'n— hunts,' beating West Indians in the streets and attacking frightened individuals who had locked themselves in their homes" (Hansen 2000: 81). As Wills (2017: 160) put it, "the riots were by white people against black, and no amount of fudging could disguise that fact." The intensity of racial feeling was exemplified in 1964, when a Conservative Party candidate in Smethwick was elected on the slogan "if you want a n— for a neighbour, vote Liberal or Labour" (Hansen 2000: 132).

Campbell (1984: 210) argued that the racism of young unemployed white men "seemed less a theory of Blacks' inferiority, more a feeling of their own," as they struggled with the frustrations of unemployment. Stuart Hall (quoted in Wills 2017: 166) called these white youth "the alienated generation." The poor educational and employment opportunities facing many working-class youth had them leaving school, in many cases by age thirteen. The National Front and other right-wing organizations worked with these white youth, "and their youth-oriented publications reveal an impressive ability to relate to and express the needs of powerless White boys on their own front lines in the alleys of 'slum city'" (Gilroy and Lawrence 1988: 151).

For Black youth it was worse: "they are not the unemployed, but the never employed … the youth know, viscerally, that there will be no work for them, ever, no call for their labour" (Sivanandan 1982: 49). By 1978–1979, unemployment among Black youth in major urban centres had reached "crisis proportions" (Solomos 1988: 173).

Packed in urban slums with bad housing and no jobs—"ghettoized and locked into the decaying areas of the inner city" (Sivanandan 1982: 103)—Black youth resisted. The National Front, formed in 1967 by a merger of several existing racist groups, fuelled the conflict. Their fierce racism was typified by the comment of their leader following the death of eighteen-year-old Gurdip Singh Chaggar. In 1976 he was "set upon by a gang of white youths and stabbed to death." The NF leader responded with: "one down, one million to go" (Sivanandan 1982: 39). Chagger's death crystallized for Black youth that "Black was their political colour—the colour of the oppressed, and that it reflected the experience and structural position of Black people in Britain" (Mukherjee 1988: 223). Conflict accelerated dramatically from the mid-1960s and throughout the 1970s, as the British economy continued its decline.

The result was the emergence of a crisis of public order, a crisis of governance, a "moral panic" (Hall et al. 1978: 29). Fear of Black "ghetto" youth was further fuelled by the urban riots in the US in the mid-1960s and by the emergence in Britain at that time of a Black Power movement and a variety of politically radical, left-wing Black movements (Wills 2017: 335). The fear was tapped into, and accentuated, by the 1968 "Rivers of Blood" speech by Conservative MP Enoch Powell, which contributed to the emergence of a "race problem" narrative—i.e., the argument that the cause of the problems was the presence in Britain of those of a different "race" (Solomos 2018: 3). In his speech, made just over two weeks after the April 4, 1968, assassination of Martin Luther King Jr., Powell said that continued immigration would create "a total transformation to which there is no parallel in a thousand years of British history." He called not only for the cessation of immigration but also for repatriation (Solomos 2018: 3), offering himself as a future Minister of Repatriation (Nairn 1977: 278). In April and May, in response to his Rivers of Blood speech, Powell received over 100,000 letters, "mostly saying thank you" (Wills 2017: 329). Four separate public opinion polls recorded levels of support for Powell ranging from 67 to 82 percent (Addison 2010: 253). When Margaret Thatcher expressed the fear a decade later, in 1978, that "this country might be rather swamped with people of a different culture," she too received "a deluge of letters in support." Her comments were endorsed by 58 percent of Labour supporters, 71 percent of Liberals and 84 percent of Conservatives (Schofield 2012: 106–7). "England's coloured population" had "become a scapegoat for capitalism's ills" (Nairn 1977: 257).

Many Black youth resisted by "making shift"—"surviving by alternative means, by a process of hustling activities such as gambling, undeclared part-time work, ganja selling, shoplifting, street crime, housebreaking and distributing stolen goods" (Friend and Metcalf 1981: 156).

The state responded aggressively. The chief constable of Greater Manchester said that "hooligans" should "be placed in penal work camps where through hard labour and unrelenting discipline they should be made to sweat as they have never sweated before" (quoted in Friend and Metcalf 1981: 162). This was the centuries-old "punish the poor" approach, used especially aggressively since the 1960s in the US (Alexander 2010; Wacquant 2009). Blacks were blamed and punished.

Immigration laws reflected both changing economic needs and these broadly held public attitudes. The 1948 *Nationality Act* had opened Britain's doors to Commonwealth citizens in response to Britain's labour shortage by affirming that colonial citizens had the right to enter the UK. "Some 500,000 primary migrants—migrants without families in the UK—entered the country" (Hansen 2000: 19). The *Commonwealth Immigrants Act* of 1962 slammed the door shut, creating "one of the strictest migration policies in the western world" (Hansen 2000: 20). Commonwealth citizens now needed work vouchers to work in the UK. The purpose of the *Act* "was to restrict, not merely to regulate, the movement of Commonwealth immigrants and particularly that from predominantly coloured countries" (Peach 1968: 51). Gallup polls conducted in 1961 and 1965 found that 76 percent and 87 percent of those polled approved of these restrictions on immigration (Peach 1968: 52). "At each successive phase of the racial storm in the 1960s, more strict immigration controls were imposed" (Nairn 1977: 274). Immigrants were blamed for the re-emergence of poverty and a host of other problems. "Leaching off the welfare state, clogging up the NHS, putting pressure on primary school places, exacerbating the housing shortage, lowering wages—despite little evidence of these abuses, and often considerable evidence to the contrary, the popular image of the immigrant was a negative one" (Wills 2017: 66).

Racist ideas about immigration had become what Smith (1994: 17) calls a "symbolic nodal point," around which Thatcher and her supporters would build a populist, right-wing campaign. The Conservatives connected with many of the real grievances experienced in Britain—grievances not dealt with adequately by either of the political parties who supported the postwar consensus. Rex (1973: 132) points out that "for this hell's brew of problems the welfare state has little in the way of answers, for this is not the set of problems with which the welfare state is designed to deal." Enoch Powell, especially with his 1968 Rivers of Blood speech, had connected these general dissatisfactions to race. "Race was re-coded through the 1970s and 1980s, concealed within euphemisms and tensions around crime waves, law and order, inner-city unrest," the loss of empire and related matters (Smith 1994: 9). In his 1968 speech, Powell located himself as the voice of "a quiet ordinary working man" and asserted that he spoke for "the people." In doing so, he showed that "a radical right-wing program would be profoundly popular with large numbers of British voters" (Smith 1994: 53, 169).

Thatcher would build on this. She constructed herself as the voice of ordinary working families who felt their needs were not being heard. She appealed to what many saw as a growing permissiveness, especially around immigration, excessive trade union power, racially defined riots and a host of related matters.

"Race" was a key thread knitting these issues together and made possible Thatcher's "authoritarian populism." This became fully evident, it can be argued, with Powell's Rivers of Blood speech. As Gamble (1988: 71) has said, "Powell's speech was of decisive importance in launching a new politics of the nation, and in turn demonstrating the possibilities of a populist assault upon some of the central aspects of postwar social democracy." Thatcherism represented a decisive turning point in postwar Britain—a right-wing populist approach to governance that would have, and continues to have, a dramatic impact on the growth of poverty and inequality.

Chapter 9

Thatcherism

An Explosion of Poverty and Inequality

The Conservative Party led by Margaret Thatcher was elected May 4, 1979, in response to what was clearly a crisis of capitalism and Labourism. The Labour Party, like social democratic parties everywhere (Piketty 2020), was out of ideas, even while presiding over an economy in chaos and a culture seen by many to be in a state of decay and even anarchy. A space was open for a new approach to governance and to management of the economy. Thatcher and her governments—she was re-elected, again with large majorities, in 1983 and 1987 before being forced out of office in 1990—sought to deliver that new approach. Their first objective was to restore the conditions for capital accumulation. She was committed to "reversing Britain's economic decline, for without an end to the decline there was no hope of success for our other objectives" (Thatcher 1993: 15). Among the other objectives was to shift the country's culture to "deconstruct the social democratic hegemonic framework," the "consensus of the post-war period" and to construct a new "common sense," a new "hegemonic project" (Jessop et al. 1988: 73). The result would be deep and deliberate damage to the already atrophying welfare state.

I will refer to Thatcher more than might be thought appropriate. This is in part because I believe that the importance of agency in historical change is often underestimated. Thatcher was a dominant political figure in the 1980s. She was a relentless and fearless exponent of right-wing ideas. As Panitch and Leys (2020: 48) put it, "It is a mistake to put too much emphasis on the role of any one individual; but it is also a mistake to deny it when an individual's significance is exceptional." Thatcher's significance was exceptional.

As Thatcher told *The Times* in January 1984, she wanted her government to be remembered as the one which decisively broke with the debilitating consensus of a paternalistic government and a dependent people; which rejected the notion that the State is all powerful and the citizen is merely its beneficiary; which shattered the illusion that Government could somehow substitute for individual performance. (Quoted in Lowe 2005: 3)

In *The Downing Street Years* (Thatcher 1993: 8), she elaborated: "Welfare benefits, distributed with little or no consideration of their effects on behaviour, encouraged illegitimacy, facilitated the breakdown of families, and replaced incentives favouring work and self-reliance with perverse encouragement of idleness and cheating."

Welfare was the problem. It created dependency, which then led to all the problems related to the undeserving poor. This, to her, was socialism. In *The Downing Street Years* (1993: 625) she wrote, "Socialism had failed. And it was the poorer, weaker members of society who had suffered worst as a result of that failure. More than that, however, socialism ... had literally demoralized communities and families, offering dependency in place of independence." She saw her job as "killing Socialism in Britain" (quoted in Schwarz 1987: 145). That meant attacking welfare, along with the undeserving poor that, she believed, welfare produced.

An Intended and Inevitable Outcome: A Price Worth Paying

An explosion of poverty and inequality was the inevitable result. This was a conscious and deliberate choice, for which no apologies would be made. The employment minister, Lord Young, said, referring to Victorian entrepreneurs, "we need not feel guilty that their success was at the expense of the poor" (quoted in Byrne 1987: 37). The growth of poverty and inequality was a price worth paying. It was part of a "two nations" strategy, far from Macmillan's One Nation approach, in which some would benefit while others were necessarily left behind. It is no surprise, then, that in 1999, after almost two decades of Thatcher-led and Thatcher-inspired Conservative governments,

> there were more people living in or on the margins of poverty than at any time in British history. According to the most rigorous survey of poverty and social exclusion ever undertaken, by the end of 1999 approximately 14 million people in Britain, or

25 percent of the population, were objectively living in poverty. (Pantazis, Gordon and Levitas 2006: 1)

What is more, it was these growing numbers in poverty that were seen to be responsible for the crisis of capitalism, a view that had preceded the Conservatives taking office and of which they took full advantage:

> In the 1970s, the poor came to be blamed not just for their own problems, but also for the nation's. Britain was increasingly seen to be in rapid decline. In the desperate search for explanations, the poor became scapegoats. Welfare spending, it was claimed, was too high.... The incentive to work hard had, it was said, been taken away by the "generosity" of public "handouts." The poor were scroungers. (Mack and Lansley 1984: 4)

It was based on such a "theory of poverty" that Thatcher's Conservatives governed. The poor were causing Britain's social and economic problems. Actions would have to be taken against the poor. Doing so would necessarily deepen poverty and inequality.

At first blush, it may seem deeply troubling that an essential element of the solution to the economic and social crisis of the 1970s featured a conscious, deliberate and massive increase in poverty and inequality. However, it is important to recall that capitalism has always involved, and indeed necessitated, the production of poverty. That was the case during the centuries when capitalism was beginning to emerge and hundreds of thousands were forced off the land and into poverty as vagrants and vagabonds and masterless men. That was the case during the industrial revolution, when a new and horrifying form of poverty was an essential element in Britain's emergent industrial dominance. From the late nineteenth century, some steps began to be taken to at least alleviate poverty, and this was accelerated in the postwar period, especially during the Attlee years. The incidence of poverty declined significantly at that time, in large part because of deliberate government efforts. However, Thatcher reversed that process with deliberate efforts to create poverty and accentuate inequality. This was necessitated by the need to restore the conditions for capital accumulation, for profitability.

Winning the Battle of Ideas

Thatcher led ideas-driven governments. These ideas—support for an individualist, market-oriented, anti-government and anti-union approach to governance—had grown gradually since being articulated in the 1930s and 1940s by, among others, Friedrich von Hayek. Thatcher promoted them fiercely. In a 1979 election speech she said,

> If you've got a message, preach it! The Old Testament prophets didn't go out into the highways saying, 'Brothers, I want consensus.' They said, 'This is my faith and my vision! This is what I passionately believe!' And they preached it. We have a message. Go out, preach it, practice it, fight for it—and the day will be ours. (Quoted in Smith 2015: 69)

She fought for an "ideological insurgency mobilized against the spirit of egalitarianism," featuring an attack on the trade union movement, the redistributive state and the poor (Campbell 2015: 42).

In doing so, she tapped into people's fears of cultural change and their fears of what many had come to see as a culture descending into anarchy, as evidenced by rising conflicts around immigration, race and crime, and dramatic changes in the structure of the family, the changing role of women and especially the growth in the numbers of lone mothers. Thatcher saw these phenomena as expressions of the "excessive permissiveness" of the 1960s and 1970s.

In populist fashion, she drew on people's fears and anxieties with a move toward law and order. Hall (2017: 325) labels it "authoritarian populism," which includes "a concentrated ideological assault on the new rights which women and Blacks secured during the 1960s and 1970s" (Gamble 1988: 197). The fears driving this ideological approach were further intensified when in 1981, "Brixton exploded in rebellion" and there followed across the country "rebellion in slum city" (Sivanandan 1982: 48–49), with riots or "serious street disorders" across major British cities and annually during the Thatcher years (Benyon and Solomos 1988: 402). The result was massive media condemnation of Blacks, who were widely blamed for violence in the inner cities (Sim 1982: 62).

Thatcher's authoritarian populism appealed to those who feared this disorder. It responded to and accentuated their anxieties and sense of loss. Thatcherism would become "the authentic voice of white working class patriarchal values, preaching the importance of a strong nation and a strong family for social cohesion" (Gamble 1988: 198).

The complement to the strong state would be a "free" market—the neoliberal commitment to unleashing its forces. Thatcher's neoliberalism had its roots in the works of von Hayek, who had been appointed to a chair at the London School of Economics in 1920. His radical right-wing ideas were seized upon from the time of the Beveridge Report in 1942 by a small minority of Conservative Party members with a "deep-seated hostility" to state intervention (Green 1999: 22). This was an "individualist counter-revolution" (Skidelsky 1988: 3).

Although severely marginalized by the Conservative One Nation governments of the 1950s, those promoting these radical right-wing ideas persisted and eventually developed the institutional capacity to produce and disseminate their new ideological approach—which was in fact a return to nineteenth-century classical liberalism. In 1958 the Institute of Economic Affairs (IEA) was established. By 1979 the IEA was securing financial support from "big companies like ICI, Unilever, Shell, Lucas, Courtaulds and Guest, Keen and Nettlefold" (MacGregor 1981: 161). Corporate donors to the IEA grew from 110 in 1962 to 299 in 1968, and in the range of 250–300 in the 1970s and early 1980s (Jackson 2012: 47). Neoliberal ideas were being normalized.

The IEA played "a major role in publicizing the ideas of Hayek" (Kavanagh 1990: 81), who was himself directly involved from its beginnings. Part of the organization's strategy was to influence "second-hand dealers in ideas" (Desai 1994b)—journalists, editors, academics, senior civil servants, political advisors—by developing social relationships with and moving in the same circles as such people (Jackson 2012). Gradually through the 1970s, "these seeds began to bear fruit. First in the learned journals, then in the senior common rooms, and finally in the informal exchanges between the 'new academics' and the more 'sensitive' senior civil servants" (Hall 1988: 47).

When Edward Heath had been forced in 1972 to abandon his attempted hard turn to the right, in what the apostles of the free market came to see as "Mr. Heath's U-turn" (Gamble 1988: 73), this, and his defeat in 1973–1974 by the miners, were for Mrs. Thatcher "important signposts on her road to Damascus" (Skidelsky 1988: 14), leading both her and Keith Joseph to immerse themselves in the work of von Hayek and Friedman.

In 1974, Joseph and Thatcher established the Centre for Policy Studies (CPS). Thatcher explained its formation by saying that she "had always been an instinctive Conservative, but I had failed to develop these instincts either into a coherent framework of ideas or into a set of practical policies for government.... Keith [Joseph] and I established the Centre for Policy Studies to do just that" (Thatcher 1993: 14). While the IEA was an independent but market-oriented body, the CPS was a Conservative Party instrument of which Joseph was chairman and Thatcher president (Kavanagh 1990: 89). Joseph and Thatcher were close:

> encouraged by Joseph, Thatcher began to question the basis of Conservative politics that had prevailed since she had entered public life; she re-read Hayek and devoured more recent works by such writers as Milton Friedman; and she engaged with the free-market ideas being put forward by Ralph Harris and Arthur Seldon at the Institute of Economic Affairs. (Cannadine 2017: 21)

The Adam Smith Institute was established in 1977 to develop free-market policies, particularly with respect to privatization and outsourcing of public services (Irvin 2008: 77), as well as the promotion of workfare programs (Dolowitz 1998: 18–19). Hayek at one time chaired its advisory board (Kavanagh 1990: 87). This ideological work had an impact. "If the Webbs, Keynes, and Beveridge were the formative figures for the social democratic policies of 1945–75, then Sir Keith Joseph, Milton Friedman, the IEA, and the CPS are the main figures of the right-wing reaction to them" (Kavanagh 1990: 22).

Keith Joseph said at the Conservative Party conference in London in 1975, "We are a national party and we have a double task—to win the next election and to win the battle of ideas" (quoted in Jones and Lowe 2002: 31). In many important respects, they won the battle of ideas. Thatcher was sufficiently successful in shifting the country's culture, in creating a new hegemony, that even after her departure "British politics have been conducted in her monstrous shadow" (Marquand, quoted in Jackson 2014: 76). Hay (2007: 189), writing almost thirty years after her initial election victory, adds, "a Thatcherite settlement has replaced the post-war settlement."

The Thatcherite settlement involved a full-fledged denigration of the poor, which included consciously chosen shifts in language. For example, social security became "welfare dependency," and such terms as the "benefits culture" and the "culture of dependency" were widely used. Implicit in this is the centuries-old condemnation of the "undeserving poor"—those whose poverty is seen to be caused by their own degenerate behaviour and, according to Thatcher, whose poverty is fuelled by the excesses of the welfare state.

Thatcher believed in Victorian values. She claimed to have been influenced by a Victorian grandmother who taught her the value of hard work, self-reliance, the need to live within one's means, pride in country. As Addison (2010: 279) says, "She spoke the language of English middle-class individualism with absolute moral conviction."

Regarding poverty, "Victorian values" were rooted in the belief that the poor were to blame for their poverty—they were degenerate, lazy, irresponsible. Interventions by the state, according to Victorian values, would worsen these character flaws, reinforcing the poor in the very behaviour that was the cause of their poverty. These beliefs were little removed from the Poor Law era, when responses to the poor were sufficient only to keep them from starving or rebelling and when punishing the poor was the norm. Indeed, Thatcher's commitment to such Victorian values is evidenced by the fact that prior to becoming prime minister, she had voted along with five other Conservative MPs in favour of the restoration of flogging (Dorling 2014a: 247).

The attack on the postwar consensus, and the ambition to create a new hegemony, included getting rid of universal social programs and eroding the principle of universality. This went back to the earliest wartime meetings of select Conservative Party members. A committee chaired by Ralph Assheton had been set up during the war to examine the Beveridge Report. Assheton told Rab Butler in 1942, "one of the chief troubles of the Beveridge Report is that whereas his diagnosis relates to Want, his proposals are very largely devoted to giving money to people who are not in want." This was at its core "a critique of universality, a principle at the heart of Beveridge's proposals and which represented his attempt to remove Poor Law stigmatization from the post-war welfare structure" (Green 1999: 22). These Conservatives' wartime argument—echoed decades later by Thatcher—was that "a successful economy requires incentives, and a welfare system based on universality hampers incentives, first by offering 'a sofa rather than a springboard' of benefits and, second, by requiring a level of taxation that reduced the rewards of productive enterprise" (Green 1999: 22–23).

The attack on universality carried on through the early 1950s. In 1952, Enoch Powell and Iain Macleod published *The Social Services: Needs not Means,* in which they opposed universality and promoted means tests (Green 1999: 25). After the 1959 election, "the party's Advisory Committee on Policy established that a key long-term issue was 'the future financing of the social services as a whole and to what extent we should break away ... from the principle of universality'" (quoted in Green 1999: 30). Abandoning universality in favour of means-tested programs more narrowly targeted at the poor leaves those programs vulnerable to erosion or even elimination by the many who believe that the poor are to blame for their poverty. Although Powell was severely marginalized within the Conservative Party at the time, his "extraordinary success as a tribune of the people revealed how fragile were the defenses of social democracy" (Gamble 1988: 177). The principle of universality was among those fragile defenses. It was increasingly abandoned as part of the Conservatives' efforts to replace the remaining vestiges of social democracy in their rush to the market.

Keith Joseph not only opposed universality; he also attacked any form of redistribution. "Redistribution is unwise. But it is also morally indefensible, misconceived in theory and repellant in practice" (Joseph and Sumption 1979: 19). It followed that the welfare state—rooted in the practice of redistribution—was to be dismantled. This included that targeted, means-tested programs should replace universal programs. To do otherwise "weakened the work ethic and lessened the recipient's sense of personal reliance and responsibility" (Kavanagh 1990: 132).

What would become of the poor? It was up to families and charity to look after the poor. Thatcher said, "We are committed to a civilized society where the poor and the sick, the disabled and the elderly are properly cared for. By the community, by their families, by voluntary organizations" (quoted in Mack and Lansley 1984: 232). She famously said, "there is no such thing as society," but added, "there are individual men and women, and there are families ... it's our duty to look after ourselves and then to look after our neighbour." This was not a role for the state. She maintained, "the root cause of our contemporary social problems ... was that the state had been doing too much" and she acknowledged that she was "reinforced in this view by the writings of conservative thinkers in the United States on the growth of an 'underclass' and the development of a dependency culture" (Thatcher 1993: 626–27).

Among those conservative thinkers was American sociologist Charles Murray, whose 1984 book, *Losing Ground,* is described by Teles (1996: 148) as being so important that there "is no way to overestimate the effect" it had on "the intellectual debate on poverty" in the US. Murray was invited to Britain on two separate occasions by *The Sunday Times,* first in 1989 and again in 1994. His essays, *The Emerging British Underclass* (Murray 1990) and *Underclass: The Crisis Deepens* (Lister 1996), were subsequently published by the IEA after appearing in *The Sunday Times.* In the first study, Murray argued that a rapidly growing underclass was emerging in Britain, characterized not just by a shortage of income but more importantly by their behaviour, which included violent crime, dropping out from the labour market and especially "illegitimacy," which he identified as "the best predictor of an underclass in the making" (Murray 1990: 4). Murray (1990: 5) referred to evidence showing a rapid rise at the end of the 1970s in the proportion of births to unmarried mothers—from 10.6 percent in 1979 to 14.1 percent in 1982, 18.9 percent in 1985 and 25.6 percent—one in four—in 1988. Rates of poverty among lone mothers were high and rose with additional children (Layard et al. 1978: 98–99).

Kiernan and her colleagues (1998), like their American counterparts Edin and Kefalas (2005) in their aptly titled *Promises I Can Keep: Why Poor Women Put Motherhood Before Marriage,* located the explanation for the rise in lone parenthood in poor women's lack of job prospects. They also argue that "there is copious evidence that a majority are poor before they become pregnant," and "would have been poor if they had married" (Kiernan et al. 1998: 279, 292). Murray, by contrast, argued that overly generous welfare benefits were the explanation and advocated the virtual elimination of state benefits and their replacement with Victorian-era voluntary or "autonomous" associations (Murray 1990: 30). Thatcher agreed and governed accordingly.

No Economic Miracle: Restructuring and Deindustrialization

The objective was to restore the conditions for enhanced capital accumulation, and the poor would be among those who, consciously and deliberately, would pay the price. Thatcher's long-term project was to replace the Keynesian/mild social democratic consensus of the postwar era with a new consensus involving a reduced role for the state, a weakening of union power and the unleashing of market forces, together with an attempt to shift the country's culture to a more individualist and pro-enterprise orientation. However, an immediate start was made in the Conservative government's first budget, where Geoffrey Howe slashed the top rate of income tax from 83 to 60 percent. Continued cuts dropped the top income tax rate to 40 percent (Addison 2010: 330). Cutting the top tax rates was the "signature issue of the 'conservative revolution' waged by the Republican Party under Ronald Reagan in the United States and the Conservative Party under Margaret Thatcher in Britain" (Piketty 2020: 31). For the poor and the working class, the value-added tax (VAT) was doubled from 8 to 15 percent, and later to almost 18 percent in 1991 (H. Thompson 2014: 55) and 20 percent by 2013 (Walker 2014: 294), and the costs of prescriptions, school meals and council house rents were raised (Gamble 1988). For example, when subsidies to council tenants were cut by 60 percent, rents rose at "double the rate of inflation" (Mack and Lansley 1984: 6).

> Overall, the well-off and the rich have gained about 2,600 million [2.6 billion] pounds between 1979 and 1984 from tax concessions ... benefit cuts over the life of Mrs. Thatcher's first term in office amounted to some 1600 million pounds, most of which represented a cut in the incomes of the poorest sections of the community. (Mack and Lansley 1984: 6)

As Leys (1985: 10) describes it, "Thatcherite tax policies have had an unambiguously 'upward' redistributive effect." Inequality skyrocketed—at a rate greater than any other Western nation (Dorey 2015).

Some economic gains were made as the result of these neoliberal policies. Real growth from 1981 to 1989 averaged 3.2 percent a year; it had been negative for sixteen months in 1980 and 1981. By 1983, inflation was less than 5 percent (Cannadine 2017: 42); by July 1986, it was at 2.5 percent, the lowest it had been since 1967 (Kavanagh 1990: 226), although by 1990 it was back up to 8 percent (Marsh and Rhodes 1992: 174). Job creation grew faster than other countries from 1983 (Kavanagh 1990: 233). In her second term, starting in 1983, there was even talk of a "British economic miracle."

"There was, however, no economic miracle" (Addison 2010: 260). Britain's annual average growth rate during the 1980s was about equal to France and behind Germany, the US and Japan, and any gains made were "partial and fragile" and built on North Sea oil and the proceeds from privatization (Cannadine 2017: 91). In 1986, "industrial investment was still lower than it had been when Thatcher become Prime Minister, and the following year Britain's gross national product fell behind that of Italy" (Cannadine 2017: 91).

New jobs were created—more than three million between 1983 and 1990, "mostly in the service sector." They were "largely confined to the south-east of the country, and the old manufacturing regions were devastated by de-industrialization: the closure of the factories, mills, steelworks, and mines on which the livelihoods of entire communities depended" (Cannadine 2017: 81–82). For many in Britain, the 1980s were experienced not as an "economic miracle" but as "years of cruel illusion and deception" (Leys 2003: 254).

The long erosion of British manufacturing continued, and even accelerated after 1979. While it is true, as Tomlinson (2009: 240) observes, that "de-industrialization has been the common fate of the OECD world since the 1970s," resulting in declining levels of manufacturing employment in all industrialized countries, British capitalism was hit especially hard. "The decline in industrial output between June 1979 and December 1980 was the fastest in recorded history. Industrial production fell by 14 percent while unemployment increased by two-thirds" (quoted in Skidelsky 1988: 21). From 1979 to 1981, "output fell in the textile industry by 26 percent, in metal manufacturing by the same amount, and in timber and furniture by 21 percent. Unemployment rose by about 250 percent overall at the time" (Hopkins 1991: 215). By 1981, it was being asserted that "the industrial base of the country [is] being destroyed" (Crick 1981: Preface). Some five thousand factories closed between 1979 and 1982 (Thane 2018: 351). Total manufacturing output fell by just under 20 percent between June 1979 and January 1981, and almost one in four manufacturing jobs that had existed in 1979 were lost (Jackson 1992: 16). "Gross real fixed investment in manufacturing fell by a massive 31 percent between 1979 and 1983, and it did not match the former level until 1988." The number of miners employed in Britain "fell from around 600,000 in the later 1940s to 200,000 in the early 1980s and a mere 30,000 by the early 1990s" (Miles and Savage 1994: 11). In 1982, for the first time in two hundred years, the UK had a manufacturing trade deficit—more manufactured goods were imported than exported (Jackson 1992: 22). Manufacturing had constituted 40 percent of the British economy in 1979; that proportion was 30 percent by 1997 when the Conservatives were finally voted out of office (H. Thompson 2014: 37). As Sassoon (1997: 457) observes, "By 1993, unemployment in the UK was, in real terms, at an all-time postwar high, while British manufacturing industry was in ruins." Thatcher's policy was to open the doors to global competition; an already long-weakened manufacturing sector was unable to compete, after decades of the failure of British capitalists to invest and innovate, throwing millions out of work. Mass unemployment, the scourge of the early 1920s and 1930s, returned to Britain in full force in the 1980s. Margaret Thatcher saw herself as a saviour of British capitalism. Not all British capitalists were behind globalization and free trade; many were hurt by it. Thatcher acted in the interests of capitalism, not necessarily of all capitalists.

Acting in the interests of British capitalism, Thatcher was determined to crush the 1984–1985 miners' strike after the miners had defeated Heath in 1973–1974. She had to win "if there was to be any chance of implementing other New Right policies" (Gamble 1988: 33). One of her closest advisors told her, "To lose might not be the end of civilization as we know it but it would be the end of Thatcherism as we know it" (quoted in Jenkins 1988: 229). Thatcher won that fight, in part through aggressively using the power of the state—200 million pounds were spent on a mobile police force drawn from forty-three separate police forces, and eleven thousand arrests were made (Thane 2018: 362). Ian MacGregor, who "had become renowned in American business circles as a skillful and relentless breaker of strikes" (Beynon and Hudson 2021: 107), was brought to Britain to chair the National Coal Board in 1983 and played a key role in the state's attacks on the miners. MacGregor used such language as "field commanders" and "second fronts," and he established both a "strategic warfare" and an "economic warfare" committee (Beynon and Hudson 2021: 114). The number of pits dropped from 170 in 1985 to 76 in 1990, by which time the National Union of Mineworkers had lost 70 percent of its members (Hopkins 1991: 227). By 1993, seventeen pits remained in operation.

The impact on mining communities was overwhelming and demonstrated the consequences of deindustrialization across the UK. A miner's wife, when asked about the impact of a pit's closure, had replied,

> We died. Once all the mines closed, all the community had gone. It's just been a big depression ever since, just struggling to sur-

vive, that's all.... We owed not just our livelihoods, but our *lives* to the pits as well. My dad retired, and then he died. My marriage broke up.... The community just disintegrated. (Quoted in Jones 2012: 185–86, emphasis in original)

Taming the unions was a major component of the Thatcher strategy, because doing so would eliminate the most dangerous opposition to her radical reform agenda, and because she believed that unless unions were tamed, "national recovery [would] be virtually impossible" (Dorey 2014: 98–99). Sassoon (1997: 506) described her "ferocious anti-trade union legislation, unparalleled in Europe." By the mid-1980s, unions "were steadily reduced to the role of minor players" (Addison 2010: 289), partly the result of laws passed during the 1980s specifically to restrict trade union activities. Jones (2012: 10) argued that Thatcher's approach was

> an all-out assault on the pillars of working-class Britain. Its institutions, like trade unions and council housing, were dismantled; its industries, from manufacturing to mining, were trashed; its communities were, in some cases, shattered, never to recover; and its values, like solidarity and collective aspiration, were swept away in favour of rugged individualism. Stripped of their power and no longer seen as a proud identity, the working class was increasingly sneered at, belittled and scape-goated.

Mrs. Thatcher attacked the unions not only with regressive legislation, but also, as with her treatment of the poor, with aggressive rhetoric. Trade unions were the "enemy within," and union leaders were "trade union barons and bully boys"—the oppressors, Thatcher argued, of "the home-owning, car-owning, respectable and responsible citizen" (Campbell 2015: 43). Thatcher appealed over the heads of union leaders to rank-and-file members; by doing so, "the Conservatives were able to portray themselves as the 'liberators,' not the 'oppressors,' of ordinary union members, freeing them from the tyranny of union bosses and 'bully boys' on picket lines" (Dorey 2014: 102).

However, it was not just Thatcher's policies and rhetoric that weakened the union movement. "The changes in the economic structure and, in particular, the process of restructuring and deindustrialization have played a crucial role in weakening the unions' bargaining position" (Marsh 1992: 188). By the early 1990s, union membership had declined by 25 percent since 1979 (Marsh 1992: 242); days lost to strikes declined from twenty-nine million in 1979 to 761,000 in 1991 (Jackson and Saunders 2012: 16); and by 2011 union membership had declined to 6.4 million from its peak of thirteen million in 1979 (Farrall and Hay 2014: 324). Union density went from 50 percent in 1979 to 35 percent in 1989 and 27 percent in 1997 (McKnight 2005: 25).

The deliberate assault on trade unions, driven by British capitalists and actively supported by Thatcher's governments, was an important part of the effort to restore the conditions for capital accumulation, and it was also a key part of the process by which capitalism produces poverty.

Mass Unemployment: More of It and Longer than the 1930s

Mass unemployment, a defining feature of the 1980s, contributed significantly to the growth of poverty. "In fact, the eighties constitute a longer period of mass unemployment than even the 1930s" (Hopkins 1991: 221); by 1986, unemployment had reached its highest-ever level in the twentieth century; the unemployed became "the largest group in poverty" (Taylor-Gooby 1988: 3 and 13).

Unemployment went from about 1.2 million in 1979 to almost three million by 1983, and it exceeded three million until 1987 (Lowe 2005: 315). It was rising in other countries at that time as well, but not as fast as in Britain. By 1983 it was at 13.1 percent in the UK, compared to 8.7 percent in the OECD (Addison 2010: 281). As in the 1930s, it was concentrated especially in the north of England and the industrial areas of south Wales and the Scottish lowlands (Addison 2010: 285). "By 1987, nearly a third of the unemployed had been on the register for over a year and in the North, the North West and West Midlands, roughly half of those unemployed had been unable to find work within a year" (Addison 2010: 285).

Unemployment fell in each of 1987 and 1988, dropping below three million in 1987 and reaching about 1.75 million by 1990 (Hopkins 1991: 216). However, after the recession of the early 1990s, unemployment was back to 2.9 million (Goodman, Johnson and Webb 1997: 88). Thane (2018: 363) argues that unemployment might have reached four million by 1986, the total number masked by the fact that "from 1979 to 1996 the basis for calculating unemployment was adjusted thirty-one times, always in a downward direction."

Ethnic minorities were hit disproportionately hard. Their unemployment rates were more than double those of the white population. The unemployment rate for young Black men was three times that of young white men—51 percent versus 18 percent (Bloch 1997: 112–13). Walker and Walker (1997: 286) argue that the evidence accumulated "stands as a huge indictment of the disastrous record of four Conservative governments towards Britain's most vulnerable and insecure citizens."

Further, the problem was not just unemployment. Growing numbers of working-age people were economically inactive—that is, neither working nor looking for work and thus not counted as unemployed. In 1996 in Merseyside, "37 percent of all working age men are *not employed*," and just under one in five households in Britain were without a working adult (Convery 1997: 185, 187, emphasis in original). The number of adults living in households without work had more than doubled between 1979 and 1993–1994 (Pile and O'Donnell 1997: 32). Ironically, given her views on the issue, Thatcher's economic strategy "greatly exacerbated the problem of welfare dependency by creating a permanent class of workless citizens who could not be absorbed into the new economy" (Gamble 2015: 12). For Norman Lamont, the chancellor of the exchequer, this was a "price worth paying" to restore the British economy (quoted in Convery 1997: 170). High unemployment would drive down wages, thus making Britain more competitive (Dolowitz 1998: 169). When asked in 1980 how much responsibility he felt for the rapid growth of unemployment, Keith Joseph had replied, "None. None" (quoted in Jenkins 1988: 98).

In Thatcher's third term, her government introduced, particularly via the *Social Security Act 1988* and the *Social Security Act 1989*, a full-fledged, American-style workfare system (Dolowitz 1998: 126) in response to the mass unemployment and the "welfare dependency" she believed it created. The practice of borrowing ways of understanding and responding to poverty from the US continued. Sir Geoffrey Holland, a permanent secretary and one of the architects of British workfare, said, "We counted ourselves lucky to have a model of something that seemed to have worked well. We took the United States model and in a sense we translated it almost literally … into English" (quoted in Dolowitz 1998: 143). In the early 1980s, there was a "constant stream" of British civil servants and politicians visiting American states to examine various workfare schemes. Between 1979 and 1984, "Department of Employment ministers made 70 overseas visits to examine employment programmes" (Dolowitz 1998: 82).

To be able to implement workfare successfully, Thatcherism had to do the ideological work to gain acceptance of the program. "The key to successful implementation of workfare was the continual emphasis upon individualism, self-help, welfare dependency and scroungers" (Dolowitz 1998: 22). This ideological/cultural work was necessary "because of the public's distaste for such [workfare] schemes and its lingering belief in a universal right to welfare entitlement" (Dolowitz 1998: 75). That lingering belief had to be undermined. For the most part it was, not least because of the relentlessly withering attacks upon the poor, described by Palmer (2014: 41) as "ideological assaults of unprecedented vigour."

Unforgiveable Treatment of the Poor

Public support for the poor and unemployed was weak. There was, however, strong public support for maintaining public spending on the core of the welfare state—the NHS, education and pensions—which benefited the middle class and skilled workers in particular. However, support was much weaker "for needy social minorities—the unemployed, single parents, the homeless—who are often seen as morally undeserving" (Taylor-Gooby 1988: 11). Thatcher's strategy was to position herself, populist style, as the supporter of honest, hard-working, respectable and deserving workers and businesspeople, while denigrating the "undeserving" poor who were consistently blamed for their poverty and blamed also by many for Britain's economic woes. Thatcher's belief in the poor as the authors of their own misfortune was reinforced by the fact that while poverty was growing, many in Britain were experiencing rising incomes. This fact

> served strongly to sustain a perception that if a minority of society has not shared in this prosperity, then it must be because of some deficiency specific to that minority. In this context, being poor is pathologized: it is attributed to the attitudes or aptitudes of those individuals who are poor or living in poverty. (Dorey 2011: 227)

Hill and Walker (2014: 96–97) argued that the 1980s "represented a huge ratcheting up of the rhetorical climate surrounding social security and the poor. It is difficult to convey now the strength of this rhetorical onslaught, or "scrounger-mania," that was sustained for the whole of Thatcher's premiership." Claims of fraud and abuse committed by social security recipients were frequent, and regional fraud units were established (Walker 2014: 286). One Nation Conservative Ian Gilmour was moved to say, "the Thatcherite treatment of the poor was unforgiveable" (quoted in Dorey 2011: 101).

Given that so much of the pain of poverty is a function of what Lister (2004: 7) described as the "non-material aspects of poverty such as: lack of voice; disrespect, humiliation and an assault on dignity and self-esteem; shame and stigma; powerlessness," Thatcher's rhetorical attacks on the poor were especially damaging. Thatcher went so far as to assert that few in Britain were "disadvantaged," and "real" poverty no longer existed. The word *poverty* disappeared from official documents. Poverty became "dependency ... a behavioural problem caused by the welfare state itself" (Walker 2014: 286).

Keith Joseph believed the same—"a family is poor if it cannot afford to eat.... By any absolute standard there is very little poverty in Britain today" (Joseph and Sumption 1979: 27–8). It followed that those being defined as poor had only themselves to blame. In a September 1975 speech, Joseph had asserted that among the supposed unemployed are "scroungers, unemployables and people who will not make their share of the effort, who expect the government or their fellow men to do everything for them" (quoted in MacGregor 1981: 131). Therefore, Conservatives, when elected, "would be after the layabouts and work shirkers" (quoted in Alcock 1987: 119).

The claim that there was "very little poverty in Britain today" echoed the earlier comments of Conservative minister Sir Kingsley Wood, who said in 1934 during the Great Depression, "with old age pensions and unemployment insurance, there was no poverty in the country" (Atkinson 1989: 44).

But Poverty Had Not Disappeared

Mrs. Thatcher's and Keith Joseph's opinions notwithstanding, several major studies provide the empirical evidence that poverty grew dramatically during the 1980s and 1990s. Mack and Lansley (1984: 7, emphasis in original) show that when defined by one's income relative to the supplementary benefit—a standard measurement—poverty grew in the late 1970s and early 1980s:

> The minimum income level provided by supplementary benefit is sometimes called the "state's poverty line." From 1960 to 1977, the estimated number of people living *below* the supplementary benefit level remained roughly constant at around 2 million. From 1977 to 1979, the number rose slightly to around 2.13 million. In the next two years this number rose by nearly a quarter to reach 2.64 million…. In 1983 over 7 million people were dependent on supplementary benefit.

In addition, Mack and Lansley (1984: 9) developed a new and innovative way of defining and measuring poverty. They defined poverty as "an enforced lack of socially perceived necessities." By this definition, poverty is based on "the social perception of needs," and "items become 'necessities' only when they are *socially* perceived to be so" (Mack and Lansley 1984: 37–38, emphasis in original). To determine what were socially perceived as necessities, they asked a representative sample of 1,174 people across Britain to judge the necessities for living in Britain in the 1980s (Mack and Lansley 1984: 44). Those who could not afford three or more of these socially perceived necessities were deemed by Mack and Lansley (1984: 178) to be living in poverty.

By this definition, five million adults and 2.5 million children were in poverty in 1983, a total of 7.5 million—"around 1 in every 7 people"—about 14 percent of the population (Mack and Lansley 1984: 182). A follow-up study in 1997 used the same methodology to examine 1990 data. The results were "clear and unambiguous." They showed that "the number of people living in poverty rose during the 1980s from 14 percent of households (approximately 7.5 million people) in 1983, to 20 percent of households (approximately 11 million people) in 1990" (Gordon and Pantazis 1997: 235). Further, "40 percent of families in poverty have a head of household in full-time work" (Mack and Lansley 1984: 185), suggesting that in addition to unemployment, low pay and irregular employment were major causal factors—evidence of the growth of the centuries-old problem of precarious labour.

In 2000, David Gordon and a team of researchers conducted yet another major study, which they described as "the most comprehensive survey of poverty and social exclusion ever undertaken in Britain." They found that "on any measure, poverty at the turn of the new millennium remains one of the greatest social problems challenging Britain" (Gordon et al. 2000: 5). Two measures of poverty were used, one based on what the majority of the population considered to be necessities, as done by Mack and Lansley (1984). Gordon and his colleagues (2000: 5, 68) conclude that "the proportion of households living in poverty in terms of both low income and multiple deprivation of necessities has increased from 14 percent in 1983 to 21 percent in 1990 to over 24 percent in 1999," two years after the Conservatives lost the 1997 election. "Over a third of British children were living in households with incomes below 50 percent of the average—the measure of childhood poverty most commonly used," so that by the mid-1990s, "the UK's child poverty rate was the third highest of the 25 nations for whom information was available" (Gordon et al. 2000: 32, 8). Child poverty grew in tandem with overall poverty, rising from 1.4 million in 1979 to 4.2 million in 1994–1995, or from 10 percent to 32 percent of all children—almost one in every three (Oppenheim 1997: 19).

Childhood poverty matters.

> Children from poor homes have lower life expectancy and are more likely to die in infancy or childhood; they have a greater likelihood of poor health, a lower chance of high educational attainment, a greater risk of unemployment, a higher probability of involvement in crime and enduring homelessness. (Oppenheim 1997: 26)

Among the results was "disturbing evidence of desperate poverty on a scale not witnessed in Britain since the 1930s ... diseases associated with poverty and malnutrition, such as rickets and tuberculosis, which most health experts had hoped were banished forever, had returned" (Walker 1997: 9).

Women continued to be more likely than men to be poor. At the start of the twentieth century, 61 percent of adults on poor relief were women. Almost a century later, this number had scarcely moved—in the early 1990s, 60 percent of those on supplementary benefits were women (Lewis and Piachaud 1992: 27). Women throughout the centuries have been paid less than men, so that "the great majority of women are trapped in a vicious circle of domestic responsibilities and low-paid, low-status employment" (Lewis and Piachaud 1992: 43). Black and Asian women were even more likely than white women to be living in poverty (Cook and Watt 1992: 16–17).

Lone parents, especially mothers, were likewise disproportionately affected, as their numbers grew. The proportion of births occurring outside marriage had been 9 percent in 1945, and stayed at roughly that level until 1977, when it started to climb. "In 1980 12 percent of births were recorded as being born outside marriage, by 1990 the proportion had increased to 28 percent, and by the mid-1990s had plateaued at one in three of all births" (Kiernan et al. 1998: 28). About half of children under age sixteen in lone-parent families "are in poverty and many are in intense poverty" (Mack and Lansley 1984: 189), but their benefits were consistently eroded. "In the 1990s there has been a new determination to make sure that they are 'less eligible' than married couples, to use the language of the nineteenth-century poor law" (Kiernan et al. 1998: 279–80). As a result, the proportion of lone parents with incomes less than half the national average rose from 29 percent in 1979 to 59 percent in 1988, while the proportion of lone mothers receiving supplementary benefits rose from about 45 percent in the late 1970s to over 70 percent by the late 1980s (Millar 1992: 150–51). All of this was consistent with what Keith Joseph had said in the mid-1970s: in defending the traditional, male-dominated family, he verbally attacked "mothers, the under twenties in many cases, single parents … [those] least fitted to bring children into the world" (quoted in Hall 1988: 27).

Drab, Dreary, Depressing: Housing under Thatcher

The 1985 report of the Archbishop of Canterbury's Commission on Urban Priority Areas, titled *Faith in the City: A Call for Action by Church and Nation* (Archbishop 1985), found terrible poverty in inner city areas—"Urban Priority Areas"—and in peripheral council estates.

> Huge impersonal housing estates, many post-war, can be found in all our cities. They are … drab, dreary, depressing, with no vitality, colour or beauty … with packs of dogs roaming around, filth in the stairwells, one or two shuttered shops…. Unemployment rates are typically 30–40 percent, and rising. Bored, out of work young people turn to vandalism, drugs, and crime—the estate takes the brunt, and the spiral of decline is given a further twist. (Archbishop 1985: 176)

Council estates were stigmatized. "Policemen talk of residents as 'scum.' Residents themselves believe that 'we are rubbish,' this is a sink estate" (Archbishop 1985: 229). Benyon and Solomos (1988: 413–14) identify five common characteristics of those urban areas where the rioting and serious street disorder so common in the Thatcher years occurred: racial disadvantage and discrimination; high unemployment; widespread deprivation, such as inadequate housing and social service provision; feelings of political powerlessness and exclusion; and mistrust of and even hostility to the police. These describe the conditions on many urban housing estates.

While the decline of council housing estates was of long standing, Conservative housing policy made it worse. Conservative governments adopted a twofold approach: selling off council housing to those who could afford to buy; and slashing spending on repairs and maintenance of the remaining housing and on the construction of new council housing.

The sale of council housing was the core of Thatcher's "popular capitalism" strategy. That strategy also included denationalizing (privatizing) British Telecom and British Gas, selling their shares at below-market value (Gamble 1988: 138) and implementing a massive privatization of previously nationalized industry (for a long list of companies that were privatized, see Addison 2010: 290–92; for analysis of particular privatizations, see Meek 2014). A result was that "by 1990 the number of private shareholders had risen from 3 to 9 million" (Lowe 2005: 493).

However, as Meek (2014: 15, 21) points out, most of the shares in companies that had been privatized did not remain in the hands of individuals, so that Thatcher's "vision of a shareholding democracy failed to come to pass through privatization," which "undermines the justification for the way the companies were taken out of public ownership." On the contrary, "it put more money into the hands of the very wealthiest people, at the expense of the elderly, the sick, the jobless and the working poor."

The Conservatives sold—commodified, in effect—vast numbers of council houses, peaking at 200,000 per year in 1982 (Addison 2010: 305), contributing significantly to the rise of owner-occupancy—from 55 percent in 1979 to almost 68 percent in 1990 (Pierson 1994: 105). Massive inducements were offered to council housing tenants to buy their houses:

> These inducements started at a discount of 30 percent on a property's market value for tenants who had lived there for three years, with an extra one percent reduction for each additional

year of the tenancy. By the end of the 1980s, to maintain the momentum of sales, the discount had risen to a remarkable 70 percent. As a result, annual sales exceeded 100,000 throughout the 1980s and by 1992, approximately 1.75 million tenants had bought their homes. This permanently transformed the nature of the housing stock. (Lowe 2005: 366)

Council housing tenants took up the offer to buy not because they wanted to flee public housing, but, on the contrary, "because what the state had built was popular." In parts of Britain, council housing was "the robust, redistributive pinnacle of the local welfare state" (Murie 2014: 146–47). Tenants acted on the Right to Buy (RTB) because they liked living in their council estate and because council houses were offered at such a deep discount from market price.

Those who exercised the RTB were disproportionately skilled workers or families with two wage earners. They were "typically more affluent, middle-aged tenants living in attractive properties and likely to have remained as tenants had they not exercised the RTB" (Murie 2014: 151). Many benefited economically from the chance to purchase good quality housing at deeply discounted prices, and undoubtedly there would be those who would be grateful for that opportunity.

For that reason, the sale of council housing is usefully seen as part of a deliberate strategy to weaken the electoral base of the Labour Party:

> Housing tenure is strongly correlated with voting behaviour, and some research has suggested it is a stronger indicator than class itself. Working class owner-occupiers have proven themselves much more likely to vote Conservative than working class council tenants. (Waller 1994: 594)

"By 1995, 1.7 million tenants in Great Britain had bought a quarter of the 1980 stock" (Thane 2018: 353), in what amounted to a "dismantling of Britain's council housing" supply (Hanley 2007: 135). Further, many of those who exercised the Right to Buy later sold their unit to a private landlord who in turn rented it out "to people on housing benefit who couldn't get a council house, at double or triple the levels of council rent" (Meek 2014: 193).

For those who remained in council housing—disproportionately those unable to afford to purchase a council house—conditions worsened. The Conservatives slashed the housing budget, "from 7.3 billion pounds to 1.9 billion pounds." The rental subsidy ended and rents rose by about 40 percent (Addison 2010: 306). The proceeds from the sale of council houses, almost 3.5 billion pounds in 1988–1989, went to local authorities, who were forbidden from using the money for new housing (Addison 2010: 305). Nor was this money ploughed back into "long overdue infrastructural repairs" (Cannadine 2017: 82). Housing became dilapidated. "Houses are deteriorating faster than they can be renovated or replaced. At the 1983/84 rate of clearance it would take 1000 years to replace the existing stock" (Archbishop 1985: 241). The building of new council houses slowed to a crawl, reaching the lowest level since 1920 and was "negligible" by 1997 (Murie 2014: 154). As Lowe (2005: 367) argues,

> The converse of council house sales was the collapse of council housing building. In 1975, there were 145,600 completions by local authorities and new towns. In 1995 the figure had fallen to a mere 1900 … a lack of social housing was a major reason for increasing homelessness.

Indeed, homelessness grew, at least in part because of Conservative housing policies. "The 1980s saw an unparalleled rise in homelessness, with the figures doubling in England between 1978 and 1986" (Pierson 1992: 105–6). Census data for 1991 show 430,000 households that were homeless (Ginsburg 1997: 140). Their growing numbers added to the ranks of those deemed to be the undeserving poor.

Meanwhile, the most "vulnerable, transient and 'troublesome' households" were left on council estates. It was a process of "ghettoization of large sections of the inner city," which then became "sink estates" (Farrall and Hay 2014: 2018–19). This spatial concentration of the poorest of the poor reinforced the distinction between the deserving and undeserving poor—the deserving poor exercised the Right to Buy, the undeserving poor were left in sink estates where they "were cut adrift on islands of grotesque disadvantage compared with the rest of society, exposed as losers who cannot provide for themselves" (Hanley 2007: 215). This process "further delegitimized council housing, reinforcing its perceived associations with inner-city deprivation and high crime rates now firmly enshrined within the dominant ideology" (Hay 1992: 59).

Empirical evidence supports this interpretation. "Between 1980 and 1993 the average income of household heads in council housing fell from

48 to 35 percent of the average income of household heads in mortgaged owner occupation"; just under half of council housing tenants' incomes came from social security, compared to just over 9 percent for those who owned their homes (Ginsburg 1997: 142). If we consider the poorest 30 percent of households in Britain in 1968, 31 percent of them lived in council housing; by 1988, 61 percent lived in council housing. The poorest of the poor were increasingly being spatially concentrated in council housing that was deliberately being allowed to degrade, a process strikingly similar to what was occurring in most large American cities (Venkatesh 2000; Wacquant 2008).

Living in these increasingly deteriorating conditions in turn added to the psychological damage caused by poverty—the sense of hopelessness and despair. The dispiriting character of this poverty was accentuated by relentlessly rising inequality. "The UPAs (Urban Priority Areas) lie at the centre of an unequal society, their poverty obscured by the busy shopping precincts of mass consumption, their bare subsistence of dole and supplementary benefit existing alongside material opulence" (Archbishop 1985: 21).

Young people were particularly damaged by this "deepening polarization.... We cannot overstress the seriousness of this situation. The loss of hope and morale in many UPA schools borders on the catastrophic" (Archbishop 1985: 294–95). Addison (2010: 315, 326) made the same case:

> There were riots in the inner cities where large numbers of young people were out of work with little hope of finding a job. No longer was it unusual to see a beggar in the street, or the homeless sleeping in shop doorways.... Officials recognized that unemployment was slowly blighting parts of urban Britain, and especially the inner cities, where there were higher concentrations of the unskilled and the unemployed. For the first time since the 1930s, there were economic wastelands in which working class teenagers were growing up demoralized by lack of hope or incentive.

The dominant explanation was that the poor were to blame: "it is the poor who are seen by some as 'social security scroungers,' or a burden on the country, preventing economic recovery. This is a cruel example of blaming the victim" (Archbishop 1985: 17).

Police repression followed, driven in part by a massive media campaign blaming Black youth for inner city violence (Sim 1982). The *Faith in the City Report* (Archbishop 1985: 16–17) estimated that "55 percent of Black youths under nineteen [were] unemployed compared with a national rate for that age group of under 20 percent." The response was more policing. In 1982, since the 1979 Conservative election win,

> The police force had increased in strength by 8000. Expenditure had more than doubled in four years. Police pay was at an all-time high. There was to be a 500 million pound prison building and repair programme. New prisons were to be built at the rate of two per year over the next four years. The short sharp shock in detention centre regimes for young offenders was to become shorter and sharper. (Sim 1982: 69)

This was the authoritarian part of authoritarian populism; it was the strong state part of *The Free Economy and the Strong State* (Gamble 1988). Echoes of the *Poor Law*, when punishment was such a common response to poverty, were loud and clear.

The John Major Conservative governments of the 1990s continued with the Thatcher approach. "The rightwards, ideological trajectory was largely sustained," including "disdain for the 'undeserving poor'" and especially single mothers (Dorey 2011: 107). While Major appeared initially to be more liberal than Thatcher, "over time his actions seemed hardly distinguishable from hers" (Thane 2018: 396).

Inequality

During the Thatcher and Thatcher-inspired years, inequality, like poverty, rose dramatically. It rose substantially from 1980 in all of Europe and the US (Piketty 2020), but its growth in Britain was "exceptional compared with international trends" (Hills 1998: 5). And like the rise in poverty, it was deliberate. According to the Conservative Party's 1976 policy document *The Right Approach*, "if the able and enterprising are discouraged from the creation of wealth, the poor and the weak will suffer," because egalitarianism, "by levelling down ... dries up the springs of enterprise and endeavour, and ultimately means there are fewer resources for helping the disadvantaged" (Dorey 2011: 23).

As Gordon and his colleagues (2000: 8) found, "between 1979 and 1994–5, the incomes of the richest tenth of the population grew by 68 percent, while those of the poorest grew by only 10 percent, before housing costs, and fell 8 percent after housing costs." Goodman, Johnson and Webb (1997: 112, 274) observed, "the increase in inequality in the 1980s dwarfed the fluctuations in inequality seen in previous decades." They added, "all the evidence suggests that the experience of the 1980s is historically highly unusual, if not unprecedented." The Gini coefficient (a measure of total societal inequality), which had fallen by about four percentage points from 1949 to 1976–1977, rose by a remarkable ten percentage points between 1977 and 1990 (Hills 1996: 3).

The poor were paying the price for the prosperity of the majority. What was being created was "a one-third/two-thirds society—the poor, the unskilled and the unemployed forming a minority facing a majority of citizens with jobs, reasonable security and rising real incomes" (Gamble 1988: 214).

Thatcher saw this as a good thing. In a 1975 speech in New York, when leader of the Opposition, she had said,

> The pursuit of equality itself is a mirage. What's more desirable and more practical than the pursuit of equality is the pursuit of equality of opportunity. And opportunity means nothing unless it includes the right to be unequal … I believe you have a saying…. "Don't cut down the tall poppies. Let them grow tall." I would say, "Let our children grow tall and some taller than others if they have the ability in them to do so.' (Quoted in Walker 2014: 283)

Universality Erodes, Means-Testing Soars, Workfare and Private Delivery Emerge

While some were being encouraged to grow taller, Thatcher's Conservative governments accelerated the erosion of universality, replacing it with means-tested benefits. The latter doubled from less than 16 percent of the benefits bill in 1979 to 32 percent by 1997 (Walker 2011: 137). Narrowly targeted, means-tested programs were justified because they would target resources "on those of greatest need" (Walker 1993: 123).

However, targeted, means-tested programs, unlike universal programs, cut the poor off from the rest of society, which "no longer has a real stake in defending and improving what is becoming an increasingly stigmatized system associated with failure" (Walker 1993: 179). Means testing divides society into superior and inferior ranks and works to control the behaviour of those in the inferior ranks. As Townsend (1979: 823) puts it, "In different ways, benefits under means-tested schemes have to be conditional upon behaviour and upon the readiness of potential beneficiaries to submit themselves to test. The function of the schemes is as much to control behaviour as to meet need."

Further, the uptake of means-tested benefits is typically low. As Walker (2011: 142) argues, "the continued failure of many people to claim their entitlement is an inevitable and intended consequence of all means-tested systems." In 1981, 25 percent of those eligible for supplementary allowances, 33 percent of those eligible for supplementary pensions and 50 percent of those eligible for family income supplement were not receiving the benefit (Atkinson 1989: 190). This is in part because of the complexity involved in applying for benefits. For example, "the application form for Pension Credit, one of the simpler means-tested benefits, is 23 pages long" (Walker 2011: 138). The intent of these targeted programs is not at all to solve poverty by targeting resources at those in greatest need. The intent is to hold down costs. This was done, with reductions in virtually all means-tested benefits (Dorey 2011: Walker 2014), as Thatcher argued consistently that benefit levels were excessive and being abused by claimants (Loney 1987: 12).

Changes to the benefits regime produced "feelings of powerlessness, loss of self-esteem, a sense of guilt and stigma" (Cohen et al. 1992: vi). Dealing with staff in Department of Health and Social Security (DHSS) offices often added to the stress. "Encountering unsympathetic staff in a physically depressing environment ('it's a depressing place, cold, the clocks don't work'), many women found the experience alienating and impersonal: 'I just sign my name, feel like a convict, lining up and all that'" (Callender 1992: 140).

At the same time, offices that administered benefits were operating "under severe stress":

> Claimants often wait all day to be seen. Staff turnover in London is around 50 percent annually and the error-rate in some offices is over 50 percent.... Across the country hundreds of thousands of claims remain outstanding for many weeks, in spite of the urgency of the need. (Loney 1987: 15)

This was a product of Thatcher's neoliberal commitment to reducing the size of the state. Panitch and Leys (2020: 245) report that "between 1979 when Thatcher took office, and 2015, the central civil service was cut by about half."

Black and Asian claimants appear to have been treated particularly poorly in DHSS offices, subjected to stereotypical assumptions, and were even less likely than their white counterparts to claim benefits (Cook and Watt 1992).

Equally frustrating and demoralizing were efforts to force those on benefits into the paid labour force—welfare-to-work and workfare initiatives. As per the *Social Security Act* 1989, claimants had to be "actively seeking work" each week—effectively the "genuinely seeking work" test of the 1930s. However, the job centres intended to move claimants into jobs were ineffective. "There was a good deal of agreement among the claimants we spoke to that jobcentres were of little use to them," and back-to-work plans were described as suggesting the "stunningly obvious" (Bryson and Jacobs 1992: 231).* Interviewees referred to "fruitless efforts at chasing non-existent jobs" (Bryson and Jacobs 1992: 231–32). Based on their thorough study, Bryson and Jacobs (1992: xii) conclude that "we go some way to disposing with the 'scrounger' myth." Nevertheless, it was the enduring belief that those on benefits were scroungers who motivated the endless demands that they chase non-existent jobs. Thatcher believed there was no poverty and that improved benefit levels would worsen the "dependency culture" eroding Britain's economic strength. Benefit levels were cut, making it inevitable and deliberate that poverty would worsen.

Thatcher's governments also began a reorganization in the way social services were delivered. The postwar welfare state came to be seen as old-fashioned. "The wave of the future lay with care by 'informal networks,' 'voluntary action,' and families as well as the private sector" (Glennerster 1991: 26). The Conservative government adopted market models, or "quasi-markets"—the government pays, but a non-governmental body delivers the service. This was called the "purchaser-provider split," because "although services continued to be financed (or purchased) by

---

* The same was found to be the case in 2011. Interviewees found that obligatory back-to-work courses were a "waste of time" and served "little or no practical purpose in terms of helping them find work" (Chase and Walker 2012: 746). Patrick (2017: 87) found the same in her longitudinal interviews with benefits recipients.

government, they were delivered (or provided) under contract by a range of competing agencies" (Jones and Lowe 2002: 15). The stress was on flexibility and customer orientation, theories "created in the USA in the late 1970s as a response to the USA's declining economic competitiveness" (Clarke and Langan 1993: 67). The term "customers" replaced citizens, and managers replaced bureaucrats and professionals. "It is not that the state has been simply replaced by the market, but that what has remained of state welfare has been reconstructed to mimic the market through the creation of quasi-markets and quasi-customers" (Clarke and Langan 1993: 69). This was "a sustained attempt to dismantle the social democratic features of the post-war welfare settlement.... Heavily influenced by US theory and practice, this has pulled the state sector towards a more residualist position in relation to both welfare benefits and the provision of welfare services" (Clarke and Langan 1993: 73).

As social services were privatized and contracted out, labour was casualized. This disproportionately affected women because women held a high proportion of public-sector social service jobs. "Since the 1980s the trend has been to casualize even more women's work in the welfare services, and this has also made contracting out and privatization easier to put into effect" (Williams 1992: 61–62). Privatization meant job losses for women in the public sector, and "those who have transferred to the private cleaning and catering companies have seen their pay and conditions deteriorate" (Millar 1997: 106). This accentuated women's poverty.

The Importance of Redistribution

Left to itself, capitalism inevitably produces poverty and inequality. To drive down poverty and inequality, redistribution is essential. Mack and Lansley (1984: 285) make that case, arguing that "tackling the problem of poverty requires a substantial redistribution in society from the top half to the bottom half, and in particular to the bottom 15 percent." Not only was Thatcherism ideologically opposed to redistribution, but also it is unlikely that there existed in the 1980s and 1990s sufficient public support for the degree of redistribution that was needed. "The scale of the problem is such that ... the measures that would be required would not, at present, gain public support. While the public are generally sympathetic to the needs of the poor, the extent to which people are prepared to make personal sacrifices is limited" (Mack and Lansley 1984: 283).

Support would need to be built for such an approach to the elimination of poverty. As Leys (1995: 11) argues, "the market's power must be confronted, and this requires a sustained, sophisticated struggle to win the battle of ideas about the future of the country." That struggle would be a challenge, because support for a redistribution to the lower reaches of the income scale is weak. The British Social Attitudes Survey of 2010 revealed that Thatcherite attitudes deepened in the two decades *after* she left office. For example, "support for wealth redistribution has fallen to its lowest level in three decades, reflecting the extent to which poverty and gross inequality in Britain are blamed on the poor themselves" (Dorey 2010: 333). The survey results suggest that moral or character deficiencies are seen to be the primary causes of poverty, social security benefits are too high and recipients are abusing the system. Support still exists for the "deserving" but not for the "undeserving" poor—a centuries-old distinction:

> For example, whereas 80 percent of respondents [to the British Social Attitudes Survey of 2010] prioritized old age pensions for any additional social security expenditure, and 52 percent opted for disability benefits, only 15 percent cited benefits for single parents, while higher benefits for the unemployed were the preference of a mere 7 percent of respondents. (Dorey 2010: 341)

Hobsbawm (1995: 308) made a similar case about the growing gap between those who benefited economically under Thatcher and those who fell further behind:

> The bottom fifth of the workers actually became worse off compared to the rest of the workers than they had been a century earlier. And as the top 10 percent of workers, with gross earnings three times as high as those in the bottom tenth, congratulated themselves on their improvement, they were increasingly likely to reflect that, as national and local tax-payers, they were subsidizing what came, in the 1980s, to be called by the sinister term 'the underclass,' who lived on the public welfare system which they themselves could, they hoped, do without except in emergencies…. The skilled and respectable thus found themselves, perhaps for the first time, potential supporters of the political right.

The gap between skilled workers and the residuum that had emerged late in the nineteenth century had returned as an important by-product of Thatcherism, accentuating the centuries-old belief that the poor are themselves the cause of their poverty and making any attempt to solve poverty via redistribution even more difficult.

Chapter 10

New Labour, New Revisionism

Thatcherism in Redux

In the wake of Thatcherism, New Labour "inherited levels of poverty and inequality unprecedented in post-war history" (Stewart et al. 2009: 2). By 1997, when New Labour took office, "more than one in four UK children lived in relative poverty, compared to one in eight when Labour had left office in 1979…. Poverty among pensioners stood at 21 percent." More than one in six households had nobody in the paid labour force—double the rate in 1979 (Stewart and Hills 2005: 1–2).

New Labour made some gains, especially in reducing the levels of child and pensioner poverty, because "there is no doubt that, since 1997, the government has taken poverty and social exclusion very seriously" (Hills and Stewart 2005: 343). Some of the deserving poor—children and pensioners in particular—experienced reduced levels of poverty. However, inequality, which reached historically high levels under Thatcher, grew still further during the thirteen years of New Labour. Any gains made, especially with respect to child poverty, unraveled upon New Labour's leaving office in 2010. Given that New Labour made serious attempts to reduce poverty, it is important to understand why so much less was achieved than was both possible and necessary.

It was not the state of the economy that prevented significant reductions in poverty and inequality. Gordon Brown, chancellor of the exchequer, boasted in his 2004 budget that between 1997 and 2004, Britain had enjoyed "its longest period of sustained growth since the Industrial Revolution" (Lowe 2005: 380). The IMF praised the UK's economic performance: "During 1996–2005, the growth of real GDP per capita was higher and less volatile than in any other G7 country" (quoted in Lee 2008: 17). Davis and Rentoul (2019: 175) describe an "unprecedented sixteen years of unbroken growth between 1992 and 2008," when "the UK's gross domestic product rose by 48 percent … against 35 percent in France, 22 percent in Germany, 19 percent in Italy and 16 percent in Japan." Strong growth supported "one of the largest sustained increases in public spending of any government since 1945" (Meredith 2006: 239).

Further, New Labour enjoyed enormous electoral majorities in 1997 and 2001, as well as a smaller majority in 2005. In a parliamentary system, this gives a government considerable freedom to do what they think needs doing. Ed Balls, Brown's chief economic advisor and close political confidante, said,

> This was a really unprecedented time in British politics where you had a government for ten years which had a huge working majority, it had relatively strong public finances, it had no financial crisis knocking us off course ... which meant that we could do what we wanted to do and we weren't fighting events, we weren't on the defensive and we had big choices to make which we could deliver.... It was, we can make big decisions about how to reshape things and what are we going to do. (Quoted in Davis and Rentoul 2019: 249)

Yet gains in reducing poverty—with the partial and temporary exception of child and pensioner poverty—were modest, and inequality rose beyond the levels reached under Thatcherism.

The Labour governments headed by Attlee made very significant gains in reducing poverty and inequality, and they did so not while the economy was booming, as in the New Labour years, but while facing enormous economic challenges. Why was New Labour's performance with respect to poverty and inequality so modest?

The New Party of Middle Britain

The Labour Party, while out of office for eighteen years from 1979, "modernized" to secure middle-class votes. This was common among European social democratic parties, although New Labour likely led the way (Moschonas 2002). Labour leader Tony Blair said, "we are the party of Middle Britain" (quoted in Lister 1998: 216), and in many respects the party, calling itself New Labour, abandoned its traditional ideological trajectory and adopted a new and "modern" approach labelled the "Third Way." In 1998, Blair published *The Third Way: A New Politics for a New Century,* the purpose of which "was similar to that of Crosland:

to adapt social democracy to changed circumstances" (Lowe 2005: 32). Like Crosland and Gaitskell in the 1950s, Blair's and New Labour's was a revisionist project. Peter Mandelson (2020) xxviii, xxvix), one of the intellectual founders of New Labour along with Blair and Brown, argued that New Labour's "approach follows on logically from the revisionist thinking of the 1950s and 1960s ... by the Labour minister and theorist Anthony Crosland."

While the Third Way was described by New Labour as centre-left, "what appeared and was presented as the 'centre-left' is in reality the centre right" (Levitas 1998: 4). The move was further than just to the centre-right. "Tony Blair's government owes more to a neoliberal appreciation of the world than to any social democratic perspective," and modernization is "a metaphor for Labour's accommodation with Thatcherism" (Heffernan 2000: viii–ix). Dorling (2014a: 260) described New Labour as "Thatcherism continued"; Crouch (1999: 70) called New Labour "Thatcher's well-behaved step-children, her direct progeny"; and Piketty (2020: 845) wrote that New Labour "largely validated and perpetuated the fiscal reforms of the Thatcher era."

Modernization began under Neil Kinnock's leadership from 1983 to 1992. Kinnock's policy review of 1988 "marked a clear shift away from the political economy of socialism, ethical or otherwise" (Driver and Martell 1998: 18). The shift continued during John Smith's brief tenure and took full flight from 1994 when Tony Blair became Party leader. Blair became prime minister in 1997 when New Labour was elected with the largest majority in the Party's history. New Labour would remain in office until 2010, although Blair left in 2007. Blair had no real experience in left politics and has been described as having "no roots, no clear grounding, in politics [or] the Labour Party" (Norton 2008: 90). Hannah (2018: 199) argues that Blair did not betray his roots, "as he had no roots to betray." Rawnsley (2010: 6) argues that "ideologically, Blair appeared to be of no fixed abode," he "didn't have a socialist bone in his body." This was confirmed when in 2015 Blair said, in response to the then likelihood that Jeremy Corbyn would become Labour leader, "Let me make my position clear: I wouldn't want to win on an old-fashioned leftist platform. Even if I thought it was the route to victory, I wouldn't take it" (quoted in Wayne 2021).

This abandonment of Labour's social democratic roots was reflected in changes to the Labour Party itself. First, Kinnock effectively marginalized the Bennite Campaign for Labour Party Democracy and other left elements (Heffernan and Marqusee 1992; Hannah 2018). Under Blair, power within the Party was centralized and activism atrophied (Panitch and Leys 1997). Party membership "collapsed after 1997" from 405,000 to 248,000 by 2004 (Lowe 2005: 383–84), 198,026 in 2005, 182,370 by the end of 2006 (Lee 2008: 195) and 153,140 by 2009 (Panitch and Leys 2020: 157). This was part of the collapse of the working-class vote for left parties in Europe (Piketty 2020). In May 2006, a Labour MP said, "The Party has disappeared. There are no local parties. There's nothing to campaign with. It's all top down and instructed from Party headquarters; all the regional organizers have gone" (Hannah 2018: 213; for the case of Burnley, as an example, see Makin-Waite 2021).

The Party abandoned its long-held commitment to equality of outcomes, in the Thatcherite belief that such efforts would be a constraint on the economy (Blair 2010: 45). During the 1997 election campaign, New Labour committed to not raising income tax rates and to stay with Conservative spending plans for the first two years. New Labour's program included promoting "free trade, flexible labour markets, sound money and the spirit of entrepreneurial capitalism, not to mention greater individual self-help and private initiative in welfare" (Driver and Martell 1998: 2). Blair said,

> I think one of the great changes that has happened in the whole Labour culture is to recognize that we need entrepreneurs and people who are going to go out and be wealth creators and who are going to become wealthy by their own efforts. I support that, I want that, a successful economy needs that. (Quoted in Driver and Martell 1998: 26)

Blair held numerous meetings prior to 1997 with businesspeople "to ram home the seriousness of their commitment to working in partnership with business and securing their support" (Driver and Martell 1998: 67–68). Corporate taxes were cut in the 1997 and 1998 budgets, bringing them to "the lowest level in British history" (Sheldrick 2000: 111) and the lowest in major industrial countries (Callinicos 2001: 53). He "packed his team with business and City figures and has missed no chance to declare Labour 'the party of business'" (Marqusee 1997: 128). Gordon Brown, like Blair, reached out in particular to the City—London's financial centre, as Wall Street is to the US. In 1997 Brown asserted, "The

City has demonstrated the best qualities of our country, what I describe as the British genius," and in 2005 he thanked the City for "the invaluable contribution you make to the prosperity of Britain" (Rawnsley 2010: 476). As Coates (2013: 49) described it, "Between 1997 and 2010 New Labour went to bed with global bankers." Blair, like Brown, took it "as a given that globalization imposes very severe limits on all social and economic policies, so that the only ones worth promoting are those that capital—'the market'—will accept" (Leys 2003: 250). In a 1995 speech to the British Chamber of Commerce, Blair said, "old Labour thought the role of government was to interfere with the market. New Labour believes the role of government is to make the market more dynamic, to provide people and business with the means of success" (quoted in Heffernan 2000: 22). New Labour was "every bit as much geared by the aspirations of the up-and-coming as the anxieties of the down-and-out" (Blair 2010: 28) Blair himself appears to have been similarly aspiring. He earned an enormous amount of money after leaving office, lived in luxurious surroundings and moved among the rich and famous—as described by Murray (2019: 118), "pimping for dictators and oligarchs." In that respect, as in so many others, he set himself apart from Old Labour (Marcetic 2017). The result was to severely restrict the kinds of state-driven, redistributive anti-poverty measures so desperately needed in the wake of eighteen years of Thatcherism.

While building links with business, New Labour loosened its historic relationship with labour. "Blair, Brown and company have actually behaved as if they really liked businessmen far more than workers—they probably do" (Sassoon 1999: 31). Blair described unions as just another interest group, to be "treated with fairness but not favours.... In 1997, if Labour had friends and a special relationship, it was at least as much with sections of the business community as with the unions" (Driver and Martell 1998: 69). The TUC [Trades Union Congress] General Secretary likened unions' presence in New Labour to "embarrassing elderly relatives at a family reunion" (quoted in Thane 2018: 439). New Labour maintained most of Thatcher's restrictive policies on picketing, strike ballots and union elections (Heffernan and Marqusee 1992: 143), so that "the UK legal regime regulating industrial action persists as one of the most restrictive in the EU" (Shaw 2008: 124).

This was in part a function of Britain's changing class structure. Manufacturing had declined to a mere 20 percent of the British economy in 1997; by 2007, it was just over 12 percent. While 16 percent of jobs had been in manufacturing in 1997, by 2007 it was less than 10 percent. There were 4.3 million manufacturing workers in 1997, but just over 2.5 million in 2010 (Coates 2013: 44). Every year New Labour was in office "around 100,000 manufacturing jobs were lost" (Murray 2019: 107). Capitalist firms—which for many decades had failed to invest and modernize and which were hurt by the loss of their colonial empire—were continuing to relocate to low-wage jurisdictions, to use automation to replace workers and to shift investments from manufacturing to finance. In the 1980s, while manufacturing investment grew by just under 13 percent, investment in financial and business services had grown by just over 320 percent (Coates 2002: 17). The traditional industrial working class, the electoral mainstay of old Labour, was rapidly diminishing, increasingly replaced by finance and service-sector workers. By 2000, "twice as many people worked in retailing and banking as in the entirety of British-based manufacturing" (Coates 2002: 4).

Further, Britain, which had been a relatively high-wage economy immediately after the war, had as early as the 1970s become a low-wage economy, with the lowest labour costs in Western Europe except for Ireland (Coates 2002: 18). Growing numbers of the poor were the working poor. They were poor because capitalist firms, supported by New Labour, took the steps to ensure that their wages were low, their work part-time, their jobs insecure and they were in and out of work—the low-pay/no-pay/no-future phenomenon discussed below. This was the return of the centuries-old phenomenon of precarious labour on a massive scale.

As part of its modernization, Blair continued New Labour's emphasis on image, begun under Kinnock. Desai (1994a: 185) calls Kinnock's policy review "a cynical image-building capitulation to a seemingly hegemonic Thatcherism." In 1985 Kinnock created the "Communications and Campaign Directorate" under the direction of Peter Mandelson, "New Labour's most fervent advocate" (Peck 2001: 279). Mandelson "believed that Labour's basic problem was that it appeared too left-wing and 'extreme'" (Heffernan and Marqusee 1992: 209). Mandelson worked aggressively to sell New Labour to the mainstream media. As Panitch and Leys (1997: 221) describe it,

> electors were now seen primarily as consumers of party programmes, with already-given attitudes and interests, rather than

as people who could be persuaded to find their needs and aspirations met in the party's project for social change…. [This was] a decisive shift away from the concept of the party as a shaper and leader of opinion, towards the idea of the party as marketing products—products which could themselves be more or less indefinitely modified in the light of "market testing."

Alistair Campbell became press secretary, "the personification of spin," as Rawnsley (2010: 9) describes him. As early as 1986, a survey conducted as part of image shaping concluded the Party was "too associated with the poor, the unemployed, the sick, the disabled, pacifists, trade unions and minorities, all of which placed it at a great disadvantage to the Tories, who were increasingly seen to be 'for everyone'" (Heffernan and Marqusee 1992: 211).

Leys (2003: 236) argues that whatever its limitations, the Labour Party's original ethos was comprised of "the most egalitarian, humanistic, unselfish, internationalist and brave elements of progressive British culture." However, Blair "operates in a milieu based on a different ethos, an ethos of professional politics based on higher education management skills, and the culture of the communications industry. Some of the chief exponents of this ethos more or less openly despise that of the old Labour movement." Roy Hattersley, typically seen as a part of the Old Labour right, said about New Labour, "the present leadership had abandoned ideology so completely, and was so preoccupied with winning middle-class support, that its commitment to the fundamental needs of the 'disadvantaged' was no longer clear." He added that socialism "requires the bedrock of principle to be the redistribution of power and wealth" (quoted in Panitch and Leys 1997: 232). Blair and New Labour were adamantly opposed to the redistribution of power and wealth.

Old Labour was committed, at least in principle, to redistribution. New Labour's approach "progressively undermines a redistributive agenda" (Levitas 1998: 47). As Driver and Martell (1998: 40) put it, "The succession of Tony Blair marked the beginning of the end of Labour as a party committed to the politics of redistribution." Stuart Hall (2005: 321) writes that "The welfare state had been Labour's greatest achievement. It had been savaged and weakened under Mrs. Thatcher. But its wholesale destruction was to be New Labour's historic mission."

Any real solution to poverty requires redistribution, which in turn requires confronting the market. However, "The market was accepted under Kinnock. Under Blair it has become positively celebrated" (Driver and Martell 1998: 40).

Part of New Labour's image was that the party was pragmatic, dispensing with old ideologies, pursuing policies that would "work" (Kavanagh 2007: 10). The objective was to reach beyond Old Labour's core vote (Heffernan 2007: 144). New Labour targeted voters who were "female, in the south-east, homeowners, and among the aspirational working class who had switched to Margaret Thatcher" (Kavanagh 2007: 9). New Labour's values changed, "because of fear of alienating a Middle England electorate" deemed sympathetic to Thatcherite values (Lister 2001: 441). The result was an accommodation with much of Thatcherism. As Lister (2002: 6) describes it, Blair's "what matters is what works" approach, his "dogmatic pragmatism, diverts attention from the need for more systemic structural change." New Labour was opposed to systemic structural change.

In his memoir, Blair (2010: 317) wrote,

> Where Mrs. Thatcher was absolutely on the side of history was in recognizing that as people became more prosperous, they wanted the freedom to spend their money as they chose; and they didn't want a big state getting in the way of that liberation by suffocating people in uniformity, in the drabness and dullness of the state monopoly. It was plain that competition drove up standards, and that high taxes were a disincentive. Anything else ignored human nature.

At the same time, there continued to be little public support for efforts to reduce poverty and inequality. As Sefton (2009: 225, 238), drawing upon national surveys and opinion polls, concludes,

> poverty in Britain is low down the general public's list of policy priorities.... Qualitative studies find little evidence of empathy for the poor and an overwhelming tendency to attribute poverty to deficiencies of personal behaviour, such as poor parenting or financial mismanagement, rather than structural explanations.

Peoples' attitudes to poverty can change, but a government would have to set out consciously to provide the kind of information and analysis to create such a change. New Labour did not do so (Sefton 2009)—theirs was a different approach. This is perhaps exemplified by the fact that in his 566-page volume describing his central role in the New Labour project, Mandelson (2010) makes no mention whatever of poverty or inequality. He confirms the centrality to New Labour of middle-class voters and those who aspired to be middle class.

Thatcher took much of the credit "for what seemed to be Labour's abandonment of socialism and nationalization, and its embrace of the free market, free enterprise and wealth creation" (Cannadine 2017: 125). She said, when asked what her greatest achievement was, "Tony Blair and New Labour. We forced our opponents to change their minds" (quoted in Panitch 2009: xiv). *The Guardian,* in an April 30, 2017, editorial on the twentieth anniversary of New Labour's initial election victory, concurs:

> The 13 years of New Labour did not transform the country as Attlee's 1945 government had done. They left none of the radical and lasting institutional change. They did more to affirm than to challenge the Thatcherite idea of the small state, and they never did enough to challenge the supremacy of market forces.

To many Labour Party members, *The Guardian* continued, "New Labour felt like 'politics as usual' rather than a radical force … it changed the party rather than the country." New Labour would not stand up to moneyed interests, "mainly for fear of being considered anti-business" (*Guardian,* April 30, 2017). New Labour's acceptance of much of Thatcherism, and its embrace of the free market, had major implications for social security, poverty and inequality.

New Welfare State: Make the Poor "Take Responsibility"

Blair was intrigued by new, more conservative communitarian ideas (Patrick 2017), especially the seemingly reasonable notion that with rights came responsibilities (Blair 1998: 3–4). However, taking responsibility came to mean ending what Blair called a "dependency culture." In this, Blair followed directly in Thatcher's footsteps, and Thatcher in turn had borrowed heavily from the US, and their belief in the obligation of those on welfare to "take responsibility." This set New Labour on the road, well-trodden by Thatcherism, to welfare-to-work and workfare—Brown's first budget in 1997 was described as a "welfare-to-work budget"

(R. Walker 1999: 684). Britain under New Labour would become a leading "workfare state" (Peck 2001).

The justification was the centuries-old belief that the undeserving poor were the authors of their own misfortunes. In his 1999 Beveridge lecture, Blair is paraphrased as having said, "In Beveridge's time the welfare state was associated with progress and advancement. Today it is often associated with dependency, fraud, abuse, laziness" (Dorling 2014a: 264). Powell (2002: 31) writes that "Labour phrases about 'hard-working families who play by the rules' and the end of the 'something for nothing welfare state' draw on deeply entrenched views about the 'deserving' and 'undeserving.'" Those on social security were the "undeserving," the "Other" (Lister 2001: 431).

Creating the conditions that enable those without employment to find jobs is in principle a good thing. A good job is the best road out of poverty, as long argued. For many of those long mired in poverty, finding a job and contributing to family well-being is a source of dignity and self-esteem.

However, it is not just any job that lifts people out of poverty. It is a good job—well paid, with benefits, job security and union protection. New Labour's approach was to push the unemployed and lone mothers into the low end of an increasingly precarious labour market. This was "social inclusion." People were to be moved from being excluded to being "included" via work, but the work in most cases would be precarious and poorly paid.

As a result, growing numbers of the poor in the Blair years were the working poor. In addition, "in certain parts of the country there are simply not the jobs there" at all (Lister 1998: 220). By 2011, the year after New Labour left office, there were twenty-three job seekers in the UK for every vacancy. "For every retail job, there were forty-two applications; in customer services it was forty-six" (Jones 2012: xii). To move people into those low-wage jobs, New Labour subsidized low-wage employers. The main policy was the Working Families Tax Credit. As a *Guardian* journalist puts it, tax credits are "essentially the state subsidizing poverty wages" (quoted in Jones 2012: 205).

Little effort was made to create "good" jobs. Job creation was left to the market, consistent with Blair's ideological orientation. To create "good" jobs—jobs that were well-paid, with benefits and job security and union protections, and that put people to work doing the multiplicity of things that need doing—would have required the redistribution and state intervention to which New Labour was firmly opposed. There was a "complete absence of any industrial policy" (Moschonas 2002: 194), other than that promoted by capitalists and by New Labour, which involved the creation of precarious jobs to drive down costs and maximize profits.

Some of the steps taken were positive, in principle, but were not enough to have the impact that the colossal levels of poverty left by Thatcherism required. For example, protections against unfair dismissal were improved, maternity leave was extended, women could not be dismissed for any reason related to pregnancy, all workers were entitled to four weeks of annual paid leave, and the Child Benefit was raised, among other changes (Thane 2018). A minimum wage was introduced in 1999, but it "was set at the lowest possible level" and was two-tiered, with even lower wages for young workers (Jones 2012: 204). If it had any effect on poverty levels, that effect was "modest" (Joyce and Sibieta 2013: 197; for life on the minimum wage, see Toynbee 2003).

Rather than create good jobs, New Labour's employment efforts were almost entirely on the supply side. Thatcher had done the same. New Labour helped people to search for work and improve work-related skills and imposed "greater coercion to find work" (McKnight 2005: 23). The New Deal for Young People, implemented in 1998 and compulsory for those aged eighteen to twenty-four and out of work for six months, provided tailored preparation for work and job search assistance by a personal advisor (McKnight 2005). Young people were to be assisted in moving into precarious and often dead-end jobs, and compulsion was involved. Labour's New Deals—for young people, lone parents, people with disabilities and others—were how welfare-to-work, or workfare, was delivered (Driver 2008: 52–53).

However, the long history of British efforts to place people in jobs, first through labour exchanges established in 1909 and later in various successors, has been uninspiring. As King (1995: 6, 16) writes, "Their placement records were dismal." Labour exchanges "not only failed effectively to place many of those seeking work, but institutionalized the systematic exclusion and political weakness of the most disadvantaged job seekers and welfare recipients." New Labour was treading old ground—ground that in the past had been proved not to be fertile.

Pushing those on assistance into the paid labour force in this fashion was a major part of New Labour's commitment to social inclusion, and social inclusion was being substituted for social equality, particularly equality of outcomes, despite social equality having historically been the central purpose of social democracy.

Levitas (1998: 7) unpacked Blair's concept of "social inclusion," saying the concept assumes the main division in society is that "between an included majority and an excluded minority."* This suggests a simple, bimodal social structure—those who are included, and those who are excluded. With such a conceptualization, social class disappears, and the wealthy capitalist class is rolled in with the working class, "their power and privilege slipping out of focus if not wholly out of sight." The poor are not a part of this social structure. They are outside of it—excluded. The solution is to push them toward inclusion, but inclusion at the bottom of an increasingly hierarchical and precarious labour market. "The solution implied by a discourse of social inclusion is a minimalist one: a transition across the boundary to become an insider rather than an outsider in a society whose structural inequalities remain largely uninterrogated" (Levitas 1998: 7). Steadily worsening poverty and inequality were too substantial to be addressed with minimalist efforts at the margins.

Borrowing from America: Force Them to Work

Much of New Labour's thinking about the welfare state and the responsibilities of social assistance recipients had its origins in the US, especially with former president Bill Clinton. Giddens (2008: xv) argues that "Labour drew too much upon the New Democrats in the US, and not enough from avant-garde social democracy, such as practiced in the Scandinavian countries." Blair was exceptionally close to Clinton. The six-page introduction to Blair's *A Journey: My Political Life*, is virtually entirely about America, how "I came to love America" and how Blair's philosophy "echoed many of the sentiments of Bill Clinton" (Blair 2010: xii, 29). A report in the *Financial Times*, April 26, 1997, said of Blair that "he designed and built New Labour, using blueprints faxed from Little Rock" (quoted in King and Wickham-Jones 1999: 279). Clinton told Blair and the New Labour modernizers that a left party had to move to the centre. This required getting tough on welfare recipients and push-

---

* It is important to note that the term "social exclusion" can be and has been used in a wide variety of ways. Hilary Silver (1994: 572) concludes her study by saying "just as the idea of exclusion has many meanings, it can also serve a variety of political purposes." Levitas provides useful insight into how New Labour used the concept.

ing them into paid employment. Clinton did this with his 1996 *Personal Responsibility and Work Opportunity Reconciliation Act* (foreshadowed by Newt Gingrich's *Contract with America*)—punitive legislation that "got tough" with those on welfare. Blair followed suit.

Patriquin (2001: 72) describes the import of Clinton's *Personal Responsibility and Work Opportunity Reconciliation Act*:

> The individual's right to cash assistance from the federal government was abolished, replaced by a lifetime maximum of five years in which a citizen can receive welfare benefits. People are ineligible for monetary assistance after they reach this maximum, regardless of demonstrated needs.

Such measures were unprecedented, Patriquin argues, and New Labour copied them. Alistair Darling, speaking in 2002 as New Labour's minister of work and pensions, said, "there is no unconditional right to benefit" (quoted in Lister 2002: 2). Yet even the 1601 *Elizabethan Poor Law* required that those in need be paid out of the rates. The whole purpose of the *Personal Responsibility and Work Opportunity Reconciliation Act* was to force people to work by reducing or even cutting off payments. The *Act* especially targeted the "undeserving" poor.

One of Clinton's measures was the Earned Income Tax Credit (EITC), the inspiration for New Labour's Working Families Tax Credit (WFTC). The EITC is "a refundable tax credit that is delivered to about 19 million working households, mostly those with children." This moved a significant number of children out of poverty, clearly a positive outcome. However,

> the program provides little to individuals without dependents.... Most importantly, the EITC is a *work* supplement. It does not provide any assistance to those who are completely unemployed, nor does it address the issue of the absence of an adequate number of well-paying jobs. (Patriquin 2001: 89, emphasis in original)

It was a form of compulsion, pushing people into any jobs available at pain of losing entitlement to social security benefits. In 1999, when New Labour introduced the WFTC, the *Wall Street Journal* was clear about what was happening: "Britain launches workfare subsidy" (quoted in Peck 2001: 324).

The harshness of this workfare approach can be seen in the remarkable case of Wisconsin, where all claimants were required to work and "lone mothers were required to work when their youngest child was twelve weeks old" (Levitas 1998: 18). It is little exaggeration to equate such measures with the 1834 *New Poor Law*—an argument compellingly advanced by Somers and Block (2005). The Wisconsin example is significant because, as Robert Walker (1999: 684) observes, "civil servants, cabinet ministers and Members of Parliament all made trips to Wisconsin, considered a bellwether state for welfare reform." Wacquant (quoted in Slater 2012: 952) calls it the "mental colonization of British policy makers by the United States."

Workfare was designed, at least in part, to appeal to the middle-class voters that New Labour so anxiously courted. "The 2012 British Social Attitudes (BSA) Survey found that 'negative perceptions of welfare recipients are a pretty constant strand in British public opinion,'" as is 'an increasing belief that the welfare system encourages dependence'" (Walker 2014: 299). The widely held public belief that social assistance promoted dependency and that such people were therefore "undeserving"—a belief long encouraged by Thatcherism—led to policies aimed at pushing "scroungers" into the paid labour force. New Labour made no efforts to educate middle-class opinions, as would have been needed to create broad support for a different approach to poverty.

The resort to compulsion via workfare was a sharp break from the previous beliefs of the Labour Party, whose national executive had, in the 1980s, signed a "Charter against Workfare" (Patrick 2017: 43). The postwar Labour Party opposed any kind of compulsion in the provision of welfare. "Labour's rejection of workfare, an arrangement under which claimants must take work in exchange for social security benefits, was unequivocal.... This commitment to universal social rights was a benchmark of the Party's welfare programme between 1945 and 1992" (King and Wickham-Jones 1999: 257). As Deacon (2002: 108) writes, "The introduction of compulsion represented a massive U-turn for the Labour Party."

New Labour set out their welfare-to-work/workfare approach prior to 1997. The *Financial Times* (November 10, 1995) quoted Gordon Brown, then shadow chancellor of the exchequer, saying, "Simply remaining unemployed and permanently on benefit will no longer be an option" (quoted in King and Wickham-Jones 1999: 258). Brown was committed to the workfare programs, especially for those ages eighteen to twenty-five, introduced by Thatcher in 1988, on loan from America (Dolowitz 1998).

However, if we go further back in history, the matter of requiring that people work for wages in return for benefits can be seen as more complex. Early in the twentieth century, progressive Labour Party members supported the idea that those on benefits should be required to work. Keir Hardie held that this was a moral obligation. George Lansbury said that "everyone should do their share of the work of the community" (quoted in Jackson 2005: 141). This was considered a matter of fairness—an egalitarian principle. Beveridge (1942: 58) advanced the same case in laying the foundations for the welfare state, saying the quid pro quo for its benefits was "enforcement of the citizen's obligation to seek and accept all reasonable opportunities of work."

The fairness principle, however, requires that the obligation to work be extended to the rich as well. As Jackson (2005: 144) puts it,

> This long-standing and powerful egalitarian vision sees individuals as equal participants in social co-operation, entitled to equal rights but also bound by the same obligations as their fellow citizens. This captures the essence of a desirable egalitarian society: free and equal citizens working together to create a prosperous and just community.

However, Blair wanted to force those aged eighteen to twenty-four years to take poorly paid jobs in the precarious labour market, jobs with no future and no security and no benefits, while those in the City were making millions annually. This was simply not consistent with "free and equal citizens working together to create a prosperous and just community." Blair opposed any limits on what the rich could accumulate, while he forced the poor into precarious jobs that would leave them in poverty. As Thane (2000: 115) puts it: "Labour entered the twentieth century behind the slogan 'The Right to Work or Full Maintenance.' It ended the century offering 'Welfare to Work.' There had been a shift from a conception of work as a right, to work as an obligation."

New Labour's adoption of workfare is best understood in the context of the dramatic changes in Britain's economy and social structure. The welfare state—identified so closely with "Old Labour"—was part of the Fordist regime, based on mass production, mass consumption, the nuclear family with a male breadwinner, and low levels of unemployment. The Fordist regime came apart in the 1970s and especially in Thatcher's 1980s—as it did throughout the Western world. Unemployment soared. Manufacturing employment plummeted. Lone parenthood grew. Precarious jobs ballooned. The social structure changed. The Keynesian welfare state did not fit this new, post-Fordist socio-economic structure.

Thatcher had come to office determined to drive down public spending but could not because the costs of social security, especially unemployment benefits, rose steadily. To solve this, people had to be put to work. However, the jobs available were unattractive. They were precarious. So, from the late 1980s, workfare—which took a wide variety of forms and was implemented to a greater or lesser extent in virtually all Western industrial countries—emerged to force people into such jobs. Workfare was needed for "regulating flows of labour around the bottom of the labour market" (Peck 2001: 39). New Labour would, however, go further than Thatcher in imposing workfare.

To make this possible, those not in the paid labour force had to continue to be reviled and denigrated. Thus, it necessitated the resurgence of the age-old narrative that the poor had only themselves to blame for their poverty and so were undeserving of rights-based benefits. New Labour perpetuated the use of "welfare dependency," a US import adopted by Thatcherism, and described welfare as "passive." More than that, Alan Walker (1999: 299) describes how "Labour continued the 'scrounger' rhetoric and launched increasingly uncompromising advertising campaigns drawing attention to 'benefits thieves.'" The "benefits thieves" were warned by "the menacing voice-over of the television advertisements, 'we're closing in.'" The implication was that if you are not working we will find you and force you to work. This was aimed especially at young people and poor single mothers—who "should be dependent on a man or a wage, not on welfare" (Peck 2001: 34). It was aimed also at what were seen by many as the demoralized and degenerate ghettoes of Britain's inner cities, where "dependency" was thought to be rampant. The workhouse and Poor Laws had performed this role in earlier centuries; workfare was to function similarly in the post-Fordist, late twentieth and early twenty-first centuries.

In the absence of any attempt to use the redistributive powers of the state to create good jobs, a strategy to which New Labour was ideologically opposed, the post-Fordist era of precarious labour necessitated the replacement of welfare with workfare. Too many people were dependent upon benefits. Their numbers had to be reduced. The numbers working for wages had to be increased. As Peck (2001: 6, my emphasis) writes, "workfare is not about creating jobs for people that don't have them; *it is about creating workers for jobs that nobody wants*. In a Foucauldian sense, it is seeking to make 'docile bodies' for the new economy: flexible, self-reliant, and self-disciplining."

As had been the case in the Industrial Revolution of the nineteenth century, capitalism created thoroughly unattractive jobs; force was required to fill them.

To some extent, New Labour's shift to compulsion "worked." By 2001, "unemployment had fallen below a million for the first time since 1975, long-term unemployment was lower than at any time since 1979 and over 280,000 young people had left the New Deal for jobs" (Deacon 2002: 109).

However, a closer look at the numbers suggests otherwise. Real rates of youth unemployment remained high: "as many as 20 percent of the young aged sixteen to twenty-four in 2005—nearly a million—were not in education, training or employment, with a calculated loss to the economy of 10 million pounds a day," a number little changed from the mid-1990s (Taylor 2007: 237).

In 2011, the year after New Labour left office, "unemployment rates amongst young black men rose again to above 50 percent. Rates for young black women had reached that level in 2009" (Dorling 2014a: 266). At the beginning of 2014, one in five residents of the UK under twenty-five years of age was still out of work (Dorling 2014b: 71). This was seventeen years after the announcement of the "New Deal for Young People."

Near the end of New Labour, Toynbee and Walker (2008: 82) wrote that "over half of families in poverty are in work: paid the minimum wage, what they earn does not lift the household out of poverty." Three-quarters of those who moved from welfare to work found employment in the poorly paid, precarious jobs that capitalists were creating (Peck 2001: 284). These jobs did not necessarily lift the children in such families out of poverty. "The UK has one of the highest employment rates of the industrialized world but it also has significant problems of in-work poverty with over half of poor children living in a household with a parent in work" (Fons 2011: 19).

Large numbers were simply deterred from applying for benefits—a "huge number of people who would simply walk away from welfare upon learning about the new quid pro quo of work for benefits" (quoted in Peck 2001: 348). Overall, poverty did not decline, unemployment—especially among young adults and ethnic minorities—remained high, and low-wage, precarious jobs kept many who were working below the poverty line. Pushing people into low-paid, precarious jobs proved not to be a solution to poverty.

Nevertheless, New Labour made some gains in reducing child and pensioner poverty. It is important that this be acknowledged and that its limitations be understood.

A Scar on Britain's Soul

When New Labour took office in 1997, following almost two decades of Thatcherism, the level of child poverty in Britain was staggering. New Labour "inherited one of the poorest records on child poverty in the developed world," and in fact "the 1980s and 1990s had seen a three-fold increase in the numbers of children in poverty" (Millar and Ridge 2002: 87). In 2000, Britain's child poverty rate was 32 percent, the highest in the European Union (Fabian Society 2006: 9). By comparison, the child poverty rate was 12 percent in France, 13 percent in Germany and an average of 20 percent in the European Union (Lowe 2005: 408). It was, Gordon Brown (1999: 8) wrote, "a scar on Britain's soul."

To his credit, Blair committed to ending this moral and economic tragedy. In the 1999 Beveridge Lecture, he committed to eliminating child poverty by 2020: "It is a 20 year mission, but I believe it can be done" (Blair 1999: 7). Shortly after, he set a goal of cutting child poverty by 25 percent by 2004–2005, and by one-half by 2010. As Millar and Ridge (2002: 99) argued, "the goal to end child poverty is one of the most radical of the government's promises and few would disagree with the importance of this goal."

Among the reasons for the rapid growth of child poverty were the growing number of households with no one in the paid labour force. "One in five children lived in a household with no member in work in 1997, compared to just 8 percent in 1979. This in turn was partly due to the fact that more children were living with a single parent—22 percent in 1995/96, up from 10 percent in 1979" (Stewart 2005: 144).

Numerous policies aimed at child poverty were implemented early by New Labour. Stewart (2007: 424) described these as "a sea change in the support, services and opportunities available to pre-school children and their parents" (for details, see Stewart 2009). Poor parents who were working benefited from tax credits intended to make work pay; those out of work benefited from improved levels of means-tested benefits; the New Deal for Lone Parents provided supports in preparing for and finding employment. Largely because of the Working Families Tax Credit, by 2010–2011,

> 25 billion pounds per year was spent on tax credits, most of which went to low-income households with children.... Overall, reforms between 1997 and 2010 amounted to an 18 billion pounds annual increase in spending on benefits for families with children and an 11 billion pound annual increase in spending on benefits for pensioners. (Joyce and Sibieta 2013: 195)

As early as 2000, the annual income of poor families had been increased, on average, between 1,300 and 3,000 pounds, amounting to about a third of the average poor families' annual income (Lowe 2005: 407). Stewart and Obolenskaya (2016: 35) report that New Labour's spending on cash benefits for families with children doubled between 1997 and 2007. Investment in a wide range of services for young children—including a National Childcare Strategy launched in 1998—was increased substantially.

An example was Sure Start Local Programmes (SSLPs), started in 1999, which "brought together a range of health and social workers in a variety of initiatives, such as toddler groups and toy libraries. The objective was to ensure that, on entering school, children from the most deprived areas were not at a disadvantage" (Lowe 2005: 407). A 1998 report, *Bringing Britain Together,* identified some 3,000 neighbourhoods with high rates of poverty, unemployment, crime and poor health. In 2000, New Labour launched the National Strategy for Neighbourhood Renewal (Lupton and Power 2005), rooted in a "vision that within 10 to 20 years, no-one should be seriously disadvantaged by where they lived" (Social Exclusion Unit 2001, quoted in Lister 2002: 8). Sure Start, modelled on the American Head Start Program, was a central part of this strategy. It was "hugely ambitious" and "aimed to change the long-term development trajectories of young children" (Stewart 2009: 66).

The SSLPs were focused initially on 250 of the most deprived areas, increased to 522 by 2004 (Stewart 2005: 147), in each of which all children under five were enrolled. In 2006, they became children's centres under local authority control.

A 2010 evaluation found there were some gains—for example, in school readiness, by five-year-old children involved in the SSLPs—but the gains were modest (Melhuish et al. 2010). The evidence revealed that meaningful gains would require sustained investment over time (Power 2009: 122). Also, Sure Start and related programs had been conceived of and rolled out so quickly that residents and parents in these low-income neighbourhoods could not possibly have been involved in a meaningful way in determining what was needed and what might work best (Lister 1999: 94). This itself would increase the likelihood that Sure Start initiatives would not produce large benefits, as would the fact that in such neighbourhoods, there are no quick fixes. Investment must be maintained consistently over time.

It was not. After New Labour left office, the Sure Start children's centres eroded. Between 2011 and 2016, more than 350 Sure Start children's centres closed in England, and spending on the program was cut by more than half. Between 2010 and 2018, five hundred child centres closed (Alston 2018: 3).

Lupton (2003) argues that New Labour's various New Deal for Communities programs were unsuccessful at least in part because they were not linked to broader programs of redistribution. In the absence of such broader efforts—to which New Labour was ideologically opposed—micro-level initiatives confined to the community level could not be successful. The causes of decline in the poorest neighbourhoods were "structural, originating in the organization of the economy and of society." Their solution required structural change (Lupton 2003: 96).

In 2007, when Blair stepped down, more than "a million citizens cannot read and every year some 35,000 illiterate children leave primary school in England to join those ranks, nearly one in ten of all eleven-year old boys" (Toynbee and Walker 2008: 147). In addition, during New Labour's time there was a 55 percent reduction in the number of sports and social clubs, a 21 percent reduction in swimming pools and a 6 percent reduction in public libraries (Jones 2012: 212).

Nevertheless, child poverty dropped significantly, as did pensioner poverty, which had stood at 21 percent in 1997 and was "all but ended" (Lowe 2005: 411). It is a fact that in 2010–2011, when New Labour left office, there were still some 2.3 million UK children living in poverty. However, this was more than one million fewer than in 1998, "and the lowest level since they began to rise in the 1980s under Thatcher" (Walker 2014: 297). Further, "persistent poverty"—children living in poverty for at least three out of four consecutive years—declined sharply (Stewart 2009: 55). It is impossible not to give credit to New Labour for these important gains.

These gains notwithstanding, 20 percent of children in the UK were still in poverty in 2007 (Toynbee and Walker 2008: 77). "Four million children were living in low-income households in 2008" (Fons 2011: 12). Remaining to be solved were "the most intractable cases of poverty," which would require "measures more radical than the ones already implemented" (Lowe 2005: 409). The Institute for Fiscal Studies estimated that the amount invested in child poverty was only one-quarter of what was needed to reach the 2010 target of cutting child poverty in half (Stewart et al. 2009: 15).

The overall numbers—when poverty is measured as those whose incomes are 50 percent or more below median income—were still twice those in 1979 (Walker 2014: 297). For those without children, poverty levels did not improve and may have risen. As Joyce and Sibieta (2013: 179) put it: "the incomes of low-income working-age adults without dependent children, a group not favoured by tax and benefit reforms, rose very little over the period, and hence their relative rate actually increased." Overall poverty "remained very significantly higher than when Thatcher came to office."

In 2008, 22 percent of the UK population, more than thirteen million people, were in households below the low-income threshold, one of the highest rates in EU countries (Fons 2011: 27).

New Labour's concern was to support people in moving out of poverty. But Roy Hattersley was surely correct that "a Labour government should not be talking about escape routes from poverty and deprivation." The task, rather, ought to be "to change society in such a way that there is no poverty and deprivation from which to escape" (quoted in Meredith 2006: 244).

That poverty persisted under New Labour is attributable largely to their ideological shift away from a commitment to redistribution and equality of outcomes. New Labour accepted the limitations imposed by an increasingly globalized capitalism and catered to the interests of corporate capitalists and especially financiers in the City. This placed a lid on the extent to which the needs of those struggling with poverty could be addressed. The determination to secure middle-class votes, and the refusal to engage in meaningful efforts to explain the structural causes of poverty to middle-class voters, also limited the room available to New Labour (Hay 1997). In fact, there is strong evidence that Blair and New Labour did not accept a structural explanation of poverty; they saw the causes in the moral and behavioural failings of the poor.

Also limiting New Labour's anti-poverty efforts was Blair's growing involvement with, and the escalating costs of, the war against Iraq. After 9/11, which happened just three months after New Labour's second overwhelming election victory in June 2001, Blair spent ever more time and energy on the international stage in support of President George W. Bush and the war against Iraq. Opposition was massive, "producing a social movement unrivalled in modern British history," as well as "one of the largest backbench rebellions in parliamentary history" (Hannah 2018: 211). This did not deter Blair. As a result, "Iraq consumed his second term and cast its baleful shadow into the third" (Rawnsley 2010: 445). Senior Blair advisor and pollster Philip Gould said, "Iraq bent Tony out of shape"; it became "the defining issue of Blair's premiership" (Rawnsley 2010: 149, 249). Nelson Mandela said that Blair was becoming "America's Foreign Secretary," and it became obvious that Blair loved his role on the global stage (Rawnsley 2010: 48). Labour MP Alan Simpson (2014) called Blair's commitment to the war against Iraq "Blair's unforgiveable sin—the lie that will dog him to the end of his days."

Public sector "reform" also became a major objective, especially in Blair's second and third terms (Stewart 2009: 13). He worked to bring the discipline and competitiveness of the market to the public sector via public-private partnerships, private finance initiatives, subcontracting of services to private profit makers and other forms of marketization (Taylor 2007). Thatcher started down this road, but "what is indisputable is that these innovations were accepted, and expanded, by New Labour" (Jones and Lowe 2002: 15).

The result was that especially from 2004–2005, New Labour's focus shifted away from child poverty. Gains eroded and were virtually gone within years of their being voted out of office (Hills et al. 2009: 343–44).

Public support for large-scale redistribution in the interests of the poor did not exist. It had not been built by New Labour.

A Record beyond Abysmal: New Labour and Housing

Nor did New Labour make any serious gains in housing. Poor housing had for centuries been a particularly damaging aspect of British poverty; capitalism does not produce decent quality affordable housing for those with low incomes. This continued to be the case under New Labour. They did little to improve housing for the poor; conditions on council estates worsened (Lund 2002). New Labour's "record on social housing was beyond abysmal, contriving to be worse than Thatcher's" (Murray 2019: 72).

Council estates were increasingly seen as homes to the undeserving poor. "Aspirational" tenants moved away, "replaced by transient tenants whose behaviour—quite apart from their very transience—made the estate even less desirable to live on" (Hanley 2007: 117). Those thought of as "problem families," those who were "the poorest households who found it hardest to cope," were concentrated on housing estates "in an attempt to contain their disruptiveness: a policy that would only cause further alienation and, eventually, nihilism and a creeping sense of lawlessness" (Hanley 2007: 124).

Mckenzie (2013: 1346) described tenants at St. Ann's council housing in Nottingham feeling acutely the stigma because of where they lived. They felt "demeaned," "looked down on" and made to "feel small." They developed their own distinct culture as a means of survival but remained cut off from "mainstream" society (see also Mckenzie 2015). Coates and Silburn had written about St. Ann's in 1960, as part of the "rediscovery of poverty." Conditions at that time, as described in Chapter 8, were very bad. Conditions in the New Labour years changed little.

The physical condition of council housing had deteriorated after eighteen years of Thatcherism. Capital spending dropped by more than half from 1993 to 1999/2000 (Lund 2002: 114), so that when New Labour took office in 1997, "20 billion pounds worth of investment was needed to bring every council house up to a reasonable standard." By 2000, it was estimated "that 42 percent of the entire council housing stock—1.7 million homes—provided sub-standard living conditions" (Hanley 2007: 144, 194). The problem was worsened because the rental revenue available to council housing had declined sharply when so many tenants became homeowners.

New Labour did little about these problems, cutting in half—"to the extraordinarily low figure of 0.3 percent"—the proportion of GDP spent on council housing. At the same time, "the building of new homes fell to its lowest point since the war, with only 179,160 units completed in 2000/1 (of which a mere 25,527 were public built). Given concurrent demolition, this was insufficient to meet long-term need. It was also insufficient in the short term" (Lowe 2005: 429).

Approximately 1.5 million people languished on wait lists for a council or housing-association home (Hanley 2007: 225). Despite the massive need, "New Labour was ideologically opposed to building council housing" (Jones 2012: 230). This occurred even though, as Boughton (2018: 251) argues, council estates should be viewed "not as a problem but as a solution—offering secure and affordable housing—to the low pay and insecure employment that affects so many." Complaints about the lack of availability and high costs were constant, in large part because of Thatcher's Right to Buy, which had "massively depleted" the supply of council housing (Jones 2012: 229).

Instead, New Labour sought funding via private finance initiatives (PFI), of which Brown and Blair were enthusiastic proponents. Between 1997 and 2004 alone, more than 600 PFI deals were entered into, especially but not only for schools and hospitals. "From 1997 onwards, nearly all hospital schemes—either complex hospitals or major extensions—have been financed and built under PFI" (Driver 2008: 58).

By 2009, some 920 PFI projects had been undertaken (Hare 2013: 97–98). In a PFI, a private developer provides upfront financing, relieving the public sector of the requirement to borrow, and is paid back over time in installments or in access to land or other real estate–related benefits. In the long run, such financing arrangements make projects more expensive, because governments can borrow at lower rates of interest than developers (Lee 2008: 26) and because complex legal contracts must be negotiated and policed (Hare 2013; Hodkinson 2011). Workers are typically disadvantaged under such schemes, too, relative to working in the public sector.

Williams (2017) describes problems in a south London PFI housing complex with multiple private for-profit participants. Residents were pushed from one corporate entity to another, and then to the local authority, with no one taking responsibility for issues as they arose and with no transparency with respect to where responsibility rested. The result was a culture in which "the idea of civic engagement was lost," and "the tenants aren't players but pawns; it is a kind of purgatory, where you are neither citizen nor consumer, caught in a limbo of impotence ... the housing serves only the interests of those who profit from it" (Williams 2017: 29).

PFIs facilitate contracting out, the financial "benefits" of which arise from low pay and poor working conditions—the NHS, for example, "is using casual workers employed by agencies at pay and conditions it would never itself dare to offer in public" (Toynbee 2003: 32). The poor, increasingly concentrated in housing estates and working at poverty-level wages, pay the price.

Part of New Labour's housing strategy took the form of "state-led gentrification," by which council housing estates were to be demolished and replaced by mixed-income housing, which would result in the displacement of existing lower-income tenants by middle-class residents. This was the case, for example, at the Aylesbury estate in south London, called derisively by many a "sink estate"—the term used for council housing estates with high levels of social problems. Targeted by New Labour as part of their "urban renaissance" strategy, ostensibly intended to regenerate troubled housing estates, Aylesbury was in fact subjected to a process of "state-led gentrification premised on mixed communities policy" (Lees 2014: 933). The goal was to bulldoze the estate on the grounds that it was too expensive to renovate and refurbish. The new build was to include far fewer homes for low-income residents. Residents resisted, including by voting against demolition. The entire process was informed, Lees (2014: 925) argues, by an American "moral underclass perspective," which was effectively "an example of capitalism rendering parts of the population (council tenants) disposable, a process of accumulation by dispossession."

Council housing under New Labour was no longer seen as an integral part of Britain's housing stock. Rather, much of it became "single class concentration camps surrounded by invisible barbed wire," creating "a new class of alienated, damaged, highly pressurized people whose links with mainstream society range from incomplete to tenuous" (Hanley 2007: 231). This was a function of New Labour's failure to invest in council housing. Mckenzie (2013: 6.3), referring to St. Ann's in Nottingham, observes that when people in a community are rejected by the wider society, when they are demeaned and devalued, negative consequences follow:

> The underground economy thrives in this neighbourhood, as it does in all neighbourhoods where there is a lack of employment linked to financial autonomy and self respect. Long term joblessness and the proliferation of low pay and part time employment, the widening gap between rich and poor, and dissatisfaction and disillusionment with mainstream politics has meant a build up of internal and internalized social decay.

These are the "undeserving" poor, and when they responded to their marginalized and stigmatized lives by engaging in illegal activities, New Labour responded with "law and order" and more poverty propaganda.

Law, Order and Poverty Propaganda

New Labour boasted in their 1997 manifesto that "Labour is the party of law and order. Labour promised the electorate more police on the beat, a crackdown on youth crime, 'effective sentencing', 'zero tolerance' of anti-social behaviour and crime" (Driver and Martell 1998: 117). The police "were at the heart of New Labour's new agenda." They adopted a "zero tolerance" approach to anti-social behaviour, drawing on the American 'broken windows' theory" (Charman and Savage 2002: 217, 215). "More than 3,600 new criminal offences were put on the statute book during New Labour's time in office and the prison population reached record levels" (Rawnsley 2010: 349–40). This was an approach to poverty—punishing the poor (Wacquant 2009)—put most fully into effect in the America that Blair so admired.

The government's response to the 2001 riots in especially low-income areas in the north, which involved clashes between South Asians and whites in some of Britain's most deprived areas (Rhodes 2009), revealed New Labour's blame-the-victim understanding of poverty. Rather than emphasizing structural causes for the riots, such as racism and poverty, the government focused on cultural factors, effectively laying the blame on South Asian communities for their insularity and on young South Asian males for their criminality:

> Discussions of racism and structural exclusion are replaced with a UK version of the "cultures of poverty" or "cultures of deprivation" debates that have marked out discussions of the "underclass" in the United States (Murray 1984). This results in a pathologization of Muslim cultures and a simplistic blame the victim approach to understanding complex processes of social exclusion. (Alexander 2004: 534)

Rhodes (2009: 4.2) argues that New Labour's understanding of the riots shifted close to that of the new right and was intellectually consistent with their lack of concern about inequalities of income and wealth, their "reluctance to engage in any significant consideration of structural inequality, particularly racial inequality."

This happened even though, as Alexander (2004: 528) points out in quoting *The Guardian* in May of 2001, the riots "were the result of tensions that have been brewing for years and whose sources are not mysterious. The first is poverty. As in every other British riot, the struggle erupted in a place of desperate economic hardship." This is confirmed in the case of Burnley, which experienced deindustrialization and poverty in the years leading up to 2001, resulting not only in conflict but also electoral success at the local level by the far-right British National Party (Makin-Waite 2021).

The easier explanation, the one consistent with centuries of past practice, is to blame those who are poor and who lash out against their poverty. "This perspective lays the blame clearly at the feet of the rioters and the community pathologies that have generated them" (Alexander 2004: 529).

The same was the case a decade later. The riots that occurred in August 2011, the year after New Labour left office—what *The Guardian* called "the worst bout of civil unrest in a generation" (quoted in De Benedictis 2012: 1)—were framed by much of the media as the product of a vicious "underclass." How the media describe such events matters, because it is "language about political events and developments that people experience" (quoted in Solomos 1986: 14). Media coverage used such language as "scum, thugs, feral rats…. The term 'scum' was the favourite pejorative: 'the scum class,' 'verminous waste'" (Tyler 2013: 3.1). *The Telegraph* ran an article titled "London Riots: The Underclass Lashes Out," in which the riots were described as "a Hobbesian dystopia of chaos and brutality" inflicted by a "ruined generation." It was an "explosion of hate speech" directed at the poor (Tyler 2013: 3.2 and 3.3). As the justice minister, Kenneth Clarke, asserted, "Our feral underclass is too big, has been growing, and needs to be diminished" (quoted in Tyler 2013: 4.2). Prime Minister David Cameron explained the riots as a "slow motion moral collapse that has taken place in parts of our country these past few generations" and insisted that "these riots were not about poverty" nor inequality but rather "about behaviour" (quoted in Tyler 2013: 6.1). Much blame for such behaviour was placed on lone mothers, the "feral" parents of "feral" children. "The depiction of the deviant lone mother responsible for societal collapse through male juvenile delinquency is especially prevalent" (De Benedictis 2012: 3). Boris Johnson, then mayor of London, warned that it would be "revolting" to advance explanations for the rioting rooted in economic and sociological phenomena (Tyler 2013: 3.4).

All of this is what Shildrick (2018: 785) calls "poverty propaganda," which has the effect that "punitive and divisive policies toward poverty become more palatable—and even desired"—by the general public:

> poverty propaganda is a mighty tool that orchestrates widespread consent for a political system that affords punishing life opportunities for significant numbers of its citizens whilst continuing to bolster the weight and strength of the cushions that protect the few. Neoliberal capitalism operates in this way and poverty propaganda plays an important role in its legitimation. (Shildrick 2018: 793)

Such attacks on the poor—"poverty propaganda"—have a long and troubling history in Britain. Their more immediate history is the complete failure of New Labour to educate the British public about the real causes of poverty. In what was his first speech about poverty, in 1997, Blair described the biggest challenge facing New Labour as "an underclass of people cut off from society's mainstream ... dependent on benefits and the black economy" (Blair 1997). New Labour championed the cause of "hard-working families" and the "aspirational working class"— the "deserving poor"—while imposing workfare on jobless youth to force them into precarious jobs, thus reinforcing the view that the poor had only themselves to blame for their poverty. The result, in the immediate wake of the New Labour years, was that "the idea of the existence of this parasitical underclass has become thoroughly entrenched as popular common sense" (Tyler 2013: 6.1, 6.3).

A more informed explanation can be located in the words of a twenty-two-year-old man involved in the August 2011 riots:

> All I can tell you is that me, myself and the group I was in, none of us have got jobs, yeah? I been out of work now coming up two years … and it's just like a depression, man, that you sink into.… I felt like I needed to be there as well to just say "look, this is what's gonna happen if there's no jobs offered to us out there." (Lewis and Newburn 2011: 25)

The study found that 86 percent of the rioters who were interviewed cited poverty as an important or very important cause of the riots (Lewis and Newburn 2011: 11).

Low-Pay/No-Pay/No-Future

Young adults in marginalized housing estates told researchers that the measures used by the New Deal for Young People were "wholly ineffective" (MacDonald et al. 2005: 882). Virtually all of these young adults

> displayed work histories—into their mid- and late-20s—that consisted of various combinations of: government schemes that rarely led to lasting employment; unfinished and/or low-level education courses; low/no skill, low paid, insecure employment; and recurrent periods of unemployment. Individuals transited between these labour market statuses with little sense of forward motion toward more secure, rewarding employment. (MacDonald et al. 2005: 880–81)

These young people "inhabit a cycle of no-pay/low-pay job insecurity. This indeed is the end of social progress" (Toynbee 2003: 5–6).

A later study found this pattern persisted well into their thirties:

> Contrary to the widely held view that "employment is the best route out of poverty," the sort of work available to our interviewees kept them in poverty rather than lifting them out of it. The pattern of low-paid and insecure jobs that recurrently returned young adults to unemployment found in our earlier studies had

not changed. The same individuals, now aged 30 to 40, still contend with the same vicious circle. (Shildrick et al. 2010: 5)

They are relegated "to churning low-pay, no-pay careers at the bottom of the labour market" (Shildrick et al. 2010: 38)—the jobs that capitalists are creating. This despite the fact that most of these adults "maintained an active search for employment, investing huge amounts of physical and emotional effort in these searches" (Shildrick et al. 2010: 18). Women are "trapped in low-paid, part-time work and increasingly this is the only work on offer," with growing numbers on zero-hour contracts requiring them "to be available for work permanently whilst guaranteeing them no set hours of employment" (Zipfel et al. 2015: 30). The job insecurity and low wages keeps them below or barely (and typically temporarily) above the poverty line, in a manner reminiscent of earlier centuries.

In the face of these dead ends—"the wreckage of the collapsed economic scaffolding that previously enabled transitions to a stable, working class, adult life" (MacDonald et al. 2005: 885)—young people rioted in August 2011. In their difficult neighbourhoods they develop cultures of toughness and mutual support, largely disconnected from "mainstream" society and the political process, their poverty long neglected. "Close family ties, mutual aid and voluntarism are often strong features of poor areas. It is these qualities which may enable people to cope with poverty, unemployment and wider processes of social exclusion" (Forrest and Kearns 2001: 2141). They survive by "making shift," as the poor have done for centuries—today known in some areas as "fiddly work" or being "on the fiddle" (MacDonald and Marsh 2005: 112–13). This process includes not only the illegal drug trade, but also, as a youth worker in a council estate described it, various more "entrepreneurial" activities— "one lad would do your leccy [fix the electricity meter so that bills were reduced] and another would bring round [stolen] kids' clothes for you. It's just a way of getting by" (MacDonald et al. 2005: 879). It's making shift, as the poor have done for centuries.

A Savagely Unequal Society

As if to add salt to the deep wounds of such poverty, inequality under New Labour continued its upward climb. Inequality had soared during the eighteen years the Conservatives held office, from 1979 to 1997, as had been the case across the industrialized capitalist world (Piketty

2020). Neither Blair nor Brown cared how rich the rich became. They were close to business, especially the City, and saw the accumulation of wealth as positive. Mandelson (2010: 265), one of the "founding triangle" (Rawnsley 2010: 4) of New Labour, famously said, "We are intensely relaxed about people becoming filthy rich, as long as they pay their taxes"—taxes that had been reduced by New Labour immediately upon their taking office:

> *The Sunday Times* described 1997–2007 as a "golden" age for the very rich, estimating that in 1997 the wealth of the UK's wealthiest 1000 totaled 98.99 billion pounds; by 2007 it was 359.943 billion. Blair, who amassed a considerable fortune after resigning as premier, never criticized this burgeoning of wealth. (Thane 2018: 438)

In 2006, the city paid some nine billion pounds in bonuses to just over 4,000 employees, each of whom "received an extra 1 million pounds" (Irvin 2008: 2). At the same time, New Labour was cutting social security benefits and using workfare to force people into the bottom rungs of the precarious, low-pay/no-pay/no-future labour market.

Labour's historic commitment to equality of outcomes was abandoned. As Brown said in 1999:

> The search for equalities of outcome, and even to talk as if that is the aim of the Labour Party, has led us up the wrong roads. The pursuit of equality of outcome is someone else's nightmare about socialism rather than a genuine socialist dream. (Quoted in Powell 2002: 22–23)

Blair's education advisor, Andrew Adonis, said, "while New Labour wants to help the poor as a matter of principle, it refuses to hit the rich as a matter of principle," and this is what, Adonis said, "separates Old Left from New Left" (quoted in Deacon 2002: 114).

New Labour rejected equality of outcomes in favour of "equality of opportunity." This was deeply flawed as an approach to poverty. Equality of opportunity is simply not possible without considerable equality of outcomes; it certainly is not possible in the face of massive inequality. Lister (2001: 438) argued that neither "genuine equality of opportunity nor meaningful recognition of equal worth is achievable in our savagely unequal society." That Britain had become "savagely unequal" is made clear by the evidence.

The share of total income taken by the top 1 percent grew from 5.7 percent in 1978—its lowest point in the postwar era—to 15.8 percent in 2008 and back to 13.9 percent in 2010. "The trend in the share of income received by the top 1 per cent has taken the pattern of a U-curve, falling from 1937 (when it stood at 17 percent) until its lowest point in 1978 and then rising again" (Lansley and Mack 2013). This was a global trend (Piketty 2020), and New Labour did nothing to resist that shift. In 2010, it was reported that "London is one of the most unequal cities on earth: the richest 10 percent is worth 273 times more than the poorest 10 percent" (Jones 2012: xxiii). By 2014, four years after New Labour left office, the richest one hundred people in the UK had as much wealth as the poorest 30 percent of all UK households, and "the five richest families now own more wealth between them than the poorest 20 percent" (Dorling 2014b: 91). Dorling (quoted in Murray 2019: 77) calculated that "No British Prime Minister since Stanley Baldwin had seen the bottom 90 percent take so little as they did under New Labour."

There was strong public support for narrowing what had become, under Thatcherism, Britain's massive inequality. The sixteenth British Social Attitudes Survey revealed that

> four-fifths of the population believed that the gap between those with high and low incomes is too large and almost three-quarters that it is definitely or probably the Government's responsibility to reduce it. Such findings suggest that a government that made a convincing case for redistribution could take the majority of the electorate with it. (Lister 2001: 437)

New Labour made no such case. They were committed to the corporate community and especially the City, as well as to the imperatives of the global market, and they took no steps to prevent the rich from becoming ever richer:

> The Prime Minister's unsettling adoration of corporate wealth seemed at odds with any recognizable moral values and principles once associated with the Labour movement. Both Blair and Brown were unwilling to challenge the excesses of boardroom sleaze, greed and corporate corruption. (Taylor 2007: 224)

Post–New Labour: It Just Keeps Getting Worse

Whatever gains were made by New Labour in reducing child poverty were not sustained after 2010, despite Prime Minister Cameron saying when he took office that he would keep New Labour's commitment to eliminate child poverty by 2020 (McAnulla 2010: 306). Far from that happening, there followed "the most comprehensive assault on the welfare state anyone living has yet seen" (Seabrook 2015: 395), "the most radical transformation of the welfare state in the UK since its inception" (O'Hara 2015: 193), what Taylor-Gooby (quoted in Lehtonen 2018: 86) called "the deepest and most precipitate cuts ever made in social provision," leaving the social security safety net in "tatters" (Patrick 2017: 55). Rules governing payment of benefits have become increasingly "punitive and degrading" (Zipfel et al. 2015: 30). By 2018, four million people in the paid labour force were in poverty; that number had increased by half a million in the previous five years; this was "driven almost entirely by increasing poverty among working parents" (JRF 2018: 3). By 2016, manufacturing had declined so far that the UK was twenty-sixth in the world in manufacturing output per capita, and 118th in the world in manufacturing as a proportion of national economic output (Merrick 2020: 168). According to the United Nations special rapporteur on extreme poverty and human rights, fourteen million people—20 percent of the population—were in poverty, four million of whom were more than 50 percent below the poverty line and 1.5 million of whom he described as "destitute, unable to afford basic essentials." This growth in poverty and destitution was happening while "the overall social safety net is being systematically dismantled" (Alston 2018: 1, 12).

At the same time, life expectancy in England stalled, and "female life expectancy declined in the most deprived 10 percent of areas between 2010–12 and 2016–18." The time that people spent in poor health had grown for men and women since 2010 (Marmot 2020: 10). Women have been particularly hard hit (O'Hara 2015). The numbers of people on zero-hour contracts "has risen significantly since 2010. In Autumn 2018 there were nearly 900,000 people on zero hour contracts in the UK, compared with 168,000 in 2010." The numbers working and still in poverty grew over that period (Marmot 2020: 14).

Even for children and pensioners, where New Labour had made gains, "this progress has begun to unravel; poverty rates are rising, especially among children, due to weakening support through benefits and tax credits, low pay and rising housing costs with less help in meeting them" (JRF 2018: 3). In 2010–2011, 2.3 million UK children had been living in poverty. By 2018, that number had almost doubled to 4.1 million children (JRF 2018: 4). New Labour's commitment to eliminate child poverty by 2020 was not even close to being realized. Spending on children under five and on early education was cut sharply, and spending on Sure Start experienced a "dramatic drop" of 41 percent in real terms between 2009–2010 and 2012–2013 (Lupton et al. 2016: 43). Some sources, the United Nations special rapporteur on extreme poverty and human rights reported, were predicting that child poverty rates could rise even further, to as high as 40 percent (Alston 2018: 1).

Meanwhile, inequality continued its precipitous growth. "In Britain today, the richest 1000 people own more wealth than 40 percent of households, or 10.2 million families," while the UK "now has more billionaires per capita than any other country in the world" (Shildrick 2018: 786, 791). In 2013, eighteen of twenty-nine coalition government Cabinet ministers were millionaires. At the same time, "Twenty-eight percent of children in the UK are growing up in poverty with the figure rising all the time" (O'Hara 2015: 36).

Lack of social housing—a product of Thatcher's Right to Buy policy and New Labour's failure to build social housing—drove housing costs up for renters, pushing rapidly growing numbers into the private rental market. "The proportion of children in the bottom quintile living in the private rented sector rose from 17 percent in 2005/6 to 37 percent in 2016/17. At the same time housing benefit has been weakened" (JRF 2018: 4).

The availability of social housing has further deteriorated. Mckenzie (2017: 274) described the case of a woman in London's East End, where poverty has produced a profound sense of hopelessness that exists cheek-by-jowl with the stately housing of the well-to-do. The woman, without housing and "in dire housing need," was told "her wait for social housing would likely take 12–15 years." In this part of London alone, 25,000 people were on the wait list.

According to the 2018 report of the UN special rapporteur:

> In England, homelessness is up 60 percent since 2010, rough sleeping is up 134 percent. There are 1.2 million people on the social housing waiting list, but less than 6000 homes were built

last year. Food bank use is up almost four-fold since 2012, and there are now about 2000 food banks in the UK, up from just 29 at the height of the financial crisis. (Alston 2018: 17)

Food banks emerged in growing numbers especially after 2010. "In 2010 foodbanks were a largely unfamiliar concept, but five years later, over 1 million people have used them," and between 2014 and 2015, "one in five family doctors were asked to refer a patient to a foodbank" (Garthwaite 2016: 57, 115). The number of people making use of three-day food supplies from food banks grew from 25,889 in 2008–2009 to 1,109,309 in 2015–2016, an increase of 4,183 percent (Patrick 2017: 53). Those who were poor relied increasingly upon pawnbrokers and cheque-cashing institutions—described as "legal loan sharks" (O'Hara 2015: 75)—reminiscent of earlier centuries. Health inequalities reached shocking proportions, with men in the lowest income ward in Stockton-on-Tees in the north living on average 17.3 years less than a man in the highest income ward in that city (Garthwaite 2016: 18). Suicide rates increased, "the consequence of a deliberate policy choice: that of austerity" (quoted in Garthwaite 2016: 133). Growing numbers engaged in "survival shoplifting" (O'Hara 2015: xix). A "welfare adviser" said in a 2015 interview, "It's always been tough but I tell you, never as tough as it is now…. You are watching people crumble right in front of you. It is soul-destroying…. I never dreamt we'd ever be in a situation so horrendous" (O'Hara 2015: 207). And yet the demonization of the poor continued relentlessly, including the growth of television "poverty porn"—"shows that seemingly take pleasure in depicting people as lazy, criminal, violent, undisciplined and shameless, playing into the media and government rhetoric around people living on low income" (Garthwaite 2016: 137; Patrick 2017: 190).

After four decades of attacking and denigrating the working class and promoting and extolling the virtues of the rich, Britain had come full circle to the unimaginable extremes of inequality that had prevailed in previous centuries and the associated demonization of those left far behind—those known for centuries as the "undeserving poor." As always, they were subjected to fear, loathing and a form of class hatred. They were the residuum, the vagrants and vagabonds, the scoundrels and shirkers, the dangerous class, who in more recent years—hatred for the poor sparks endless creativity in nomenclature—have been called scum and verminous waste, a feral underclass and chavs (Jones 2012: 7). "Chavs" appears to have emerged in the 1990s to describe someone "ensconced in a culture of low level criminality" (Shilliam 2018: 126). During the New Labour years a whole range of terms, derivatives of the word "chav," emerged as "ubiquitous terms of abuse for the white poor," expressing "intense class-based abhorrence," "middle class contempt for the lower classes," British versions of what in America is called "white trash" (Tyler 2008: 21, 22, 25). The "blame-the-poor" approach to understanding poverty has gained increasing currency in the post-New Labour years. In the immediate aftermath of New Labour's 2010 defeat, the coalition government "drew upon well-trodden discourses, framed in terms of the 'Broken Society,' focusing upon individual motivations, behaviour and pathology ... reminiscent of the scroungerphobia period of the late 1970s" (Pantazis 2016: 4).

As always, this interpretation of the causes of poverty was fuelled by right-wing think tanks; in this period the Centre for Social Justice engaged in what Slater (2012: 961) described as the "production of ignorance," deliberately obfuscating the structural causes of poverty.

The demonization of the poor is functional. It has always been. If the poverty and related behaviours of the poor come to be understood as self-inflicted, then the fault is theirs and theirs alone, and society need not worry that some are becoming ultra-rich while the conditions of the poor steadily worsen. We can justifiably demonize the poor, and such demonization becomes "the ideological backbone of an unequal society" (Jones 2012: xiii). This is poverty propaganda. New Labour, in carrying on with Thatcherism, taking its distance from and even being contemptuous of the working class in favour of the "middle class" and promoting the uber-rich, had contributed to this appalling outcome. Their approach to poverty was a failure.

Chapter 11

Solving Perpetual Poverty

Can Capitalism Be Undone?

For centuries, poverty has been a constant presence in the daily lives of the British people, and until relatively recently, a large proportion of the British people. This is because capital accumulation simultaneously produces both massive profits and massive poverty—they are part of the same process. Marx wrote, "A matter of a million paupers in the British workhouse is as inseparable from British prosperity as the existence of eighteen to twenty millions in gold in the Bank of England" (quoted in Palmer 2014: 54). The price paid over the centuries in terms of human suffering and early death of the countless numbers who were poor has been staggering and is literally incalculable. Capitalism did indeed come into the world "dripping from head to toe, from every pore, with blood and dirt" (Marx 1976: 926).

This was the case through the centuries-long enclosure movement, which pushed peasants off the land, forcing them into a desperate search for a means of survival, creating vagrants and vagabonds, rogues, scoundrels and sturdy beggars, paupers and masterless men. They were the undeserving poor—feared, despised and punished. It was the case throughout the sixteenth to the eighteenth centuries as capitalism emerged and Britain became an imperial power. People continued to be pushed off the land and increasingly into urban centres, where survival was difficult and making shift a necessity. The *Elizabethan Poor Law* provided just enough to keep the poor from dying of starvation or rebelling. Many were exported to the colonies. The emergence in the mid- to late eighteenth century of industrial capitalism created new and horrifying forms of poverty in dark, dangerous mills. The *New Poor Law*, the workhouse and fear of destitution were necessary to force those who were resistant into the poorly paid and dangerous work that industrial capitalism produced.

By the late nineteenth and early twentieth centuries, conditions were being created by which poverty could be significantly reduced. Three things were especially important: British industrial capitalism, with its vast colonial empire, was producing enormous wealth. Trade unions and other left political organizations were emerging and demanding that at least some of that wealth be shared with at least some of the workers who were its creators—pressure from below is and always has been an essential ingredient in any effort to significantly reduce poverty. Militancy, and the fear of the consequences of militancy—the fear of socialism in particular—led those with power to realize that the state must redistribute some of the wealth to the working poor, growing numbers of them now voters, to maintain the prevailing social and economic arrangements. These developments, this organized pressure from below, found expression in the mildly redistributive but conceptually important policies initiated by the 1906–1914 Liberal governments.

These early and partial gains were placed on hold for almost a third of a century by the emergence in the early 1920s and especially the 1930s of mass unemployment, with all the poverty and related hardships that entailed, including the indignities associated with the "genuinely seeking work" requirement, the hated household means test and the constant charges of malingering. When the Second World War ended, a decade and a half after the onset of the Great Depression, British workers—many of whom had organized through trade unions and at the municipal level and in multiple other ways—were anxious to be rewarded for their many sacrifices. They elected a Labour government that had the courage to implement genuinely social democratic measures, the most important being the National Health Service, building more than a million good quality rental homes for working people, the *National Insurance Act* and promoting full employment. These policies were rooted in commitments to collectivism, egalitarianism and redistribution. They were made possible by the pressure from below that had been building in multiple ways for a century, starting with the Factory Acts in the early to mid-nineteenth century, and by the courage of the 1945–1951 Labour governments in the face of economic adversity and political opposition. Thus was laid the basis for the modern welfare state, which would significantly reduce the incidence and severity of poverty and would do so in the face of the enormous financial challenges facing postwar Britain and the fierce opposition of capitalists and their supporters.

Important though they were, the measures implemented in six short years were incomplete. Much was left to be done. "The post-1945 welfare state was not in itself a final destination" (Briggs 1961: 222). It ought to have been "merely the first installment of a much more far reaching program of radical reform" (Harris 1977: 434). That did not happen. The huge steps taken by the postwar Attlee governments were not built upon by later Labour governments in the ways that were both necessary and possible. Britain moved from being a social policy leader in the immediate postwar years to a social policy laggard—gradually at first, as the result in part of revisionist Labour Party policies, and then more deliberately and dramatically with the elections starting in 1979 of Margaret Thatcher's Conservative governments.

During the thirty years following the Second World War, the British economy and especially British manufacturing continued their long decline relative to other capitalist nations. British capitalists were automating their operations, moving jobs offshore and investing in financial and service sector activities rather than manufacturing, creating job losses and precarious jobs and thus producing poverty. All of this led to crisis in the mid- to late 1970s, to which Thatcherism was the harsh response. For almost twenty years, Thatcher and Thatcher-inspired Conservative governments, first elected in 1979, successfully attacked trade unions, promoted individualism, introduced workfare and eroded the redistributive character of the welfare state in an attempt to restore the conditions for capital accumulation. The result was mass unemployment that returned to the levels of the 1930s, a severely eroded welfare state and dramatic growth of poverty and inequality.

New Labour replaced Thatcherism in 1997. Their "modernized" form of Labourism accepted and even encouraged the dominance of capital, and especially finance capital, in ways largely consistent with Thatcherism, while implementing narrowly targeted measures to reduce poverty, especially child and pensioner poverty. Some success was achieved, but it was limited and short-lived and had no impact on the capitalist power relations that produce perpetual poverty. Under pressure from capitalists, Blair's New Labour governments expanded workfare, a mechanism aimed at forcing people into the lower reaches of the increasingly precarious labour market, just as the *New Poor Law* of 1834 was aimed at forcing reluctant workers into the accursed mills of the Industrial Revolution. From the leading welfare state under Attlee's postwar Labour governments, Britain became the leading "workfare state" under Blair's New Labour (Peck 2001). With New Labour's defeat in 2010, any gains in reducing poverty among the deserving poor were quickly washed away in a tidal wave of austerity that reproduced in accentuated form the harsh destitution of Thatcherism.

Capitalism produces poverty. This has always been the case; this is the case today. The evidence makes clear that Blackwell and Seabrook (1985: 39) were correct: "The single most unifying factor in working class culture has been poverty; the threat of poverty, the fear of poverty, the certainty of poverty." Precarious labour, seemingly new and resurgent today, is in fact a centuries-long phenomenon. It is the norm. "Work has never been anything but a precarious foundation of life lived on the razor's edge of dispossession" (Palmer 2014: 44). The poverty that the fundamental logic of capitalism inevitably produces is complex and multifaceted, often brutalizing the poor. Yet it is the poor themselves who are blamed, who are scorned and reviled and feared, who are marginalized, punished and incarcerated.

Poverty continues to be a massive problem in Britain in the third decade of the twenty-first century. Housing conditions for many are appalling. Homelessness grows relentlessly. Precarious labour abounds. Food banks are ubiquitous. Fuel poverty is widespread. The poor suffer depleted health and shortened lives. Drug addiction is rampant and destructive, especially for the poor, as gin was in the eighteenth century. Punishment and imprisonment of the poor is a staple of today's response to poverty, as it was under the Poor Laws. Hopelessness and despair weigh heavily on those who are poor. Vast human suffering is the result of this age-old scourge—today, as ever. And the poor continue to be blamed, even reviled and hated, for their poverty—a poverty caused not by their moral and behavioural failings, but by the fundamental logic of capitalism.

Is Perpetual Poverty Inevitable?

It is reasonable to fear that this will continue. Today, capitalism produces a "surplus population" that Barrow (2020: 147) argues "will not disappear—ever—so long as the fundamental logic of capitalist development remains intact, and in fact it will continue to grow in size." The fundamental logic of capitalism requires that the vast profits that it produces are allocated to wherever capitalists believe still more profits are to be made. The profits are not allocated to where the needs are greatest if doing so is not expected to produce profits. They are not invested in a living wage, for example, because it is believed that doing so would reduce the total amount of profits to be earned. Capitalists keep wages low and labour precarious in order to maximize profits, even though it is known that doing so will produce still more poverty. The result is the production not only of goods and services and of profits, but also and necessarily, of poverty. The entire point of the capitalist system is the maximization of profit, not the meeting of human needs, and certainly not the elimination of poverty.

There is little political will to address what is by now a massive and deeply entrenched poverty. Social democratic parties have, for the most part, dropped their commitment to redistribution. "Social redistribution, traditionally the first plank in social-democratic reformist action, is practically abandoned" (Moschonas 2002: 294; Piketty 2020). Charity continues in its haphazard fashion, but as has been the case for centuries, it does not solve poverty. So-called anti-poverty programs narrowly targeted at the poor are frequently advanced, but are simply ineffective in addressing the root causes of destitution.

The problem is deepened by the way people imagine poverty—the "bundle of beliefs," the "ideas beyond question, assumptions so deep that the very fact that they are assumptions is only rarely brought to light" (Hall, Massey and Rustin 2013: 9). At the core of these assumptions is that the poor are to blame for their poverty. They are poor because of their moral failings and degenerate behaviour. They are lazy, they drink too much, they are undisciplined and sometimes violent, they have too many children, their homes are dirty and unkempt, they are poor parents and thus contribute to the reproduction of poverty. This has particularly been the case made regarding the "undeserving" poor—those able-bodied but not in the full-time paid labour force. They have been blamed, feared, reviled and humiliated. Poverty propaganda relentlessly ramps up the hostility directed at the ever-growing surplus population.

Such enduring beliefs serve to mask and divert attention from the underlying, structural causes of poverty, reproducing a definition of poverty as a moral issue that is about personal failings. When understood in this way, there is no need to make significant changes to structural realities and power relations, nor even to implement significant redistributive policies. Without such changes, capitalism will, indeed, perpetually produce poverty.

Universal, Redistributive Strategies

Poverty can be very significantly reduced, but only by governments fully committed to doing so by means of state-directed redistributive policies and strategies designed to put people to work in good jobs—jobs with a living wage, benefits, job security, opportunities for advancement and union protections—doing the vast amount of work that so obviously needs to be done. The Labour governments of 1945–1951 did this to a considerable extent and under particularly challenging conditions. Three things are notable about their poverty-reducing achievements.

First, they had broadly based public support for what they did. This was in large part because of the deprivation and hardship experienced by the majority of the British people who, having struggled and sacrificed through the Great Depression and the Second World War, were eager for, and demanded, the kind of change that would meet the repressed needs of working people. The Great Depression and the Second World War had led the British public to believe that a better way was possible and necessary, and Labour and liberal (Beveridge; Keynes) intellectuals had built a roadmap for that better way. The widely held belief that a better way is possible is a precondition for solving poverty. If a serious effort were to be made to dramatically reduce poverty and inequality, progressive political parties would have to take the lead in rebuilding such a belief. "The market's power must be confronted, and this requires a sustained, sophisticated struggle to win the battle of ideas about the future of the country" (Leys 1995: 11). Winning the battle of ideas is the precondition for the organized pressure from below, the organized struggle, that is necessary if a significant reduction in poverty and inequality is to be achieved.

Second, although those Labour governments were successful in significantly reducing poverty, none of what they did was framed as "anti-poverty" programs, targeted narrowly at "the poor." Theirs was a broadly based, social democratic approach that was collective, egalitarian and redistributive. It included universal, single-payer health care, the building of good quality, affordable council housing and the promotion of full employment, each aimed at meeting the needs of the majority of working people. So-called anti-poverty programs that narrowly target the poor will not win broadly based public support, in large part because of the prevailing belief that the poor are the authors of their own misfortune. Only universal, redistributive policies can earn the wide support needed to drive down the incidence of poverty and inequality.

Third, any government that would introduce the kind of universal, redistributive programs needed to dramatically reduce poverty would need the courage to act boldly, because such efforts will inevitably be challenged aggressively by the rich and powerful. Human agency matters. Aneurin Bevan, for example, was steadfastly committed to socialist principles and courageous enough to put them into practice, even in the face of fierce opposition. His actions exemplify the argument advanced by Frances Fox Piven (1995: 114): "the realm of politics—of agency, imagination, of demonic and heroic intent—matters in creating the structures which then limit human possibilities. And which sometimes expand possibilities as well."

However, in the past half-century and more, social democratic governments have "gradually abandoned any ambition to mould populations intellectually and morally, and simply sought to expand and diversify their electoral base" (Moschonas 2002: 40). This has been accompanied, and to a considerable extent caused, by the weakening of the trade union movement—a weakening hastened dramatically by the deliberate actions of the Thatcher governments of the 1980s. The result, importantly, has been the large-scale abandonment of the redistribution that was at the core of the 1945–1951 Labour governments' efforts. So long as this continues to be the case—that is, so long as there is no deliberate government commitment to redistribution and the creation of very large numbers of good jobs—capitalism will continue its relentless production of poverty and inequality, with all the immense human misery that causes.

Two Roads

Thus, two roads lie before us. One is to continue on the current path—a commitment to the largely unrestricted market, punctuated by charity and narrowly constructed "anti-poverty" programs that are, for the most part, ineffectual. Down this road lies the continued and perpetual production of poverty and of an ever-expanding surplus population, which will accentuate the growth of human misery and produce dangerous political outcomes—various forms of fascism in particular—that are already evident. The other is to impose dramatic limits on capitalism's otherwise perpetual production of poverty by committing to collectivism, egalitarianism and redistribution via the state.

This second road, if pursued with the intent of dramatically reducing poverty and inequality, would be a massive undertaking and would generate enormous opposition. Its success would require governments committed to this purpose and prepared to act with courage—thus the importance of human agency—and it would require large-scale support from a public that had been prepared by a long-term, sustained and sophisticated struggle at the level of ideas. The British people would have to be convinced that a better future is possible and that it can be built with a commitment to collectivism, egalitarianism and redistribution. This will not be easy. Pessimism about the likelihood of success on this second path is intellectually justifiable.

Movement down this second road is, nevertheless, possible. It is possible to drive the incidence of poverty down to a bare minimum. To do so would require a government with a genuinely social democratic or socialist commitment, prepared to act with courage and resolve to put in place a sustained program of redistribution from those who have wealth and power to those who do not, including putting people to work in good jobs doing the many things that have to be done to build a better world. This is what I believe Miliband (2009: 73) meant when he acknowledged the many difficulties of moving in such a direction, while suggesting that overcoming such obstacles is possible. He argued,

> But there is more than one way to deal with the adverse conditions which these new governments encounter on their assumption of office. One of them is to treat these conditions as a challenge to greater boldness, as an opportunity to greater radicalism, and as a means, rather than an obstacle, to swift and decisive measures of reform. There is, after all, much that a genuinely radical government, firm in purpose and enjoying a substantial measure of popular support, may hope to do on the morrow of its electoral legitimation, not despite crisis conditions but because of them. And doing so, it is likely to receive

the support of many people, hitherto uncommitted or half-committed, but willing to accept a resolute lead.

The 1945–1951 Labour governments, although often criticized from the left, showed that this is possible when public support for redistribution exists and when a social democratic government acts with courage and resolve:

> As the example of the Attlee government reveals, social democratic administrations have indeed been elected that did not successfully appease capital (at least to capital's satisfaction), that managed to enact significant social and economic reform, and that did not precipitate economic crisis. (Hay 1997: 238)

Social democracy has withered, even atrophied, over the long, post–Second World War period. Many on the left have read last rites over the seemingly lifeless body of a form of governance committed to collectivism, egalitarianism and redistribution. However, I believe that there is nothing fundamentally wrong with the core ideas of social democracy. Its decline has not been caused by any law of necessity. "The problem is one of ideas and politics, rather than of ineluctable economic necessity" (Keating and McCrone 2015: 10). The problem, as has always been the case, is one of organizing from below to demand that governments act in a collective, egalitarian and redistributive fashion. Enormously difficult though it may be, poverty can be reduced to a bare minimum with a commitment to these principles.

In the absence of governments that are prepared to act in this way and that are supported by a population made ready, at the level of ideas, for such a struggle, those with power will continue to make the case, despite centuries of evidence to the contrary, that the only way to solve poverty is to create the conditions for more economic growth, more capital accumulation. This does not solve poverty; it produces poverty. Yet the purveyors of this myth argue endlessly and repetitively that promoting economic growth by unleashing the forces of the market will generate the wealth that can then be used to fuel anti-poverty efforts. This is not to be believed.

Capitalism will continue to produce poverty as long as it exists. The empirical evidence over the centuries in Britain makes that clear, as does capitalism's internal logic. Poverty can be minimized, by doing still more of what the 1945–1951 Labour governments began to do. However, the challenges are huge, given the magnitude of the task and the ferocity of the opposition that will be generated. Thus, courage, along with building public support and ideological commitment, will be required. The alternative is perpetual poverty.

References

Abel-Smith, Brian, and Peter Townsend. 1965. *The Poor and the Poorest*. London: G. Bell and Sons Ltd.
Addison, Christopher. 1922. *The Betrayal of the Slums*. London: Herbert Jenkins Ltd.
Addison, Paul. 2010. *No Turning Back: The Peacetime Revolutions of Post-War Britain*. Oxford: Oxford University Press.
_____. 1975. *The Road to 1945: British Politics and the Second World War*. London: Jonathan Cape.
Alcock, Pete. 1987. *Poverty and State Support*. London: Longman.
Alexander, Claire. 2004. "Imagining the Asian Gang: Ethnicity, Masculinity and Youth after 'the Riots.'" *Critical Social Policy* 24, 4.
Alexander, Michelle. 2010. *The New Jim Crow: Mass Incarceration in the Age of Colorblindness*. New York: The New Press.
Alston, Philip. 2018. *Statement on Visit to the United Kingdom, by Professor Philip Alston, United Nations Special Rapporteur on Extreme Poverty and Human Rights*. Geneva: United Nations Human Rights Office of the High Commissioner.
Archbishop of Canterbury's Commission on Urban Priority Areas. 1985. *Faith in the City: A Call for Action by Church and Nation*. London: Church House Publishing.
Aston, T.H., and C.H.E. Philpin (eds.). 1987. *The Brenner Debate: Agrarian Class Structure and Economic Development in Pre-Industrial Europe*. Cambridge: Cambridge University Press.
Astor, John Jacob, A.L. Bowley et al. 1922. *The Third Winter of Unemployment: The Report of an Enquiry undertaken in the Autumn of 1922*. London: P.S. King and Son, Ltd.
Atkinson, A.B. 1989. *Poverty and Social Security*. Hertfordshire: Harvester Wheatsheaf.
Attlee, Clement. 1954. *As It Happened*. London: Odhams Press Limited.
August, Martine. 2008. "Social Mix and Canadian Public Housing Redevelopment: Experiences in Toronto." *Canadian Journal of Urban Research* 17, 1.
Ayers, Pat, and Jan Lambertz. 1986. "Marriage Relations, Money and Domestic Violence in Working Class Liverpool, 1919–1939." In Jane Lewis (ed.). *Labour and Love: Women's Experience of Home and Family 1850–1940*. Oxford: Basil Blackwell Ltd.
Bakke, E. Wight. 1933. *The Unemployed Man: A Social Study*. London: Nisbet and Co. Ltd.
Banting, Keith. 1979. *Poverty, Politics and Policy: Britain in the 1960s*. London: Macmillan.
Baptist, Edward. 2016. "Toward a Political Economy of Slave Labour: Hands, Whipping-Machines, and Modern Power." In Sven Beckert and Seth Rockman (eds.), *Slavery's Capitalism: A New History of American Economic Development*. Philadelphia: University of Pennsylvania Press.
_____. 2014. *The Half Has Never Been Told: Slavery and the Making of American Capitalism*. New York: Basic Books.
Barnett, Corelli. 1986. *The Audit of War: The Illusions and Reality of Britain as a Great Nation*. London: Macmillan.
Barrow, Clyde. 2020. *The Dangerous Class: The Concept of the Lumpenproletariat*. Ann Arbor: University of Michigan Press.

Beckert, Sven. 2015. *Empire of Cotton: A Global History.* New York: Penguin.
Beckert, Sven, and Seth Rockman (eds.). 2016. *Slavery's Capitalism: A New History of American Economic Development.* Philadelphia: University of Pennsylvania Press.
Beier, A.L. 1985. *Masterless Men: The Vagrancy Problem in England 1560–1640.* London: Methuen.
⸺. 1983. *The Problem of the Poor in Tudor and Early Stuart England.* London: Lancaster Pamphlets, Methuen.
Bennett, Judith. 1997. "Conviviality and Charity in Medieval and Early Modern England." *Past and Present* 154, 1.
Beynon, Huw, and Ray Hudson. 2021. *The Shadow of the Mine: Coal and the End of Industrial Relations.* London: Verso.
Benyon, John, and John Solomos. 1988. "The Simmering Cities: Urban Unrest During the Thatcher Years." *Parliamentary Affairs* 41, 3.
Berry, Helen. 2019. *Orphans of Empire: the Fate of London's Foundlings.* Oxford: Oxford University Press.
Berthoud, Richard, and Joan C. Brown, with Steven Cooper. 1981. *Poverty and the Development of Anti-Poverty Policy in the United Kingdom: A Report to the Commission of the European Communities.* London: Heinemann.
Beveridge, William. 1942. *Social Insurance and Allied Services.* New York: Macmillan.
Blackmon, Douglas. 2009. *Slavery by Another Name: The Re-Enslavement of Black Africans from the Civil War to World War II.* New York: Anchor Books.
Blackwell, Trevor, and Jeremy Seabrook. 1985. *A World Still to Win: The Reconstruction of the Post-War Working Class.* London: Faber and Faber.
Blair, Tony. 2010. *A Journey: My Political Life.* New York: Alfred A. Knopf.
⸺. 1999. "Beveridge Revisited: A Welfare State for the 21st Century." R. Walker (ed.). *Ending Child Poverty: Popular Welfare for the 21st Century.* Bristol: Policy Press.
⸺. 1998. *The Third Way: New Politics for the New Century.* London: Fabian Society.
⸺. 1997. "Speech at the Aylesbury Estate," Southwark. June 2.
⸺. 1995. *Let Us Face the Future—the 1945 Anniversary Lecture.* London: Fabian Society.
Blake, William. 1810. "And Did Those Feet in Ancient Times." In *Milton: A Poem.*
Blaug, M. 1974. "The Myth of the Old Poor Law and the Making of the New." In M.W. Flinn and T.C. Smout (eds.), *Essays in Social History.* London: Oxford University Press.
Blewett, Neal. 1965. "The Franchise in the United Kingdom." *Past and Present* 32, 1.
Bloch, Alice. 1997. "Ethnic Inequality and Social Security Policy." In Alan Walker and Carol Walker (eds.), *Britain Divided: The Growth of Social Exclusion in the 1980s and 1990s.* London: CPAG Ltd.
Booth, Charles. 1889. *Life and Labour of the People in London, Volume 1.* Edinburgh: Williams and Norgate.
Bosanquet, Nick, and Peter Townsend (eds.). 1980. *Labour and Equality: A Fabian Study of Labour in Power, 1974–79.* London: Heinemann.
Boughton, John. 2018. *Municipal Dreams: The Rise and Fall of Council Housing.* London: Verso.
Bowley, A.L., and A.R. Burnett-Hurst. 1915. *Livelihood and Poverty.* London: G. Bell and Sons, Ltd.
Boyd, Kelly, and Rohan McWilliam. 2007. "Introduction: Rethinking the Victorians." In

Kelly Boyd and Rohan McWilliams (eds.), *The Victorian Studies Reader*. London: Routledge.

Boyer, George. 1990. *An Economic History of the English Poor Law 1750–1850*. New York: Cambridge University Press.

Braidwood, Stephen. 1994. *Black Poor and White Philanthropists: London's Blacks and the Foundation of the Sierra Leone Settlement 1786–1791*. Liverpool: Liverpool University Press.

Brenner, Robert. 1987a. "Agrarian Class Structure and Economic Development in Pre-Industrial Europe." In T.H. Aston and C.H.E. Philpin (eds.), *The Brenner Debate: Agrarian Class Structure and Economic Development in Pre-Industrial Europe*. Cambridge: Cambridge University Press.

_____. 1987b. "The Agrarian Roots of European Capitalism." In T.H. Aston and C.H.E. Philpin (eds.), *The Brenner Debate: Agrarian Class Structure and Economic Development in Pre-Industrial Europe*. Cambridge: Cambridge University Press.

Briggs, Asa. 1990. *Victorian Cities*. London: Penguin Books.

_____. 1963. *Victorian Cities*. London: Odhams Books Limited.

_____. 1961. "The Welfare State in Historical Perspective." *European Journal of Sociology* 2, 2.

Brockway, Fenner. 1932. *Hungry England*. London: Victor Gollancz Ltd.

Brodie, Marc. 2004. *The Politics of the Poor: The East End of London 1885–1914*. Oxford: Clarendon Press.

Brooke, Stephen. 1991. "Problems of 'Socialist Planning': Evan Durbin and the Labour Government of 1945." *Historical Journal* 34, 3.

Brown, Derek. 2001. "1945–51: Labour and the Creation of the Welfare State." *The Guardian*, March 14.

Brown, Gordon. 1999. "A Scar on the Nation's Soul." *Poverty*. London: Child Poverty Action Group.

Brown, John. 1968. "Charles Booth and Labour Colonies, 1989–1905." *Economic History Review* 21, 2.

Brundage, Anthony. 2002. *The English Poor Laws, 1700–1930*. Basingstoke: Palgrave.

Bryan, Beverly, Stella Dadzie and Suzanne Scafe. 1985. *The Heart of the Race: Black Women's Lives in Britain*. London: Virago.

Bryson, Alex, and John Jacobs. 1992. *Policing the Workshy: Benefit Controls, the Labour Market and the Unemployed*. Aldershot: Ashgate Publishing.

Burnett, John. 1986. *A Social History of Housing 1815–1985*, 2nd edition. London: Methuen.

Butchart, Ed. 1997. *Unemployment and Non-Employment in Interwar Britain*. University of Oxford: Discussion Papers in Economic and Social History, 16.

Byres, Terence J. 2006. "Differentiation of the Peasantry under Feudalism and the Transition to Capitalism: In Defense of Rodney Hilton." *Journal of Agrarian Change* 6, 1.

Byrne, Dominic. 1987. "Rich and Poor: The Growing Divide." In Alan Walker and Carol Walker (eds.), *The Growing Divide: A Social Audit 1979–1987*. London: Child Poverty Action Group.

Callender, Claire. 1992. "Redundancy, Unemployment and Poverty." In Caroline Glendinning and Jane Millar (eds.), *Women and Poverty in Britain, the 1990s*. Hemel Hempstead: Harvester Wheatsheaf.

Callinicos, Alex. 2001. *Against the Third Way*. Cambridge: Polity Press.

Campbell, Beatrix. 2015. "Margaret Thatcher: To be or not to be a Woman." *British Politics* 10, 1.

———. 1984. *Wigan Pier Revisited: Poverty and Politics in the '80s*. London: Virago Press.

Campbell, John. 1987. *Nye Bevan and the Mirage of British Socialism*. London: Weidenfeld and Nicolson.

Cannadine, David. 2017. *Margaret Thatcher: A Life and Legacy*. Oxford: Oxford University Press.

———. 1984. "The Present and the Past in the English Industrial Revolution 1880–1980." *Past and Present* 103, 1.

Cantor, Norman F. 2001. *In the Wake of the Plague: The Black Death and the World It Made*. New York: Simon and Schuster.

Carby, H. 1982. "Schooling in Babylon." In Centre for Contemporary Cultural Studies (ed.). *The Empire Strikes Back*. London: Hutchinson.

Chambliss, William J. 1964. "A Sociological Analysis of the Law of Vagrancy." *Social Problems* 12, 1.

Chapman, Stanley (ed.). 1971. *The History of Working-Class Housing: A Symposium*. London: David and Charles Publishers.

Charlesworth, Lorie. 2010. *Welfare's Forgotten Past: A Socio-Legal History of the Poor Law*. New York: Routledge.

———. 2006. "Readings of Begging: The Legal Response to Begging Considered in its Modern and Historical Context." *Nottingham Law Journal* 15, 1.

Charman, Sarah, and Stephen P. Savage. 2002. "Toughing it Out: New Labour's Criminal Record." In Martin Powell (ed.). *Evaluating New Labour's Welfare Reforms*. Bristol: Policy Press.

Chater, Kathleen. 2009. *Untold Histories: Black People in England and Wales during the Period of the British Slave Trade, c.1660–1807*. Manchester: Manchester University Press.

Chinn, Carl. 1991. *Homes for People: 100 Years of Council Housing in Birmingham*. Birmingham: Birmingham Books.

Clarke, Peter. 2004. *Hope and Glory: Britain 1900–2000*. London: Penguin.

Clarke, John, and Mary Langan. 1993. "The British Welfare State: Foundation and Modernization." In Allan Cochrane and John Clarke (eds.), *Comparing Welfare States: Britain in International Context*. London: Sage Publications.

Coates, David. 2013. "Labour after New Labour: Escaping the Debt." *British Journal of Politics and International Relations*. 15.

———. 2003. "Labour Governments: Old Constraints and New Parameters." In David Coates (ed.). *Paving the Third Way: the Critique of Parliamentary Socialism*. London: Merlin Press.

———. 2002. "The New Political Economy of Post-War Britain." In Colin Hays (ed.). *British Politics Today*. Cambridge: Polity Press.

———. 1983. "The Character and Origin of Britain's Economic Decline." In David Coates and Gordon Johnston (eds.), *Socialist Strategies*. Oxford: Martin Robertson.

———. 1975. *The Labour Party and the Struggle for Socialism*. Cambridge: Cambridge University Press.

Coates, David, and Richard Silburn. 1970. *Poverty: The Forgotten Englishmen*. London: Penguin Books.

Cody, Lisa Forman. 2000. "The Politics of Illegitimacy in an Age of Reform: Women, Reproduction, and Political Economy in England's New Poor Law of 1834." *Journal of Women's History* 11, 4.

Cohen, Steve. 1985. "Anti-Semitism, Immigration Controls and the Welfare State." *Criti-

cal Social Policy 13.
Cohen, Ruth, Jill Coxall, Gary Craig and Azra Sadiq-Sangster. 1992. *Hardship Britain: Being Poor in the 1990s.* London: Child Poverty Action Group.
Coldrey, Barry M. 1999. "'…a place to which idle vagrants may be sent,' The First Phase of Child Migration during the Seventeenth and Eighteenth Centuries." *Children and Society* 13.
Cole, G.D.H. 1941. *British Working Class Politics 1832–1914.* London: The Labour Book Service.
Colwill, Jeremy. 1994. "Beveridge, Women and the Welfare State." *Critical Social Policy* 14, 41.
Convery, Paul. 1997. "Unemployment." In Alan Walker and Carol Walker (eds.), *Britain Divided: The Growth of Social Exclusion in the 1980s and 1990s.* London: CPAG Ltd.
Cook Juliet, and Shantu Watt. 1992. "Racism, Women and Poverty." In Caroline Glendinning and Jane Millar (eds.), *Women and Poverty in Britain, the 1990s.* Hemel Hempstead: Harvester Wheatsheaf.
Cooney, E.W. 1974. "High Flats in Local Authority Housing in England and Wales Since 1945." In Anthony Sutcliffe (ed.). *Multi-Storey Living: The British Working Class Experience.* London: Croom Helm.
Cooper, John. 2017. *The British Welfare Revolution, 1906–14.* London: Bloomsbury.
CRE (Commission for Racial Equality). 1984. *Race and Housing in Liverpool: A Research Report.* London: Commission for Racial Equality.
Crick, Bernard (ed.). 1981. *Unemployment.* London: Methuen.
Crosland, Anthony. 1956. *The Future of Socialism.* London: Jonathan Cape.
Crossman, Richard. 1952. "Towards a Philosophy of Socialism." In Richard Crossman (ed.). *New Fabian Essays.* London: Turnstile Press.
Crouch, Colin. 1999. "The Parabola of Working Class Politics." In Andrew Gamble and Tony Wright (eds.), *The New Social Democracy.* Oxford: Blackwell Publishers.
Crowther, M.A. 1981. *The Workhouse System 1834–1929: The History of an English Social Institution.* Athens: University of Georgia Press.
Cruickshank, Marjorie. 1978. "Factory Children and Compulsory Education: The Short-Time System in the Textile Areas of North-West England 1833–1864." *Vocational Aspect of Education* 30.
Cunningham, Hugh. 1992. *The Children of the Poor: Representations of Childhood Since the Seventeenth Century.* Oxford: Blackwell.
_____. 1990. "The Employment and Unemployment of Children in England c.1680–1851," *Past and Present* 126, 1.
Daunton, Martin. 2002. *Just Taxes: The Politics of Taxation in Britain 1914–1979.* Cambridge: Cambridge University Press.
Davis, Jennifer. 1989. "Jennings' Buildings and the Royal Borough: The Construction of the Underclass in Mid-Victorian England." In David Feldman and Gareth Stedman Jones (eds.), *Metropolis London: Histories and Representations since 1800.* London: Routledge.
Davis, John. 2001. "Rents and Race in 1960s London: New Light on Rachmanism." *Twentieth Century British History* 12, 1.
Davis, Jon, and John Rentoul. 2019. *Heroes or Villains? The Blair Government Reconsidered.* Oxford: Oxford University Press.
Davis, Mike. 2006. *Planet of Slums* New York: Verso.
Deacon, Alan. 2002. *Perspectives on Welfare: Ideas, Ideology and Policy Debates.* Buckinghamshire: Open University Press.

———. 1981. "Unemployment and Politics in Britain since 1945." In Brian Showler and Adrian Sinfield (eds.), *The Workless State: Studies in Unemployment*. Oxford: Martin Robertson.

———. 1978. "The Scrounging Controversy: Public Attitudes towards the Unemployed in Contemporary Britain." *Social and Economic Administration* 12, 2.

———. 1976. *In Search of the Scrounger: the Administration of Unemployment Insurance in Britain 1920–1931*. Occasional Papers on Social Administration 60. London: G. Bell and Sons.

Deacon, Alan, and Jonathan Bradshaw. 1983. *Reserved for the Poor: The Means Test in British Social Policy*. Oxford: Martin Robertson and Company Ltd.

De Benedictis, Sara. 2012. "Feral Parents: Austerity Parenting under Neoliberalism." *Studies in the Maternal* 4, 2.

Dench, Geoff, Kate Gavron and Michael Young. 2006. *The New East End: Kinship, Race and Conflict*. London: Profile Books.

Desai, Radhika. 1994a. *Intellectuals and Socialism: "Social Democrats" and the Labour Party*. London: Lawrence and Wishart.

———. 1994b. "Second-Hand Dealers in Ideas: Think-Tanks and Thatcherite Hegemony." *New Left Review* 203.

Dobb, Maurice. 1946. *Studies in the Development of Capitalism*. London: George Routledge and Sons.

Dobson, R.B. 1987. "The Risings in York, Beverley and Scarborough, 1380–1381." In Rodney Hilton and T.H. Aston (eds.), *The English Rising of 1381*. Cambridge: Cambridge University Press.

Dolowitz, David. 1998. *Learning from America: Policy Transfer and the Development of the British Welfare State*. Brighton: Sussex Academic Press.

Donnison, David. 1982. *The Politics of Poverty*. Oxford: Martin Robertson.

Donnison, David, and Clare Ungerson. 1982. *Housing Policy*. Harmondsworth: Penguin.

Dorey, Pete. 2015. "A Farewell to Alms: Thatcherism's Legacy of Inequality." *British Politics* 10, 1.

———. 2014. "The Stepping Stones Programme: The Conservative Party's Struggle to Develop a Trade-Union Policy, 1975–1979." *Historical Studies in Industrial Relations* 35.

———. 2011. *British Conservatism: The Politics and Philosophy of Inequality*. London: I.B. Tauris.

———. 2010. "A Poverty of Imagination: Blaming the Poor for Inequality." *The Political Quarterly* 81, 3.

Dorling, Danny. 2014a. "Mapping the Thatcherite Legacy: The Human Geography of Social Inequality in Britain Since the 1970s." In Stephen Farrall and Colin Hay (eds.), *The Legacy of Thatcherism: Assessing and Exploring Thatcherite Social and Economic Policies*. Oxford: Oxford University Press.

———. 2014b. *Inequality and the 1%*. London: Verso.

———. 2010. *Injustice: Why Social Inequality Persists*. Bristol: Policy Press.

Driver, Cecil. 1946. *Tory Radical: The Life of Richard Oastler*. New York: Oxford University Press.

Driver, Stephen. 2008. "New Labour and Social Policy." In Matt Beech and Simon Lee (eds.), 2008. *Ten Years of New Labour*. London: Palgrave Macmillan.

Driver, Stephen, and Luke Martell. 1998. *New Labour: Politics after Thatcherism*. Cambridge: Polity Press.

Dunkley, Peter. 1982. *The Crisis of the Old Poor Law in England 1795–1834: An Interpre-*

tative Essay. New York and London: Garland Publishing.
Dunleavy, Patrick. 1981. *The Politics of Mass Housing in Britain, 1945–1975*. Oxford: Clarendon Press.
Durbin, Elizabeth. 1985. *New Jerusalems: The Labour Party and the Economics of Democratic Socialism*. London: Routledge and Kegan Paul.
Dutton, H.I., and J.E. King. 1982. "The Limits of Paternalism: The Cotton Tyrants of North Lancashire, 1836–1854." *Social History* 7, 1.
Dyer, Christopher. 2012. "Poverty and its Relief in Late Medieval England." *Past and Present* 216.
Dyos, H.J. 1967. "The Slums of Victorian London." *Victorian Studies* 11, 1.
Eckstein, Harry. 1960. *Pressure Group Politics: The Case of the British Medical Association*. Stanford: Stanford University Press.
Edin, Kathryn, and Maria Kefalas. 2005. *Promises I Can Keep: Why Poor Women Put Motherhood Before Marriage*. Berkeley: University of California Press.
Eichengreen, Barry, and T.J. Hatton. 1988. "Interwar Unemployment in International Perspective: An Overview." In Barry Eichengreen and T.J. Hatton (eds.), *Interwar Unemployment in International Perspective*. Dordrecht: Kluwer Academic Publishers.
Engels, Friedrich. 1987. *The Condition of the Working Class in England in 1844*. London: Penguin.
Erickson, Arvel, and Martin Havron (eds.). 1967. *Readings in English History*. New York: Charles Scribner's Sons.
Evans, Tanya. 2005. *'Unfortunate Objects': Lone Mothers in Eighteenth-Century London*. London: Palgrave Macmillan.
Fabian Society. 2006. *Narrowing the Gap: The Final Report of the Fabian Commission on Life Chances and Child Poverty*. London: Fabian Society.
Farrall, Stephen, and Colin Hay (eds.). 2014. *The Legacy of Thatcherism: Assessing and Exploring Thatcherite Social and Economic Policies*. Oxford: Oxford University Press.
Feinstein, Charles H. 1998. "Pessimism Perpetuated: Real Wages and the Standard of Living in Britain during and after the Industrial Revolution." *Journal of Economic History* 58, 3.
Fiegehen, G.C., P.S. Lansley and A.D. Smith. 1977. *Poverty and Progress in Britain 1953–73*. Cambridge: Cambridge University Press.
Field, Frank. 1982. *Poverty and Politics: The Inside Story of the Child Poverty Action Group's Campaigns in the 1970s*. London: Heinemann.
Flanagan, Richard. 1991. *"Parish-Fed Bastards": A History of the Politics of the Unemployed in Britain, 1884–1939*. Westport: Greenwood Press.
Flinn, M.W. (ed.). 1965. *Report on the Sanitary Condition of the Labouring Population of Gt. Britain by Edwin Chadwick, 1842, edited and with an Introduction by M.W. Flinn*. Edinburgh: Edinburgh University Press.
Fons, Jean-Philippe. 2011. "Poverty and Inequality: Has New Labour Delivered?" *Observatoire de la Societe Britannique* 10.
Forrest, Ray, and Ade Kearns. 2001. "Social Cohesion, Social Capital and the Neighbourhood." *Urban Studies* 38, 12.
Francis, Martin. 1997. *Ideas and Policies under Labour, 1945–1951*. Manchester: Manchester University Press.
_____. 1995. "Economics and Ethics: The Nature of Labour's Socialism, 1945–51." *Twentieth Century British History* 6, 2.

Fraser, Derek. 1984. *The Evolution of the British Welfare State: A History of Social Policy Since the Industrial Revolution*, 2nd edition. Basingstoke: Palgrave.

Fried, Albert, and Richard Elman. 1968. *Charles Booth's London*. New York: Pantheon Books.

Friend, Andrew, and Andy Metcalf. 1981. *Slump City: The Politics of Mass Unemployment*. London: Pluto Press.

Fryer, Peter. 1984. *Staying Power: The History of Black People in Britain*. London: Pluto Press.

Gamble, Andrew. 2015. "The Thatcher Myth." *British Politics* 10, 1.

———. 1988. *The Free Economy and the Strong State: The Politics of Thatcherism*. London: Macmillan.

Garside, W.R. 1990. *British Unemployment 1919–1939: A Study in Public Policy*. Cambridge: Cambridge University Press.

Garthwaite, Kayleigh. 2016. *Hunger Pains: Life Inside Foodbank Britain*. Bristol: Policy Press.

Gauldie, Enid. 1974. *Cruel Habitations: A History of Working Class Housing*. London: George Allen and Unwin Ltd.

Gazeley, Ian. 2003. *Poverty in Britain, 1900–1965*. Basingstoke: Palgrave.

Gazeley, Ian, and Pat Thane. 1998. "Patterns of Visibility: Unemployment in Britain during the Nineteenth and Twentieth Centuries." In Gail Lewis (ed.). *Forming Nation, Framing Welfare*. London/New York: Routledge, The Open University.

George, Dorothy. 1965. *London Life in the Eighteenth Century*. New York: Harper and Row.

———. 1953. *England in Transition: Life and Work in the Eighteenth Century*. London: Penguin.

George, V. 1968. *Social Security: Beveridge and After*. London: Routledge and Kegan Paul.

Giddens, Anthony. 2008. *The Third Way: The Renewal of Social Democracy*. Cambridge: Polity Press.

Gilbert, Bentley. 1970. *British Social Policy 1914–1939*. Ithaca: Cornell University Press.

Gilroy, Paul, and Errol Lawrence. 1988. "Two-Tone Britain: White and Black Youth and the Politics of Anti-Racism." In Philip Cohen and Harwant Bains (eds.), *Multi-Racist Britain*. London: Macmillan.

Ginsburg, Norman. 1997. "Housing." In Alan Walker and Carol Walker (eds.), *Britain Divided: The Growth of Social Exclusion in the 1980s and 1990s*. London: CPAG Ltd.

Glennerster, Howard. 2004. "Poverty Policy from 1900 to the 1970s." In Howard Glennerster, John Hills, David Piachaud and Jo Webb (eds.), *One Hundred Years of Poverty and Policy*. York: Joseph Rowntree Foundation.

———. 1991. "Social Policy Since the Second World War." In John Hills (ed.). 1991. *The State of Welfare: The Welfare State in Britain since 1974*. Oxford: Clarendon Press.

Golding, P., and S. Middleton. 1982. *Images of Welfare: Press and Public Attitudes to Welfare*. London: Basil Blackwell and Martin Robertson.

Goldthorpe, John, David Lockwood, Frank Beckhover and Jennifer Platt. 1967. "The Affluent Worker and the Thesis of Embourgeoisement: Some Preliminary Research Findings." *Sociology* 1, 1.

Goodman, Alissa, Paul Johnson and Steven Webb. 1997. *Inequality in the UK*. Oxford: Oxford University Press.

Gordon, David, and Christina Pantazis (eds.). 1997. *Breadline Britain in the 1990s*. Aldershot, England: Ashgate Publishing Limited.

Gordon, David, Laura Adelman, Karl Ashworth, Jonathan Bradshaw, Ruth Levitas, Sue Middleton, Christina Pantazis, Demi Patsios, Sarah Payne, Peter Townsend and Julie Williams. 2000. *Poverty and Social Exclusion in Britain*. York: Joseph Rowntree Foundation.

Gramsci, Antonio. 1971. *Selections from the Prison Notebooks*. New York: International Publishers.

Great Britain. 1965 (reprinted 1972). *Report of the Committee on Housing in Greater London, Chair, Sir Milner Holland*. London: Her Majesty's Stationery Office.

_____. 1834. *Report from His Majesty's Commissioners for Inquiring into the Administration and Practical Operation of the Poor Laws*. London: King's Printer.

Green, David. 2010. *Pauper Capital: London and the Poor Law, 1790–1870*. Farnham: Ashgate Publishing Limited.

_____. 2006. "Pauper Protests: Power and Resistance in Early Nineteenth Century London Workhouses." *Social History* 31, 2.

_____. 1995. *From Artisans to Paupers: Economic Change and Poverty in London, 1790–1870*. Brookfield: Ashgate Publishing.

Green, E.H.H. (Ewen) 1999. "Thatcherism: An Historical Perspective." *Transactions of the Royal Historical Society* 9.

Haggard, Robert F. 2001. *The Persistence of Victorian Liberalism: The Politics of Social Reform in Britain, 1870–1900*. Westport: Greenwood Press.

Hall, Stuart. 2017. *Selected Political Writings: The Great Moving Right Show and Other Essays*. London: Lawrence and Wishart.

_____. 2005. "New Labour's Double-Shuffle." *Review of Education, Pedagogy and Cultural Studies* 27, 4.

_____. 1988. *The Hard Road to Renewal: Thatcherism and the Crisis of the Left*. London: Verso.

Hall, Stuart, Doreen Massey and Michael Rustin (eds.). 2015. *After Neoliberalism? The Kilborn Manifesto*. London: Lawrence and Wishart.

Hanley, Lynsey. 2007. *Estates: An Intimate History*. London: Granta Books.

Hannah, Simon. 2018. *A Party with Socialists in It: A History of the Labour Left*. London: Pluto Press.

Hansen, Randall. 2000. *Citizenship and Immigration in Post-War Britain*. Oxford: Oxford University Press.

Hare, Paul. 2013. "PPP and PFI: The Political Economy of Building Public Infrastructure and Delivering Services." *Oxford Review of Economic Policy* 29, 1.

Harley, Joseph. 2015. "Material Lives of the Poor and their Strategic Use of the Workhouse During the Final Decades of the English Old Poor Law," *Continuity and Change* 30, 1.

Harris, Bernard. 2004. *The Origins of the British Welfare State*. London: Palgrave Macmillan.

_____. 1988. "Unemployment, Insurance and Health in Interwar Britain." In Barry Eichengreen and T.J. Hatton (eds.), *Interwar Unemployment in International Perspective*. Dordrecht: Kluwer Academic Publishers.

Harris, Jose. 2000. "Labour's Political and Social Thought." In Duncan Tanner, Pat Thane and Nick Tiratsoo (eds.), *Labour's First Century*. Cambridge: Cambridge University Press.

_____. 1996. "Contract and Citizenship." In David Marquand and Anthony Seddon (eds.), *The Ideas that Shaped Post-War Britain*. London: Fontana Press.

_____. 1995. "Between Civic Virtue and Social Darwinism: The Concept of the Residuum." In David Englander and Rosemary O'Day (eds.), *Retrieved Riches: Social Investigation in Britain 1840-1914*. London: Scolar Press.

———. 1986. "Political Ideas and the Debate on State Welfare, 1940-45." In Harold L. Smith (ed.). *War and Social Change: British Society in the Second World War*. Manchester: Manchester University Press.

———. 1977. *William Beveridge: A Biography*. Oxford: Clarendon Press.

———. 1972. *Unemployment and Politics: A Study in English Social Policy 1886-1914*. Oxford: Clarendon Press.

Haseler, Stephen. 1969. *The Gaitskellites: Revisionism in the British Labour Party 1951-64*. London: Macmillan.

Hatherley, Owen. 2020. "The Government of London." *New Left Review*. 122, March-April.

Hatton, Timothy J., and Roy E. Bailey. 2000. "Seebohm Rowntree and the Postwar Poverty Puzzle." *Economic History Review* LIII, 3.

Hay, Colin. 2010. "Chronicles of a Death Foretold: the Winter of Discontent and Construction of the Crisis of British Keynesianism." *Parliamentary Affairs* 63, 3.

———. 2007. "Whatever Happened to Thatcherism?" *Political Studies Review* 5.

———. 1997. "Anticipating Accommodations, Accommodating Anticipations: The Appeasement of Capital in the "Modernization" of the British Labour Party, 1987-1992." *Politics & Society* 25, 2.

———. 1992. "Housing Policy in Transition: From the Post-War Settlement towards a 'Thatcherite' Hegemony." *Capital and Class* 16, 1.

Hay, J.R. 1975. *The Origins of the Liberal Welfare Reforms 1906-1914*. London: Macmillan.

Hayek, F.A. 1944. *The Road to Serfdom*. Chicago: University of Chicago Press.

——— (ed.). 1954. *Capitalism and the Historians*. Chicago: University of Chicago Press.

Heffernan, Richard. 2007. "Tony Blair as Labour Party Leader." In Anthony Seldon (ed.). *Blair's Britain, 1997-2007*. Cambridge: Cambridge University Press.

———. 2000. *New Labour and Thatcherism: Political Change in Britain*. London: Macmillan.

Heffernan, Richard, and Mike Marqusee. 1992. *Defeat from the Jaws of Victory: Inside Kinnock's Labour Party*. London: Verso.

Heller, Henry. 2011. *The Birth of Capitalism: A Twenty-First-Century Perspective*. London: Pluto Press.

Henriques, Ursula. 1979. *Before the Welfare State: Social Administration in Early Industrial Britain*. New York: Longman.

Hickman, Mary J. 1998. "Education for 'Minorities': Irish Catholics in Britain." In Gail Lewis (ed.). *Forming Nation, Framing Welfare*. London: Routledge, The Open University.

Hill, Christopher. 1986. *The Collected Essays of Christopher Hill, Volume Three: People and Ideas in Seventeenth Century England*. Amherst: University of Massachusetts Press.

———. 1985. *The Collected Essays of Christopher Hill, Volume 1: Writing and Revolution in Seventeenth Century England*. Amherst: University of Massachusetts Press.

———. 1972. *The World Turned Upside Down: Radical Ideas During the English Revolution*. London: Temple Smith.

———. 1964. *Society and Puritanism in Pre-Revolutionary England*. New York: Schocken Books.

———. 1955. *The English Revolution 1640*, 3rd edition. London: Lawrence and Wishart.

———. 1952. "Puritanism and the Poor." *Past and Present* 2.

Hill, Michael, and Alan Walker. 2014. "What Were the Lasting Effects of Thatcher's Legacy for Social Security?" In Stephen Carroll and Colin Hay (eds.), *The Legacy of Thatcherism: Assessing and Exploring Thatcherite Social and Economic Policies*. Oxford: Oxford University Press.

Hills, John. 1996. "Introduction: After the Turning Point." In John Hills (ed.). *New Inequalities: The Changing Distribution of Income and Wealth in the United Kingdom*. Cambridge: Cambridge University Press.

Hills, John, Tom Sefton and Kitty Stewart (eds.). 2009. "Conclusions: Climbing Every Mountain or Retreating from the Foothills?" In John Hills, Tom Sefton and Kitty Stewart (eds.), *Towards a More Equal Society? Poverty, Inequality and Policy since 1997*. Bristol: Policy Press.

Hills, John, and Kitty Stewart. 2005. "A Tide Turned by Mountains Yet to Climb?" In John Hills and Kitty Stewart (eds.), *A More Equal Society? New Labour, Poverty, Inequality and Exclusion*. Bristol: Policy Press.

Hilton, Rodney. 1985. *Class Conflict and the Crisis of Feudalism: Essays in Medieval Social History*. London: Hambledon Press.

———. 1978. "Reasons for Inequality Among Medieval Peasants." *Journal of Peasant Studies* 5, 3.

Himmelfarb, Gertrude. 1991. *Poverty and Compassion: The Moral Imagination of the Late Victorians*. New York: Knopf.

Hindle, Steve. 2004a. *On the Parish? The Micro-Politics of Poor Relief in Rural England c. 1550–1750*. Oxford: Oxford University Press.

———. 2004b. "Dependency, Shame and Belonging: Badging the Deserving Poor, c. 1550–1750." *Cultural and Social History*, 1, 1.

Hirsch, Arnold. 1983. *Making the Second Ghetto: Race and Housing in Chicago 1940–1960*. Chicago: University of Chicago Press.

Hitchcock, Tim, Peter King and Pamela Sharpe (eds.). 1997. *Chronicling Poverty: The Voices and Strategies of the English Poor, 1640–1840*. London: Macmillan.

Hitchcock, Tim, and Robert Shoemaker. 2015. *London Lives: Poverty, Crime and the Making of a Modern City, 1690–1800*. Cambridge: Cambridge University Press.

Hobsbawm, Eric. 1995. *Age of Extremes: The Short Twentieth Century 1914–1991*. London: Abacus.

———. 1981. *The Forward March of Labour Halted?* London: Verso.

———. 1977. *The Age of Capital 1848–1875*. London: Abacus.

———. 1968. *Industry and Empire: An Economic History of Britain since 1750*. London: Weidenfeld and Nicolson.

———. 1964. *Labouring Men: Studies in the History of Labour*. London: Weidenfeld and Nicholson.

———. 1962. *The Age of Revolution: 1789–1848*. New York: New American Library.

Hobsbawm, Eric, and George Rude. 1969. *Captain Swing*. London: Lawrence and Wishart.

Hodkinson, Stuart. 2011. "The Private Finance Initiative in English Council Housing Regeneration: A Privatisation too Far?" *Housing Studies* 26, 6.

Hopkins, Eric. 1991. *The Rise and Decline of the English Working Classes 1918–1990*. New York: St. Martin's Press.

Howkins, Alan and John Saville. 1979. "The Nineteen Thirties: A Revisionist History."

Socialist Register 16.
Hunt, Tristram. 2005. *Building Jerusalem: The Rise and Fall of the Victorian City*. London: Phoenix.
Inman, John. 1934. *Poverty and Housing Conditions in a Manchester Ward*. Manchester: University of Manchester Economics Research Section, Pamphlet 2.
Innes, Joanna. 1999. "The State and the Poor: Eighteenth Century England in European Perspective." In John Brewer and Eckhart Hellmuth (eds.), *Rethinking Leviathan: The Eighteenth Century State in Britain and Germany*. Oxford: Oxford University Press.
Irvin, George. 2008. *Super Rich: The Rise of Inequality in Britain and the United States*. Cambridge: Polity Press.
Jackson, Ben. 2018. "Reviews: Citizen and Subject: Clement Attlee's Socialism." *History Workshop Journal* 86.
_____. 2012. "The Think-Tank Archipelago: Thatcherism and Neo-Liberalism." In Ben Jackson and Robert Saunders (eds.), *Making Thatcher's Britain*. Cambridge: Cambridge University Press.
_____. 2005. "From Each According to His Ability: Work and Progressive Political Thought." *Public Policy Research*.
Jackson, Ben, and Robert Saunders (eds.). 2012. *Making Thatcher's Britain*. Cambridge: Cambridge University Press.
Jackson, Peter. 2014. "Commentary: The Long Run Economic Consequence of Mrs. Thatcher." In Stephen Farrall and Colin Hay (eds.), *The Legacy of Thatcherism: Assessing and Exploring Thatcherite Social and Economic Policies*. Oxford: Oxford University Press.
_____. 1992. "Economic Policy." In David Marsh and R.A.W. Rhodes (eds.), *Implementing Thatcherite Policies: Audit of an Era*. Buckinghamshire: Open University Press.
Jacobs, Sidney. 1985. "Race, Empire and the Welfare State: Council Housing and Racism." *Critical Social Policy* 13.
Jahoda, Marie, Paul Lazarsfeld and Hans Zeisel. 1971 (originally 1933). *Marienthal: The Sociography of an Unemployed Community*. Chicago: Aldine Atherton Inc.
Jenkins, Peter. 1988. *Mrs. Thatcher's Revolution: The Ending of the Socialist Era*. Cambridge, Massachusetts: Harvard University Press.
Jessop, Bob, Kevin Bonnett, Simon Bromley and Tom Ling. 1988. *Thatcherism: A Tale of Two Nations*. London: Polity Press.
Johnson, Paul Barton. 1968. *Land Fit for Heroes: The Planning of British Reconstruction 1916–1919*. Chicago: University of Chicago Press.
Jones, Esyllt. 2019. *Radical Medicine: The International Origins of Socialized Health Care in Canada*. Winnipeg: ARP Books.
Jones, Gareth Stedman. 1971. *Outcast London: A Study in the Relationship Between Classes in Victorian Society*. London: Oxford University Press.
Jones, Harriet. 1991. "New Tricks for an Old Dog? The Conservatives and Social Policy, 1951–5." In Anthony Gorst, Lewis Johnman and W. Scott Lucas (eds.), *Contemporary British History 1931–1961: Politics and the Limits of Policy*. London and New York: Pinter Publishers.
Jones, Margaret, and Rodney Lowe. 2002. *From Beveridge to Blair: The First Fifty Years of Britain's Welfare State 1948–98*. Manchester: Manchester University Press.
Jones, Owen. 2012. *Chavs: The Demonization of the Working Class*. London: Verso.
Jordan, W.K. 1961. *The Charities of Rural England 1480–1660*. London: George Allen

and Unwin Ltd.
Joseph, Keith, and Jonathan Sumption. 1979. *Equality*. London: John Murray Publishers.
Joseph Rowntree Foundation (JRF). Analysis Unit. 2018. *UK Poverty 2018*. York: Joseph Rowntree Foundation.
Joyce, Robert, and Like Sibieta. 2013. "An Assessment of Labour's Record on Income Inequality and Poverty." *Oxford Review of Economic Policy* 29, 1.
Katz, Michael. 2013. *The Undeserving Poor: America's Enduring Confrontation with Poverty*, 2nd Edition. Oxford: Oxford University Press.
Kavanagh, Dennis. 2007. "The Blair Premiership." In Anthony Seldon (ed.). *Blair's Britain, 1997–2007*. Cambridge: Cambridge University Press.
_____. 1990. *Thatcherism and British Politics*. Oxford: Oxford University Press.
Kaye, Harvey. 1984. *The British Marxist Historians*. Cambridge: Polity Press.
Keating, P. (ed.). 1976. *Into Unknown England 1866–1913, Selections from the Social Explorers*. London: Fontana.
Keating, Michael, and David McCrone (eds.). 2015. *The Crisis of Social Democracy in Europe*. Edinburgh: Edinburgh University Press.
Keeling, Dorothy. 1961. *The Crowded Stairs: Recollections of Social Work in Liverpool*. London: National Council of Social Service.
Kefford, Alistair. 2018. "Housing the Citizen-Consumer in Post-War Britain: The Parker Morris Report, Affluence and the Even Briefer Life of Social Democracy." *Twentieth Century British History* 29, 2.
Kidd, Alan. 1999. *State, Society and the Poor in Nineteenth Century England*. London: Macmillan.
Kiernan, Kathleen, Hilary Land and Jane Lewis. 1998. *Lone Motherhood in Twentieth Century Britain*. Oxford: Clarendon Press.
Kiernan, Victor. 1953. "Communication: Puritanism and the Poor." *Past and Present* 3, 1.
King, Desmond. 1995. *Actively Seeking Work? The Politics of Unemployment and Welfare Policy in the United States and Great Britain*. Chicago: University of Chicago Press.
King, Desmond, and Mark Wickham-Jones. 1999. "Bridging the Atlantic: The Democratic (Party) Origins of Welfare to Work." In Martin Powell (ed.). *New Labour, New Welfare State? The 'Third Way' in British Social Policy*. Bristol: The Policy Press.
King, Peter. 1998. "The Rise of Juvenile Delinquency in England 1780–1840: Changing Patterns of Perception and Prosecution." *Past and Present* 160, 1.
King, Steven. 2000. *Poverty and Welfare in England, 1700–1850: A Regional Perspective*. Manchester: Manchester University Press.
Kingsford, Peter. 1982. *The Hunger Marchers in Britain 1920–1940*. London: Lawrence and Wishart.
Knott, John. 1986. *Popular Opposition to the 1834 Poor Law*. London: Croom Helm.
Kynaston, David. 2014. *Modernity Britain: A Shake of the Dice, 1959–62*. London: Bloomsbury.
_____. 2013. *Modernity Britain: Opening the Box, 1957–59*. London: Bloomsbury.
_____. 2008. *Austerity Britain 1945–51*. New York: Walker and Company.
Labour Party Annual Conference. *Labour Party Annual Conference Report*. 1976.
Landes, David. 1969. *The Unbound Prometheus: Technological Change and Industrial Development in Western Europe from 1750 to the Present*. Cambridge: Cambridge University Press.
Lansley, Stewart, and Joanna Mack. 2013. "A More Unequal Country?" Poverty and Social Exclusion. <poverty.ac.uk/editorial/more-unequal-country>.
Law, Ian. 1981. *A History of Race and Racism in Liverpool, 1660–1950*. Liverpool: Mer-

seyside Community Relations Council.

Layard, D., D. Piachaud and M. Stewart. 1978. *The Causes of Poverty. Background Paper No. 5. Royal Commission on the Distribution of Income and Wealth*. London: Her Majesty's Stationery Office.

Lazonick, William. 1974. "Karl Marx and Enclosures in England." *Review of Radical Political Economics* 6, 2.

Lee, Simon. 2008. "The British Model of Political Economy." In Matt Beech and Simon Lee (eds.), 2008. *Ten Years of New Labour*. London: Palgrave Macmillan.

Lees, Loretta. 2014. "The Urban Injustices of New Labour's 'New Urban Renewal': The Case of the Aylesbury Estate in London." *Antipode* 46, 4.

Lees, Lynn Hollen. 1998. *The Solidarities of Strangers: The English Poor Laws and the People, 1700–1948*. Cambridge: Cambridge University Press.

Le Grand, Julian. 1991. "The State of Welfare." In John Hills (ed.). 1991. *The State of Welfare: The Welfare State in Britain since 1974*. Oxford: Clarendon Press.

Lehtonen, Aura. 2018. "Helping Workless Families: Cultural Poverty and the Family in Austerity and Anti-Welfare Discourse." *Sociological Research Online* 23, 1.

Levene, Alysa. 2012. *The Childhood of the Poor: Welfare in Eighteenth-Century London*. London: Palgrave Macmillan.

_____. 2010. "Poor Families, Removal and 'Nurture' in late Old Poor Law London." *Continuity and Change* 25, 2.

_____. 2008. "Children, Childhood and the Workhouse: St. Marylebone, 1769–1781." *London Journal* 33, 1.

Levine-Clark, Marjorie. 2000. "Engendering Relief: Women, Ablebodiedness, and the New Poor Law in Early Victorian England." *Journal of Women's History* 11, 4.

Levitas, Ruth. 1998. *The Inclusive Society? Social Exclusion and New Labour*. London: Macmillan.

Lewis, David Levering. 1997. *When Harlem Was in Vogue*. New York: Penguin.

Lewis, Jane. 1992. "Gender and the Development of Welfare Regimes." *Journal of European Social Policy* 2, 3.

Lewis, Jane, and David Piachaud. 1992. "Women and Poverty in the Twentieth Century." In Caroline Glendinning and Jane Millar (eds.), *Women and Poverty in Britain, the 1990s*. Hemel Hempstead: Harvester Wheatsheaf.

Lewis, Paul, and Tim Newburn. 2011. *Reading the Riots: Investigating England's Summer of Disorder*. London: The Guardian and London School of Economics.

Leys, Colin. 2003. "The British Labour Party's Transition from Socialism to Capitalism." In David Coates (ed.). *Paving the Third Way: The Critique of Parliamentary Socialism*. London: Merlin Press.

_____. 1995. "A Radical Agenda for Britain." *New Left Review* 212.

Lindert, Peter, and Jeffrey Williamson. 1983. "English Workers' Living Standards during the Industrial Revolution: A New Look." *Economic History Review* 36, 1.

Lipsey, David. 1981. "Crosland's Socialism." In David Lipsey and Dick Leonard (eds.), *The Socialist Agenda: Crosland's Legacy*. London: Jonathan Cape.

Lis, Catharina, and Hugo Soly. 1979. *Poverty and Capitalism in Pre-Industrial Europe*. New Jersey: Humanities Press.

Lister, Ruth. 2004. *Poverty*. Cambridge: Polity Press.

_____. 2002. "Investing in the Citizen-Workers of the Future: New Labour's 'Third Way' in Welfare Reform." Paper prepared for the Annual Meeting of the American Political Science Association, Boston, August.

_____. 2001. "New Labour: A Study in Ambiguity from a Position of Ambivalence."

Critical Social Policy 21, 4.

_____. 1999. "A Modern Party of Social Justice: Achievements and Missed Opportunities." In Robert Walker (ed.). *Ending Child Poverty: Popular Welfare for the 21st Century?* Bristol: The Policy Press.

_____. 1998. "From Equality to Social Inclusion: New Labour and the Welfare State." *Critical Social Policy* 18, 2.

_____ (ed.). 1996. *Charles Murray and the Underclass: The Developing Debate*. London: Institute of Economic Affairs.

Loach, Ken. 2016. *I, Daniel Blake*. Sixteen Films, Why Not Productions and Wild Bunch with support of British Film Institute and BBC Films [written by Paul Laverty].

_____. 1966. *Cathy Come Home*. BBC Television [written by Jeremy Sandford].

Loney, Martin. 1987. "A War on Poverty or on the Poor?" In Alan Walker and Carol Walker (eds.), *The Growing Divide: A Social Audit 1979–1987*. London: Child Poverty Action Group.

Longmore, Jane. 2007. "'Cemented by the Blood of a Negro'? The Impact of the Slave Trade on Eighteenth-Century Liverpool." In David Richardson, Suzanne Schwarz and Anthony Tibbles (eds.), *Liverpool and Transatlantic Slavery*. Liverpool: Liverpool University Press.

Lorimer, Douglas. 1978. *Colour, Class and the Victorians: English Attitudes to the Negro in the Mid-Nineteenth Century*. Leicester: Leicester University Press and Holmes and Meier Publishers.

Lowe, Rodney. 2005. *The Welfare State in Britain Since 1945*, 3rd edition. New York: Palgrave Macmillan.

_____. 1999. "Introduction: The Road from 1945." In Helen Fawcett and Rodney Lowe (eds.), *Welfare Policy in Britain: The Road from 1945*. London: Macmillan.

_____. 1990. "The Second World War, Consensus and the Foundation of the Welfare State." *Twentieth Century British History* 1, 2.

Lund, Brian. 2002. "Safe as Houses? Housing Policy under New Labour." In Martin Powell (ed.). *Evaluating New Labour's Welfare Reforms*. Bristol: The Policy Press.

Lupton, Ruth. 2003. *Poverty Street: The Dynamics of Neighbourhood Decline and Renewal*. Bristol: Policy Press.

Lupton, Ruth, T. Burchardt and John Hills (eds.). 2016. *Social Policy in a Cold Climate: Policies and their Consequences since the Crisis*. Bristol: Policy Press.

Lupton, Ruth, and Anne Power. 2005. "Disadvantaged by Where You Live? New Labour and Neighbourhood Renewal." In John Hills and Kitty Stewart (eds.), *A More Equal Society? New Labour, Poverty, Inequality and Exclusion*. Bristol: Policy Press.

MacDonald, Robert, and Jane Marsh. 2005. *Disconnected Youth? Growing up in Britain's Poor Neighbourhoods*. Basingstoke: Palgrave Macmillan.

MacDonald, Robert, Tracy Shildrick, Colin Webster and Donald Simpson. 2005. "Growing Up in Poor Neighbourhoods: The Significance of Class and Place in the Extended Transitions of 'Socially Excluded' Young Adults." *Sociology* 39, 5.

MacGregor, Suzanne. 1981. *The Politics of Poverty*. London: Longman.

MacKinnon, Shauna, and Jim Silver. 2018. "Decolonizing for Equity and Inclusion in Winnipeg's North End." In Fran Klodawsky, Janet Siltanen and Caroline Andrew (eds.), *Toward Equity and Inclusion in Canadian Cities: Lessons from Critical Praxis-Oriented Research*. Montreal: McGill-Queen's University Press.

Mack, Joanna, and Stewart Lansley. 1984. *Poor Britain*. London: George Allen and Unwin.

Macnicol, John. 1999. "From 'Problem Family' to 'Underclass,' 1945–95." In Helen Fawcett and Rodney Lowe (eds.), *Welfare Policy in Britain: The Road from 1945.*" London:

Macmillan.

———. 1989. "Eugenics and the Campaign for Voluntary Sterilization in Britain Between the Wars." *Society for the Social History of Medicine* 2, 1.

———. 1987. "In Search of the Underclass." *Journal of Social Policy* 16, 3.

———. 1980. *The Movement for Family Allowances 1918–1945: A Study in Social Policy Development*. London: Heinemann.

Makin-Waite, Mike. 2021. *On Burnley Road: Class, Race and Politics in a Northern English Town*. London: Lawrence Wishart.

Mandelson, Peter. 2010. *The Third Man: Life at the Heart of New Labour*. London: HarperPress.

Mann, Kirk. 1994. "Watching the Defectives: Observers of the Underclass in the USA, Britain and Australia." *Critical Social Policy* 14, 41.

———. 1992. *The Making of an English Underclass? The Social Divisions of Welfare and Labour*. Buckinghamshire: Open University Press.

Manning, Roger B. 1988. *Village Revolts: Social Protest and Popular Disturbances in England, 1509–1640*. Oxford: Clarendon Press.

Marcetic, Branko. 2017. "Tony Blair's Ghoulish Last Decade." *Jacobin*, September.

Marmot, Michael. 2020. *Health Equity in England: The Marmot Review 10 Years On, Executive Summary*. London: Institute of Health Equity.

Marqusee, Mike. 1997. "New Labour and its Discontents." *New Left Review* 224.

Marsh, David. 1992. *The New Politics of British Trade Unionism: Union Power and the Thatcher Legacy*. Ithaca: ILR Press.

Marsh, David, and R.A.W. Rhodes (eds.). 1992. *Implementing Thatcherite Policies: Audit of an Era*. Buckinghamshire: Open University Press.

Marshall, Dorothy. 1969. *The English Poor in the Eighteenth Century*. London: Routledge and Kegan Paul.

Martin, John E. 1983. *Feudalism to Capitalism: Peasant and Landlord in English Agrarian Development*. New Jersey: Humanities Press.

Martin, Tara. 2009. "The Beginning of Labor's End? Britain's 'Winter of Discontent' and Working Class Women's Activism." *International Labor and Working-Class History* 75.

Marx, Karl. 1976. *Capital: A Critique of Political Economy, Volume One*. London: Penguin Books.

Matthews, David. 2018. "The Working Class Struggle for Welfare in Britain." *Monthly Review* 69, 9.

———. 2017. "The Struggle for Shelter: Class Conflict and Public Housing in Britain." *Monthly Review* 69, 4.

Mauro, Ian, and Jim Silver. 2017. Video. *A Good Place to Live: Transforming Public Housing in Lord Selkirk Park*. Manitoba Research Alliance and the University of Winnipeg. <mra-mb.ca/publication/good-place-live-transformation-public-housing-lord-selkirk-park/>.

McAnulla, Stuart. 2010. "Heirs to Blair's Third Way? David Cameron's Triangulation Conservatism." *British Politics* 5, 3.

McArthur, Daniel, and Aaron Reeves. 2019. "The Rhetoric of Recessions: How British Newspapers Talk about the Poor When Unemployment Rises, 1896–2000." *Sociology* 53, 6.

McGarvey, Darren. 2018. *Poverty Safari: Understanding the Anger of Britain's Underclass*. London: Picador.

Mckenzie, Lisa. 2017. "The Class Politics of Prejudice: Brexit and the Land of No-Hope and Glory." *British Journal of Sociology* 68, S1.

_____. 2015. *Getting By: Estates, Class and Culture in Austerity Britain*. Bristol: Policy Press.

_____. 2013. "Fox-Trotting the Riot: Slow Rioting in Britain's Inner City." *Sociological Research Online* 18, 4.

McKibbin, Ross. 2010. *Parties and People: England 1914–1951*. Oxford: Oxford University Press.

McKnight, Abigail. 2005. "Employment: Tackling Poverty Through 'Work for Those who Can.'" In John Hills and Kitty Stewart (eds.), *A More Equal Society? New Labour, Poverty, Inequality and Exclusion*. Bristol: Policy Press.

Meacher, Molly. 1974. *Scrounging on the Welfare: The Scandal of the 4 Week Rule*. London: Arrow Books.

Meek, James. 2014. *Private Island: Why Britain Now Belongs to Someone Else*. London: Verso.

Melhuish, Edward, Jay Belsky and Jacqueline Barnes. 2010. "Sure Start and Its Evaluation in England." In R. Tremblay, R.G. Barr, R.D Peters and M. Boivin (eds.) *Encyclopedia on Early Childhood Development*. Montreal: Centre of Excellence for Early Childhood Development.

Meredith, Stephen. 2006. "Mr. Crosland's Nightmare? New Labour and Equality in Historical Perspective." *British Journal of Politics and International Relations* 8.

Merrick, John. 2020. "Gilding Postwar Britain." *New Left Review* 122.

Middlemas, Keith. 1979. *Politics in an Industrial Society: The Experience of the British System Since 1911*. London: Andre Deutsch.

Miles, Andrew, and Mike Savage. 1994. *The Remaking of the British Working Class, 1840–1940*. London: Routledge.

Miliband, Ralph. 2009. *The State in Capitalist Society*. Pontypool: Merlin Press.

_____. 1972. *Parliamentary Socialism: A Study in the Politics of Labour*, 2nd edition. London: Merlin Press.

_____. 1960. "The Sickness of Labourism." *New Left Review* 1, 1.

Millar, Jane. 1997. "Gender." In Alan Walker and Carol Walker (eds.), *Britain Divided: The Growth of Social Exclusion in the 1980s and 1990s*. London: CPAG Ltd.

_____. 1992. "Lone Mothers and Poverty." In Caroline Glendinning and Jane Millar (eds.), *Women and Poverty in Britain, the 1990s*. Hemel Hempstead: Harvester Wheatsheaf.

Millar, Jane, and Tess Ridge. 2002. "Parents, Children, Families and New Labour: Developing Family Policy? in Martin Powell (ed.). *Evaluating New Labour's Welfare Reforms*. Bristol: Policy Press.

Mooney, Gerry. 1998. "Remoralizing the Poor? Gender, Class and Philanthropy in Victorian Britain." In Gail Lewis (ed.). *Forming Nation, Framing Welfare*. London: Routledge, The Open University.

Morgan, Carol E. 1992. "Women, Work and Consciousness in the Mid-Nineteenth-Century English Cotton Industry." *Social History* 17, 1.

Morgan, Kenneth. 1984. *Labour in Power, 1945–51*. Oxford: Clarendon Press.

Morris, John. 1953. "Early Christian Orthodoxy." *Past and Present* 3, 1.

Moschonas, Gerassimos. 2002. *In the Name of Social Democracy. The Great Transformation: 1945 to the Present*. London: Verso.

Moynihan, Daniel Patrick. 1965 (reprinted 1967). *The Negro Family: the Case for National Action*. Washington, DC: Office of Planning Policy and Research. Reprinted in Lee Rainwater and William Yancey (eds.), *The Moynihan Report and the Politics of Controversy*. Cambridge: MIT Press.

Mukherjee, Tuku. 1988. "The Journey Back." In Philip Cohen and Harwant Bains (eds.), *Multi-Racist Britain*. London: Macmillan.

Murie, Alan. 2014. "The Housing Legacy of Thatcherism." In Stephen Carroll and Colin Hay (eds.), *The Legacy of Thatcherism: Assessing and Exploring Thatcherite Social and Economic Policies*. Oxford: Oxford University Press.

Murray, Andrew. 2019. *The Fall and Rise of the British Left*. London: Verso.

Murray, Charles. 1990. *The Emerging British Underclass*. London: Institute of Economic Affairs.

_____. 1984. *Losing Ground*. New York: Basic Books.

Myers, Norma. 1996. *Reconstructing the Black Past: Black in Britain 1780–1830*. London: Frank Cass and Co.

Nadasan, Premilla. 2007. "From Widow to Welfare Queen: Welfare and the Politics of Race." *Black Women, Gender and Families* 1, 2.

Nairn, Tom. 1977. *The Break-Up of Britain*. London: NLB.

Norton, Philip. 2008. "Tony Blair and the Office of Prime Minister." In Matt Beech and Simon Lee (eds.), *Ten Years of New Labour*. London: Palgrave Macmillan.

Novak, Tony. 1988. *Poverty and the State: an Historical Sociology*. Buckinghamshire: Open University Press.

Oakeshott, Michael. 1962. "On Being Conservative." In *Rationalism in Politics and Other Essays*. New York: Methuen.

O'Connor, Alice. 2001. *Poverty Knowledge: Social Science, Social Policy and the Poor in Twentieth Century US History*. Princeton: Princeton University Press.

O'Connor, James. 1973. *The Fiscal Crisis of the State*. London: St. James.

O'Hara, Mary. 2015. *Austerity Bites: A Journey to the Sharp End of Cuts in the UK*. Bristol: Policy Press.

Oppenheim, Carey. 1997. "The Growth of Poverty and Inequality." In Alan Walker and Carol Walker (eds.), *Britain Divided: The Growth of Social Exclusion in the 1980s and 1990s*. London: CPAG Ltd.

Oppenheimer, Peter. 1970. "Muddling Through: The Economy, 1951–1964." In Vernon Bogdanor and Robert Skidelsky (eds.), *The Age of Affluence 1951–1964*. London: Macmillan.

Orsi, Cosma. 2017. "The Political Economy of Inclusion: The Rise and Fall of the Workhouse System," *Journal of the History of Economic Thought* 39, 4.

Orwell, George. 1962 (originally 1937). *The Road to Wigan Pier*. Penguin: Harmondsworth, England.

O'Tuathaigh, M.A.G. 1985. "The Irish in Nineteenth Century Britain." In Roger Swift and Sheridan Gilley (eds.), *The Irish in the Victorian City*. London: Croom Helm.

Oxley, Geoffrey. 1974. *Poor Relief in England and Wales 1601–1834*. London: David and Charles.

Palmer, Bryan. 2019. "The *New* New Poor Law: A Chapter in the Current Class War Waged from Above." *Labour/Le Travail* 84.

_____. 2014. "Reconsideration of Class: Precariousness as Proletarianization." In Leo Panitch, Greg Albo and Vivek Chibber (eds.), *Socialist Register 2014: Registering Class*. Halifax: Fernwood Publishing.

_____. 2002. "E.P. Thompson, British Marxist Historians, and the Making of Dissident Political Mobilization." *Labour/Le Travail* 50.

Panitch, Leo. 2009. "Foreword: Reading the State in Capitalist Society." Ralph Miliband. *The State in Capitalist Society*. Pontypool: Merlin Press.

_____. 2003. "Socialist Renewal and the Labour Party." In David Coates (ed.). *Pav-

ing the Third Way: The Critique of Parliamentary Socialism. London: Merlin Press.
_____. 1986. *Working Class Politics in Crisis: Essays on Labour and the State*. London: Verso.
_____. 1976. *Social Democracy and Industrial Militancy*. Cambridge: Cambridge University Press.
Panitch, Leo, and Colin Leys. 2020. *Searching for Socialism: The Project of the Labour New Left from Benn to Corbyn*. London: Verso.
_____. 1997. *The End of Parliamentary Socialism: From New Left to New Labour*. London: Verso.
Pantazis, Christina. 2016. "Policies and Discourses of Poverty During a Time of Recession and Austerity." *Critical Social Policy* 36, 1.
Pantazis, Christina, David Gordon and Ruth Levitas. 2006. *Poverty and Social Exclusion in Britain: The Millennium Survey*. Bristol: Policy Press.
Parker, David. 2008. *Ideology, Absolutism and the English Revolution: Debates of the British Marxist Historians 1940–1956*. London: Lawrence and Wishart.
Parr, Joy. 1980. *Labouring Children: British Immigrant Apprentices to Canada, 1869–1924*. London and Montreal: Croom Helm and McGill-Queen's University Press.
Patrick, Ruth. 2017. *For Whose Benefit? The Everyday Realities of Welfare Reform*. Bristol: Policy Press.
Patriquin, Larry. 2001. "The Historical Uniqueness of the Clinton Welfare Reforms: A New Level of Social Misery?" *Journal of Sociology and Social Welfare* XXVIII, 3.
Peach, Ceri. 1968. *West Indian Migration to Britain: A Social Geography*. London: Oxford University Press.
Pearce, Robert. 1994. *Attlee's Labour Governments 1945–51*. London: Routledge.
Peck, Jamie. 2001. *Workfare States*. New York and London: The Guilford Press.
Pederson, Susan. 2004. *Eleanor Rathbone and the Politics of Conscience*. New Haven: Yale University Press.
Pelling, Henry. 1984. *The Labour Governments, 1945–51*. New York: St. Martin's Press.
_____. 1968. *A Short History of the Labour Party*, 3rd edition. London: Macmillan and St. Martin's Press.
_____. 1965. *The Origins of the Labour Party 1880–1900*. Oxford: Clarendon Press.
Perry, Matt. 2000. *Bread and Work: The Experience of Unemployment, 1918–1939*. London: Pluto Press.
Perry, Matt, and Matthias Reiss. 2011. "Beyond Marienthal: Understanding Movements of the Unemployed." In Matthias Reiss and Matt Perry (eds.), *Unemployment and Protest: New Perspectives on Two Centuries of Contention*. Oxford: Oxford University Press.
Pierson, Christopher. 1996. "Social Policy." In David Marquand and Anthony Seddon (eds.), *The Ideas that Shaped Post-War Britain*. London: Fontana Press.
_____. 1994. "Continuity and Discontinuity in the Emergence of the 'Post-Fordist' Welfare State." In Roger Burrows and Brian Loader. *Towards a Post-Fordist Welfare State?* London: Routledge.
Piketty, Thomas. 2020. *Capital and Ideology*. Cambridge: Harvard University Press.
_____. 2017. *Capital in the Twenty-First Century*. Cambridge: Harvard University Press.
Pile, Helga, and Catherine O'Donnell. 1997. "Earnings, Taxation and Wealth." In Alan Walker and Carol Walker (eds.), *Britain Divided: The Growth of Social Exclusion in the 1980s and 1990s*. London: CPAG Ltd.
Pimlott, Ben. 1995. "The Myth of Consensus." In *Frustrate Their Knavish Tricks: Writings*

on *Biography, History and Politics*. London: Harper Collins.

———. 1971. "The Socialist League: Intellectuals and the Labour Left in the 1930s." *Journal of Contemporary History* 6, 3.

Pinchbeck, Ivy. 1957. "The State and the Child in Sixteenth Century England—II." *British Journal of Sociology* 8, 1.

———. 1956. "The State and the Child in Sixteenth Century England—I." *British Journal of Sociology* 7, 4.

Pinchbeck, Ivy, and Margaret Hewitt. 1973. *Children in English Society Volume II: From Tudor Times to the Eighteenth Century*. London/Toronto: Routledge and Kegan Paul and University of Toronto Press.

———. 1969. *Children in English Society Volume I: From Tudor Times to the Eighteenth Century*. London/Toronto: Routledge and Kegan Paul and University of Toronto Press.

Pinto-Duchinsky, Michael. 1970. "Bread and Circuses? The Conservatives in Office, 1951–1964." In Vernon Bogdanor and Robert Skidelsky (eds.), *The Age of Affluence 1951–1964*. London: Macmillan.

Piven, Frances Fox. 1995. "Is it Global Economics or Neo-Laissez Faire?" *New Left Review* 213.

Plumb, J.H. 1981. *England in the Eighteenth Century*. New York: Penguin.

Polanyi, Karl. 1944. *The Great Transformation*. Boston: Beacon Press.

Poovey, Mary. 2007. "Representing the Manchester Irish." In Kelly Boyd and Rohan McWilliams (eds.), *The Victorian Studies Reader*. London: Routledge.

Pope, Rex. 2000. "Unemployed Women in Inter-War Britain: The Case of the Lancashire Weaving District," *Women's History Review* 9, 4.

Porter, Roy. 1991. *English Society in the Eighteenth Century*. London: Penguin.

Powell, Martin (ed.). 2002. *Evaluating New Labour's Welfare Reforms*. Bristol: The Policy Press.

Power, Anne. 2009. "New Labour and Unequal Neighbourhoods." In John Hills, Tom Sefton and Kitty Stewart (eds.), *Towards a More Equal Society? Poverty, Inequality and Policy since 1997*. Bristol: Policy Press.

Poynter, John. 1969. *Society and Pauperism: English Ideas on Poor Relief, 1795–1834*. London: Routledge and Kegan Paul.

Pugh, Martin. 2008. *We Danced all Night: A Social History of Britain Between the Wars*. London: Bodley Head.

Quigley, William P. 1997. "Five Hundred Years of English Poor Laws, 1349–1834: Regulating the Working and Nonworking Poor." *Akron Law Review* 30, 1.

Rathbone, Eleanor. 1913. *The Condition of Widows Under the Poor Law*. Liverpool: Liverpool University.

Rawnsley, Andrew. 2010. *The End of the Party*. London: Penguin.

Reeves, Maude Pember. 1914. *Round About a Pound a Week*. London: G. Bell and Sons, Ltd.

Rex, John. 1973. *Race, Colonialism and the City*. London: Routledge and Kegan Paul.

Rhodes, James. 2009. "Revisiting the 2001 Riots: New Labour and the Rise of 'Colour Blind Racism.'" *Sociological Research Online* 14, 5.

Ridley, F. F. 1981. "View from a Disaster Area: Unemployed Youth in Merseyside." In Bernard Crick. *Unemployment*. London: Methuen.

Roberts, David. 1963. "How Cruel Was the Victorian Poor Law?" *Historical Journal* 6, 1.

Roberts, Robert. 1971. *The Classic Slum*. Manchester: University of Manchester Press.

Romyn, Michael. 2016. "The Heygate: Community Life in an Inner-City Estate, 1974–

2011." *History Workshop Journal* 81.
Rose, Michael. 1972. *The Relief of Poverty, 1834–1914*. London: Macmillan.
Rose, Richard. 1960. "How the Party System Works." In Mark Abrams and Richard Rose (eds.), *Must Labour Lose?* Harmondsworth: Penguin.
Ross, Ellen. 1993. *Love and Toil: Motherhood in Outcast London 1870–1918*. Oxford: Oxford University Press.
Ross, Ellen. 1986. "Labour and Love: Rediscovering London's Working-Class Mothers, 1870–1918." In Jane Lewis (ed.). *Labour and Love: Women's Experience of Home and Family 1850–1940*. Oxford: Basil Blackwell Ltd.
Rowntree, Seebohm. 1901. *Poverty: A Study of Town Life*. London: Macmillan.
Rowntree, Seebohm, and G.R. Lavers. 1951. *Poverty and the Welfare State*. London: Longman's, Green and Co.
Rozworski, Michal. 2018. "Lessons from the 70th birthday of the National Health Service." *Canadian Dimension* 52, 2.
Rubin, Miri. 1994. "The Poor." In Rosemary Horrox (ed.). *Fifteenth-Century Attitudes: Perceptions of Society in Late Medieval England*. Cambridge: Cambridge University Press.
_____. 1987. *Charity and Community in Medieval Cambridge*. Cambridge: Cambridge University Press.
Rude, George. 1971. *Hanoverian London*. Berkeley: University of California Press.
Russell, A.K. 1973. *Liberal Landslide: The General Election of 1906*. Newton Abbot: David and Charles.
Samuel, Raphael. 1981. *East End Underworld: Chapters in the Life of Arthur Harding*. London: Routledge and Kegan Paul.
_____. 1977. "Workshop of the World: Steam Power and Hand Technology in mid-Victorian Britain," *History Workshop Journal* 3, 1.
_____. 1960. "The Deference Voter." *New Left Review* 1, 1.
Samuel, Raphael, James Kincaid and Elizabeth Slater. 1962. "But Nothing Happens." *New Left Review* 13–14.
Sanghera, Sathnam. 2021. *Empireland: How Imperialism Has Shaped Modern Britain*. London: Penguin.
Sassoon, Donald. 1999. "European Social Democracy and New Labour: Unity in Diversity?" In Andrew Gamble and Tony Wright (eds.), *The New Social Democracy*. Oxford: Blackwell Publishers.
_____. 1997. *One Hundred Years of Socialism: The West European Left in the Twentieth Century*. London: Fontana Press.
Saunders, Robert. 2007. "The Politics of Reform and the Making of the Second Reform Act, 1848–1867." *Historical Journal* 50, 3.
Savage, Mike, Fiona Devine, Niall Cunningham, Mark Taylor, Yaojun Li, Johs Hjellbrekke, Brigitte Le Roux, Sam Friedman and Andrew Miles. 2013. "A New Model of Social Class? Findings from the BBC's Great British Class Survey." *Sociology* 47, 2.
Saville, John. 2003. "Labourism and the Labour Government." In David Coates (ed.). *Paving the Third Way: The Critique of Parliamentary Socialism*. London: Merlin Press.
_____. 1957. "The Welfare State: An Historical Approach." *New Reasoner*, 3.
Schneer, Jonathan. 1988. *Labour's Conscience: The Labour Left 1945–51*. Boston: Unwin Hyman.
Schofield, Camilla. 2012. "A Nation or No Nation? Enoch Powell and Thatcherism." In Ben Jackson and Robert Saunders (eds.), *Making Thatcher's Britain*. Cambridge: Cambridge University Press.
Schwarz, Bill. 1987. "The Thatcher Years," *The Socialist Register* 23.

Seabrook, Jeremy. 2015. "Review of Mary O'Hara. *Austerity Bites: A Journey to the Sharp End of Cuts in the UK*." *Sociology* 49, 2.
_____. 2013. *Pauperland: Poverty and the Poor in Britain*. London: C. Hurst and Co.
_____. 1985. *Landscapes of Poverty*. Oxford: Basil Blackwell.
_____. 1981. "Unemployment Now and in the 1930s." In Bernard Crick (ed.), *Unemployment*. London: Methuen.
Searle, G.R. 2004. *A New England? Peace and War 1886–1914*. Oxford: Clarendon Press.
_____. 1979. "Eugenics and Politics in Britain in the 1930s." *Annals of Science* 36.
Sefton, Tom. 2009. "Moving in the Right Direction? Public Attitudes to Poverty, Inequality and Redistribution." In John Hills, Tom Sefton and Kitty Stewart (eds.), *Towards a More Equal Society? Poverty, Inequality and Policy since 1997*. Bristol: The Policy Press.
Seyd, Patrick. 1987. *The Rise and Fall of the Labour Left*. New York: St. Martin's Press.
Shankland, Graeme, Peter Willmott and David Jordan. 1977. *Inner London: Policies for Dispersal and Balance. Final Report of the Lambeth Inner Area Study*. London: Her Majesty's Stationery Office.
Shapely, Peter, Duncan Tanner and Andrew Walling. 2004. "Civic Culture and Housing Policy in Manchester, 1945–79." *Twentieth Century British History* 15, 4.
Shaw, Eric. 2008. "New Labour and the Unions: The Death of Tigmoo?" In Matt Beech and Simon Lee (eds.), *Ten Years of New Labour*. London: Palgrave Macmillan.
Sheldrick, Byron. 2000. "The Contradictions of Welfare to Work: Social Security Reform in Britain." *Studies in Political Economy* 62, 1.
Shildrick, Tracy. 2018. "Lessons from Grenfell: Poverty Propaganda, Stigma and Class Power." *Sociological Review Monographs* 66, 4.
Shildrick, Tracy, Robert MacDonald, Colin Webster and Kayleigh Garthwaite. 2010. *The Low-Pay, No-Pay Cycle: Understanding Recurrent Poverty*. York: Joseph Rowntree Foundation.
Shilliam, Robbie. 2018. *Race and the Undeserving Poor*. Newcastle upon Tyne: Agenda Publishing.
Shyllon, Folarin. 1977. *Black People in Britain 1555–1833*. London: published for The Institute of Race Relations by Oxford University Press.
Silver, Hilary. 1994. "Social Exclusion and Social Solidarity: Three Paradigms." *International Labour Review* 33, 5–6.
Silver, Jim. 2011. *Good Places to Live: Poverty and Public Housing in Canada*. Winnipeg: Fernwood Publishing.
Silver, Jim, Janice Goodman, Cheyenne Henry and Carolyn Young. 2016. "A Good Place to Live: Transforming Public Housing in Lord Selkirk Park." In Jim Silver. *Solving Poverty: Innovative Solutions from Winnipeg's Inner City*. Halifax: Fernwood Publishing.
Sim, Joe. 1982. "Scarman: The Police Counter-Attack." *Socialist Register* 19.
Simpson, Alan. 2014. "Inside New Labour's Rolling Coup: the Blair Supremacy." *Red Pepper*, December 1.
Sinfield, Adrian, and Brian Showler. 1981. "Unemployment and the Unemployed in 1980." In Brian Showler and Adrian Sinfield (eds.), *The Workless State: Studies in Unemployment*. Oxford: Martin Robertson.
Sivanandan, A. 1982. *A Different Hunger: Writings on Black Resistance*. London: Pluto Press.
Skidelsky, Robert (ed.). 1988. *Thatcherism*. London: Chatto and Windus.
Slack, Paul. 1990. *The English Poor Law, 1531–1782*. Cambridge: Cambridge University Press.

———. 1988. *Poverty and Policy in Tudor and Stuart England*. New York: Longman.
———(ed.). 1975. *Poverty in Early-Stuart Salisbury*. Devizes: Wiltshire Record Society, Volume XXXI.
———. 1974. "Vagrants and Vagrancy in England, 1598–1664." *Economic History Review* 27, 3.
Slater, Tom. 2012. "The Myth of 'Broken Britain': Welfare Reform and the Production of Ignorance." *Antipode* 46, 4.
Smith, Anna Marie. 1994. *New Right Discourse on Race and Sexuality: Britain, 1968–1990*. Cambridge: Cambridge University Press.
Smith, Martin J. 2015. "From Consensus to Conflict: Thatcher and the Transformation of Politics." *British Politics* 10, 1.
Snell, K.D.M. 1985. *Annals of the Labouring Poor: Social Change and Agrarian England, 1660–1900*. New York: Cambridge University Press.
Snow, C.E. 1931. "Emigration from Great Britain." In Walter Wilcox (ed.). *International Migrations Volume II: Interpretations*. London: National Bureau of Economic Research.
Solar, Peter. 1995. "Poor Relief in English Economic Development Before the Industrial Revolution," *Economic History Review* XLVIII, 1.
Solomos, John. 2018. "Strangers in Their Own Land: Powellism's Policy Impact." *Patterns of Prejudice* 53, 2.
———. 1988. "Institutionalized Racism: Policies of Marginalization in Education and Training." In Philip Cohen and Harwant Bains (eds.), *Multi-Racist Britain*. London: Macmillan.
———. 1986. "Political Language and Violent Protest: Ideological and Policy Responses to the 1981 and 1985 Riots." *Youth and Policy* 18.
Somers, Margaret, and Fred Block. 2005. "From Poverty to Perversity: Ideas, Markets, and Institutions Over 200 Years of Welfare Debate." *American Sociological Review* 70.
Starkey, Pat. 2000. "The Feckless Mother: Women, Poverty and Social Workers in Wartime and Post-War England." *Women's History Review* 9, 3.
———. 1998. "The Medical Officer of Health, the Social Worker, and the Problem Family, 1943–1968: The Case of Family Service Units." *Society for the Social History of Medicine* 11.
Stenberg, Kim Yoonok. 1998. "Working Class Women in London Local Politics, 1895–1914." *Twentieth Century British History* 9, 3.
Stevenson, John, and Chris Cook. 1994. *Britain in the Depression: Society and Politics 1929–1939*. London: Pearson.
Stewart, Kitty. 2009. "A Scar on the Soul of Britain: Child Poverty and Disadvantage under New Labour." In John Hills, Tom Sefton and Kitty Stewart (eds.), *Towards a More Equal Society? Poverty, Inequality and Policy since 1997*. Bristol: Policy Press.
———. 2007. "Equality and Social Justice." In Anthony Seldon (ed.). *Blair's Britain, 1997–2007*. Cambridge: Cambridge University Press.
———. 2005. "Towards an Equal Start? Addressing Childhood Poverty and Deprivation." In John Hills and Kitty Stewart (eds.), *A More Equal Society? New Labour, Poverty, Inequality and Exclusion*. Bristol: Policy Press.
Stewart, Kitty, and John Hills. 2005. "Introduction." In John Hills and Kitty Stewart (eds.), *A More Equal Society? New Labour, Poverty, Inequality and Exclusion*. Bristol: Policy Press.
Stewart, Kitty, and Polina Obolenskaya. 2016. "Young Children." In Ruth Lupton, Tania

Burchardt, John Hills, Kitty Stewart and Polly Vizard (eds.), *Social Policy in a Cold Climate: Policies and their Consequences since the Crisis*. Bristol: Policy Press.

Stewart, Kitty, Tom Sefton and John Hills. 2009. "Introduction." In John Hills, Tom Sefton and Kitty Stewart (eds.), *Towards a More Equal Society? Poverty, Inequality and Policy since 1997*. Bristol: Policy Press.

Stokes, Peter M. 2001. "Bentham, Dickens and the Uses of the Workhouse," *Studies in English Literature 1500-1900* 41, 4.

Swift, Roger, and Sheridan Gilley (eds.). 1985. *The Irish in the Victorian City*. London: Croom Helm.

Tawney, R.H. 1912. *The Agrarian Problem in the Sixteenth Century*. London: Longman, Green and Co.

Taylor, Michael. 2020. *The Interest: How the British Establishment Resisted the Abolition of Slavery*. London: Bodley Head.

Taylor, Robert. 2007. "New Labour, New Capitalism." In Anthony Seldon (ed.). *Blair's Britain, 1997–2007*. Cambridge: Cambridge University Press.

Taylor-Gooby, Peter. 1988. "The Future of the British Welfare State: Public Attitudes, Citizenship and Social Policy under the Conservative Governments of the 1980s." *European Sociological Review* 4, 1.

Tebbutt, Melanie. 1983. *Making Ends Meet: Pawnbroking and Working Class Credit*. New York: St. Martin's Press.

Teles, Steven M. 1996. *Whose Welfare? AFDC and Elite Politics*. Lawrence: University Press of Kansas.

Thane, Pat. 2018. "Poverty in the Divided Kingdom." *History and Policy* September. <historyandpolicy.org/policy-papers/rss_2.0>.

_____. 2010. "Older People and Equality." In Pat Thane (ed.). *Unequal Britain: Equality in Britain since 1945*. London: Continuum.

_____. 2000. "Labour and Welfare." In Duncan Tanner, Pat Thane and Nick Tiratsoo (eds.), *Labour's First Century*. Cambridge: Cambridge University Press.

_____. 1984. "The Working Class and 'State Welfare' in Britain, 1880–1914." *Historical Journal* 27, 4.

_____. 1982. *Foundations of the Welfare State*. London: Longman.

_____. 1978a. "Women and the Poor Law in Victorian and Edwardian England." *History Workshop* 6.

_____ (ed.). 1978b. *The Origins of British Social Policy*. London: Croom Helm.

Thatcher, Margaret. 1993. *The Downing Street Years*. New York: HarperCollins Publishers.

Thomas, Mark. 1988. "Labour Market Structure and the Nature of Unemployment in Interwar Britain." In Barry Eichengreen and T.J. Hatton (eds.), *Interwar Unemployment in International Perspective*. Dordrecht: Kluwer Academic Publishers.

Thompson, E.P. 1974. "Time, Work-Discipline and Industrial Capitalism." In M.W. Flinn and T.C. Smout (eds.), *Essays in Social History*. London: Oxford University Press.

_____. 1971. "The Moral Economy of the English Crowd in the Eighteenth Century." *Past and Present* 50.

_____. 1967. "The Political Education of Henry Mayhew," *Victorian Studies* 11, 1.

_____. 1963. *The Making of the English Working Class*. New York: Penguin Books.

Thompson, E.P., and Eileen Yeo. 1984. *The Unknown Mayhew: Selections from the Morning Chronicle 1849–50*. London: Penguin.

Thompson, Helen. 2014. "The Thatcherite Economic Legacy." In Stephen Carroll and Colin Hay (eds.), *The Legacy of Thatcherism: Assessing and Exploring Thatcherite*

Social and Economic Policies. Oxford: Oxford University Press.

Thompson, Paul. 1967. *Socialists, Liberals and Labour: The Struggle for London 1885–1914.* London: Routledge and Kegan Paul.

Tierney, Brian. 1959a. *Medieval Poor Law: A Sketch of Canonical Theory and Its Application in England.* Berkeley: University of California Press.

———. 1959b. "The Decretists and the 'Deserving Poor.'" *Comparative Studies in Society and History* 1, 4.

Tiratsoo, Nick. 1991. "Popular Politics, Affluence and the Labour Party in the 1950s." In Anthony Gorst, Lewis Johnman and W. Scott Lucas (eds.), *Contemporary British History 1931–1961.* London: Pinter.

Titmuss, Richard. 1962. *Income Distribution and Social Change.* Toronto: University of Toronto Press.

———. 1960. *The Irresponsible Society.* London: Fabian Society.

———. 1958. *Essays on the Welfare State.* London: George Allen and Unwin Ltd.

———. 1950. *Problems of Social Policy.* London: Longmans.

Tomlinson, Jim. 2009. "Thrice Denied: 'Declinism' as a Recurrent Theme in British History in the Long Twentieth Century." *Twentieth Century British History* 20, 2.

———. 2000. "Labour and the Economy." In Duncan Tanner, Pat Thane and Nick Tiratsoo (eds.), *Labour's First Century.* Cambridge: Cambridge University Press.

———. 1995. "Welfare and the Economy: The Economic Impact of the Welfare State, 1945–1951." *Twentieth Century British History* 6, 2.

Townsend, Peter. 1979. *Poverty in the United Kingdom.* Berkeley: University of California Press.

———. 1975. *Sociology and Social Policy.* London: Allan Lane.

———. 1973. *The Social Minority.* London: Allan Lane.

———. 1972. *Labour and Inequality.* London: Fabian Society.

———. 1970. *The Concept of Poverty.* London: Heineman.

———. 1966. *Poverty, Socialism and Labour in Power.* London: Fabian Society.

Toynbee, Polly. 2003. *Hard Work: Life in Low-Pay Britain.* London: Bloomsbury.

Toynbee, Polly, and David Walker. 2008. *Unjust Rewards: Exposing Greed and Inequality in Britain Today.* London: Granta Publications.

Tully, John. 2014. *Silvertown: The Lost Story of a Strike that Shook London and Helped Launch the Modern Labor Movement.* New York: Monthly Review Press.

Tyler, Imogen. 2013. "The Riots of the Underclass? Stigmatization, Mediation and the Government of Poverty and Disadvantage in Neoliberal Britain." *Sociological Research Online* 18, 4.

———. 2008. "Chav Mum Chav Scum." *Feminist Media Studies* 8, 1.

United Kingdom (UK). 1842. *Report on the Condition and Treatment of the Children Employed in the Mines and Collieries of the United Kingdom. CAREFULLY COMPILED FROM THE APPENDIX TO THE FIRST REPORT OF THE COMMISSIONERS APPOINTED TO INQUIRE INTO THIS SUBJECT.*

Valverde, Marianna. 1988. "'Giving the Female a Domestic Turn': The Social, Legal and Moral Regulation of Women's Work in British Cotton Mills, 1820–1850." *Journal of Social History* 21, 4.

Venkatesh, Sudhir. 2000. *American Project: The Rise and Fall of a Modern Ghetto.* Harvard University Press.

Vincent, David. 1991. *Poor Citizens: The State and the Poor in Twentieth Century Britain.* London and New York: Longman.

Wacquant, Loic. 2009. *Punishing the Poor: The Neoliberal Government of Social Insecu-*

rity. Durham: Duke University Press.

———. 2008. *Urban Outcasts: A Comparative Sociology of Advanced Marginality*. Cambridge: Polity Press.

Walker, Alan (ed.). 1999. *Ending Child Poverty: Popular Welfare for the 21st Century?* Bristol: Policy Press.

———. 1997. "Introduction: The Strategy of Inequality." In Alan Walker and Carol Walker (eds.), *Britain Divided: The Growth of Social Exclusion in the 1980s and 1990s*. London: CPAG Ltd.

Walker, Alan, and Carol Walker (eds.). 1997. *Britain Divided: The Growth of Social Exclusion in the 1980s and 1990s*. London: CPAG Ltd.

Walker, Carol. 2014. "Don't Cut Down the Tall Poppies: Thatcherism and the Strategy of Inequality." In Stephen Farrall and Colin Hay (eds.), *The Legacy of Thatcherism: Assessing and Exploring Thatcherite Social and Economic Policies*. Oxford: Oxford University Press.

———. 2011. "For Universalism and Against the Means Test." In Alan Walker, Adrian Sinfield and Carol Walker. *Fighting Poverty, Inequality and Injustice: A Manifesto Inspired by Peter Townsend*. Bristol: Policy Press.

———. 1993. *Managing Poverty: The Limits of Social Assistance* New York: Routledge.

Walker, Robert. 1999. "The Americanization of British Welfare: A Case Study of Policy Transfer." *International Journal of Health Services* 29, 4.

Waller, Robert. 1994. "Conservative Electoral Support and Social Class." In Anthony Seldon and Stuart Ball (eds.), *Conservative Century: The Conservative Party since 1900*. Oxford: Oxford University Press.

Ward, J.T. 1962. *The Factory Movement: 1830–1855*. London: Macmillan and Co. Ltd.

Ward, Stephanie. 2013. *Unemployment and the State in Britain: The Means Test and Protest in 1930s South Wales and North-East England*. Manchester: Manchester University Press.

———. 2011. "'The Workers are in the Mood to Fight the Act': Protest against the Means Test, 1931–1935." In Matthias Reiss and Matt Perry (eds.), *Unemployment and Protest: New Perspectives on Two Centuries of Contention*. Oxford: Oxford University Press.

Wayne, Mike. 2021. "Roadmaps After Corbyn: Parties, Classes, Political Cultures." *New Left Review* 131.

Webb, Sidney, and Beatrice Webb. 1929. *English Poor Law History, Part II: The New Poor Law*. London: Longman's, Green and Company.

———. 1927. *English Poor Law History, Part 1: The Old Poor Law*. London: Longman's, Green and Company.

Webster, Charles. 1990. "Conflict and Consensus: Explaining the British Health Service." *Twentieth Century British History* 1, 2.

———. 1983. "The Health of the School Child During the Depression." In Nicholas Perry and David McNair (eds.), *The Fitness of the Nation: Physical and Health Education in the Nineteenth and Twentieth Centuries*. London: History of Education Series.

Welshman, John. 2013. *The Underclass: A History of the Excluded Since 1880*, 2nd edition. London: Bloomsbury.

———. 1996. "In Search of the 'Problem Family': Public Health and Social Work in England and Wales 1940–1970." *Society for the Social History of Medicine* 9.

White, Jerry. 2016. "Life in Nineteenth Century Slums: Victorian London's Homes from Hell." *BBC History Magazine*. London.

―――――. 2013. *A Great and Monstrous Thing: London in the Eighteenth Century.* Cambridge: Harvard University Press.

―――――. 1979. "Campbell Bunk: A Lumpen Community in London Between the Wars." *History Workshop Journal* 8, 1.

Whiteside, Noel. 1987. "The Social Consequences of Interwar Unemployment." In Sean Glynn and Alan Booth (eds.), *The Road to Full Employment.* London: Allen and Unwin.

Wilkinson, Ellen. 1939. *The Town that was Murdered: The Life-Story of Jarrow.* London: Victor Gollancz Ltd.

Williams, Eric. 1944. *Capitalism and Slavery.* Chapel Hill: University of North Carolina Press.

Williams, Fiona. 1993. "Gender, 'Race' and Class in British Welfare Policy." In Allan Cochrane and John Clarke (eds.), *Comparing Welfare States: Britain in International Context.* London: Sage Publications.

―――――. 1992. "Social Relations, Welfare and the post-Fordism Debate." In Roger Burrows and Brian Loader. *Towards a Post-Fordist Welfare State?* London: Routledge.

Williams, Samantha. 2016. "The Maintenance of Bastard Children in London, 1790–1834," *The Economic History Review* 69, 3.

Williams, Zoe. 2017. "How Profit Corrupts Social Housing." *The Guardian,* July 22.

Wills, Clair. 2017. *Lovers and Strangers: An Immigrant History of Post-War Britain.* London: Allen Lane.

Wilson, Elizabeth. 1977. *Women and the Welfare State.* London: Tavistock.

Wohl, Anthony S. 1977. *The Eternal Slum: Housing and Social Policy in Victorian London.* London: Edward Arnold Ltd.

―――――. 1971. "The Housing of the Working Classes in London, 1815–1914." In Stanley Chapman (ed.). *The History of Working-Class Housing: A Symposium.* London: David and Charles Publishers.

―――――. 1968. "The Bitter Cry of Outcast London," *International Review of Social History* 13, 2.

Wood, Ellen Meiksens. 2012. *Liberty and Property: A Social History of Western Political Thought from Renaissance to Enlightenment.* London: Verso.

Woodall, Ann. 2005. *What Price the Poor? William Booth, Karl Marx and the London Residuum.* Aldershot: Ashgate.

Woodroofe, Kathleen. 1962. *From Charity to Social Work: In England and the United States.* London: Routledge and Kegan Paul.

Woodward, Donald. 1980. "The Background to the Statute of Artificers: The Genesis of Labour Policy, 1558–63." *Economic History Review* 33, 1.

Wootton, Barbara. 1963. "Is There a Welfare State? A Review of Recent Social Change in Britain." *Political Science Quarterly* 78, 2.

Zipfel, Tricia, Jo Tunnard, Josephine Feeney, Audrey Flannagan, Loretta Gaffney, Karen Postle, Frances O'Grady, Sally Young and Fran Bennett. 2015. *Our Lives: Challenging Attitudes to Poverty in 2015,* updated and presented in Parliament November 2015.

Zweig, Ferdinand. 1961. *The Worker in an Affluent Society.* London: Heinemann.

Zweiniger-Bargielowska, Ina. 2000. *Austerity in Britain: Rationing, Controls and Consumption, 1939–1955.* Oxford: Oxford University Press.

―――――. 1994. "Rationing, Austerity and the Conservative Party Recovery after 1945." *Historical Journal* 37, 1.

Index

Abel-Smith, Brian (*The Poor and the Poorest*), 140, 159–60, 163–4
able-bodied poor, 24, 31, 106
   beliefs about, 18–19, 48–9, 110, 205
   forced work for, 25, 43, 51–2, 57, 91
   legislation for, 28, 67
Addison, Christopher (*The Betrayal of the Slums*), 122
Addison, Paul, 119, 202
African people, 172–3
   depictions of, 40–1, 121, 165
   slave trade, 38–40, 59–60
   see also Black people
anti-poverty measures, 15–16, 142, 254
   Labour government, 101, 130–4, 138, 214, 231
   persistence of poverty amid, 3, 9–10, 250–2
Asian people, 235
   jobs for, 8, 121, 172
   racism faced by, 41, 174–5, 197–8, 206
Attlee, Clement, 89, 128, 254
   policy retreat following, 146, 150, 154, 161, 218, 248–9
   welfare state shifts under, 89, 130, 144–6, 159, 181, 211
Australia, 2, 46

badges, required wearing of, 41–2
Banting, Keith, 161, 164
Barbados, 38, 83
Barnardo, Dr., 81
Barnett, Corelli, 143
Barnett, Samuel and Henrietta, 89
Barrow, Clyde, 71, 249
Beckert, Sven, 59–60
begging, 171, 202
   badges for, 41–2
   enclosure movement and, 22–3, 246
   legislation against, 23, 25–6, 28,
   making shift and, 33–4, 41
   punishment/removal of, 24–5, 31, 45–6
Beier, A.L. 23–4, 31–2
beliefs about poverty, 159, 206
   bundle of, 12, 250
   capitalist/neoliberal, 3, 9, 99, 183, 195, 227, 237–8
   causes of, 81–8, 106, 171–2, 186
   changes in, 112, 168–70
   Christian, 18–19, 32
   Conservative, 20, 180, 193
   left-wing, 102, 124–6, 218
   poor people's, 20, 31, 50, 199
   shaping responses to the poor, 11–13, 29, 57, 120, 130–1, 241
Bentham, Jeremy, 42
Bevan, Aneurin, 118
   council housing efforts, 133–4, 166
   creation of NHS, 131–3
   welfare state measures, 140–1, 145, 149–50, 252
Beveridge, William (*The Problem of the Unemployed*), 86, 102, 184, 227
   1942 Report, 126–7, 134–7, 185
   political resistance to, 142, 150, 153, 170, 183, 219
   on postwar welfare state, 125–7, 134–7, 162, 224, 251
Birmingham, 78–9, 142, 166
Bismarck, Otto von, 93–4
Blackburn, 111–12
Black Death, 22, 24–5, 77
Black people,
   populations in England, 41
   poverty of, 193, 197
   racism faced by, 39–41, 121, 172–5, 182, 206
   youth, 8, 143, 154, 176–7, 203

see also African people; slavery
Blackwell, Trevor, 4, 249
Blair, Tony, 229
    capitalist neoliberal stance, 13, 212–19, 227, 240–1
    private finance initiatives, 231, 233–4
    revisionism of, 150–2, 211–12
    social inclusion, 219–21
    ties to US, 221–2, 231, 235
    workfare under, 2, 224, 237–8, 248–9
boards of guardians, 51, 56, 95, 110
Boer War, 85, 100, 124
Booth, Charles (*Life and Labour of the People in London*), 91
    categorizations of poverty, 6, 82–3, 163
    survey of poverty, 69–70, 73, 82–5, 98
    pension advocacy, 82, 101
Bowley, A.L., 84, 105, 163
bread, 48–50, 84
Briggs, Asa, 100, 124
Bristol, 39–41
Britain, 1
    as imperialist power, 2, 246
    as social policy laggard, 2, 248
    social policy leadership, 2, 29, 130–4, 148, 248
British Union of Fascists, 115, 119
Brown, Gordon, 227
    budget of, 210–12, 218–19
    policies, 213–14, 223, 233, 240–2
Brundage, Anthony, 50
Burnett-Hurst, A.R., 84, 105

Callaghan, James, 157–8, 170
Cameron, David, 237, 242
Canada, 2, 15, 81, 168
capitalism, 2
    agrarian, 17, 32
    brutality of poverty under, 8, 56–61, 64, 109, 249
    crisis of, 12, 170, 179, 181
    as filter, 7–8
    industrial, *see* industrial capitalism
    necessity of poverty in, 1, 3, 8, 80
    production of poverty, 1–10, 13–14, 40, 181, 250
    productivity of, 1, 10, 60
    profit maximization, impacts of, 8–9, 169, 220, 250
    surplus, production of, 8–10, 249, 252–3
    "uselessness" under, 6–7
    war, 60
capitalist economies, 4, 86, 96, 170
Caribbean, 37–8, 41
Centre for Policy Studies, 184
charitable organizations, 47, 101
    intrusive inspections by, 68
    support for exporting the poor, 81
    women's involvement with, 88
charity, 35
    deservingness and, 4, 18, 21, 114
    as dominant response to poverty, 11, 20–1, 86
    as haphazard and threadbare, 21, 91, 186, 250–2
    medieval, 19–20
    meekness and, 42, 47
    morality and, *see* morality
    redistribution versus, 14–15, 98, 131
    resistance by the poor to, 47
    "scientific" casework, 87–9
    system of, 29, 47, 50, 87, 175
Charity Organization Society, 81, 87–9, 102
Charlesworth, Lorie, 23
Chartism, 50, 56, 93
Child Poverty Action Group, 161, 165
children, 210
    apprenticeships for, 25, 37–8, 44, 57–8, 62
    charitable organizations and, 84, 87–9
    colonial exporting of, 37–8, 81–3
    dislike of poor, 36–8, 81–2
    "feeble-minded," 171–3
    illegitimate, 67, 180, 187
    Irish, 81–2
    as labourers, 57–8, 61–6, 69, 72, 83
    legislation to protect, 63–4, 91, 100–1, 128, 222, 228–9
    in makeshift economies, 33–7, 70–2, 120
    in mills, 57–60, 72, 83
    in mining, 61–2
    mortality/malnutrition, 32, 45, 84, 92, 113–14, 123–4
    poverty of, 81–3, 159–62, 196–7,

226–30, 243
  separation from mothers, 30, 55, 67–8, 164
  on the streets, 36–7, 74–5, 237
  of vagrants, 5, 22–5, 47
  in workhouses, 43–5, 67–8
Christianity, 40
  beliefs on poverty, 18–21, 87, 97, 99
  charity and, 47, 87
  medieval, 18–21
Churchill, Winston, 103, 107, 128, 132, 139, 142
civil servants, 40, 183, 206
  beliefs on poverty, 89, 102, 161
  trips to United States, 193, 223
class, 131
  capitalist, 17, 32, 221
  changes, 152, 214, 221
  conflict, 46, 96, 108, 145, 151
  "dangerous," 39, 71–2, 99, 171, 244
  divisions, 38–41, 120–1, 126, 193, 245
  "lowest," 6, 35, 82–3, 236
  middle, *see* middle class
  working, *see* working class
Clinton, Bill, 221–2
coal mines, 111, 131, 152, 189–91
  women and children in, 57, 61–2, 72, 83
Cole, G.D.H., 55, 112, 125
collectivism, 9–10, 139, 247
  moral economy and, 27, 51, 99
  retreat from, 13, 141, 148–54, 161, 191
  social service provision and, 99, 127–8, 142–5, 251
  state intervention, 96, 124, 129, 150, 253–4
colonialism, 173
  capitalist expansion, 28, 31–2, 59–60, 215, 223
  exporting of poor in, 37–8, 80–1, 246–7
  legacy of, 8, 79, 177
  see also settler colonies; slavery
commodities, 139
  consumerism and, 147, 199
  labourers as, 7, 39
  profits from selling, 1, 66
Communist Party, 116–18

community work, charity, 89, 91
Conservative Party governments,
  beliefs about poverty, 14, 145, 181, 195
  electoral politics, 100, 132, 139–42, 148–9, 179
  housing, 197–9, 201
  impacts of, 180–1, 190–3, 197–9, 239
  neoliberal policy shifts, 2, 166–70, 184, 188, 203–6, 248
  One Nation, 147, 153, 180, 183, 195
  political stances, 101, 130, 147, 151–3, 183–6
  racism in, 175–8
conservativism, 110
  beliefs about poverty, 20–1, 187, 218
  labour movement and, 117
  working class and, 41, 93, 200
Cooper, John, 89, 97
Corbyn, Jeremy, 212
Cotton Mills and Factories Act (1819), 63
cotton production, 108
  mills, 57, 59–63, 66–9, 78, 165
  slavery, 39–40, 59–61, 165
council housing, 238–9
  allocation of, 174–5
  building of, 133, 251
  decline of, 191, 198–9, 201, 232–5
  Labour Party disconnection from, 143, 154, 201
  legislation for, 162, 167
  perceptions of, 167–9, 198, 201–2, 232
  Right to Buy, 199–200
  wait lists for, 142, 174
criminality, 100, 171
  children and, 24–5, 34, 74, 197–8
  development of, 7, 31, 33–5, 165, 177–8, 201
  exporting the poor for, 23, 46
  notions of poverty and, 19, 45, 82–3, 182, 187, 244–5
  policies to address, 25, 228, 235
  see also illegal activities; prisons
Crosland, Anthony (*The Future of Socialism*), 125, 159, 172
  revisionist movement, 151–2, 155, 211–12
Crossman, Richard, 151, 154

deaths,
 of children, 32, 37, 44–5, 58, 121–3, 176
 early, 35, 71
 industrialization-related, 8, 70
 poverty-related, 8, 14, 46, 53, 65, 77, 246
 see also Black Death; infant mortality; suicide
decommodification, 133–4
Decretum (Gratian), 18
Department of Health and Social Security (DHSS), 205–6
deservingness, 246
 charity based on, 4, 18, 21, 114
 distinctions of, 2–3, 19, 87–8, 194, 201, 219
 legislation based on, 29, 97–9, 101
 marginalization and, 7–8, 103–4, 208
 means testing and, 101, 120, 205
 meekness and, 21, 30, 41–2, 109–10
 for social assistance, 18–19, 33, 54, 88, 109, 237
Dickens, Charles (*Oliver Twist*), 55
disease, 132
 poor living conditions and, 53, 71, 76–7, 197
 societal narratives of, 19, 33, 71, 77, 81, 99
 workhouses and, 56, 58
dispossession, razor's edge of, 4, 33, 249
dock labour, 7, 77, 89–90, 175
 strikes, 69–70, 94
Dorling, Danny, 12, 212, 241
drug use, 198, 239
 rampant, 14, 249
 resorting to, 7, 61
drunkenness, 78
 domestic, 70–1
 perceptions of working class, 7, 120, 250
 public, 31, 34, 82
Dunkirk, 119, 128, 140
Durbin, Evan (*The Politics of Democratic Socialism*), 125

egalitarianism, 152, 168, 224
 anti-, 182, 203, 216

popular rebellions, 31–2, 253–4
state-driven, 124, 128, 131, 134, 247, 251
Elizabethan Poor Law (1601), 67
 approach to poverty, 2, 18–19, 49, 99, 222
 establishment of, 18–19, 28
 parish-based relief system of, 48
 poor people's unrest and, 5, 21, 27
 stinginess of, 48, 246
 see also Poor Laws
employment, 193–4
 able-bodied poor and, 19, 221–2
 capitalist, 9–10, 156
 children's see children
 exclusion from, 5, 41, 104
 goal of full, 130, 137–8, 142, 148, 238–9, 247
 investments in opportunities for, 9, 127, 157, 170, 219, 228
 lack of, 4–5, 70, 106, 175, 189, 225
 legislation, 26, 64, 220, 251
 partial, 5, 75, 90–1, 233–5
 precarious, 33, 68–9, 72, 82–4, 196–8, 226
 women's, 35, 91, 104, 197–8
 see also unemployment; wages
enclosure movement, 22
 impacts of, 17, 28, 32, 45–7, 246
 riots against, 23–4, 26
Engels, Friedrich, 53, 75, 79, 94, 97
England,
 parishes in, 29, 51
 populations in, 22, 32, 41, 75
English Revolution, 32; see also revolution
eugenics, 85, 171–2

Fabian Society, 85, 94, 97, 102–3, 125
factories, 39, 77–8
 conditions in, 52–3, 57, 59–60, 64
 decline and closure of, 152, 169, 173–4, 189
 legislation for, see Factory Acts
 resistance to entering, 45, 49–52, 65–6
 see also mills; workhouses
Factory Acts, 77
 as policy shift, 63–4, 247

struggle for, 11, 93, 96
families,
　fragility of, 35, 180
　housing for, 122, 134, 163–4, 174, 200
　inspections of, 68, 88, 114
　making shift for, 7, 65, 72–3
　minimal relief for, 112–14, 137, 159–63
　poverty of, 61, 84, 92, 106, 198
　"problem," 6, 99, 165, 171–2, 232
　separation in, 22, 36, 55
　struggling, 15, 33, 70, 118–21, 196
　see also Working Families Tax Credit
feeble-mindedness, 53, 101
　association with residuum, 85–6, 99, 171–2
feudalism, 25
　capitalist transition from, 1, 5, 17, 28, 32
　enclosure and, see enclosure movement
First World War, 75, 95
　poverty since, 112
　unemployment following, 129, 137
　wage increases, 105–6, 121–2
food,
　riots, 49–50
　rising costs of, 49–50
　subsidies, 48, 50
　see also bread
food bank use, 14, 244, 249
Fordism, 224–5
France, 32, 188, 211, 227; see also Paris Commune
Fraser, Derek, 54, 102
Friedman, Milton, 183–4
friendly society movement, 92

Gaitskell, Hugh, 125, 150–1, 212
Gazeley, Ian, 82, 114
genuinely seeking work test, 108–9, 206, 247
gin, as temporary relief, 14, 34–5, 249
gender, 4, 7, 148
George, Lloyd, 122, 135
Germany, 93–4, 100, 104, 227
　economic growth, 188, 211
Gramsci, Antonio, 12
Great Depression, 149
　pressure for poverty reduction, 9, 130, 247, 251
　unemployment during, 24, 138
　welfare state development and, 124, 195
Great Harwood, 111–12
Great Unrest, The, 94–5
Greenwich, 112, 118

Habergram, Joseph, 59
Haggard, Robert F., 97
hanging, 26
　public, 24, 37, 46
Hardie, Kier, 106, 224
Hay, Colin, 96, 158, 184
Haygarth, 76–7
health, 81
　erosion of, 4–5, 31, 61, 100
　family, 84, 92, 197, 242
　industrialization and, 65, 77, 131
　insurance, 75, 97, 104–5, 114, 131
　legislation, 93, 96–7, 165–6
　poverty and poor, 14, 53, 123–4, 133, 249
　women's, 120, 123–4, 242
　working class, 97, 100, 104, 121, 143
　see also malnourishment; National Health Service; rickets
health care,
　reforms, 130–3, 140, 228
　single-payer system of, 142, 251
　spending, 117, 127
　see also National Health Service
Heath, Edward, 153, 183, 190
Henriques, Ursula, 63–4
Hill, Christopher, 22–3
Hill, Octavia, 88
Himmelfarb, Gertrude, 98
Hitchcock, Tim, 34, 44, 46
Hobsbawm, Eric, 52, 97, 208
　on Great Depression, 112, 124
　impacts of industrialization, 47–8, 60
　societal values and, 10, 147
Hollingshead, John (*Ragged London*), 76
home-based work, 136
　clothing, 65–6, 72
homelessness, 34, 94, 197
　growth of, 14, 38, 164, 201–2, 243, 249

House of Commons, 141
  committees of, 44, 55, 101
  petitions to, 118, 149
housing, 90
  building, 117, 133–4, 138, 155
  council, *see* council housing
  deservingness for, 88, 122, 163–4, 174, 200
  displacement from, 78, 165–8, 174, 234
  families, *see* families
  health impacts of poor, 53–4, 77–9, 85–6, 123–4, 131
  inadequate, 14, 31, 161, 168–71, 199–201
  lack of supply, 76, 79–80, 122
  legislation, 79, 93, 96, 161–4
  London, *see* London
  middle class, *see* middle class
  overcrowding, 76, 79–80, 90, 123, 163–5, 174
  poverty and, 4–5, 78–80, 134, 138, 149
  private finance (PFI), 233–4
  public, 15, 153, 166–8, 200
  Right to Buy, *see* Right to Buy
  shortage, 164–7, 178
  social, 15, 139, 168, 201, 232, 243
  studies on, 78–80, 123, 173
  subsidies, 117, 121–2, 142
  unaffordable, 9, 79–80, 243
  see also slums
human needs, meeting, capitalism's lack of, 8–9, 122, 147, 250
hunger, 34, 49, 84
hunger marches, 94, 116–18, 124

illegal activities, 4, 14, 91, 235, 239
immigrants, treatment of, 75–7, 149, 173–8, 182
immorality, beliefs about, 19, 68, 72, 85
imperialism, Britain's, 2, 121, 246
Independent Labour Party (ILP) 94, 97, 106, 125, 145
India, cotton production in, 60–1
individualism, 88, 96
  collectivism versus, 127, 144, 148, 151
  consumerism and, 147–54
  Thatcherism and, 182–5, 188, 191, 194, 248
industrial capitalism, 1
  Britain's, 2, 10, 59–60, 247
  suffering caused by, 47–52, 64, 96, 246
Industrial Revolution, 210, 248
  Britain's, 39, 57–8, 111
  forced labour under, 14, 42, 45–7, 59–60, 83, 226
  laissez-faire ideas, 11, 65
  necessity of poverty for, 52–3, 57–60, 66, 80, 131, 181
infant mortality, 121, 123, 159; *see also* deaths
inner-city life,
  escape from, 90, 174
  poverty, 15, 133, 201
  racialized communities and, 174–8, 203
  studies of, 164, 169, 198
Interdepartmental Committee on Physical Deterioration, 100–1
International Monetary Fund (IMF), 156–8, 170, 210
Iraq War, 231
Irish, the, 39
  difficult conditions facing, 33, 65, 77
  English resentment of, 33, 75, 78–82
  housing of, 78–9
  poverty of, 33, 75, 215
Institute of Economic Affairs, 153, 183–4, 187

Jamaica, 31–2, 38, 83
Jarrow, 111, 113–14
Jewish people, 75
jobs, 7, 35
  competition for, 63–6, 69, 115, 163, 174
  creation of, 3, 39–40, 188–9, 219–20, 252
  forced, 14–15, 57, 222–7
  full-time, 3, 111, 204, 219–20, 251–3
  lack of, 2–4, 24, 69–70, 111, 155, 176
  low-wage, 113, 169, 215, 219, 227
  menial, 8, 121
  poorly paid, 2, 75, 82–4, 163, 235
  precarious, 68–9, 91, 224–7, 248–50
  searching for, 95, 109, 199, 202, 206, 219

unionized, 66
women's, 43, 66, 72, 163, 187, 207
youth, 8, 175–7, 198–202, 220, 225–6, 237–9
see also employment; labour; unemployment
Johnson, Boris, 237
Jones, Gareth Stedman, 75, 89–90, 193–5, 198
Jones, Owen, 191
Joseph, Keith, 183–4, 186

Keynes, John Maynard, 125, 140
writing of, 126–7, 138, 251
Keynesianism, 127
adoption of, 140–1
replacement of, 184, 187–8, 225
King, Desmond, 220
King, Steven, 34, 46–8, 56
Kingsford, Peter, 118
Kinnock, Neil, 212–13, 215, 217

labour,
child, *see* children
colonies, 83–5, 101–2, 106
exchanges, 102–3, 106, 220
farm, 45, 47–8, 65, 86
market, *see* labour market
precarious, 4–5, 9, 13, 98–9, 196, 237
relationship to poverty, 4
shortages, 22, 24, 30, 134, 173, 177
skilled, *see* skilled labour
unskilled, *see* unskilled labour
labour market, 7
casual, 69–70, 72, 75
children in, 36
forced entry into, 23–4, 52, 57, 68–9, 225
legislation, 36, 108
people outside of, 3, 6, 69, 71, 187
precarious, 76, 219–21, 224, 238–40, 248
women in, 163
Labour Party governments (1945–1951), 89, 103, 161, 254
building of welfare state, 1–5, 64, 124–6, 130–9, 141–7
creation and election of, 97, 100, 117
critiques of, 132, 139–42, 146–9, 179

disconnection from movements, 154–5
erosion of gains by, 3, 13, 161–2, 170, 212
financial crises during, 130, 139–44, 247
housing, *see* council housing
ideology of, 130–3, 139–46, 150–1, 159
National Health Service, *see* National Health Service
policymaking, 130–3, 140, 144–6, 150–8
poverty reduction attempts, 3, 8–11, 128–30, 142–4, 165, 251–2
revisionism and, *see* revisionist movement
social reform programs, 94, 125–6, 132, 137–9, 144–6, 150
support for poor people, 106, 110, 113–17
taxation, 131–3, 135–7, 142–3
see also National Insurance Act; New Labour
labour-power, value only for, 6–7
Labour Representation Committee (LRC), 94, 100
laissez-faire ideology,
on poverty, 11, 96–7, 141, 151
state intervention versus, 63–4, 77, 80, 92–3, 127–9, 139
Lancashire, 77, 120
mills, 57–61, 65, 111–12
left wing, 254
ideas, 72, 97, 130, 152, 215
organizing, 115, 124–5, 143, 176
see also socialist organizing
liberalism, 203, 251
classical, 96, 183
new, 11, 96–7, 104
Liberal Party, 89, 175
election of, 100
government reforms, 5, 64, 96–7, 100–5, 142
ideology, 86
policies of, 75, 85, 99–105, 131, 247
social service provision, 100–2, 122
Liverpool, 38
Irish population in, 77, 79, 82

poverty in, 70, 114–15, 119–21
slave trade economy, 39–41, 165
loans, small-scale, 244
    interest rates on, 73–4, 120
London, 46, 213
    casual employment in, 34–5, 69–72, 91
    charitable organizing in, 47, 87–8, 103
    children in, 33–8, 44, 57–8, 74
    demographics and growth of, 77–8, 121, 241
    dockyards, 69–70
    East End, 33–5, 72, 75, 88–90, 145, 174
    housing in, 76–80, 82, 88–90, 164–8, 233–4, 243
    perceptions of the poor in, 6, 23, 31, 90–1
    poverty in, 83–4, 112, 139
    protests in, 26, 80, 94, 115–16, 236–7
    racism in, 33, 122, 156, 174–5
    slave trade in, 39–41
    women's work in, 34–5, 54, 72–4, 91
    workhouses in, 34, 42–5, 54
London Foundling Hospital, 36, 44
low-pay/no-pay/no-future cycle, 13, 82, 215, 224, 238–40
Luddite protests, 50, 93

MacLeod, Iain, 153, 186
MacMillan, Harold, 148, 153, 166, 180
making shift, 4, 33–5, 72–3, 91–3, 177, 239
malnourishment, 58, 101, 124, 197
Manchester, 36, 52–3, 71, 74, 89, 177
    housing in, 76, 78–9, 123, 143, 167–8
Mandelson, Peter, 212, 215, 218, 240
manufacturing sector, 144, 163, 225, 242
    jobs, 155–6, 173–5, 189–91, 214–15, 248
Marshall, Dorothy, 43, 45
Marshall Plan, 138, 140
Marx, Karl, 6, 28, 45, 143
    on capitalism's brutality, 8, 55, 59, 246
masterless men, 106
    creation of, 5, 17, 181, 246
    threat of, 22–4, 31, 99
Mayhew, Henry, 69–70, 73

means testing, 68, 128, 247
    introduction of, 108–10, 113
    notions of deservingness and, 101, 120, 205
    opposition to, 110, 113–18, 124–6, 160–1
    supplementary benefits, 134–5, 160, 228
    universality versus, 126, 142, 153, 171, 186, 204–5
Mearns, Andrew, 78
Middle Ages, 17, 20
middle class, 97, 137, 151
    beliefs about poverty, 120–1, 245
    charitable and settlement work, 87–90, 175
    housing, 79, 234
    political voting of, 95, 150, 211, 216–18, 223, 231
    welfare state measures versus, 139–43, 148, 194
Midlands Revolt, 24
mills, industrial, 14, 111–12, 165, 246
    children in, 57–60, 72, 83
    cotton, 57, 59–63, 65–9, 78, 165
    forced work in, 48–9, 52, 123, 248
Milner-Holland Report, 164, 173
minimum wage, 103, 115, 125, 220, 226
mining, *see* coal mines
Minority Report of the Poor Law Commissioners, 102, 132
monasteries, medieval, 19, 21
moneylending, 5, 17, 119–20
moral economy and, 27, 51, 99
morality, 234, 241
    charity and, 45–7, 87, 224
    Christian, 47
    poor people and, 6, 19, 42, 53, 69–72, 85
    poverty as failure of, 3, 11, 75–81, 101, 171–2
    snooping and, 68
    structural causes of poverty versus, 112, 127, 208, 231, 245, 249–50
Mosley, Oswald, 115, 119
mothers, 120, 136, 162, 223–5
    blame on, 43, 172, 182, 203, 219, 237
    children in workhouses, 34, 54–5, 61
    as parish "burdens," 35–6

single, 30, 34–6, 43, 67–8, 71–2, 187
  working-class, 72–3, 84, 121, 149, 169, 198
Murray, Charles (*Losing Ground*), 187
mutual aid, 21, 91–2, 194, 213, 239

National Assistance Act, 131, 135–8
National Front, 174, 176
National Health Service (NHS), 178, 234, 247
  creation of, 11, 131–2, 145–6
  as welfare state provision, 134, 137–9, 173, 194
National Insurance Act, 131, 247
  as social insurance plan, 103–4, 134–5, 138
  see also National Assistance Act
nationalization, 132, 138, 141, 146, 218; see also privatization
National Unemployed Workers' Movement (NUWM), 116–19
neoliberalism,
  global capitalism and, 12–13, 183, 206, 212, 237
  policy shifts to, 2, 153, 188
New Deal for Communities programmes, 220, 226–9, 238
New Labour,
  capitalist accommodation, 13, 213–18, 233–4, 240–1, 248–9
  criminalization of the poor, 235–7, 245
  electoral politics, 211–12
  housing under, 232–5
  New Deal, *see* New Deal for Communities programmes
  poverty under, 210, 215–18, 228–30, 239–42
  as revisionist project, 211–12
  Sure Start, *see* Sure Start Local Programmes
  workfare under, 2, 14, 218–26, 237, 240, 248–9
  see also Labour Party governments
New Poor Law (1834), 36, 51
  forced work through, 28, 50, 57, 68, 223
  less eligibility for relief, 2, 51–4, 65–6, 87
  poor rebellion and, 5, 56, 93
  workhouses under, 14, 43, 53–7, 246–8
  working class, creation of, 53, 67, 93
  see also Poor Laws
Nordic countries, lower child poverty in, 10

Old Poor Law, 36, 67, 87, 90, 135
  reform of, 48–51
Ordinance of Labourers, 25–6

Palmer, Bryan, 4, 194
Paris Commune, 50, 80
parishes, 121
  poor children in, 25, 35–7, 43–4, 57–8, 62
  relief system of, 21, 29–37, 41–2, 46–51, 58, 83, 90
  removal of poor from, 30–2, 35–8, 56, 83
  single mothers in, 35–6, 67
pauperism, 32, 105–6
  exercising agency and, 41–2
  children, 32, 57–8, 62
  fear of, 23, 33, 57, 69–71
  forced work for, 26, 37, 43–9, 65
  rise of, 17, 19, 38, 52
  undeservingness and, 5–7, 33–4, 98, 101, 109–10
  women and, 67–8, 71
  workhouses and, 54–7, 65–7, 246
pawning, 73–4, 119–20, 244
peasants, 24
  evicted, 22, 246
  landowning, 17
pensions, 105, 126, 131, 159
  advocacy, 82, 85
  gains in, 148, 155, 162, 194
  introduction of, 101–2
  means testing for, 101, 134–6, 205, 208
  poverty, 210–11, 222, 227–9, 242, 248
Perry, Matt, 115, 118
pickpocketing, 6, 31, 37, 91
Piketty, Thomas, 12, 212
Pinchbeck, Ivy, 22, 25, 38
police, 74, 199, 235
  repressive tactics, 56, 115–16, 190,

202–3
poor, the, 78, 85, 91, 121
   able-bodied, *see* able-bodied poor
   blaming, 3–7, 23, 71, 128, 170–2, 178–82, 247–50
   brutalization of, 4, 35–8, 56–62, 64, 249
   deserving, *see* deservingness
   distinctions between, 2–4, 19, 87, 201–2, 208
   exporting, 38, 80–1, 83, 246
   humiliation of, 4–5, 195, 250
   lowest stratum of, 3, 5–8, 102
   poorest of, 3–8, 85, 168, 201–2
   responsibility for own poverty, 11–14, 93, 185–6, 218–22, 237
   as "scum," 6, 99, 199, 235–7
   self-help among, 21, 91–2, 194–5, 213, 239
   stigmatization of, 2, 98, 105, 135, 163, 195, 232
   undeserving, *see* undeserving poor
   working, 2–3, 48, 99, 199, 215, 219, 247
   see also poverty
Poor Law Commission, 51, 132
   deplorable conditions and, 55, 57
   views of poor, 49, 53
Poor Laws, 14, 128, 225
   calls to reform, 48–9, 67
   historical influence of, 18–21, 25, 49, 249
   reports on, 55, 57, 102, 106
   see also Elizabethan Poor Law (1601); *New Poor Law* (1834)
poverty,
   anti-, *see* anti-poverty measures
   beliefs about, *see* beliefs about poverty
   complexity of, 4, 12–15, 164, 169
   constant changes in, 1–2, 14–16
   definitions of, 82
   perpetual production of, 1–10, 13–14, 40, 61, 181, 250
   "porn," 6, 244
   propaganda, 235, 237, 245, 250
   reducing, *see* poverty reduction
   re-emergence of, 2–3, 8–9, 158–9, 163, 171
   see also poor, the

poverty reduction, 105–6, 253
   Labour government, 1, 9, 144–5, 211, 249–51
   modest attempts at, 8, 211
Powell, Enoch (Rivers of Blood speech), 153, 176–8, 186
pregnancies, 54
   as burdensome on parishes, 35–6
   poor health from repeated, 73, 120, 123
   poverty amid, 84–5, 187
pressure from below,
   components of, 5, 251, 254
   ideological, 9, 12–13
   poverty reduction and, 5, 9, 247
prisons,
   children in, 62
   conditions in, 45–6
   punishing poverty through, 14, 25, 116, 235, 149
   ubiquity of, 45, 203
private finance initiatives, 231, 233–4
privatization, 184, 189, 199, 207; *see also* nationalization
profit maximization, production of poverty, 8–9, 169, 220, 250
prostitution, 6, 23, 31, 35, 45, 73, 91
public assistance committees (PACs), 113–14
public works expenditures, 106, 114
putting-out system, 65, 69

race,
   discrimination based on, 4, 7, 41, 176–8
   the poor as different/criminal, 58, 81, 121, 182
racism, 115, 178
   colonialism, 8, 121
   employability and, 5, 41, 175–6
   poverty and, 75, 173–6, 235–6
   slavery and, *see* slavery
Reagan, Ronald, 67, 188
rebellion by the poor, 37–9, 182
   fear of, 21, 26, 48–9
   legislative change and, 5, 28, 107, 114, 185
   prevention of, 3–4, 7–8, 27, 246
   social change and, 31

Index   293

reconstruction, 160
   American South, 43
   social democratic, 122, 125–6, 139
redistribution, 32, 200, 220, 241
   charity versus, 14, 87
   levels of support for, 3, 9–10, 13, 151, 182, 186
   policies of, 3, 103–5, 139, 144–5, 169, 188
   poverty reduction and, 207–9, 214–16, 225, 229–32, 248–54
   within the working class, 127, 136–7, 143, 154
Reform Act (1832; 1867; 1884–85): 94–5
relief, poor, 50, 67, 197
   badges for, 41–2
   Christian thought in, 18
   deservingness and, *see* deservingness
   lack of poverty elimination, 20, 32
   last resort of, 34, 45, 51–2, 160
   legislation, 26, 48–9, 51, 102
   less eligibility for, 2, 51–4, 65–6, 81, 87
   outdoor, 51, 54, 68, 102
   parish, 21, 29–37, 41–2, 46–51, 58, 83, 90
   reasoning behind, 27, 48, 113
   spending on, 41, 46, 48, 58, 87
   threadbare allocations of, 21, 29–31, 67–8, 90–1, 116
   see also Elizabethan Poor Law (1601); *New Poor Law* (1834)
residuum, 6–8
   extreme poverty of, 75, 80–2, 85–6, 171
   skilled workers versus, 71–2, 90, 209
   societal perceptions of, 85–6, 98–101, 244
resistance, poor peoples', 5, 7, 23, 46–7, 234
   racialized communities, 174, 176–7
   in workhouses, 56–7, 93, 246
revisionist movement, 125, 150–2, 155
   new, 211–12, 248
revolution, social, 32, 118
   changes toward, 126, 138, 145–6
   conservative, 156–7, 183, 188
   counter-, 141, 151–3
   elite fear of, 50, 80, 86, 108

   see also English revolution; Industrial Revolution
rich people, 32, 224
   antagonism with the poor, 21, 30, 10
   disparities between poor and, 89–90, 139, 188, 203, 235, 243–5
   housing of, 243
   mortality rates, 123
   redistribution to poor from, 50, 87, 127, 137, 143, 252
   taxation and benefits, 127, 131, 136, 224, 240–1
rickets, 58, 124, 197
Right to Buy (RTB) housing, 200
riots, poor people's, 46, 94
   common explanations for, 199, 202, 236–9
   elite suppression of, 27, 50, 56
   enclosure movement, 23–4, 26
   food, 48–50
   racial dynamics and, 174–6, 178, 182, 235–6
Rowntree, Seebohm, 69, 98, 101, 163
   poverty study findings, 83–5, 91, 124, 140, 159
Royal Commission on the Aged Poor, 96, 101
Royal Commission on the Poor Laws, 67, 102, 106
rural communities,
   enclosure of, *see* enclosure movement
   impoverishment of, 22, 48

Salvation Army, 81, 121
Samuel, Raphael, 65, 164
Sanitation Act (1866), 77, 96
school meal provision, 87, 100–1, 104–5, 188
Scotland, 1, 138, 192
scoundrels, notions of poor as, 3–8, 14, 28, 98–9, 171, 244–6
Seabrook, Jeremy, 4, 249
seasonal work, 7, 17, 35, 47–8, 65, 72
Second World War, 41
   poverty during, 119, 121, 128–9, 251
   pressure for poverty reduction, 9, 128, 137, 247–8
   racism during, 173
   welfare state provisions after, 1, 11,

130, 159, 254
Settlement Act (1662), 48
settlement houses, 15, 89–90
settler colonies, 121
    approaches to poverty, 2, 106
    need for labour in, 37–8, 41, 81–6, 101–2
sexism, employability and, 5
shirkers, notions of poor as, 3–8, 19, 108, 120, 195, 244–6
Shoemaker, Robert, 34, 44, 46
skilled labour, 15, 71, 90, 167, 208–9
    economic benefits to, 170, 194, 200
slavery, 62, 72
    American Deep South, 40, 59–60
    cotton production, 39–40, 59–61, 165
    depictions of, 24, 40–1, 55, 78
    legislation, 26, 61
    profits from 32, 39–40, 59–61
    sugar production, 38–40
slums,
    clearing of, 117, 122, 165–7, 171
    conditions in, 78, 91, 145, 163–4
    depictions of, 112, 121–3, 133, 176, 182
    development of, 10, 80, 174
    disease in, 76–7, 123
    Manchester, 53, 76, 123, 167
social assistance,
    beliefs about morality, 19, 221, 223
    deservingness and, *see* deservingness
    stigmatization with, 2, 142
    stinginess of, 2, 29, 160–1
Social Democratic Federation (SDF), 82
social democratic parties, 97, 150, 184
    critiques of, 174, 178–9, 186–7, 207
    governments of, 94, 126, 129–30, 144, 211–12
    on poverty rates and, 10, 82, 142, 247
    pressure for social reforms, 5, 9–13, 80, 92, 221, 250–4
social inclusion, 219–21
socialism,
    assumptions of, 133–4, 136, 140, 142
    elite fear of, 92–4, 124–5, 247
    Labour governments and, 142–4, 151–2, 216, 240
    Thatcherism and, 180, 212, 218
Socialist League, 124–5

Socialist Medical Association (SMA), 132–3
socialist organizing, 89, 129
    poverty rates and, 9–11
    social reforms, 5, 50, 80, 96–7, 145, 252–3
Social Security Act (1988; 1989), 193, 206
social services, 14
    cutbacks to, 147, 153, 186, 199, 206–7
    government policies to deliver, 92, 104, 125–6
    reforms to, 89, 133, 154–5
    state, 99–100, 138
    worker militancy and, 93, 154
social welfare measures, 11–12, 14, 92, 128, 143
Speenhamland Scheme, 47–8
stagflation, 156, 170
state, the, 54
    capitalist, 3, 11, 32, 175, 190, 206–7
    intervention, *see* state intervention
    role of, 127–8, 180, 186–7
state intervention, 3, 64
    agreement on logic of, 11, 86, 93, 96–7, 200
    charity versus, 14, 98
    legislation on, 104–5, 126, 138, 162, 219
    opposition to, 87–8, 167, 185, 217
    redistribution, 14, 77, 99–100, 225, 247, 253
Statute of Labourers, 22, 41–2
strikes, 21, 75, 107, 174, 190
    days lost due to, 156, 192
    dockworkers, 70, 94
    wave of, 94, 104
    wildcat, 154, 156
suffrage, 14, 86, 94–6
sugar production, 38–40
suicide, rates of, 113, 120, 244
Sure Start Local Programmes (SSLPs), 228–9
surplus population, 7, 250
    capitalist production of, 6, 249, 253
Swing Riots, 50

taxation, 95, 230
    credits, 219, 222, 228, 243
    modernization of, 103, 131

Index   295

parish relief system of, 29, 30, 32, 37
perceptions of, 129, 157, 162, 170, 208
redistribution through, 101, 125–6, 133
regressive, 104, 127–8, 135–7, 159
top rates of, 185, 188, 213, 217, 240
Tawney, R.H. 22, 89
Ten Hour Act, 63–4
Thane, Pat, 114, 123, 192, 224
   Labour's welfare measures, 117, 130, 135–6, 138
Thatcher, Margaret, 157–8, 225, 248–9
   authoritarian populism of, 178, 182, 193–5, 203
   government of, 146, 177–82, 187, 191–2, 216
   housing under, 191, 198–204, 232–3, 243
   neoliberal policy shifts, 2, 141–2, 183, 188–90, 217–20
   poverty levels under, 155, 193–6, 208–11, 227–30
   racist ideas of, 178, 199–200, 203
   theory of poverty, 14, 180–1, 184–6, 204–7
   unions versus, 178, 182, 187–92
thieving, 6, 81
benefits, 225
Thompson, E.P., 47, 50, 69, 73
Tierney, Brian, 23
Titmuss, Richard, 72, 99, 128, 161, 171
Townsend, Peter, 140–1, 154, 157–61, 163–4, 171, 205
Toynbee, Polly, 52, 163, 226
Toynbee Hall, 89
Trades Union Congress (TUC), 94, 214
trade unions, 50, 66, 106, 216
   Conservative governments versus, 178, 182, 191–2, 248
   growth and militancy, 75, 80, 93–4, 97
   poverty and, 10, 116–17, 170
   pressure of, 12, 96, 101–3, 107, 151
   protections, 154, 219, 251
   struggle for National Health Service, 11–12
   weakening of, 13, 92, 174, 187, 192, 252
   welfare state development, 129, 131, 158, 247–8
   women's, 95, 103
   see also strikes
Tudor era, 19, 21, 25
typhus, 53, 76–7

undeserving poor, 33–4, 201, 232, 244
   able-bodied as, 29, 71–2, 109–10, 222–3, 250
   blamed for poverty, 7, 88, 219, 225
   punishment and exclusion of, 29, 85, 101–4, 194, 235
   vilification of, 3–8, 98–101, 180, 185, 203
   see also deservingness
unemployed, the, 86
   ex-servicemen, 107–8, 115, 119
   hostility toward, 162, 171, 176, 216, 219
   numbers of, 24, 107–8, 111, 192
   protests by, 94, 106, 114–18, 124, 202
   services for, 102–3, 114, 194, 208
   studies of, 112, 114, 204
   see also National Unemployed Workers' Movement
unemployment, 8, 34, 103, 119, 148
   beliefs about, 63, 82, 112, 115–18
   benefits, *see* unemployment benefits
   as cause of poverty, 106, 122, 159, 175–6
   cyclical, 69, 238–9
   definition of, 106
   demonstrations against, 106, 115–16
   inevitability of, 56, 165
   insurance, 103–5, 115–16
   mass, 19, 106–15, 127–9, 151, 192–6, 247–8
   rates of, 137–8, 155–7, 162–3, 169–73, 189–98, 225–8
   seasonal, 47, 72
   temporary, 56, 196
   see also employment; jobs; making shift
Unemployment Assistance Board (UAB), administration of means testing, 113–14
   study findings, 112
unemployment benefits, 225
   applicants for, 97, 111–12, 126

eligibility, 75, 134
    reasons for offering, 93–4, 103–5, 124
    seeking work versus receiving, 112
Unemployment Insurance Acts, 107–9
unionization, 10, 93–4, 191–2
unions, *see* trade unions
United Nations housing reports, 242–4
United States, 67, 190, 202
    approach to poverty, 2, 172, 186–8, 193, 225–36
    competition from, 100, 104
    exporting of poor children to, 37–8, 83
    housing in, 166–8, 174
    loans from, 129, 140
    poverty rates in, 10, 43, 203
    slavery in, 39–41, 59–61
    social democratic organizing in, 10, 176–7
    workfare in, 193, 221–4, 207
unrest, social, 178, 236
    inquiries on, 122
    Poor Laws and, 28
    preventing, 27, 114
    see also Great Unrest, The; riots, poor people's
unskilled labour, 7
    casual, 69, 83, 90
    glut of, 69, 72, 111, 202–4
    separation from skilled, 75, 90, 143, 208–9
urban areas,
    housing, 89–90, 94, 165–8, 234
    population movement to, 10, 246
    poverty in, 10, 16, 19, 71, 176
Urban Priority Areas (UPAs), 198, 202

vagabonds, 106
    creation of, 5, 171, 181, 246
    definition of, 24
    fear of, 22, 31, 98–9
    increase of, 17, 22–3, 28
    punishment of, 24, 244
vagrancy,
    beliefs about, 45, 106, 112, 171, 244–5
    creation of, 5, 17, 28, 181, 246
    exporting of, 36–7
    legislation for, 22–6, 31
    punishment of, 21, 24–6, 45, 98–9

Valverde, Marianna, 66–7
Victorian era, 78–80, 86–8, 97–8
    values, 99, 180, 185, 187
violence,
    associating poverty with, 34, 99, 182, 187, 203, 244, 250
    domestic, 119, 162, 169
    of industrial capitalism, 8, 32, 59–60
    protest, 50, 107, 116, 174
von Hayek, Friedrich, 153, 182–4
voting, 185, 231, 234
    political party, 175, 190, 200, 213, 217
    rights, *see* suffrage

wage labour, 17, 52
    forced, 24–5, 28, 66
    rejection from, 8
wages, 154, 193
    as cause of poverty, 65, 80–2, 89, 106, 234–9
    children's, 34, 60–5
    irregular, 69–70, 72–5, 84–8
    legislation for, 26, 47–9, 52, 113
    living, 9, 53, 250–1
    low, 2–5, 33, 155, 169, 215, 227
    migration for, 22–3, 65
    minimum, *see* minimum wage
    rising, 71, 98–9, 105, 110–11, 156–9
    women's, 35, 65–7, 73, 225
Wales, 22, 42, 53, 92–5, 116, 138, 192
Webb, Sidney and Beatrice, 50, 74, 82, 86, 96
    studies of workhouses, 43, 55, 65, 132
    welfare state policies, 85, 101–2, 125, 184
welfare state,
    atrophying of 147–8, 150–2, 159–62, 179
    development, 1–2, 86, 100–2, 136–8, 200, 247–8
    leadership, 11, 64, 105, 130–2, 134, 216
    new, 219, 221, 224–5, 242
    opposition to, 137, 141–4, 146, 153–5, 170, 186
    perceptions of leaching of, 174–5, 177–8, 185, 195
    public support for, 110, 124, 129, 144–5, 194

West Indian people, 8, 40, 173, 175
whippings,
    threat of, 23, 42–3
    public, 24–6, 28, 31, 46
white-collar workers, 152
whiteness, notions of, 38–9, 121
White Paper on Employment Policy (1944) (Keynes), 127, 138
white people, 192–3, 198, 206
    racism of, 173–6, 235
    working class, 152, 174–5, 182–3, 245
widows, 43, 54, 67–8, 71, 84
Wilkinson, Ellen, 111, 113–14
Wilson, Harold, 154–5, 161, 165
Winnipeg, poverty in, 15–16
women, 148–9
    charity involvement, 88
    disproportionate poverty of, 34–5, 67–8, 71
    factory work, 43, 66
    health, 120, 123–4, 242
    legislative activism, 101–2, 154
    middle-class, 88, 95, 148
    pregnancies, *see* pregnancies
    suffrage, 95
    work available for, 72, 91, 104, 163, 187, 197–8, 207
    see also gender; mothers; widows
workday length, 55, 62–4, 125
workfare,
    in Britain, 2, 184, 220, 222, 240, 248–9
    forced work under, 14, 206, 223–6, 237
    legislation, 193, 218–19
    promotion of, 184, 193–4, 223–5
workhouses,
    children in, 43–5, 67–8
    conditions in, 43–4, 56, 58
    in industrial capitalism, 44–5, 47–52, 64, 96, 246
    promotion of, 14, 42–3, 53–7, 246–8
    resistance in, 56–7, 93, 246
    studies of, 43, 55, 65, 132
    in survival strategies, 34, 54–7, 65–7, 246
    women in, 43
working class, 26, 38–40, 52, 188–91, 244
    aspirational, 217, 221, 237

capitalist production of, 1–2, 6
consciousness, 50, 65–7, 92, 147
conservativism of, 41, 93, 200
creation of, 28, 53, 67, 93
culture, 4, 70, 84, 151–2, 202, 249
depictions of, 88, 164, 169
health, 97, 100, 104, 121, 123–4, 143
housing, 76–8, 80, 121–3, 134, 174
means testing, hatred of, 114, 116–17
organizing and protest of, 11–12, 92–6, 103, 239
political pressure of, 12–13, 104, 107, 144–5
programs for, 97, 101, 117, 150
redistribution within, 127, 136–7, 143, 154
separation from poor, 71–2, 74, 98, 110, 174, 213–15
struggle for National Health Service, 11–12
white people, 121, 152, 174–5, 182–3, 245
women of, 95, 103, 119–20, 132
Working Families Tax Credit, 219, 222, 228
Workmen's Compensation Act, 96, 102–3
workshops, 64–5, 72